# Discovering the Social Mind

In the World Library of Psychologists series, international experts themselves present career-long collections of what they judge to be their finest pieces – extracts from books, key articles, salient research findings, and their major practical theoretical contributions.

Christopher D. Frith has an international reputation as an eminent scholar and pioneer in the fields of schizophrenia, consciousness, and social cognition. A specially written introduction gives an overview of his career and contextualises the selection in relation to changes in the field during this time.

This collection reflects the various directions of Frith's work, which have become increasingly philosophically oriented throughout his career, and enables the reader to trace major developments in these areas over the last forty years. Frith has had his work nominated for the Royal Society Science Book Award and, in 2009, was awarded the Fyssen Foundation Prize for his work on neuropsychology. He has also been awarded several prestigious prizes for his collaborative work with Uta Frith.

This book is an essential read for those students and researchers engaged in the fields of social cognition, cognitive neuropsychology, and consciousness studies.

**Christopher D. Frith** is a Psychologist and Professor Emeritus at the Wellcome Trust Centre for Neuroimaging at University College London, UK and Honorary Research Fellow at the Institute of Philosophy, University of London, UK.

## World Library of Psychologists

The *World Library of Psychologists* series celebrates the important contributions to psychology made by leading experts in their individual fields of study. Each scholar has compiled a career-long collection of what they consider to be their finest pieces: extracts from books, journals, articles, major theoretical and practical contributions, and salient research findings.

For the first time ever the work of each contributor is presented in a single volume so readers can follow the themes and progress of their work and identify the contributions made to, and the development of, the fields themselves.

Each book in the series features a specially written introduction by the contributor giving an overview of their career, contextualizing their selection within the development of the field, and showing how their thinking developed over time.

**Developmental Transitions across the Lifespan**
Selected works of Leo B. Hendry
*Leo B. Hendry*

**Studies of Thinking**
Selected works of Kenneth Gilhooly
*Kenneth J. Gilhooly*

**Attention, Perception and Action**
Selected works of Glyn Humphreys
*Glyn W. Humphreys*

**Facial Expression Recognition**
Selected works of Andy Young
*Andy Young*

**From Obscurity to Clarity in Psychometric Testing**
Selected works of Professor Peter Saville
*Professor Peter Saville with Tom Hopton*

**Discovering the Social Mind**
Selected works of Christopher D. Frith
*Christopher D. Frith*

# Discovering the Social Mind

## Selected works of Christopher D. Frith

**Christopher D. Frith**

Routledge
Taylor & Francis Group
LONDON AND NEW YORK

First published 2017
by Routledge
4 Park Square, Milton Park, Abingdon, Oxon OX14 4RN

and by Routledge
605 Third Avenue, New York, NY 10017

First issued in paperback 2022

*Routledge is an imprint of the Taylor & Francis Group, an informa business*



Publisher's Note
The publisher has gone to great lengths to ensure the quality of this reprint but points out that some imperfections in the original copies may be apparent.

*British Library Cataloguing in Publication Data*
A catalogue record for this book is available from the British Library

*Library of Congress Cataloging-in-Publication Data*
Names: Frith, Christopher D., author.
Title: Discovering the social mind : selected works of Christopher D. Frith / Christopher D. Frith.
Description: 1 Edition. | New York, NY : Routledge, 2016. | Includes bibliographical references and index.
Identifiers: LCCN 2016008453 | ISBN 9781138641433 (hardback) | ISBN 9781315630502 (ebook)
Subjects: LCSH: Cognitive psychology. | Social perception. | Control (Psychology)
Classification: LCC BF201 .F75 2016 | DDC 153—dc23
LC record available at https://lccn.loc.gov/2016008453

ISBN 13: 978-1-03-247721-3 (pbk)
ISBN 13: 978-1-138-64143-3 (hbk)

DOI: 10.4324/9781315630502

Typeset in Times New Roman
by Apex CoVantage, LLC

# Contents

# Acknowledgements

Kind thanks is due to the following publishers for granting permission (or waiving permissions) for the ensuing articles published in this collection.

## British Journal of Psychiatry

Frith, C. D. (1979) Consciousness, information processing and schizophrenia. *British Journal of Psychiatry*, 134, 225–235.

## Cambridge University Press

Frith, C. D. & Done, D. J. (1989) Experiences of alien control in schizophrenia reflect a disorder in the central monitoring of action. *Psychological Medicine*, 19, 359–363.

## Transactions Publishers

Frith, C. D. & Frith, U. (1991) Elective affinities in schizophrenia and childhood autism. In P. E. Bebbington (ed.) *Social Psychiatry: Theory, Methodology and Practice*. Transactions Publishers, New Brunswick, New Jersey, pp. 65–88.

## The Royal Society Publishing

Frith, C. D., Blakemore, S.-J. & Wolpert, D. M. (2000) Abnormalities in the awareness and control of action. *Philosophical Transactions of the Royal Society of London, Series B*, 355, 1771–1788.

Frith, C. D., Friston, K. J., Liddle, P. F. & Frackowiak, R. S. J. (1991) Willed action and the prefrontal cortex in man: A study with PET. *Proceedings of the Royal Society of London, Series B*, 244, 241–246.

## Elsevier

Frith, C. D. (2011) Explaining delusions of control: The comparator model 20 years on. *Conscious Cogn*, 21(1), 52–54.

Frith, C. D., Perry, R. & Lumer, E. (on behalf of the consciousness club) (1999) The neural correlates of conscious experience: An experimental framework. *Trends in Cognitive Sciences*, 3, 105–114.

Frith, C. D. (2014) Action, agency and responsibility. *Neuropsychologia*, 55, 137–142.

Amodio, D. M. & Frith, C. D. (2006) Meeting of minds: The medial frontal cortex and social cognition. *Nature Reviews Neuroscience*, 7(4), 268–277.

Shea, N. J., Boldt, A. Bang, D. Yeung, N., Heyes, C. & Frith, C. D. (2014) Supra-personal cognitive control and metacognition. *Trends in Cognitive Sciences*, 18, 186–193.

Hedge, B. J., Everitt, B. S. & Frith, C. D. (1978) The role of gaze in dialogue. *Acta Psychologica*, 42, 453–475.

## Springer

Roepstorff, A. & Frith, C. D. (2004) What's at the top in the top-down control of action? Script-sharing and 'top-top' control of action in cognitive experiments. *Psychology Research*, 68(2–3), 189–198.

Kilner, J. M., Friston, K. J. & Frith, C. D. (2007) Predictive coding: An account of the mirror neuron system. *Cognitive Processing*, 8(3), 159–166.

## AAAS

Bahrami, B., Olsen, K., Latham, P. E., Roepstorff, A., Rees, G. & Frith, C. D. (2010) Optimally interacting minds. *Science*, 329(5995), 1081–1085.

# Introduction

What does it feel like to prepare a book about a lifetime in research? I found an unexpected pleasure in stepping back to look at what I have actually done. Normally I live a week at a time, preparing the current talk, writing the current review, revising the current paper. Now I can take a longer view. If I string all these weeks together across the years, what pattern will emerge? Will there be a pattern at all?

I have some experience of creating such patterns. For many years I had to write progress reports concerning my research grants. This was always a fascinating exercise. I had to show how the various tangents along which my bright young students had diverged, cohered into a perfectly rational narrative. Now I have the chance to create such a story on a much larger scale.

As with all of us, I have lived through exciting times. I studied psychology in the period of the switch from behaviourism to cognitivism. As an undergraduate, I received lectures from the leading cognitive psychologists of their day, Donald Broadbent and Richard Gregory. At the same time, I was being supervised by a hard-line Skinnerian, John Steiner.[1] Later, I was in the right place at the right time to be among the first psychologists to have access to computers (1966) and then brain scanners (1976). These chance encounters pushed me in certain directions that I would not have followed otherwise. These are just some of the many events that shaped my career.

## Apprenticeship 1: Institute of Psychiatry – learning how to do experiments

The first event was my failure to get a good enough degree to take up a PhD on computational neuroscience (as it would now be called) with Donald MacKay. I had always wanted to do research, and my way back in was via clinical psychology. At that time the only post-graduate academic course was at the Institute of Psychiatry. My plan succeeded, and after completing a Diploma in Abnormal Psychology, I was firmly advised that I should be doing research, rather than helping patients. In 1965 I was back in research, doing a PhD in experimental psychology with Hans Eysenck. It was at this time that I started working with computers. In addition to learning how to program, I received an excellent training in statistical analysis. The topic of my PhD thesis was the performance and learning of motor skills. During the course of my studies of how people learn to track a target, I graduated from a pursuit rotor to a LINC-8 computer. The pursuit rotor is essentially a modified gramophone turntable where all you can measure is whether your volunteer is on or off the target. The LINC-8 was a great advance and was, in many ways, better than most of today's machines. It had built-in A-to-D converters for measuring the position of a joystick and an oscilloscope screen with no refresh-rate problems. I could measure precisely where my volunteer was in relation to the target and do fancy mathematical analyses to explore frequencies present in his or her tracking movements (Frith, 1973b). My bible at this time was Attneave's book on information theory (1959), which I attempted to apply to everything from motor skills to perception (Frith and Nias, 1974).

In retrospect, my ten years at the Institute of Psychiatry were a wonderful time when I didn't have to worry about where the next grant would come from and could explore many different research topics. One of these concerned schizophrenia. I had spent the early part of my clinical training at Cane Hill Hospital, one of the many mental asylums that formed a ring around London and have now mostly been 'developed' into up-market housing estates. I had been particularly fascinated by the symptoms expressed by patients with a diagnosis of schizophrenia: the bizarre hallucinations and delusions that are so difficult to understand. When the time came for Eysenck to prepare the second edition of his massive *Handbook of Abnormal Psychology*, he allocated chapters to various of his students. I was pleased to get the one on 'Abnormalities of Perception', which was mostly about schizophrenia (Frith, 1973a). Perhaps this was why, in 1975, Tim Crow asked me to join his new MRC unit, at Northwick Park Hospital, dedicated to uncovering the biological basis of schizophrenia.

## Apprenticeship 2: Northwick Park Hospital – learning about the brain

This was a very different environment from the Psychology Department at the Institute of Psychiatry. There the clinical and the experimental psychologists had little contact with each other, since they occupied different corridors, and I remember being actively discouraged from having anything to do with people in other departments, such as Physiology. The MRC unit was completely different. There were relatively few of us, with each relevant discipline being represented by one or two people. Every day we all met for coffee, lunch and tea and discussed what we were doing. For the first time I was interacting with psychiatrists, physiologists, comparative psychologists, biochemists[2] and even sociologists.

Psychology is often dismissed as a 'soft' science. At the MRC unit I learned that the 'hard' laboratory sciences were not quite as reliable as I had believed. One week the biochemical assays simply didn't work, and no one seemed to know quite why. My 'lab', a room full of gas taps and sinks that I never needed, was in the middle of the acute psychiatric ward. I was in close contact with patients and learned about the great differences between the acute and chronic phases of psychosis. But, most of all, I learned about the brain. My colleagues were sitting at their microscopes looking at the fine structure of the brain or standing at their benches measuring various metabolites relating to brain function.

One of the recurring topics of our teatime chats was dopamine. Only a decade earlier dopamine had been identified as a neurotransmitter in the human brain (Carlsson et al., 1957).[3] Shortly after that, it was shown that Parkinson's disease was associated with a dramatic loss of dopamine in the striatum (Ehringer and Hornykiewicz, 1960) and that the motor problems associated with this disorder could be dramatically reduced by treatment with L-DOPA (Birkmayer and Hornykiewicz, 1961). The role of dopamine in brain function became and remains a major topic for research. It was soon discovered that release of dopamine in the brain was related to reward: animals would work hard to achieve such release via direct electrical stimulation of the brain (self-stimulation, Olds, 1958). Tim Crow had been directly involved in this work and recognised that a brain system involved in the control of motivated behaviour would be relevant to understanding the biological basis of many psychiatric disorders (Crow, 1973).

There were many reasons why dopamine might be relevant to research in schizophrenia, in particular the observation that all antipsychotic drugs block dopamine receptors (Seeman et al., 1976).[4] We explored such treatment effects in a series of clinical trials. In one study, patients in the acute phase of a psychosis were randomly assigned to receive α-flupenthixol, β-flupenthixol or placebo (Johnstone et al., 1978). These two isomers have many properties in common, but only α-flupenthixol blocks dopamine receptors. The results were very clear. After three weeks of treatment α-flupenthixol caused a greater reduction in the severity of hallucinations and delusions than either β-flupenthixol or placebo. At the same time there was no effect on the severity of negative features, such as poverty of speech.

### *Explaining the symptoms of schizophrenia*

Clinical trials are extremely difficult to conduct and our success was entirely due to Eve Johnstone who was tireless in her endeavours to acquire sufficient numbers of volunteers and to look after them properly. A key feature of these trials was that a placebo group was always included. As a result there were groups of drug-free patients available for my psychological studies (see for example, **Article 2**). Today it is extremely difficult to study drug-free patients, which makes interpretation of results, whether behavioural or neural, problematic.

Eve Johnstone taught me many important lessons concerning the study of patients. One is the distinction between signs and symptoms. Signs are features of behaviour that can be observed. Symptoms are subjective experiences that you can only know about through what the patients tell you. Hallucinations and delusions, the defining features of schizophrenia, are such symptoms. These are subjective experiences involving perceptions and beliefs, and yet it is these symptoms, rather than behavioural signs, that are reduced in severity by blocking dopamine receptors. I realised that I needed to address the hard question of the relationship between brain activity and conscious experience. But first I needed to try to understand the symptoms of schizophrenia in terms of abnormal information processing (now known as cognition). I am still trying to develop this approach today, but the fundamental framework has remained the same. I assume that most of the cognitive processes carried out by the brain, the simpler aspects of perception, language, and thought, never lead to any conscious experience. My first idea (**Article 1**) was that symptoms arise when these processes start leaking into consciousness. As a result patients become abnormally self-aware.

It is all very well to tell stories about the cognitive processes that underlie the symptoms of schizophrenia. The problem is to derive hypotheses from these stories that can be tested experimentally. I approached this problem by focussing on a rare, but important, subgroup of symptoms. These are sometimes called passivity experiences, or first-rank symptoms. Patients report that their actions, emotions and thoughts are being controlled by external agents. Such reports raise the question of how the rest of us are able to make this distinction. For example, if an image moves across my visual field, is it because something moved or is it because I moved my eyes? Much influenced by the ideas of Helmholtz, I suggested that we make this distinction by monitoring our own actions. If I intended to move my eyes, then I know that the movement in the visual field is due to my action and not to some external event. My intention to move is accompanied by a feeling of 'effort of will', and a signal in the brain known as 'corollary discharge' or 'efference copy'. A failure to monitor such signals might lead to the various first-rank symptoms, including the belief that alien thoughts are being inserted into one's mind (Feinberg, 1978). To test this hypothesis, my postdoc, John Done, and I examined the ability of patients with these symptoms to monitor their own actions by looking at error correction in reaction time tasks (**Article 2**). We confirmed that they had a specific difficulty with monitoring their own actions.

Delusions of control do not simply involve a feeling of not being in control. There is also the feeling that some other agent is the source of the control. Indeed, delusions about other minds are a feature of other widespread symptoms of schizophrenia. For example, delusions of reference involve the false belief that other people are trying to communicate with the patient, while paranoid (persecutory) delusions involve the false belief that other people have evil intentions towards the patient. So how are the rest of us able to avoid these false beliefs and correctly perceive the hidden mental states of others?

During my time in the MRC unit, the phrase 'Theory of Mind' had burst onto the academic scene (Premack and Woodruff, 1978). This term refers to the possibly uniquely human ability to think about the mental states of the self and others. I knew about the literature on this topic because my wife, Uta Frith, and her colleagues at the MRC Developmental Psychology Unit, had shown that autism, then still known as childhood autism, was associated with a specific problem with

Theory of Mind (Baron-Cohen et al., 1985).[5] We had many conversations on this topic concerning the similarities and differences between autism and schizophrenia and wrote about this in **Article 3**. In some ways autism and schizophrenia seem to be mirror images. Autism is associated with a failure to see the intentions of others, while schizophrenia, at least when positive symptoms are present, is associated with seeing intentions that are not there. In some other ways they are very similar. The negative signs associated with schizophrenia – flattening of affect, social isolation – are also associated with autism. With Rhiannon Corcoran, my post-doc at this time, I developed various Theory of Mind tests that could be used with adults and found that patients with schizophrenia were not very good at them (e.g. Frith and Corcoran, 1996). This result has been widely replicated (see Sprong et al., 2007), but the precise nature of the problem and its relation to symptomatology remain obscure.

In contrast, the story about the cognitive basis of delusions of control and other first-rank symptoms has become much more precise. After moving to the Institute of Neurology in 1994, I was fortunate enough to meet Daniel Wolpert, a leading authority on human motor control. With the help of Daniel and our PhD student, Sarah-Jayne Blakemore, my ideas about monitoring of action were recast in terms of forward and inverse models (the comparator model, **Article 4**). Using this model we proposed explanations for a range of problems in the control of action seen in many neurological and psychiatric cases. I no longer had direct access to patients at this time, but was able to test some of these ideas through collaboration with Eve Johnstone, in Edinburgh (Blakemore et al., 2000), and Sukhi Shergill at the Institute of Psychiatry (Shergill et al., 2005). Others have taken up this story, and there have been exciting developments in theory and methodology, which I summarised (**Article 5**) as part of a special edition 'Beyond the comparator model' of *Consciousness & Cognition*.

### *Learning about the brain*

Why did the story linking delusions of control to a comparator system fare so much better than the story linking paranoia to a Theory of Mind system? I believe the reason is that the comparator model and its successors are formulated in terms that are more readily translated into computational models and, in consequence, can be more easily mapped onto brain function.

In many ways my time at the MRC unit was an apprenticeship for learning about the brain. I spent a lot of time looking at photographs of post-mortem brain slices and had to learn to recognise and name the various structures.[6] I also had to learn about brain function, including, for example, the various control loops linking frontal cortex and basal ganglia in which dopamine plays an important role. My colleagues Rosalind Ridley and Harry Baker, who are experts on brain structure and function, guided me here. It was at this time that I realised that, as a psychologist, I was actually studying the brain, since all our behaviour and experience is mediated by the brain. I also realised that to fully understand human cognition we need to compare and contrast it with cognition in other animals. For example, dopamine has a very similar distribution in the brain of the rat and the human. Furthermore, amphetamine, which stimulates the dopamine system, produces stereotyped behaviour in monkeys and in humans (Ridley et al., 1988). On the other hand, it seems unlikely that monkeys will experience the complex and culturally coloured delusions that large doses of amphetamine can cause in humans.

This was also the time when cognitive neuropsychology, through the study of patients with discrete brain lesions, was having a major impact on cognitive theory (Shallice, 1988). These ideas were typically presented in the form of box-and-arrow diagrams illustrating the flow of information through a system in which representations (e.g. of the sounds of words) were converted into other representations (e.g. of the motor programme needed to speak the words). Modularity in the brain/mind is the basic assumption of this approach. Different brain regions are dedicated to different types of representations and detailed psychological examination of patients with discrete lesions can reveal the function of the damaged area.

Clinical neuropsychologists applied the reverse of this logic. Their brief was to make a detailed psychological examination of a patient, through which it would be possible to estimate the most likely location of the lesion. Strangely this approach had not been applied to patients with schizophrenia, despite their poor performance on psychological tests. At the time, schizophrenia was considered to be a 'functional' disorder, with no evidence of brain abnormalities. Evidence for structural brain changes associated with schizophrenia was dismissed as being a consequence of drug treatment (Marsden, 1976), and poor test performance was blamed on apathy and institutionalization (Wing and Brown, 1970). Through a detailed study of more than 1,000 patients in Shenley hospital, including a subgroup which had never received any physical treatments, my colleagues at the MRC unit were able to show that both of these assumptions were wrong (Johnstone et al., 1981; Owens et al., 1985).

With Tim Shallice and Paul Burgess, I applied the neuropsychological case study approach to a series of patients with schizophrenia (Shallice et al., 1991). There were considerable individual differences, but there was a general tendency for poor performance on tests sensitive to frontal lobe lesions. However, a new technology was just emerging and neuropsychology would never be the same again. It was at this point of transition that I put together everything I had learned about schizophrenia into a book in which I attempted to explain the signs and symptoms within the framework of cognitive neuropsychology (Frith, 1992).

## Apprenticeship 3: Hammersmith Hospital/Queen Square – learning about brain scanning

For complicated reasons that we never fully understood, the MRC decided to close down all its research units at Northwick Park Hospital, including the one in which I was employed.[7] Although somewhat stressful at the time, this turned out to be greatly to my advantage. The new technology that was to revolutionize neuropsychology was, of course, brain scanning, and I was able to transfer to another MRC unit where the new scanning techniques were being developed.

This technological breakthrough depended on the use of computers to generate 3D images of the inside of an object. The first machines, CT scanners,[8] used X-rays to generate the images. The first scan of a brain was carried out in 1971 and took 2.5 hours to process. I was involved with the first application of this technique to the study of schizophrenia (Johnstone et al., 1976). CT scanners were soon upstaged by MRI[9] scanners that can, within seconds, display brain structure in exquisite detail and without exposure to X-rays. This revolutionised neurology since it was now possible to precisely locate the damage associated with strokes or tumours. Now the question for neuropsychologists was, 'The lesion is here, but what psychological changes have occurred?'

However, my primary interest was in brain function, rather than structure. After the closure of the unit at Northwick Park, I moved to the MRC Cyclotron Unit at the Hammersmith Hospital. They had just acquired one of the first PET scanners[10] in the UK with which it was possible to measure local blood flow changes in the brain by injecting volunteers with radioactive water. Local increases in blood flow are tightly coupled with local increases in neural activity.

Functional brain scanning realised the cognitive neuropsychologist's dream. We could now write the name of the relevant brain area in the boxes of our box-and-arrow models, alongside the name of the cognitive operation. This approach was first described by Posner and colleagues (1988). After reading this paper I knew I now had the possibility to do the same thing with my cognitive models of symptoms. But I rapidly realised that this aim was radically premature. We did not know what to expect when scanning the 'normal' brain, so how could we possibly interpret activity in the 'abnormal' brain? Furthermore, we had to learn how to use this new technology.

Appropriate experiments for a scanning environment are different from typical behavioural experiments. On the one hand the experiments have to be much simpler. In the early days with PET you could only take 12 measurements per volunteer, which might translate into an experiment with 6 measurements in each of two conditions. But what should be the appropriate control condition? I learned a lot from discussions with Dick Passingham, particularly concerning if and when a 'resting state' might be relevant.[11]

One the other hand we obtained enormous amounts of data, since each measurement was a whole brain scan containing thousands of data points. Analysis was equivalent to doing thousands of paired *t*-tests simultaneously. As often happens with new technology, many people invented new techniques rather than taking account of decades of development of statistical techniques. However, I was fortunate enough to be collaborating with Karl Friston who developed techniques, based on classical statistical methods, which, in the form of SPM,[12] became the most widely used method for analysing data from all kinds of brain scanning devices (Penny et al., 2011).

Of course, we did scan some patients, and found that activation during hallucinations was located in sensory brain regions roughly relating to the content of those hallucinations (Silbersweig et al., 1995). This result confirms that hallucinations are in some sense real, but tells us little about the underlying mechanism. I realised that, in order to understand the symptoms of schizophrenia, I needed first to learn more about the neural correlates of consciousness.

I believe that the symptoms of schizophrenia reflect a disorder of consciousness (**Article 1**). For example, a patient with delusions of control does not have any obvious problems with controlling his movements. It is his experience of the movements that is abnormal. He no longer experiences his movements as free since his actions are being controlled by an external agent. **Article 6** describes an early PET study in which we identified a brain area (dorsolateral prefrontal cortex) that was activated when volunteers had to freely choose which response to make. At the same time, more posterior regions showed a reduction of activity. The reduction seems to reflect processes by which sensory activity caused by our own movements is supressed. This neural suppression also occurs when we try to tickle ourselves (Blakemore et al., 1998) and is absent in patients with delusions of control (Spence et al., 1997).

Because of the need for injection of radioactive material, PET scanning was not an ideal technique. Within a short time it was superseded by fMRI.[13] This provides an indirect measure of blood flow without the need for anything to be injected. fMRI has better temporal and spatial resolution than PET, but the scanning environment is more claustrophobic and very noisy. Advances in computing power had kept pace with scanning development, and it was now possible to collect and analyse the much larger volumes of data that fMRI generated. The first fMRI scans with humans were reported in 1992 (Kwong et al., 1992).

For complicated political reasons it was not possible for the MRC cyclotron unit to develop fMRI. Fortunately for us all, Richard Frackowiak exerted his promotional and entrepreneurial skills to such an extent that we were able to set up a new imaging centre in Queen Square funded by the Wellcome Trust. In this unit I had a small research team funded to work on the neural correlates of consciousness.

Many psychologists, then and now, are not convinced that scanning adds much to our understanding of cognition beyond what can be discovered through behavioural experiments and studies of patients with brain lesions. One area where I believe scanning is useful is the study of unconscious processing. It is very tricky to obtain behavioural evidence of unconscious processing. With a scanner, in contrast, you can measure if and where a subliminal stimulus elicits brain activity without requiring any behavioural response. For example, subliminal presentation of a face will elicit activity in the fusiform gyrus (Beck et al., 2001), while consciousness of the face is associated with additional activity in frontal and parietal cortex. We discussed experiments like this at weekly meetings of a 'consciousness club'. On the basis of these discussions we published a manifesto (**Article 7**) in which we outlined experimental paradigms that would pick out neural activity that was specifically associated with consciousness and not confounded with stimulus processing or automatic motor preparation. The identification of the neural correlates of consciousness continues to be an exciting research area, although the answer remains elusive.

I also realised that, in order to understand the symptoms of schizophrenia, I needed to learn more about how social interactions work. Such patients certainly have difficulty with social interaction and many of their symptoms concern social interactions, for example, believing that other people are communicating with them (delusion of reference) or hearing a voice commenting on their actions. In addition such patients seem less affected by the beliefs of others and maintain their delusions even though they conflict with cultural norms.

I held a weekly breakfast meeting for the members of my research group in which we discussed current projects and recent publications and gossiped about all manner of topics. One of the participants in these sessions was Andreas Roepstorff. Andreas came to the functional imaging laboratory to conduct an anthropological study of how the new ideas generated by brain imaging had an impact outside the scientific community and on culture more generally. That there is such an impact is clear. In the years since the emergence of brain scanning, technology discussions in the media on topics such as compassion, psychopathy and voting behaviour, to name just a few, always mention the key role of the brain (Racine et al., 2006). Much of the content is misguided, but it is also clear that our expectations, derived from past experience and our interactions with others have an impact on how we see the world and what sort of decisions we make. This is an effect of culture on the brain (Paulesu et al., 2000).

Experimental psychologists have tended to ignore these prior expectations and assume that their subjects will simply carry out the instructions for the task they are asked to perform. The problem is highlighted when we consider top-down control, a key concept in cognitive psychology. We exert top-down control when we choose to attend to dim red stimuli, rather than bright, flashing green ones that attract our attention in a bottom-up manner. In the laboratory such top-down control typically comes from the experimenter telling the subject what to do (**Article 8**). If we want our subject to exert his or her own top-down control, then we need to have more open-ended instructions, such as 'lift your finger whenever you have the urge to do so' (Libet et al., 1983). The problem with such instructions is that they need to be interpreted. Our 'subjects' are people with minds of their own and expectations about what happens in experiments. One thing that such people might suspect is that the experimenter will not be very pleased to be told, after half an hour or so, 'I never had the urge to lift my finger'.

I had been brought up in a tradition of experimental psychology that typically studied people in isolation. Our subjects would sit in a room by themselves and interact with stimuli presented by a computer. I now began to realise that, even in this situation, the behaviour I was observing depended on an interaction between the experimenter and a 'subject' who brought with her all sorts of expectations created by previous interactions. Such considerations throw a different light on the concept of willed action and on the idea of free will more generally.

From the new discipline of experimental philosophy I learned that people closely associate free will with responsibility. We will only be held responsible for those acts that we perform freely (Nahmias et al., 2005). The concept of responsibility plays an important role in creating social cohesion, justifying sanctions against those whose actions are bad for the group. Perhaps our experience of acting freely is something that emerges as we learn to make the distinction between deliberate and accidental acts from the culture in which we are embedded. I presented these ideas in **Article 9**.

## Retirement: Denmark and All Souls – Interacting Minds and metacognition

I had a wonderful time at the Functional Imaging Laboratory, but in 2007, having reached the age of 65, it was time to retire.[14] By this point my main interest had switched from the neural correlates of consciousness to the mechanisms underlying social interactions. However, I believe that these two topics are related. I had claimed that 'the primary function of consciousness is to permit high level interactions with other conscious beings' (Frith, 1995), and I believed that Theory of Mind, our ability to read the mental states of others, required consciousness.[15] However, I also believed that the study of social interactions was more experimentally tractable than the study of consciousness. So in October 2007 Uta and I drove to Aarhus[16] in Denmark for the beginning of a five-year project on Interacting Minds.

The interest, shared with Uta, in interacting minds, and social cognition more generally, developed naturally from our earlier work on Theory of Mind (Frith and Frith, 1999). In the early days of brain imaging we had identified a neural network that was activated when people thought about the mental states of others (Fletcher et al., 1995). This result has been replicated in many subsequent studies (**Article 10**), although the precise role of the various brain regions involved remains to be determined. However, these studies are not really about interacting minds. The participants are simply thinking about or observing others. They are not actually interacting with them (Schilbach et al., 2013). We wanted to embark on a new series of experiments involving face-to-face interactions. I had already explored this approach much earlier. One of the last publications to emerge from my time at the Institute of Psychiatry involved face-to-face interactions (**Article 11**). We recorded speech and eye gaze behaviour during a dialogue and showed that aspects of this behaviour could be captured with a relatively simple mathematical model.

From the very beginning of my time in research I had wanted to go beyond the box-and-arrow accounts and develop computational models of the behaviour I was studying. I spent a lot of time playing with such models, but they rarely reached a stage suitable for publication. This was partly because suitable models did not become available until quite recently. But, in truth, I was not sufficiently skilled to achieve this without suitable collaborators. Karl Friston was particularly important in this respect. He introduced me to the Bayesian approach to perception and action. The basic idea is that perception depends not only on the evidence provided by the senses, but also on prior expectations or beliefs about the world. If these expectations are sufficiently strong, then we may perceive something that is not actually there. The framework of predictive coding, developed at the end of the 20th century (Rao and Ballard, 1999), provides a formal, Bayesian approach to ideas about perception put forward 150 years earlier by Helmholtz and later championed by Richard Gregory. The Bayes equation tells us how much we should change our beliefs, given some new sensory evidence.

The ability to read the mental states of other people can seem to have a somewhat magical aspect, since the conscious experiences of others are totally hidden from us. This is in contrast to the states of the physical world with which we experience direct contact. The Bayesian approach makes no distinction between these cases since the states of the physical world are equally hidden from us and must be inferred[17] from the crude evidence provided by our senses. Nevertheless, we have the illusion of a direct connection to the physical world. I wrote about these insights in *Making up the Mind* (Frith, 2007). But how do we make successful inferences about the mental states of others? With James Kilner and Karl Friston, I gave a Bayesian account of how we might use evidence provided by the kinematics of movements of others to make inferences about their intentions (**Article 12**). This account proposes a precise role for mirror neurons within a system for reading goals and intentions. When we set off to Aarhus, one of our aims was to spread the Bayesian gospel.

When he returned to Denmark, Andreas Roepstorff had taken up an unusual joint position at Aarhus University combining anthropology and neuroimaging. There he created the Interacting Minds Project, in which, for the first time, Uta and I had a joint appointment. In addition to helping to design experiments on interacting minds, we also interacted with a much wider range of disciplines than we had at UCL. In addition to the brain imagers, we talked to people from linguistics, semiology, political science and theology.

In Aarhus, Bahador Bahrami developed a powerful paradigm for studying interacting minds. This involves two people performing a standard signal detection task together. On each trial they give an individual report about the signal; then, if they disagree, they have a discussion and come up with a joint decision. We showed that this joint decision could be better than that of the better of the two partners (**Article 13**), and we developed a mathematical model that could accurately predict the advantage of working together on the assumption that the partners reported their confidence in what they saw on a trial-by-trial basis.[18] Analysis of what people actually said to each other confirmed this idea and showed that people developed ways of coordinating the way they talked about confidence (Fusaroli et al., 2012).

It is these experiments that revealed to me the importance of metacognition. In these experiments, reports of confidence relate to how well the subjects think they are performing the signal detection task. This involves thinking about thinking, which is the definition of metacognition. Towards the end of the interacting minds project, thanks to Cecilia Heyes, I spent two years as a fellow of All Souls College, Oxford. This college has no undergraduate students and the fellows mostly represent the humanities. Now I was interacting with philosophers, lawyers, classicists and historians. I learned about Hellenistic ideas concerning the nature of free will and responsibility and found these much more compatible with cognitive approaches to these problems than more recent philosophy (see **Article 9**). While at All Souls, I organised a series of seminars on metacognition. With my Oxford colleagues we summarised the ideas emerging from these seminars in **Article 14**.

In this paper we distinguished between implicit and explicit metacognition. Explicit, or conscious, metacognition is the process that enables us to introspect on our mental states and talk about them with others. I believe this process is fundamental in the creation of social minds. This process works in two directions. First, it enables people to influence others by broadcasting ideas about the physical world. They can make mental representations public. Second, it enables the way a person's mind works to be influenced by the ideas of others, by internalising a mental version of a public representation. This two-way traffic, which may be unique to humans, is the basis of cultural transmission and essential for the emergence of cumulative culture (Sperber, 1996).

At least since the time of T. H. Huxley, people have wondered whether consciousness has a function or is simply an epiphenomenon (Huxley, 1874). I believe that explicit metacognition, the ability to reflect upon and talk about our ideas and mental states, provides an important function for consciousness, because it is fundamental for creating truly social minds (Frith and Metzinger, 2016).

What about schizophrenia? A key feature of this disorder, and of psychosis more generally, is a lack of insight. In other words such people have major problems reflecting on their own mental states. If this reflects a disorder of explicit metacognition, then we might also expect problems with the other aspect of this process: the tendency to be influenced by the beliefs of others. This is also a characteristic feature of psychosis. People with psychotic delusions are resistant to the arguments of others. Their delusions seem less constrained by the beliefs of the people around them and by cultural beliefs more generally. Perhaps I have finally been able to bring together the three major threads of my research portfolio.

## What next?

Looking back at this story of my life in research I notice that my interests have become increasingly philosophically oriented. The philosophical relevance of my research emerged quite early on. Philosophers became very interested in the phenomenon of thought insertion, because its existence seems to go against a fundamental principle in philosophy that, when having a thought, one cannot be mistaken about whose thought it is (immunity to error, Campbell, 1999). Consciousness is also a topic that has, until recently, engaged philosophers rather than neuroscientists. Indeed one can legitimately ask whether neuroscience has made any contributions to our understanding of consciousness. Through my connections with Aarhus

I was able to collaborate with the Danish philosopher (and Bayesian) Jakob Hohwy. We suggested that neuroscience could help us to understand subjective experience (Hohwy and Frith, 2004). So it is perhaps appropriate that I now have a desk at the Institute of Philosophy at the University of London. Nevertheless, the experimental approach remains my primary commitment. I want to study how the beliefs of others can influence our behaviour and brain function. And I guess this project will see me out.

## Notes

1 He later became a psychoanalyst.
2 A few years later, the biochemists had all become molecular geneticists.
3 Meriting award of a Nobel Prize to Arvid Carlsson in 2000.
4 Despite the flurry of interest in 'atypical' antipsychotics, this still seems to be the case.
5 When writing about my time at the Institute of Psychiatry, I omitted the most important event: meeting and marrying Uta Aurnhammer.
6 Of which my favorite has to be the *substantia innominata*.
7 There's an institute nobody knows/where the staff are all kept on their toes/by insults & gibes. /The resulting bad vibes/eventually caused it to close.
8 Computerised Tomography
9 Magnetic Resonance Imaging
10 Positron Emission Tomography
11 If you're studying the motor system, then 'not moving' might be an appropriate control. But what about higher cognitive functions? Can we have volunteers not attending, not remembering, not thinking?
12 Statistical Parametric Mapping
13 Functional Magnetic Resonance Imaging
14 As I was told very firmly by the secretary of the Institute of Neurology.
15 This belief turned out to be wrong (Samson, D., Apperly, I. A., Braithwaite, J. J., Andrews, B. J., & Bodley Scott, S.E. 2010. Seeing it their way: evidence for rapid and involuntary computation of what other people see. *Journal of Experimental Psychology: Human Perception and Performance*, *36*, 1255–1266).
16 At that time there was a ferry between Harwich and Esbjerg.
17 Note for philosophers, these inferences occur at a subpersonal level.
18 I am proud to say that this model has no free parameters with which to manipulate the fit.

## References

Attneave, F. 1959. *Applications of information theory to psychology: A summary of basic concepts, methods, and results*. Henry Holt, Oxford.

Baron-Cohen, S., Leslie, A. M., & Frith, U. 1985. Does the autistic child have a "theory of mind"? *Cognition*, *21*, 37–46.

Beck, D. M., Rees, G., Frith, C. D., & Lavie, N. 2001. Neural correlates of change detection and change blindness. *Nature Neuroscience*, *4*, 645–650.

Birkmayer, W., & Hornykiewicz, O. 1961. The L-3,4-dioxyphenylalanine (DOPA)-effect in Parkinson-akinesia. *Wien Klin Wochenschr.*, *73*, 787–788.

Blakemore, S. J., Smith, J., Steel, R., Johnstone, C. E., & Frith, C. D. 2000. The perception of self-produced sensory stimuli in patients with auditory hallucinations and passivity experiences: Evidence for a breakdown in self-monitoring. *Psychological Medicine*, *30*, 1131–1139.

Blakemore, S. J., Wolpert, D. M., & Frith, C. D. 1998. Central cancellation of self-produced tickle sensation. *Nature Neuroscience, 1*, 635–640.

Campbell, J. 1999. Schizophrenia, the space of reasons, and thinking as a motor process. *Monist, 82*, 609–625.

Carlsson, A., Lindqvist, M., & Magnusson, T.O.R. 1957. 3,4-Dihydroxyphenylalanine and 5-Hydroxytryptophan as Reserpine Antagonists. *Nature, 180*, 1200.

Crow, T. J. 1973. Catecholamine-containing neurons and electrical self-stimulation: 2. a theoretical interpretation and some psychiatric implications. *Psychological Medicine, 3*, 66–73.

Ehringer, H., & Hornykiewicz, O. 1960. Verteilung von noradrenalin und dopamin (3-hydroxytyramine) in gehirn des menschen und der verhalten bei erkrankungen des extrapyramiden systems. *Klinische Wochenschrift, 38*, 1236–1239.

Feinberg, I. 1978. Efference copy and corollary discharge: Implications for thinking and its disorders. *Schizophrenia Bulletin, 4*, 636–640.

Fletcher, P. C., Happe, F., Frith, U., Baker, S. C., Dolan, R. J., Frackowiak, R. S., & Frith, C. D. 1995. Other minds in the brain: A functional imaging study of "theory of mind" in story comprehension. *Cognition, 57*, 109–128.

Frith, C. D. 1973a. Abnormalities of perception. In *Handbook of Abnormal Psychology*. H. J. Eysenck, editor. Pitman Medical, London.

Frith, C. D. 1973b. Learning rhythmic hand movements. *Quarterly Journal of Experimental Psychology, 25*, 253–259.

Frith, C. D. 1992. *The cognitive neuropsychology of schizophrenia*. Lawrence Erlbaum Associates, Hove.

Frith, C. 1995. Consciousness is for other people. *Behavioral and Brain Sciences, 18*, 682–683.

Frith, C. D. 2007. *Making up the mind: how the brain creates our mental world*. Blackwell, Oxford.

Frith, C. D., & Corcoran, R. 1996. Exploring 'theory of mind' in people with schizophrenia. *Psychological Medicine, 26*, 521–530.

Frith, C. D., & Frith, U. 1999. Interacting minds—a biological basis. *Science, 286*, 1692–1695.

Frith, C. D., & Metzinger, T. 2016. What's the use of consciousness? In *Where's the Action? The Pragmatic Turn in Cognitive Science*. A. K. Engel, K. Friston, and D. Kragic, editors. MIT Press, Cambridge, MA.

Frith, C. D., & Nias, D. K. 1974. What determines aesthetic preferences? *Journal of Generanl Psychology, 91*, 163–173.

Fusaroli, R., Bahrami, B., Olsen, K., Roepstorff, A., Rees, G., Frith, C., & Tylen, K. 2012. Coming to terms: Quantifying the benefits of linguistic coordination. *Psychological Science, 23*, 931–939.

Hohwy, J., & Frith, C. 2004. Can neuroscience explain consciousness? *Journal of Consciousness Studies, 11*, 180–198.

Huxley, T. H. 1874. On the hypothesis that animals are automata, and its history. *Nature, 10*, 362–366.

Johnstone, E. C., Crow, T. J., Frith, C. D., Carney, M. W., & Price, J. S. 1978. Mechanism of the antipsychotic effect in the treatment of acute schizophrenia. *Lancet, 1*, 848–851.

Johnstone, E. C., Crow, T. J., Frith, C. D., Husband, J., & Kreel, L. 1976. Cerebral ventricular size and cognitive impairment in chronic schizophrenia. *Lancet, 2*, 924–926.

Johnstone, E.C., Owens, D.G.C., Gold, A., Crow, T.J., & Macmillan, J.F. 1981. Institutionalization and the defects of schizophrenia. *British Journal of Psychiatry, 139*, 195–203.

Kwong, K.K., Belliveau, J.W., Chesler, D.A., Goldberg, I.E., Weisskoff, R.M., Poncelet, B.P., Kennedy, D.N., Hoppel, B.E., Cohen, M.S., & Turner, R. 1992. Dynamic magnetic resonance imaging of human brain activity during primary sensory stimulation. *Proceedings of the National Academy of Sciences USA, 89*, 5675–5679.

Libet, B., Gleason, C.A., Wright, E.W., & Pearl, D.K. 1983. Time of conscious intention to act in relation to onset of cerebral activity (readiness-potential): The unconscious initiation of a freely voluntary act. *Brain, 106*(Pt 3), 623–642.

Marsden, C.D. 1976. Cerebral atrophy and cognitive impairment in chronic schizophrenia. *Lancet, 2*, 1079.

Nahmias, E., Morris, S., Nadelhoffer, T., & Turner, J. 2005. Surveying freedom: Folk intuitions about free will and moral responsibility. *Philosophical Psychology, 18*, 561–584.

Olds, J. 1958. Self-stimulation of the brain: Its use to study local effects of hunger, sex, and drugs. *Science, 127*, 315–324.

Owens, D.G., Johnstone, E.C., Crow, T.J., Frith, C.D., Jagoe, J.R., & Kreel, L. 1985. Lateral ventricular size in schizophrenia: relationship to the disease process and its clinical manifestations. *Psychological Medicine, 15*, 27–41.

Paulesu, E., McCrory, E., Fazio, F., Menoncello, L., Brunswick, N., Cappa, S.F., Cotelli, M., Cossu, G., Corte, F., Lorusso, M., Pesenti, S., Gallagher, A., Perani, D., Price, C., Frith, C.D., & Frith, U. 2000. A cultural effect on brain function. *Nature Neuroscience, 3*, 91–96.

Penny, W.D., Friston, K.J., Ashburner, J.T., Kiebel, S.J., & Nichols, T.E. 2011. *Statistical parametric mapping: the analysis of functional brain images: The analysis of functional brain images*. Academic press, London.

Posner, M.I., Petersen, S.E., Fox, P.T., & Raichle, M.E. 1988. Localization of cognitive operations in the human brain. *Science, 240*, 1627–1631.

Premack, D., & Woodruff, G. 1978. Does the chimpanzee have a theory of mind? *Behavioural and Brain Sciences, 4*, 515–526.

Racine, E., Bar-Ilan, O., & Illes, J. 2006. Brain imaging: A decade of coverage in the print media. *Science Communication, 28*, 122–142.

Rao, R.P.N., & Ballard, D.H. 1999. Predictive coding in the visual cortex: A functional interpretation of some extra-classical receptive-field effects. *Nature Neuroscience, 2*, 79–87.

Ridley, R.M., Baker, H.F., Frith, C.D., Dowdy, J., & Crow, T.J. 1988. Stereotyped responding on a two-choice guessing task by marmosets and humans treated with amphetamine. *Psychopharmacology, 95*, 560–564.

Samson, D., Apperly, I.A., Braithwaite, J.J., Andrews, B.J., & Bodley Scott, S.E. 2010. Seeing it their way: evidence for rapid and involuntary computation of what other people see. *Journal of Experimental Psychology: Human Perception and Performance, 36*, 1255–1266.

Schilbach, L., Timmermans, B., Reddy, V., Costall, A., Bente, G., Schlicht, T., & Vogeley, K. 2013. Toward a second-person neuroscience. *Behavioral and Brain Sciences, 36*, 393–414.

Seeman, P., Lee, T., Chau-Wong, M., & Wong, K. 1976. Antipsychotic drug doses and neuroleptic/dopamine receptors. *Nature, 261*, 717–719.

Shallice, T. 1988. *From neuropsychology to mental structure*. Cambridge University Press, Cambridge.

Shallice, T., Burgess, P. W., & Frith, C. D. 1991. Can the neuropsychological case-study approach be applied to schizophrenia? *Psychological Medicine, 21*, 661–673.

Shergill, S. S., Samson, G., Bays, P. M., Frith, C. D., & Wolpert, D. M. 2005. Evidence for sensory prediction deficits in schizophrenia. *American Journal of Psychiatry, 162*, 2384–2386.

Silbersweig, D.A., Stern, E., Frith, C., Cahill, C., Holmes, A., Grootoonk, S., Seaward, J., McKenna, P., Chua, S. E., Schnorr, L., et al. 1995. A functional neuroanatomy of hallucinations in schizophrenia. *Nature, 378*, 176–179.

Spence, S.A., Brooks, D. J., Hirsch, S. R., Liddle, P. F., Meehan, J., & Grasby, P. M. 1997. A PET study of voluntary movement in schizophrenic patients experiencing passivity phenomena (delusions of alien control). *Brain, 120*, 1997–2011.

Sperber, D. 1996. *Explaining culture: A naturalistic approach*. Wiley-Blackwell, Oxford.

Sprong, M., Schothorst, P., Vos, E., Hox, J., & Van Engeland, H. 2007. Theory of mind in schizophrenia: Meta-analysis. *The British Journal of Psychiatry, 191*, 5–13.

Wing, J. K., & Brown, G. W. 1970. *Institutionalism and schizophrenia*. Cambridge University Press, London.

## Fourteen key articles

(The number at the end of each reference, in parentheses, is the number of citations.)

### *Schizophrenia*

1 Frith, C. D. (1979) Consciousness, information processing and schizophrenia. *British Journal of Psychiatry, 134*, 225–235. (423)

2 Frith, C. D., & Done, D. J. (1989) Experiences of alien control in schizophrenia reflect a disorder in the central monitoring of action. *Psychological Medicine, 19*, 359–363. (442)

3 Frith, C. D., & Frith, U. (1991) Elective affinities in schizophrenia and childhood autism. In P. E. Bebbington (ed.) *Social Psychiatry: Theory, Methodology and Practice*. Transactions Publishers, New Brunswick, New Jersey, pp. 65–88. (116)

4 Frith, C. D., Blakemore, S.-J., & Wolpert, D. M. (2000) Abnormalities in the awareness and control of action. *Philosophical Transactions of the Royal Society of London, Series B, 355*, 1771–1788. (703)

5 Frith, C. D. (2011) Explaining delusions of control: The comparator model 20 years on. *Conscious Cogn, 21*(1), 52–54. (78)

### *Will and consciousness*

6 Frith, C. D., Friston, K. J., & Liddle, P. F., & Frackowiak, R. S. J. (1991) Willed action and the prefrontal cortex in man: A study with PET. *Proceedings of the Royal Society of London, Series B, 244*, 241–246. (959)

7 Frith, C. D., Perry, R. & Lumer, E. (on behalf of the consciousness club) (1999) The neural correlates of conscious experience: an experimental framework. *Trends in Cognitive Sciences, 3*, 105–114. (345)

8 Roepstorff, A., & Frith C. D. (2004) What's at the top in the top-down control of action? Script-sharing and 'top-top' control of action in cognitive experiments. *Psychology Research, 68*(2–3), 189–198. (82)
9 Frith, C. D. (2014) Action, agency and responsibility. *Neuropsychologia, 55*, 137–142. (6)

### *Social cognition*

10 Amodio, D. M, & Frith, C. D. (2006) Meeting of minds: The medial frontal cortex and social cognition. *Nature Reviews Neuroscience, 7*(4), 268–277. (2155)
11 Hedge, B. J., Everitt, B. S., & Frith, C. D. (1978) The role of gaze in dialogue. *Acta Psychologica, 42*, 453–475. (24)
12 Kilner, J. M., Friston, K. J. & Frith, C. D. (2007) Predictive coding: An account of the mirror neuron system. *Cognitive Processing, 8*(3), 159–166 (406)
13 Bahrami, B., Olsen, K., Latham, P. E., Roepstorff, A., Rees, G., & Frith, C. D. (2010) Optimally interacting minds. *Science, 329*(5995), 1081–1085. (164)
14 Shea, N. J., Boldt, A., Bang, D., Yeung, N., Heyes, C., & Frith, C. D. (2014) Supra-personal cognitive control and metacognition. *Trends in Cognitive Sciences, 18*, 186–193. (16)

# Section 1

# Schizophrenia

# 1 Consciousness, information processing and schizophrenia

*C. D. Frith*

## Introduction

The three principal positive symptoms of schizophrenia, hallucinations, delusions and thought disorder, are all disorders that manifest themselves in the consciousness of the patient. Indeed, two of these symptoms, delusions and hallucinations, can only be assessed on the basis of the patient's introspections concerning his conscious experience. The third symptom, thought disorder, is observed in the patient's speech; however, it is inferred that this language disorder is also a reflection of another disorder of consciousness, i.e. the stream of thought. Even though some important symptoms associated with schizophrenia, such as motor retardation, flattening of affect and muteness, can be assessed on the basis of the patient's behaviour rather than of his reported conscious experience, none of these symptoms would be sufficient on their own to allow an unequivocal diagnosis of schizophrenia. The only two symptoms which are both necessary and sufficient for a diagnosis of schizophrenia, according to some widely used standardized procedures (Wing, Cooper and Sartorius, 1974; Feighner, Robins, Guze, Woodruff, Winokur and Munoz, 1972), are hallucinations and delusions.

In this paper I shall try to show that a basic disorder of consciousness can account not only for the three principal symptoms of schizophrenia but also for a number of cognitive disorders associated with the illness. In order to throw some light on the nature of this disorder it will first be necessary to discuss some recent experiments concerning the differences between conscious and preconscious processing.

In the last 20 years experimental psychologists have made considerable advances in understanding the various cognitive processes that must be involved when a person interacts with the environment. These studies have provided a vocabulary and a methodology for studying the hypothetical processes carried out by the brain. For example, Broadbent's (1958) suggestion that human information processing involves a limited capacity system and the 'filtering' of information has had a considerable influence. This has lead to various models of schizophrenic cognitive deficit in terms of a defective filtering system (e.g. Payne, Matussek and George, 1959; Cromwell, 1968) and to a number of ingenious experiments on perception in schizophrenic patients.

This model has had success in explaining some of the cognitive disorders found in schizophrenia, but how it accounts for the principal symptoms of the disorder is much less clear. A more serious criticism of the theory is its assumption that stimulus selection in general has become defective. Perception is so dependent on selection that such a defect would result in a reduction in cognitive abilities to a level approaching severe subnormality. In contrast, many schizophrenic patients can function and communicate remarkably well in spite of continuous hallucinations and all-pervasive delusions. Thus a defect in filtering cannot be of a general kind, and it is necessary to specify at what level of processing a breakdown occurs. In addition, the defective filter model does not account for deficits in response selection, although such a defect is clearly an important component in the cognitive abnormalities found in schizophrenia (Broen and Storms, 1967; Chapman, 1966).

The model of schizophrenic cognitive deficit to be presented here, while being closely related to these defective filter theories, attempts to overcome these problems. It incorporates recent evidence on the nature and function of conscious awareness and specifies more precisely the nature and extent of the cognitive deficit. In addition, the model considers deficits in output as well as input processes.

## The properties and functions of conscious and preconscious process

### *1 Preconscious processes*

It is by no means a novel idea that certain processes operate outside consciousness (i.e. cannot be observed by introspection). There is now good evidence that these unconscious processes are multitudinous and extremely sophisticated.

Among these unconscious processes, I shall be particularly concerned with those which have been or can become conscious, that is, what Freud termed the preconscious. This restriction excludes various complex control systems, such as those carried out by endocrine or spinal mechanisms. A simple demonstration of one of these preconscious processes is given by Sperling's (1960) partial report technique. When people are shown very briefly a large array of letters, they can report only about four of these. If, however, they are asked after presentation to report letters from a particular row or a particular column of the array, they can still report about four. Thus for a brief period of time virtually the whole array of letters must have been available in the preconscious. Only about four letters from any part of the array can actually become conscious, although subjects are aware that other letters were present. This is taken as evidence for the existence of a brief, high-capacity 'iconic' store below the level of consciousness.

Preconscious processes include not only perceptual inputs but also motor outputs. Almost any repetitive skilled movement, such as typing or riding a bicycle, is carried out without conscious attention, and indeed rapid skilled movements can only be achieved by processes operating below consciousness since the reaction time to consciously perceived signals is too slow to provide the necessary control (Poulton, 1966; Frith, 1973).

Perhaps the best example of a highly sophisticated preconscious process is that involved in word recognition. In order to recognize a written or spoken word the sensory input must undergo graphical or phonological analysis; and, probably at the same time, semantic properties of the word must be processed. The final result of the interaction between these processes is that some model of the actual word presented (its meaning and form) reaches consciousness (Allport, 1976; Marcel and Patterson, 1977).

There are a number of studies indicating that much of this processing occurs at the preconscious level. For example, Mewhort (1967) showed that some processing occurred in iconic memory before items reached awareness. Subjects were asked to report one of two rows of letters; which row was to be reported on was indicated after presentation. More letters could be reported from the target row if the letters in the other row obeyed the laws of English orthography (e.g. CERNALIT) than if they were random, even though the subject was unable to report what was in this second row. Thus subjects must have processed this second row to the extent of making use of the regular sequence of the letters, even though the contents of this row never reached awareness.

Preconscious and conscious processes do not differ from one another simply in their availability for awareness. There are a number of additional properties on which the two kinds of process differ.

## *2 Capacity*

As we have already seen, there is evidence that some preconscious processes involve the storage of large numbers of items (Sperling, 1960). It is not only the iconic store that has a large capacity: the long-term store has an even larger capacity. Material in this latter store is clearly preconscious in the sense given above, and the processes by which material (such as one's telephone number) is retrieved from this store are largely unavailable to introspection. We also have an enormous preconscious store of English words and their meanings, but we can only be conscious of a very few such words at any time. Atkinson and Shiffrin (1971) and Erdelyi (1974) have argued that the contents of consciousness may be equated with the contents of a short-term memory system of limited capacity (roughly seven items, Miller, 1956). Thus, in contrast to preconscious processes, the capacity of conscious processes is very small.

## *3 Multiple vs single meanings*

If a stimulus is ambiguous and has more than one meaning, only one of these interpretations can be in consciousness at one time. Marcel (1976) has demonstrated experimentally this difference between preconscious and conscious processes, using a word recognition paradigm. The perception of a word is facilitated if a word of similar meaning has just been seen (e.g. BREAD—BUTTER). This also occurs with ambiguous words. Thus PALM will be facilitated if it is preceded by either TREE or HAND. However, once one meaning of PALM has become conscious the other meaning is inhibited. Thus, WRIST will be facilitated if preceded by HAND—PALM, but not facilitated if preceded by TREE—PALM. If, however, by a masking technique, PALM is prevented from reaching consciousness and is only processed in the preconscious, then alternative meanings are not inhibited and WRIST is facilitated when preceded by TREE—PALM.

### *4 Serial vs parallel processing*

We have great difficulty in attending consciously to more than one task at a time. On the other hand, many different preconscious processes can be carried on simultaneously without difficulty. This difference between the two systems is perhaps a consequence of, or another way of describing, the differences in capacity. In conscious processing the relevant items must be dealt with one at a time, in other words serially. If items from more than one task are present, they will interfere with one another (Posner and Klein, 1973; Posner and Snyder, 1975). In a number of experimental situations, such as the dichotic listening task (Broadbent, 1958), people function as if all information had to be processed through a single 'channel' of limited capacity. These are all tasks demanding conscious attention. When a task does not demand conscious attention (as when a trained pianist or typist is required to touch a particular key), the person behaves as if the task were controlled by one of many channels simultaneously available for processing information (Shaffer, 1975).

### *5 Automatic vs strategic processing*

Turvey (1974) and Erdelyi (1974) have suggested that preconscious processing is regulatory or automatic, whereas conscious processing is strategic, implying that the crucial feature of conscious processing is flexibility. Automatic or regulatory processing does not involve flexibility; in such processing the repertoire of appropriate stimuli and responses is already known, and there is a fixed relationship between stimulus and response. Such tasks are those that can be carried on in spite of the fact that conscious attention is directed elsewhere, and they can be maintained in parallel with other tasks. Novel tasks in which the repertoire of stimuli and responses is not known and for which there is no fixed relationship between input and output have to be carried out by conscious processes. The learning of a skill involves the development of knowledge about the repertoire of stimuli and responses and the construction of fixed relations between them. Thus the performance of a skill is gradually transferred from a conscious process to an automatic preconscious process (Eysenck and Frith, 1977). To the extent to which our environment is continually presenting novel situations which require novel reactions, conscious processing is crucial for successful interactions with the environment.

### *6 The role of consciousness*

Shallice (1972) has suggested that the role of consciousness is that of a high-level executive system. Such an executive system must select one course of action from among many and then carry it out without hesitation or interruption unless the need for change becomes very strong. To achieve this aim there must be an unambiguous representation of the current situation and the desired goal. In addition, the system must have a certain amount of inertia so that a chosen course of action will not be abandoned simply because an alternative action seems momentarily more desirable. Thus, crucial for the successful functioning of such a system are the various limitations of consciousness discussed above: small capacity, intolerance of ambiguity, and serial processing. What we are conscious of is the selection and carrying out of the chosen course of action (the dominant action system, in Shallice's terminology). The chosen course of action is dominant both in relation to other possible courses of action and in relation to any automatic processes that may be going on simultaneously. In particular, the dominant action system has priority in the interpretation of perceptions and the selection of responses if there is any conflict with other on-going processes.

### *7 A mechanism for consciousness*

Shallice has shown that a simple mechanism can have the properties desired for this executive system. Although this mechanism is not of relevance to the symptoms of schizophrenia, it is of interest in relation to the possible causes of the breakdown, as it suggests the manner in which consciousness may lose its normal role. If each of many possible actions is represented by a single hypothetical neurone, then a network in which each neurone inhibits all the others will have the property that when many of the neurones are stimulated only one will finally become activated. In addition to this capability of selection, the network also has the property of inertia. Once one neurone has 'captured' the system it is relatively more difficult for others to take over.

## Schizophrenia as a disorder of consciousness

I suggest that the symptoms of schizophrenia occur when the selective capacity of consciousness breaks down. In terms of the filter theory, the filter that has become defective in schizophrenia is the one that determines which items in preconsciousness shall enter awareness. As a result, the patient becomes aware of ambiguous and multiple interpretations of events and finds it difficult to select and carry through an appropriate course of action. He also becomes aware of the functioning of various automatic processes. Why does this breakdown occur? We know that schizophrenic breakdown probably results from a combination of two factors. The first is some genetic predisposition, probably associated with an abnormality in brain biochemistry (Crow, Deakin, Johnstone and Longden, 1976). The second is some kind of social or environmental stress (Brown, Birley and Wing, 1972; Vaughn and Leff, 1976). Analogous factors could operate in the nerve net model for the selection of material to enter awareness. As the various component neurones become more strongly stimulated (in analogy with increasing stress and arousal), more overall inhibition would have to be generated in order that only one could finally become activated. If the system did not have the capacity to generate sufficient inhibition (in analogy with the genetic predisposition and biochemical abnormality), the system would break down and many neurones would become activated simultaneously. In the remainder of this essay I shall try to show how this disorder of consciousness can account for the various symptoms of schizophrenia and associated cognitive abnormalities.

## *1 Hallucinations*

Not only are the majority of schizophrenic hallucinations auditory, but they specifically involve the hearing of words (Fish, 1962). Thus, one of Schneider's (1957) first-rank symptoms of schizophrenia is 'hearing one's thoughts spoken out aloud'. The understanding of speech must rely to a considerable extent on sophisticated preconscious processing devices. Such processing probably involves a sequence of 'guesses' and 'checks', and a system of this type has been described by Lesser, Fennell, Firman and Reddy (1974). A similar model has been applied to reading by Rumelhart (1976).

When a speech sound is heard a number of hypotheses are made about its physical nature, its phonemic properties and its meaning. These hypotheses will depend partially on prior expectations and will interact with one another. Thus, for example, a hypothesis as to the meaning of the sound will suggest hypotheses about its physical characteristics which can then be checked. Finally a set of hypotheses that are mutually consistent at the various levels will emerge, and if the evidence for them is sufficiently strong this interpretation of the speech sound will enter awareness. (Note that it is not the speech sound itself that enters awareness but a hypothetical reconstruction of it). Only the final result of this very rapid process normally arrives into consciousness, but clearly a number of incorrect interpretations of the sound will be present in the preconscious while the correct interpretation is being made. Naturally this processing will be carried out for all sounds, not just speech sounds, and the possibility that any sound may be speech must usually be considered in the early stages of processing. I propose that the awareness of these incorrect early interpretations is the basis of auditory hallucinations in schizophrenia.

This explanation requires that hallucinations should have a basis in real sounds and involve the same processing channels as speech and other auditory stimuli. There is a certain amount of evidence for this point of view. Some schizophrenic patients report that their hallucinations are based on real sounds. 'When the door slams I hear the words "Get out".' This type of hallucination is known as a functional hallucination (Fish, 1962) but is only rarely described.

It follows from this explanation of hallucinations that schizophrenics should misinterpret genuine speech as well as other sounds. Bull and Venables (1974) found that schizophrenic patients were more likely than controls to misinterpret auditorily presented words, even though there was no evidence of any hearing loss for pure tones. Similar results have been obtained by Moon, Mefferd, Wieland, Pokorny and Falconer (1968).

Misinterpretation of sounds should be reduced if the correct interpretation is made to stand out from the incorrect alternatives. This is more likely to occur when we actively attend to some particular auditory signal as opposed to the situation in which we listen passively to sounds from a number of unrelated sources. Clearly auditory hallucinations should be more apparent in this latter situation (Prediction 1). It is in line with this prediction that Slade (1974) has shown that auditory hallucinations decrease in intensity when patients are required to perform some complex auditory processing task.

It also follows from the model of hallucinations proposed here that if no sound impinges on the patient then no misinterpretation is possible, and thus no hallucinations should occur. However, in practice it is impossible to place someone in a noiseless environment. Even in a situation of complete sensory deprivation a person eventually adapts to the new low level of sound, and low intensity noises, such as the heart beat, air molecules hitting the ear drums and breathing, enter awareness. Harris (1959) has reported that schizophrenics placed in a situation of sensory deprivation show a temporary reduction in hallucinations. This may have been a response to the initial 'quiet' period before adaptation had occurred. However, Harris's method of recording the presence of hallucinations was not entirely satisfactory. A corollary of this prediction concerns the effects of reducing the possibility for making correct interpretations (reducing the signal to noise ratio in the language of signal detection theory). If, as far as possible, all meaningful sounds are removed, as in the perceptual or sensory deprivation situation, any attempts to interpret the remaining sounds are doomed to failure. Since people apparently have a need to find 'meaning' in their environment (Bartlett, 1932; Garner, 1966), some of these incorrect interpretations will be accepted. This seems to be what happens to normal people in the later stages of sensory deprivation (Schulman, Milton and Weinstein, 1967).

Deafness also will increase the relative amount of meaningless noise that is to be interpreted. It is thus very interesting that Cooper, Garside and King (1976) have found that deafness is more common in elderly psychotic patients than in other types of elderly patient. It would be interesting to know if auditory hallucinations were predominant among their symptoms.

Misinterpretation of sounds also seems to underly the verbal transformation effect demonstrated by Warren and Gregory (1958), in which a word repeated over and over again seems to transform into other words or sounds. It is as if the dominant (correct) interpretation satiates, and less likely interpretations are allowed to enter awareness. Slade (1976) has found that people prone to auditory hallucinations hear particularly extreme transformations in this situation. Once again, this is consistent with the idea that hallucinations occur when unlikely interpretations of sounds fail to be inhibited from entering awareness.

Complex preconscious processing is as much involved in the reading as in the hearing of words, and this, too, probably depends on the selection of the most likely from a number of alternative hypotheses. One would therefore expect that schizophrenics should also have difficulty in reading. As far as I am aware this ability has never been systematically studied in schizophrenic patients. Misread words can of course be checked by re-reading (unless they are present tachistoscopically), which is not the case for misheard words. However, one would still expect that the flow of reading in schizophrenic patients would be considerably disrupted (Prediction 2).

## 2 *Delusions*

Matussek (1952) and Maher (1974) have argued that the abnormality that results in delusions is not one of thought process, but one of the original perception on which it is based. Thus delusions can be seen essentially as attempts to explain and understand, using entirely normal principles of reasoning and experience, the basic misperceptions we have already discussed. At first sight this might be thought to imply that delusions are secondary to hallucinations and therefore cannot occur in their absence. However, it is quite possible for a percept to arrive in consciousness abnormally and not to give rise to an hallucination, since the original environmental event has been correctly interpreted. The abnormality lies in the fact that normally we would not bother to interpret such an event. The very arrival of this percept in awareness means (normally) that it is important and therefore needs to be explained. This hyper-awareness, noting and remembering, for example, the colours of the ties of all the guests at a party, is frequently observed in deluded patients, and these irrelevant details form an important part of their delusional system (Payne, Caird and Laverty, 1964).

The model of schizophrenic cognition presented here certainly emphasizes the initial perception as the primary cause of delusions. However, it is also clear that the thought process itself would not be expected to remain entirely normal. If thought is essentially a form of inner speech, we would expect that schizophrenic thought would be beset by all the problems of schizophrenic speech, the stream of thought being diverted by irrelevant associations and so on. This could account for the way in which some delusional systems become strangely generalized. Nevertheless, the prime cause of these delusional systems must be the initial erroneous percepts.

It could be that the greater intelligence and intactness of personality often found in patients with paranoid delusions compared to those with other types of schizophrenia occurs because only such people are capable of constructing the very complex systems necessary to explain all the irrelevant percepts of which they have become aware. Individuals without the knowledge or ability to construct such explanations might not develop delusions even when experiencing the same degree of hyper-awareness.

It should be possible to induce delusions of a paranoid type by requiring people to attend to large amounts of 'irrelevant' information (Prediction 3). A natural setting for such an effect would be an intelligence collection agency. The personnel of such an agency would be required to pay close attention to minor events concerning foreign countries or political organizations. Eventually a system for discovering the 'secret' significance of such events would be constructed.

### *3 Thought disorder*

Thought disorder is diagnosed on the basis of abnormal use of language. Typical abnormalities include 'knight's move', 'thought blocking', 'neologisms' or simply talking incomprehensible nonsense (Fish, 1962). These abnormalities can be seen as manifestation of the same defect as that causing the misperception of words, but at the level of production. The process by which the required meaning is converted into appropriate articulations is clearly very complex and requires the same process of guessing and checking as the understanding of spoken words. Thus, en route to the required word many related words will be selected as possible hypotheses. Once again we are not normally aware of these intermediate steps, but the schizophrenic will be distracted by these irrelevant words and will be likely to lose the thread of his conversation. In particular, one can see that the failure to inhibit alternative meanings of ambiguous words would be extremely distracting. Since we are assuming that the neologisms or unexpected words in this case are a result of too readily accepting inappropriate hypotheses, we would predict that the pauses before such words would be shorter than those before expected words (Prediction 4). This is the opposite of what happens in 'jargon aphasia' (Butterworth, 1977), in which there is a longer than normal pause before the unexpected words, suggesting a failure of the selection process to generate suitable hypotheses.

Lecours and Vanier-Clement (1976) have shown that in schizophrenic language disorders the underlying language-generating devices are working, but if anything too well, producing novel forms such as puns at a level normal speakers would find difficult to maintain. These neologisms may result from an attempt to describe the patient's abnormal experiences. Aphasic language disorders, in contrast, are characterized by a poverty of production, so that the afflicted patient cannot generate the words he wants at either the phonemic, morphemic or semantic level.

This model of schizophrenia clearly predicts that patients should fail to inhibit alternative meanings of ambiguous words. This failure should disrupt both the perception and the production of speech. Furthermore, if this deficit is associated with schizophrenia two very specific predictions about their performance on certain experimental tasks can be made.

As already discussed, the perception of a word is facilitated if a word of similar meaning has been seen previously. Only one of the meanings of an ambiguous word can produce this facilitation in normal people (Schvanevelt, Meyer and

Becker, 1976). In contrast, for schizophrenic patients more than one meaning should be available. Thus for them the perception of TREE should be facilitated even when preceded by HAND—PALM (Prediction 5).

Essentially the same phenomenon can be investigated by another technique. Subjects are required to learn a list of words, such as JAM. During several recall trials they are given cues for each word, such as TRAFFIC. If they are then asked to recall the list when provided with equally associated cues, such as STRAWBERRY, they do very poorly, even worse than with no cues at all (Tulving and Thompson, 1973). Schizophrenics should not do so poorly when asked to recall the original list using a different set of cues, since the alternative meanings of the original words should not have been inhibited (Prediction 6).

## *4 Problems of movement and action*

In his important study of the early symptoms of schizophrenia Chapman (1966) describes certain disturbances of motor function and suggests that patients lose the ability to carry out automatic skilled movements. This hypothesis is based on statements such as 'none of my movements come automatically to me now'. 'I've been thinking too much about them, even walking properly, talking properly, and smoking – doing anything' and 'if I do something like going for a drink of water, I've got to go over every detail – find cup, walk over, turn tap, turn tap off, drink it'. I would interpret these data differently and would suggest that the patients have not lost the ability to carry out the skilled movements, but feel compelled to attend to these movements as they are carried out although this attention is unnecessary for correct performance. This awareness may in fact interfere with the performance, since the patient feels compelled to attend to and integrate the isolated elements of performance of which he is aware rather than letting the automatic procedures carry on.

A partial simulation of this aspect of schizophrenic deficit can be achieved by requiring subjects to attend to two activities simultaneously since they will then at least attempt to be conscious of both. Posner and Keele (1969) required subjects to perform a reaction time task at various stages during the performance of a task requiring movement towards a target. In these circumstances the reaction time was slowed, particularly when it coincided with initiation of movement in the aiming task. Posner and Boies (1971) also looked at reaction times performed during a perceptual matching task and found that reaction times were slowed by response selection, but not by perceptual encoding. The general slowing of reaction time in schizophrenia is well known (e.g. Marshall, 1973). However Hemsley (1976), by studying RT tasks in which number of stimuli and number of responses are varied independently, has shown that this is due to slowness in response selection rather than stimulus selection. Thus schizophrenics perform in a manner similar to Posner and Boies (1971) subjects even though there is no other task competing for their attention. This is consistent with a failure of a system which should normally inhibit all but one response from becoming dominant.

### *5 Awareness of automatic processes*

#### *a Size constancy*

The model predicts that schizophrenics should have particular problems with any situation which involves the use of complex processing systems which normally function below the level of awareness. A very basic system of this type is used to estimate the size of objects. People are normally very good at this task even though it involves the integration of many diverse aspects, such as retinal size, depth cues, object recognition and so on. They are also largely unaware of how they arrive at their estimate. There have been a large number of studies of size constancy in schizophrenia which have tended to produce equivocal results, some studies finding under-constancy and some over-constancy. In their review of this literature, Price and Eriksen (1966) concluded that essentially schizophrenics are bad at this task and can show either kind of error. This sort of result is precisely what would be expected from our model of schizophrenic deficit. The patient is abnormally aware of the many cues involved in the performance of this task and in attempting to make use of them consciously over-rides the correctly functioning automatic system, and over-emphasizes one or another of the cues, thus producing various kinds of error.

#### *b Non-verbal communication*

A much more complex system that processes information below the level of awareness is the one concerned with non-verbal communication. In a conversation, we are principally aware of what the other person says to us, but are also making use of a number of non-verbal cues to interpret what he says and to control the flow of the dialogue. Thus, eye gaze has been shown to play an important role in the transition from one speaker to another, although the speakers are usually unaware of this (Kendon, 1967; Argyle and Ingham, 1972). The schizophrenic will have particular difficulty in this situation, since he will not only be distracted by his awareness of the non-verbal cues being presented by the other person but will also, through over-awareness, disrupt the non-verbal cues he is contributing to the conversation. It would be predicted that this particular disruption would result from a 'double bind' situation (Bateson, Jackson, Haley and Weakland, 1956). If one message is presented verbally while a contradictory message is presented non-verbally no problem arises, since we are conscious only of the verbal message although we react to the non-verbal one as well. The schizophrenic is aware of both messages at once and naturally finds this extremely difficult to comprehend and to deal with. Better communication with schizophrenic patients should be achieved if the communicant minimizes the number of non-verbal cues used in his part of the dialogue (Prediction 7).

## Conclusions

In this essay I have presented a model of the cognitive deficits associated with schizophrenia in terms of a modification of 'defective filter' theory. In presenting this model I have had three basic aims: (1) To describe recent psychological experiments that seem to throw some light on the nature of consciousness and hence on the nature of schizophrenia. (2) To show how the hypothesized cognitive deficit relates to the principal clinical symptoms of schizophrenia. (3) To make some specific and testable predictions about the behaviour of schizophrenics derived from the hypothetical cognitive deficit.

In essence, it is suggested that the basic cognitive defect associated with schizophrenia is an awareness of automatic processes which are normally carried out below the level of consciousness but are available to consciousness. These processes are primarily concerned with the selection of the appropriate interpretation of stimuli and the selection of appropriate responses.

The consequences of this defect may be summarized as follows:

1 The patient is aware of erroneous and multiple interpretations of incoming stimuli, giving rise to hallucinations. Reducing the ambiguity of stimulation (increasing signal-to-noise ratio) should reduce hallucinations. (Prediction 1).
2 These misperceptions and multiple interpretations occur particularly with words, since these are very complex and arbitrary stimuli. This should give rise to problems with reading as well as with listening to words. (Prediction 2).
3 The patient is aware of stimuli/events normally rejected from consciousness as unimportant. Attempting to understand why such events are apparently important gives rise to paranoid delusions. (Prediction 3).
4 Awareness of the multiple meanings of words will also affect the patient's speech, giving rise to the typical features of thought disorder. He will be unable to inhibit alternative verbal responses, and this will lead to the rapid production of neologisms and inappropriate words. (Prediction 4).
5 In certain experimental situations the patient's hyperawareness of multiple meanings should lead to better than normal performance. (Predictions 5 and 6).
6 The patient is at a disadvantage whenever his situation involves information processing normally carried out in an automatic manner, but involves stimuli that can be perceived consciously. For example, he is aware of the many and frequently ambiguous components of a conversation (e.g. non-verbal aspects of communication). He should find communication easier if these aspects are eliminated. (Prediction 7).

The strength of this proposal for the basic cognitive deficit associated with schizophrenia lies not only in its ability to account for the symptoms of this disorder and for many of the performance abnormalities revealed by cognitive testing, but also in its ability to make a number of precise and testable predictions about the behaviour of schizophrenic patients.

## Acknowledgements

I am grateful to Geoff Riley for many helpful discussions while I was writing this paper, and to Tim Crow, Uta Frith, Narinder Kapur, Tony Marcel, Rosalind Ridley and Tim Shallice for their comments on earlier drafts of the paper.

## References

Allport, D. A. (1976) In: S. Dornic (ed). *Attention and Performance VI.* London and New York: Academic Press.

Argyle, M. & Ingham, R. (1972) Gaze, mutual gaze and proximity. *Semiotica,* **6,** 32–49.

Atkinson, R. C. & Shiffrin, R. M. (1971) The control of short-term memory. *Scientific American,* **224,** 82–90.

Bartlett, F. (1932) *Remembering.* Cambridge University Press.

Bateson, G., Jackson, D. D., Haley, J. & Weakland, J. (1956) Toward a communication theory of schizophrenia. *Behavioural Sciences,* **1,** 251.

Broadbent, D. F. (1958) *Perception and Communication.* London: Pergamon Press.

Broen, W. E. Jr. & Storms, L. H. (1967) A theory of response interference in schizophrenia. In: B. A. Maher (ed.), *Progress in Experimental Personality Research,* Vol. IV. New York: Academic Press.

Brown, G. W., Birley, J. L. T. & Wing, J. K. (1972) Influence of family life on the course of schizophrenic disorders; a replication. *British Journal of Psychiatry,* **121,** 241–58.

Bull, H. C. & Venables, P. H. (1974) Speech perception in schizophrenia. *British Journal of Psychiatry,* **125,** 350–4.

Butterworth, B. (1977) Hesitation and the production of neologism in jargon aphasia. Paper presented to the Experimental Psychology Society, Sheffield Meeting.

Chapman, J. (1966) The early symptoms of schizophrenia. *British Journal of Psychiatry,* **112,** 225–51.

Cooper, A. F., Garside, R. F. & Kay, D. W. K. (1976) A comparison of deaf and non-deaf patients with paranoid and affective psychosis. *British Journal of Psychiatry,* **129,** 532–8.

Cromwell, R. J. (1968) Stimulus redundancy and schizophrenia. *Journal of Nervous and Mental Disease,* 146 (5), 360–75.

Crow, T. J., Deakin, J. F. W., Johnstone, E. C. & Longden, A. (1976) Dopamine and schizophrenia. *Lancet, ii,* 563–6.

Dixon, N. F. (1971) *Subliminal Perception: The Nature of a Controversy.* London: McGraw-Hill.

Erdelyi, M. H. (1974) A new look at the new look: perceptual defence and vigilance. *Psychological Review,* **81,** 1–25.

Eysenck, H. J. & Frith, C. D. (1977) *Reminiscence, Motivation and Personality.* New York: Plenum Press.

Feighner, J. P., Robins, F., Guze, J. B., Woodruff, R. A., Winokur, G. & Munoz, R. (1972) Diagnostic criteria for use in psychiatric research. *Archives of General Psychiatry,* **26,** 57–63.

Fish, F. J. (1962) *Schizophrenia.* Bristol: John Wright; 2nd Ed. *Fish's Schizophrenia*, ed. M. Hamilton, 1976.

Frith, C. D. (1973) Learning rhythmic hand movements. *Quarterly Journal of Experimental Psychology,* **25,** 253–9.

Garner, W. R. (1966) To perceive is to know. *American Psychology,* **21** (1), 11–19.

Harris, A. (1959) Sensory deprivation and schizophrenia. *Journal of Mental Science,* **105,** 235.

Hemsley, D. R. (1976) Attention and information processing in schizophrenia. *British Journal of Social and Clinical Psychology,* **15,** 199–209.

Kendon, A. (1967) Movement co-ordination in social interaction. *Acta Psychologica,* **32,** 100–25.

Lecours, A. R. & Vanier-Clement, M. (1976) Schizophasia and jargon aphasia. *Brain and Language,* **3,** 516–65.

Lesser, V. R., Fennell, R. D., Firman, L. D. & Reddy, D. R. (1974) Organization of the Hearsay II speech understanding system. (Working papers in speech recognition III). Carnegie-Mellon University, 1974, 11–21.

Maher, B. A. (1974) Delusional thinking and perceptual disorder. *Journal of Individual Psychology,* **30,** 98–113.

Marcel, A. J. (1976) Unconscious reading. Paper given to the British Association for the Advancement of Science, Lancaster.

Marcel, A. & Patterson, K. (1976) Word recognition and production: reciprocity in clinical and normal studies. In: *Attention and Performance VII* (ed.) J. Requin. New Jersey: Lawrence Erlbaum.

Marshall, W. L. (1973) Cognitive functioning in schizophrenia. *British Journal of Psychiatry,* **123,** 413–33.

Matussek, P. (1952) Untersuchungen über der Wahnwahrnehmung. Erste Mitteilung: Veränderungen der Wahrnehmungswelt bei beginnenden schizophrenen Wahn. *Archiv für Psychiatrie und der Nervenkrankheiten,* **189,** 279.

Mewhort, A. J. (1967) Familiarity of letter sequences, response uncertainty and the tachistoscopic recognition experiment. *Canadian Journal of Psychology,* **21,** 309–21.

Miller, G. A. (1956) The magical number seven plus or minus two: some limits on our capacity for processing information. *Psychological Review,* **63,** 81–97.

Moon, A. F., Mefferd, R. B., Wieland, B. A., Pokorny, A.D. & Falconer, G. A. (1968) Perceptual dysfunction as a determinant of schizophrenic word associations. *Journal of Nervous and Mental Disease,* **146** (1), 80–4.

Payne, R. W., Caird, W. K. & Laverty, S. G. (1964) Overinclusive thinking and delusions in schizophrenic patients. *Journal of Abnormal and Social Psychology,* **68,** 562–6.

——— Matussek, P. & George, G. I. (1959) An experimental study of schizophrenic thought disorder. *Journal of Mental Science,* **105,** 627–52.

Posner, M. I. & Boies, S. J. (1971) Components of attention. *Psychological Review,* **78,** 391–408.

——— & Keele, S. W. (1969) Attention demands of movement. In: *Proceedings of the 16th International Congress of Applied Psychology.* Amsterdam: Swetts and Zeitlirger.

——— & Klein, R. M. (1973) On the functions of consciousness. In: S. Kornblum (ed.). *Attention and Performance IV.* London: Academic Press.

——— & Snyder, C. R. R. (1975) Attention and cognitive control. In: R. L. Solso (ed.), *Information Processing and Cognition: the Loyola Symposium.* Hillsdale M.H., Erlbaum.

Poulton, E. C. (1966) Tracking Behaviour. In Bilodeau, E. A. (Ed.). *Acquisition of Skill,* London: Academic Press.

Price, R. H. & Eriksen, C. W. (1966) Size constancy in schizophrenia: a reanalysis. *Journal of Abnormal Psychology,* **71** (3), 155–60.

Rumelhart, D. G. (1976) Toward an interactive model of reading: In: S. Dornic (ed.), *Attention and Performance VI.* London and New York: Academic Press.

Schneider, K. (1957) Primäre und sekundäre Symptome bei Schizophrenie. *Fortschritte der Neurologie und Psychiatrie,* **25,** 487.

Schulman, C. A., Milton, R. & Weinstein, S. (1967) Hallucinations and disturbances of affect, cognition and physical state as a function of sensory deprivation. *Perceptual and Motor Skills,* **25** (3), 1001–24.

Schvaneveldt, R. W., Meyer, D. E. & Becker, C. A. (1976) Lexical ambiguity, semantic context and visual word recognition. *Journal of Experimental Psychology, Human Perception and Performance,* **2,** 243–56.

Shaffer, L. H. (1975) Multiple attention in continuous verbal tasks. In: P. M. A. Rabbitt and S. Dornic (eds.), *Attention and Performance V.* London: Academic Press.

Shallice, T. (1972) Dual functions of consciousness. *Psychological Review,* **79,** 383–93.

Slade, P. D. (1974) The external control of auditory hallucinations: an information theory analysis. *British Journal of Social and Clinical Psychology,* **13,** 73–9.

——— (1976) An investigation of psychological factors involved in the predisposition to auditory hallucinations. *Psychological Medicine,* **6,** 123–32.

Sperling, G. (1960) The information available in brief visual presentations. *Psychological Monographs,* **74** (11, whole no. 498).

Tulving, E. & Thompson, D. M. (1973) Encoding specificity and retrieval processes in short-term memory. *Psychological Review,* **80,** 352–73.

Turvey, M. T. (1974) Constructive theory, perceptual systems and tacit knowledge. In: W. B. Weimer and D. S. Palermo (eds.), *Cognition and the Symbolic Processes.* Hillsdale M.H.: Erlbaum.

Vaughn, C. & Leff, J. P. (1976) The influence of family and social factors on the course of psychiatric illness: a comparison of schizophrenic and depressed neurotic patients. *British Journal of Psychiatry,* **129,** 125–37.

Warren, M. & Gregory, R. L. (1958) An auditory analogue of the visual reversible figure. *American Journal of Psychology,* **71,** 612–13.

Wing, J. K., Cooper, J. E. & Sartorius, N. (1974) *The Description and Classification of Psychiatric Symptoms: An Instruction Manual for the PSE and Catego System.* London: Cambridge University Press.

# 2 Experiences of alien control in schizophrenia reflect a disorder in the central monitoring of action

*Christopher D. Frith and D. John Done*

## Introduction

Many of the symptoms of schizophrenia involve experiences that are outside the normal range. Yet they must be the consequence of impairments to normal psychological processes. We (Frith, 1987; Frith & Done, 1988) have recently proposed that symptoms such as delusions of control and thought interference are the consequence of failure in a system whereby we monitor our intended actions (see also Feinberg, 1978). This monitoring permits the distinction between internally generated (willed) and externally generated (stimulus elicited) actions. It is necessary if we are to know what we have just done and why. If thoughts and actions occurred in the absence of central monitoring they might be attributed to alien forces.

Extensive evidence for the existence of a central monitoring system comes from studies of error correction in human subjects (Rabbitt, 1966; Angel, 1976). In these experiments it has been shown that errors of movement can be detected and corrected in the absence of visual feedback and too rapidly for other kinds of exteroceptive feedback to have been used. Thus, studies of error correction can be used to test the hypothesis that those schizophrenic symptoms that relate to experiences of alien control are associated with problems in the central monitoring of action.

There is already evidence that schizophrenic patients have difficulty with central error correction (Malenka *et al.* 1982). We have designed a modified version of the task that was used in that study. Our aim was to examine not merely whether problems with central error correction relate to schizophrenia but whether they relate to specific schizophrenic symptoms experienced by many but not all schizophrenic patients.

## Method

### *Subjects*

In order to examine this precise hypothesis it was necessary to select the patients very carefully. A major requirement was that they should be drug free at the time of testing, since neuroleptic drugs in particular, might be expected to interfere with the ability to make rapid movements. In order to test the hypothesis that specific symptoms rather than general diagnosis are important in determining error correcting performance it was necessary to compare patients suffering from schizophrenia with patients suffering from affective psychosis and schizophrenic patients having experiences of alien control with those not having such experiences. For this purpose a careful examination of symptoms at the time of testing was required. Finally, it was necessary to find patients who were able and willing to carry out these rather complex tasks in spite of their acute illness. We were able to find 23 such patients in the course of an extensive ($N = 252$) study of the treatment of the functional psychoses (Johnstone *et al.* 1988). All the patients in this study were assessed using the Present State Examination (Wing *et al.* 1974) and had to have at least one definite psychotic symptom. Fourteen of the patients received a CATEGO classification of schizophrenia (S) while 9 were classified as having affective psychosis (AP) (2 manic, 7 depressed). From the PSE records we selected delusions of control, thought insertion and thought blocking as evidence of experiences of passivity or alien control. All of the patients with affective psychosis and four of the patients with schizophrenia did not have any of these symptoms. Six control subjects (C) were selected from the ward and laboratory staff matched for age and sex with the patients.

### *Procedure*

The error correcting task was closely modelled on that used by Malenka *et al.* (1982), but was presented as a video game and administered by a microcomputer. The subject's task was to shoot birds which appeared without warning on either the left or the right side of a VDU.

#### *Task 1*

Throughout the game two men aiming guns were on the VDU. A man aiming right was on the left of the top half of the screen and a man aiming left was on the right of the bottom half of the screen. A trial was initiated by the appearance of a bird opposite one of the two men. The man and the bird were separated by 13 cm. As soon as the bird appeared the subject attempted to make the man opposite fire his gun by moving the joystick to the left or the right. A bullet then appeared which moved slowly across the screen, taking 2800 msec to reach the bird. At this point the bird either fell over or jumped out of the way. If the subject fired the wrong gun and failed to correct this before the 2800 msec then the message 'you pulled the wrong trigger' appeared on the screen. At any time during the 2800 msec the subject could fire the other gun. A bullet then emerged from the other gun and travelled across the screen as before, while the first bullet stopped. In this way subjects could correct their errors. There was a gap of approximately 2 secs between the end of one trial and the beginning of the next.

It was critical to this investigation that the subjects made many errors. The task was therefore made more difficult by periodically reversing the relationship between movement of the joystick and the man selected to shoot (Malenka *et al.* 1982). Thus, for some trials moving the joystick to the left caused the left hand man to fire (type A), while on the other trials moving the joystick to the left caused the right hand man to fire (type B). The level of difficulty could be controlled by altering the number of trials on which the relationship between joystick and gun remained the same (i.e. 10 of type A followed by 10 of type B or 5 of type A by 5 of type B etc.). In the most difficult version of the task the relationship between joystick and guns was reversed on every trial (i.e. type A followed type B followed by type A and so on). The procedure was carefully explained to each subject so that they knew in advance what the sequence of trial types would be. During a practice period an appropriate level of difficulty was chosen so that each subject made approximately the same number of errors. In 26 cases the most difficult version of the task was used (i.e. strict alternations of trial type). Two of the schizophrenic patients with passivity experiences and one of the schizophrenic patients without passivity experiences were given a slightly easier version of the task with double alternations of trial type.

### *Task 2*

Task 2 was identical to task 1 except that two walls were present on the VDU between each man and the positions where the birds would appear. Each wall was 10 cm long and there was a 3 cm gap between the end of the wall and the position of the bird. The purpose of the walls was to hide the trajectory of the bullet. Thus, the bullet was invisible (behind the wall) for the first 2000 msec after the subject's response. It then appeared from behind the wall and was visible for the last 800 msec until reaching the bird. In this task, therefore, the subject did not get any visual feedback as to whether he had fired the correct gun for 2000 msec. He did have visual feedback for the last 800 msec of the trial. As in task 1 he could correct his response at any time during the 2800 msec.

Subjects viewed the VDU from a distance of approximately 40 cm in a well lit room. They manipulated the joystick with their preferred hand. After a practice period each subject performed 80 trials with task 1 followed by 80 trials with task 2. Subjects were instructed to respond as quickly as possible. If they had not responded within 670 msec a message appeared on the VDU indicating that they were too late.

## Results

In each task there were four measures of interest: the number of errors (i.e. firing the wrong gun); the proportion of these errors that were corrected within 2800 msec; the proportion of these corrections made within the first 2000 msec (since in task 2 such corrections must be made in the absence of visual feedback); and, the number of false corrections (i.e. after having fired the correct gun,

*Table 2.1* Medians and semi-interquartile ranges for the four measures of task performance. (1) Number of errors committed in 80 trials (a). (2) The percentage of these errors that were corrected (b/a). (3) The percentage of these corrections that were initiated within 2000 msec (c/b). (4) The number of times a response was changed when it was correct. The semi-interquartile range is omitted when all subjects achieved the same score.

| | *Schizophrenics with experiences of alien control (N = 10)* | *Schizophrenics without experiences of alien control (N = 4)* | *Affective (N = 9)* | *Control (N = 6)* | *Kruskal-Wallis χ2 (df = 3)* |
|---|---|---|---|---|---|
| Task 1 | | | | | |
| Errors in 80 trials | 23 (13·5) | 10·5 (9·5) | 21 (2) | 27 (16) | 2·19 |
| % Errors corrected | 100 | 100 | 100 | 100 | – |
| % Errors corrected within 2000 msec | 100 (0) | 100 | 100 (1·5) | 100 (2·5) | 1·68 |
| False corrections | 0 | 0 | 0 | 0 (0) | – |
| Task 2 | | | | | |
| Errors in 80 trials | 17 (11·7) | 8 (8·75) | 14 (6·5) | 12 (12·5) | 0·79 |
| % Errors corrected | 82 (21) | 65 (15·75) | 50 (12·5) | 66 (22·5) | 0·25 |
| % Errors corrected within 2000 msec | 8 (16·5) | 80 (22·5) | 40 (13·5) | 67 (33·5) | 13·13 |
| False corrections | 0 (0·5) | 0 (0) | 0 (0·5) | 0 (0·5) | 2·79 |

Semi-interquartile ranges are shown in parentheses.

inappropriately firing the other). The medians and semi-interquartile ranges for these four measures are shown in Table 2.1.

Since these measures were far from normally distributed all the group comparisons were made using non-parametric statistics (Kruskal-Wallis test and Page's test for paired comparisons).

### *Task 1*

In task 1 there were no differences between the groups on any of the four measures. Subjects made errors on about 25% of the trials. They corrected virtually all these errors within 2000 msec and made almost no false corrections.

### *Task 2*

There were fewer errors made in task 2 than in task 1 presumably because of practice. In all other respects, however, performance of task 2 was worse. There were no differences between the groups in the number of errors made, the proportion of errors corrected or the number of false corrections. There were, however, significant differences in the proportion of errors corrected within the first 2000 msec (in the absence of visual feedback) ($\chi^2 = 13{\cdot}1$, df $= 3$, $P < 0{\cdot}01$). The schizophrenic patients with experiences of alien control differed significantly from each of the other three groups (S + AP *v.* S, $P < 0{\cdot}001$, S + AP *v.* AP, $P < 0{\cdot}02$, S + AP *v.* C, $P < 0{\cdot}01$). The other three groups did not differ significantly from one another.

## Discussion

In order to make a correct response on either task, a subject must correctly register which side the bird has appeared and also remember which type of trial (A or B) the current one is. All groups of subjects were able to make correct responses at a much higher rate than would be expected by chance, especially on task 2. Thus they were able to keep track of the sequence of trial types most of the time. We conclude then, that neither experiences of alien control nor the more general symptoms of schizophrenia interfered with our patients' ability to make correct responses on either task. The critical question for our hypothesis is whether patients were able to correct those errors that they did commit.

It was very easy to detect and correct errors in task 1 because of the immediate visual feedback (the appearance of the bullet from the gun). As a consequence all errors were corrected and there were no false corrections (apart from one made by a control subject). It is however, important to note that virtually all errors were corrected within 2000 msec by all groups. Thus, any failure to correct errors as quickly in task 2 cannot be attributed to the non-specific slowness of reaction often observed in schizophrenic patients. Indeed reaction time would have to be extremely slow to prevent responding before 2000 msec.

Correcting errors in task 2 before the bullet appeared from behind the wall was far more difficult. Nevertheless, subjects (except those with experiences of alien control) did correct most of their errors before the bullet appeared. One reason for making an error would be that the subject had lost track of where he was in the sequence of trials. However there is no way that he could correct such an error before the bullet appeared. If he simply changed his mind as a consequence of his uncertainty, then this would result in an increase in false corrections. There were very few of these and the groups did not differ in this respect. It seems unlikely, therefore, that many errors were a consequence of failure to keep track of the sequence of trial types. In tasks of this sort the movement errors that occur are usually considered to be 'impulsive' in the sense that they are made prematurely before the subject has fully digested all the information that is available to him (Megaw, 1972; Rabbitt & Vyas, 1981). In our version of the task the subject might quickly make the most 'natural' response (e.g. moving the joy-stick towards the bird that has just appeared) and then realize that the current trial was type B and that he should have moved the joy-stick the other way. This realization depends (1) on knowing where he is in the sequence of trials and (2) on knowing in the absence of visual feedback what response he has just made. Since the groups did not differ in the number of correct responses or in the number of false corrections we would like to argue that the groups did not differ in their ability to keep track of the sequence of trials. Therefore, we infer that the problem for the patients having experiences of alien control must have been due to not knowing what response they had just made.

Given the external feedback supplied by the bullet as it eventually appeared from behind the wall these patients then usually did correct their error. This was done within the final 800 msec. For this reason it seems unlikely that the patients had a problem merely with vigilance or low motivation. We conclude that patients having experiences of alien control had a specific difficulty with using central feedback to monitor their own actions.

Our results extend those of Malenka *et al.* (1982) in showing that this problem is particularly associated with schizophrenia rather than affective psychosis. Over and above this association we have shown that it did not occur in the four schizophrenic patients who were not having experiences of alien control. Clearly this result needs to be replicated with larger samples. It is however, consistent with our suggestion that it is specifically experiences of passivity and alien control that are a consequence of a problem with the internal monitoring of actions.

Using a very different EEG paradigm, Braff *et al.* (1977) also obtained a result suggesting that schizophrenic patients have difficulty monitoring their own actions. Normally the EEG evoked response to a tone is reduced if the subject has generated the tone himself by pressing a button. This reduction was found not to appear in schizophrenic patients. Braff *et al.* attribute this to a failure in very short-term memory. We suggest that the problem is particularly to do with a failure of memory for the response the subject has just made. Hence, this is another example of a problem with the central monitoring of action. It would be desirable to repeat Braff *et al.*'s experiments to see if the result here also relates to particular symptoms rather than to schizophrenia in general.

We have deliberately chosen to discuss tasks in which performance critically depends on the subject's ability to monitor his own responses internally. Further research with other tasks will be needed to ascertain whether the problem that some schizophrenic patients have is specific to the internal monitoring of their own responses or is part of a more general problem with manipulation of internal representations.

Relating symptoms to underlying psychological processes is an essential step if we are eventually to understand symptoms in terms of brain dysfunction. It is difficult to understand how passivity experiences such as delusions of alien control might relate to the brain. However, there have already been attempts to study how central monitoring is carried out by the brain. Indeed, it is perfectly possible to study in animals which brain systems are involved in central monitoring. For example, it has been shown that neurons in the superior colliculus of rhesus monkeys distinguish real from self-induced stimulus movement (Robinson & Wurtz, 1976) and that neurons in the auditory cortex of squirrel monkeys distinguish between self-produced and loudspeaker transmitted vocalizations (Muller-Preuss, 1978). We suggest that an investigation of the sources of the signals which permit this detection of self-induced events would provide important clues to the brain disorders underlying many of the symptoms of schizophrenia.

We are grateful to Dr Eve C. Johnstone and Dr T. J. Crow for giving us access to the patients under their care and also their PSE examinations. We are grateful to Uta Frith, Rosalind Ridley and Timothy Crow for their comments on earlier drafts of this paper. This study was carried out under the auspices of the Ethical Committee of Northwick Park Hospital.

## References

Angel, R. W. (1976). Efference copy in the control of movement. *Neurology* **26,** 1164–1168.

Braff, D. L., Calloway, I. & Naylor, J. (1977). Very short-term memory dysfunction in schizophrenia. *Archives of General Psychiatry* **34,** 25–30.

Feinberg, I. (1978). Efference copy and corollary discharge: Implications for thinking and its disorders. *Schizophrenia Bulletin* **4,** 636–640.

Frith, C. D. (1987). The positive and negative symptoms of schizophrenia reflect impairments in the perception and initiation of action. *Psychological Medicine* **17,** 631–648.

Frith, C. D. & Done, D. J. (1988). Towards a neuropsychology of schizophrenia. *British Journal of Psychiatry* **153,** 437–443.

Johnstone, E. C., Crow, T. J., Frith, C. D. & Owens, D. G. C. (1988). The Northwick Park 'functional' psychosis study: diagnosis and treatment response. *Lancet* ii, 119–125.

Malenka, R. C., Angel, R. W., Hampton, B. & Berger, P. A. (1982). Impaired central error-correcting behaviour in schizophrenia. *Archives of General Psychiatry* **39,** 101–107.

Megaw, J. D. (1972). Directional errors and their correction in a discrete tracking task. *Ergonomics* **15,** 633–643.

Muller-Preuss, P. (1978). Single unit responses of the auditory cortex in the squirrel monkey to self-produced and loudspeaker transmitted vocalisations. *Neuroscience Letters Suppl.* 1, S.7.

Rabbitt, P.M. A. (1966). Error-correction time without external signals. *Nature* **212,** 438.

Rabbitt, P.M. A. & Vyas, S. (1981). Processing a display even after you made a response to it. How perceptual errors can be corrected. *Quarterly Journal of Experimental Psychology* **33A,** 223–239.

Robinson, D. L. & Wurtz, R. H. (1976). Use of an extra retinal signal by monkey superior colliculus neurons to distinguish real from self-induced stimulus movement. *Journal of Neurophysiology* **39,** 852–870.

Wing, J. K., Cooper, J. R. & Sartorius, N. (1974). *The Description and Classification of Psychiatric Symptoms. An Instruction Manual for the PSE and CATEGO System.* Cambridge University Press: Cambridge.

# 3 Elective affinities in schizophrenia and childhood autism

*Christopher D. Frith and Uta Frith*

## Do childhood autism and schizophrenia show a hidden relationship?

> "Let me anticipate," said Charlotte, "to see if I understand what you are aiming at. Just as everything is related to its own kind so it must be related to other things" . . . "Quite so" replied the Captain, . . . "We talk of affinities when things meet together and interact with each other. Take alkalis and acids. Despite their antagonism, or perhaps because of it, they seek each other most determinedly. They modify each other and form something new. Here is affinity." . . . "I must confess," said Charlotte, "when you mention these strange examples they don't make me think of blood relations, but of relationships of the mind . . . "

In Goethe's *Elective Affinities* (*Die Wahlverwandtschaften,* 1809), from which this extract is taken, the characters go along with the idea that there is greater merit in bringing together elements, opposites even, than there is in separating them. We follow their example by bringing together some very different concepts which can yet reveal surprising compatibilities. Clearly the two psychotic disorders that we have chosen to relate to each other, schizophrenia and autism, each belong to a different category of onset, one late, one early. Delusions and hallucinations commonly occur in schizophrenia, but are an exclusion criterion for the diagnosis of autism. There are major differences in epidemiological statistics, such as sex ratio, family history, and incidence of mental retardation. Nevertheless the term "autism" was originally coined by Bleuler in 1911 in order to characterize a type of social impairment that seemed characteristic of schizophrenia. Profound and intransigent social impairments are indeed a feature of both disorders, and it is no coincidence that both Kanner (1943) and Asperger (1944) independently of each other chose the label "autistic" to name the disorder that we now call childhood autism.

In some respects it is easy to see similarities in different psychiatric disorders. Impaired performance on cognitive tests or impaired emotional responses are examples of very common deficits. Such commonalities are not the areas where we would like to discover a hidden relationship. We wish to know whether there are similarities of a specific rather than a general nature, features that hold uniquely and universally true for both disorders. Our first problem is therefore to decide which features are, in fact, fundamental to both. Once chosen, we would like to explain them in terms of a similar underlying dysfunction in the processing of information and, underlying this, a similar neurophysiological dysfunction.

## The key features of autism

When identifying key features, the picture is clearer in many ways for early childhood autism. Autism research benefited from methodological advances that were made in the study of mental retardation (e.g., Ellis, 1979; Hermelin and O'Connor, 1970). The most important advance was the strategy of comparing retarded children with mental age-matched autistic children. The problem of misidentifying chronological age-inappropriate behavior as abnormal when it is, in fact, mental age-appropriate is therefore avoided. Abnormalities can be specifically attributed to autism rather than to mental retardation when this strategy is followed. Wing and Gould (1979) used this insight in order to clarify the key symptoms of autism. In an important epidemiological study, they contrasted children with and without severe social impairment. As a result of this study a cluster of signs were identified which sharply divide children with and without persistent social impairments. These signs are largely independent of other additional handicaps such as sensory or motor handicap, and of accompanying mental retardation. The three signs are: 1) impaired social relations including aloofness, passivity, and oddness, 2) impaired communication, verbal and non-verbal, and 3) impaired imaginative activity with the substitution of stereotyped behavior. This triad applies to all individuals who are diagnosed as autistic according to various diagnostic schemes (Wing, 1988a,b). It includes "pure" cases as well as cases with additional handicaps, and degree of severity can vary. For all affected individuals the triad is the common denominator. It thus defines a whole spectrum of autistic disorders.

The triad is frequently, but not necessarily, associated with general mental retardation (Wing and Gould, 1979). Thus it is possible to study cases in which the three key signs are unconfounded by general intellectual impairment. With different levels of development and different degrees of ability, the signs show different behavioral manifestations, but they are always distinctly recognizable. The able and verbally articulate individual may show a communication impairment by engaging in lengthy accounts of a favorite topic without any consideration of the listener's wish to be told. This is just as much a failure of communication as can be observed in a mute child who persists in repetitive action without regard to the teacher's efforts towards a more constructive activity. It is sometimes hard to spot impairments at the extreme ends of the spectrum. At one extreme, difficulty arises because very young or very retarded children have too limited a repertoire to allow the key behavior to be observed. At the other extreme, the difficulty is that older, well taught and able autistic individuals can show remarkable compensation, and their well-rehearsed and often wide behavioral repertoire can deceive the non-expert observer. It is therefore not surprising that the middle range of the autistic spectrum includes the most typical cases.

## The key features of schizophrenia

For schizophrenia, the question of comparison groups is not so clear. As long as schizophrenia was considered not to be associated with organic damage, it was appropriate to compare schizophrenia with the other "functional" psychoses, and even the neuroses. However, such a view is now untenable. It is generally accepted that there is an organic basis to schizophrenia (e.g., Cutting, 1985), and in the majority of cases there is evidence of significant intellectual impairment (Aylward et al., 1987). It therefore might be more appropriate to compare schizophrenia with neurodegenerative disorders. Studies of this kind on a large scale in the manner of Wing and Gould's study of social impairment in children have yet to be done. In the absence of such definitive studies, there continues to be argument about which should be considered the key features of schizophrenia. The at present undisputed contenders are the positive symptoms (particularly Schneider's first rank symptoms, i.e., specific forms of abnormal experience underlying some hallucinations and delusions). In most of the leading standardised diagnostic schemes (e.g., PSE, Wing et al., 1974; DSM IIIR; American Psychiatric Association, 1987) these symptoms are necessary, but not always sufficient for the patient to be classified as suffering from schizophrenia. On the other hand, there are also the negative signs of psychomotor slowness, affective blunting, and intellectual deficit. These often precede as well as follow the first onset of the positive symptoms which attract attention both in the early stages and in acute phases of relapse. In the later stages of the illness, only one or the other type may be shown. Crow (1980) even suggested that these symptom clusters belong to discrete syndromes with different aetiologies.

In terms of the quality of life that the patient can lead, and in terms of long-term adaptation, there is little doubt that it is the negative signs that are most important (Owens and Johnstone, 1980). This is true, too, in terms of association with neurological signs (Owens et al., 1985). However, recent speculations about the psychological abnormalities that underly schizophrenia have largely been concerned with the striking positive symptoms and have ignored the less visible negative ones. An example is the theory that positive symptoms are caused by a disorder of selective attention. The idea is that the patient cannot help but attend to irrelevant events in his environment. It is then suggested that the negative signs are merely consequences of a strategy that is deliberately adopted to overcome this failure of selective attention (Hemsley, 1977). For instance, the patient would avoid complex situations in which many competing stimuli are likely to occur and in which any attention failure would be particularly serious. In this sort of theory, social withdrawal and lack of communication are explained simply by the fact that social situations are examples of complex situations. Unfortunately, this explanation begs the question of what situations count as complex and why. A more serious problem for the theory is the finding that there are patients who show negative signs (e.g., poverty of speech), in the absence of any significant cognitive decline (Frith and Done, 1983). Presumably, their social impairment is not due to non-specific problems concerning complex information processing. Rather, their problem is in dealing specifically with *social* situations, and in particular, communication (Wing and Freudenberg, 1961).

As Bleuler (1911) originally suggested, we ourselves believe that social withdrawal and lack of communication do not reflect a coping strategy for some other cognitive impairment. Instead, they are themselves primary features and in need of explanation by a psychological theory. If we add to these a third feature, namely lack of spontaneous, creative behaviour with increased stereotyped activity (Frith and Done, 1983; Lyon et al., 1986; Frith and Done, 1990), then we have an exact parallel to Wing's triad of impairments. The negative signs of schizophrenia can therefore be seen as a distinctive cluster of social, communicative, and imaginative impairments. Because these impairments together most clearly predict long-term outcome and brain pathology (Johnstone et al., 1986; Owens and Johnstone, 1980; Owens et al., 1985), it seems justified to consider them as key features of chronic schizophrenia over and above the definitive positive features.

As in the examples elaborated in Goethe's *Elective Affinities,* there are both attractions and risks in the attempt to relate separate or opposite entities. The attraction of our attempts to relate Wing's triad of impairments to the negative symptoms of schizophrenia is that we can build on cognitive theories that have already been proposed for both autism and schizophrenia. We are therefore in a position to put together a tentative model that can link related symptoms to underlying cognitive processes and can attempt to link these cognitive processes to brain function.

What then are the risks in our search for hidden similarities? Of course, when we suggest that certain key features of autism and chronic schizophrenia are related, we do not mean to imply that the two disorders are the same. This is plainly not the case, and on no account should differences be obscured (Wing and Attwood, 1987). The single most important difference is in the age of onset. Thus, the social-cognitive impairment that is associated with autism is manifest in early childhood, while that associated with schizophrenia may not appear until middle age. It follows that social knowledge and abilities in the adult autistic person are an outcome of abnormal development, while the schizophrenic individual even in his illness can draw on a store of normally acquired skills. Epidemiological and genetic studies point to a difference in aetiology. However, given the large variety of biological causes that are likely to exist for both disorders, we do not wish to speculate here about them.

## Wing's triad and second-order representations

The theory that can explain Wing's triad of impairments as the consequence of a specific cognitive dysfunction has been presented elsewhere (e.g., Baron-Cohen et al., 1985, 1986; Leslie, 1987; Leslie and Frith, 1988; Frith, 1989), and we shall therefore consider it only briefly. Crucial to the theory is Leslie's (1987; 1988a; 1988b) distinction between two kinds of knowledge. First, there is knowledge about objects in the world, such as bananas and telephones. This knowledge concerns the properties of the objects (color, texture) and the appropriate responses to be made to them (eating, dialing). It provides a more or less "true" representation of the world, and stored knowledge of this type is referred to as a *first-order representation.* It is the mind's window to the world. Second-order representations are what the mind makes of first-order representations. These are not like a window, but are "once removed" from reality as we perceive it. By cutting themselves off from a direct view (via a decoupling mechanism, in Leslie's terminology), these representations become the basis for a different kind of knowledge from which new inferences can be drawn. This knowledge knows about knowing. The ability to form second-order representations is a quantum leap in development. According to Leslie, one of the first unequivocal manifestations is the ability to pretend, which emerges around 18 months. From now on, the child is capable of taking into account that something is the case (a real state of affairs and a first-order representation), and yet can playfully ignore or contradict this knowledge (a "pretend" state and a second-order representation). An empty cup can be treated as if full, without the child being mistaken about the real state of affairs.

A later, highly important spin-off of the ability to handle second-order representations is the development of a "theory of mind." Of course, a well developed "theory of mind" depends on a great number of other things as well, not least learning and experience (Astington et al., 1988). It is a theory because we are talking of systematic social knowledge as opposed to mere social-emotional responding. This systematic knowledge is precisely what enables fast learning of social rules, and flexible, sophisticated use of the rules. Without such a theory, learning would be a slow process.

Having a "theory of mind" crucially depends on being aware that there are mental states (thoughts, desires, beliefs) which people have *about something,* and that other people have minds with different contents to our own. It is this aspect of "theory of mind" that depends on the ability to form second-order representations. Having a "theory of mind" enables us to mind-read, in a manner of speaking. We can work out what somebody is thinking by using inferences because we know mental states have causes and effects (e.g., we know something not by magic, but because someone told us). Furthermore, being able to mind-read implies that we are aware that actions, words and expressions produced by other people are not necessarily true reflections of their state of mind. By elaborating on this discrepancy we can deceive, lie and bluff. One could mention many more aspects of sophisticated social know-how and manipulation but here we are concerned only with that aspect that critically enables this sophistication to develop at all, namely second-order representation.

Impairment of pretend play and imaginative activity is one of the components of Wing's triad which can be seen as a consequence of a failure with second-order representations. This could itself be due to a variety of problems in mechanisms that underlie our handling of second-order representations. The impairment of two-way social interaction is a more indirect consequence due to a lack of a 'theory of mind.' Autistic aloneness is not so much a lack of first-order social responsiveness (this seems to be a non-specific feature of mental retardation) but a lack of second-order social know-how. Autistic aloneness is a kind of mind-reading blindness (Frith, 1989). It implies that thinking about people is similar to thinking about very complex and unpredictable objects. However, it does not imply avoidance of people. In fact, autistic children prefer to be in the company of others rather than alone, and show attachment to particular individuals (Sigman and Ungerer, 1984; Sigman et al., 1986; Mundy et al., 1986), suggesting that primary social responsiveness is not impaired. Mind-reading blindness can accommodate also the fact that the social impairment in autism comprises the aloof, the passive, and odd. All three forms can be explained as manifestations of the inability to conceive of people as having mental states.

What of the impairment of communication? Here too we must distinguish two levels. Certainly, straightforward *instrumental* communication is possible for autistic children (Attwood et al., 1988; Landry and Loveland, 1988). On the other hand, two-way *intentional* communication depends upon making inferences about the minds of others. This requirement has been discussed in detail by Sperber and Wilson (1986). Thus, the lack of a "theory of mind" will leave communication very impoverished. For example, the appropriate response to the query "Can you get out of bed?" depends upon inferring something about the context and the speaker's intentions. In the case of the mother speaking to her adolescent son, she intends him to get up, and if he simply said "yes" without moving, this would make her angry. On the other hand, if the question was asked by a doctor of a Parkinson's patient, the answer "yes" would be noted as satisfactory, even without an accompanying demonstration. Typically, in pure autism, unconfounded by mental retardation, we find that the individual takes no account of the speaker's likely wishes and merely decodes the messages literally. "Can you get out of bed?" would be decoded as a request for information about mobility. In this way, we can explain the elusive quality of the able autistic individual's comprehension failure which includes lack of humor, irony, and make-believe. At the same time we can allow for the fact that a great deal of social competence exists in such individuals.

Difficulty with second-order representations explains Wing's triad of autistic features in terms of a single cognitive deficit. This theory also enables predictions to be made about aspects of autistic behavior that were not previously investigated. In particular, it was predicted that autistic children should have difficulty in understanding false beliefs. This prediction has been tested in a number of experiments (Baron-Cohen et al., 1985; 1986; Leslie and Frith, 1988). In one of these (Perner et al., 1989), the child is disappointed to discover that a "smarties" tube contains, not Smarties, but a small, blunt pencil. The child is then asked "What will your friend say/think is in the tube when she comes into the room?" In order to give the correct answer (Smarties), the child must recognize that, although there is really a pencil in the tube, his friend does not know this and will falsely believe that there are Smarties in the tube. Unlike normal 4-year olds, the majority of autistic children (with a mental age well above 4) incorrectly answered, "a pencil." They behaved as if they believed that when they know something, everyone else knows it too. In this sense, they do not know what causes their own knowledge (they *saw* what was in the tube) or somebody else's ignorance (they did *not see*). Many of the anecdotes about communication failure in autistic children can be understood in terms of this kind of mind-reading blindness.

The cognitive deficit we envisage is very specific: it is a difficulty in forming and applying second-order representations, not first-order representations. When there is mental retardation (with or without autism) the efficiency of both systems would be impaired, but in autism without mental retardation, only the second order system is affected. This need not be a serious deficit for adapting oneself to the physical world, but it is when it comes to adapting oneself to the social world. Here it is necessary to be able to represent and continually update the mental states of others. This must be kept separate from updating information about the true state of the world. Hence, we are aware that others can have different beliefs from us, and this drives our wish to communicate. Second-order representation is just as necessary to represent one's own mental states as it is for that of others, and thus the ability is a necessary component of self-consciousness.

## Schizophrenic symptoms and second-order representations

Having identified a triad of social and communicative impairments with stereotypes in schizophrenia, we propose that here too is a problem with second-order representations. We also propose that the cognitive dysfunction giving rise to this problem would manifest itself very differently in the two disorders. The major difference between the schizophrenic and the autistic person is that the autistic individual shows cognitive impairment from early in life, whereas the schizophrenic patient manifests the impairment long after the various cognitive abilities and language are fully developed. Thus we expect to see differences between those two groups, just as we do when comparing people who are congenitally deaf with those who acquired deafness in later life (Myklebust, 1964; Bloom and Lahey, 1978).

For the first decade or so of his life, the future schizophrenic patient will have had plenty of experience inferring the mental states of others and acknowledging (and no doubt taking advantage of) their false beliefs. Thus it is plausible that he will be able to draw on this experience when the psychosis first manifests itself, and that he will continue to take account of the fact that other people have different mental states, knowledge, and beliefs. He would still also systematically take account of possible causes and effects of mental states, his own as well as others. We propose, that as his illness progresses the schizophrenic patient will have increasing difficulty in using a theory of mind in the normal way, and will often fail to interpret mental states correctly. This difficulty will result in major problems with social interaction and communication. However, there is no reason to doubt that a well established self-awareness persists, as well as an ingrained knowledge about routine social roles and relationships.

We would expect differences too in the type of imaginative impairment that would result from problems with second-order representations, because the patient prior to his illness has fully developed normal imagination. As this becomes difficult to handle, stereotyped activities take over.

## Communication impairment in schizophrenia

There have been extensive studies of language in schizophrenia but far fewer of communication. The results of these studies suggest that schizophrenic language is remarkably intact, that is in terms of phonology, syntax, and semantics (see review by Frith and Allen, 1988). Nevertheless problems always emerge, but these have proved difficult to characterize. The problems include lack of cohesion (Rochester and Martin, 1979), failures of discourse planning (Hoffman, 1986), failure to make inferences (Allen, 1984), use of simplified syntax (Morice and Ingram, 1982) and, above all, poverty of ideas and production. All these problems can readily be interpreted in terms of failures of communication rather than of language. To reiterate, in order to communicate intentionally, it is necessary to infer the mental state of the partner. This is because we cannot understand what the point of a remark is unless we take into account what the partner intends and what he already knows and expects. These inferences determine whether to reply to a message at all, as well as the precise form of the reply. There is some evidence of a failure in schizophrenic patients to make inferences of mental states (Allen, 1984).

The problem with the use of referents and with discourse can largely be understood as a consequence of not taking into account the needs of the listener (in terms of his current knowledge). For example, we use complex rather than simple syntax only if the needs of the listener make such complexity necessary for communication. If varying needs are not taken into account then either the simplest syntax will always do, or else pedantic language is used at all times. Just such strategies are found in schizophrenic language as in the signs "poverty of speech" and "stilted speech." In the extreme, if the needs of the listener are not inferred and thus not recognized, then there is no need for communication at all and muteness results. Poverty of speech is a common sign in chronic schizophrenic patients, and is also observed in autistic patients when adults (Rumsey, et al., 1986). Thus many of the "language" problems associated with schizophrenia can be explained in terms of a failure to infer continuously the relevant mental states of others.

The expression of affect is also largely to do with communication of inner states and one's awareness of the effect this has on other people's inner feelings. Thus flattening of affect can be seen as a direct consequence of the same problem, namely a difficulty in forming and using second-order representations. At this deeper level of analysis – but not necessarily in surface behavior – similarities of autistic and schizophrenic communication failure are striking.

## Self-monitoring and willed intentions

Many of the negative and some of the positive symptoms of schizophrenia have been explained in terms of defects in the initiation and monitoring of willed actions (Frith, 1987; Frith and Done, 1988). Briefly, this refers to a fault in the ability to know whether or not an action was one's own. Certain types of symptoms, such as delusions of control by outside agencies were said to arise because the patient was not aware of his own willed intentions. A precise prediction made on the basis of this hypothesis was that patients showing these symptoms should have difficulty correcting their own errors in a reaction time task (Frith and Done, 1989). This prediction was confirmed experimentally. Negative symptoms according to this theory occur when the patient fails to form willed intentions. This account had almost nothing to say about communication problems in schizophrenia. In contrast, the triad of impairments in autism and its explanation has almost entirely been concerned with communication, and not with action and self monitoring. How will these different accounts fare when we relate them together? What are the hidden affinities?

Communication is a special kind of action. Therefore, it can be understood in the same way as other actions. Initiation and monitoring of actions play an important role in communication. Otherwise, one would not know what one said and meant as opposed to what someone else said and meant. Second-order representation is necessary for this type of monitoring, and must therefore be necessary for certain kinds of action as well. In fact, it applies whenever one needs to consider whether one did or did not do something, and also when one forms willed intentions.

Figure 3.1 is taken from Leslie (1988a) and illustrates his model for pretend play. Two sources of action are shown. The first depends on first-order representations and enables us to respond appropriately to objects (e.g., answering the telephone). The second depends on second-order representations and enables us to pretend (e.g., answering the banana). There is a striking similarity between this figure and that concerning the two routes to action discussed by Frith (1987), and by Frith and Done (1988) (Figure 3.2). This similarity suggests that stimulus elicited action depends upon first-order representation, while spontaneous or willed action depends on second-order representation. We propose therefore that both intentional communication and willed action depend upon second-order representation.

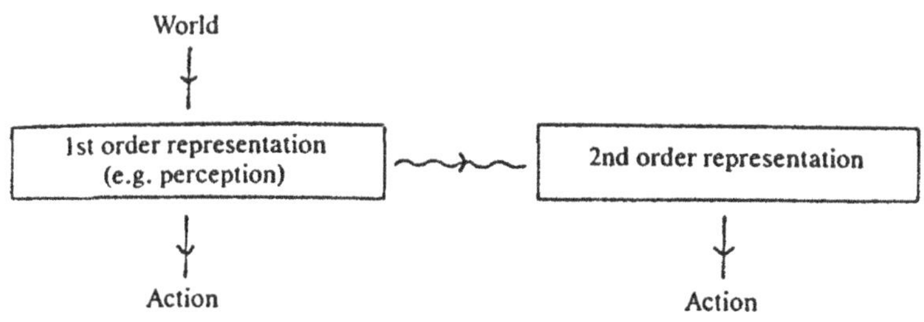


*Figure 3.1* First and Second Order Representations (after Leslie, 1988a)

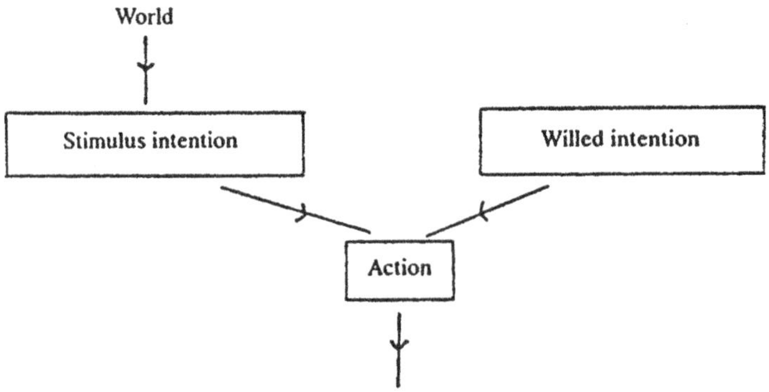


*Figure 3.2* Two Routes to Action (after Frith and Done, 1988)

The difference between these systems is that communication depends especially on representing the mental states of others, while willed action depends on representing the mental states of the actor himself, in particular his wishes and intentions. We therefore can postulate one single fault in the underlying processes that would explain the social failure as well as the poverty of ideas and actions.

Sperber and Wilson (1986) analyze in some detail the series of processes involved in a successful two-way communication. Essentially the relevance of the message has to be understood. First, the subject must recognize that there is an intent to communicate. Sperber and Wilson call an indication of an attempt to communicate an ostensive stimulus. This often takes the form of speech (as in "Oy, Jimmy"), but can also be a subtle and non-verbal stimulus (as in a raised eyebrow). Having recognized that there is an attempt to communicate, the subject must decode the message that is presented (e.g., from sound to phonology to semantics). However, decoding the message is not enough. The subject must also make inferences about the mental state of the communicator in order to extract the relevance of the message. The subject's representations of the mental state (e.g., wishes) of the communicator must be kept distant from his own wishes and also distinct from his representations of the real state of the world.

The development of a willed action can be described in a very similar way. First, the subject must recognize that one of his goals is achievable. He must then infer the series of states of the world that has to be produced in order to achieve that goal. These desired states of the world (second-order representation) must be kept distinct from the actual states of the world (first-order representations).

## Negative and positive symptoms in communication

In Table 3.1 we suggest some of the problems that might arise if there was a fault in the processes that compute relevance in communication. A fault can result in two kinds of error, false positives and false negatives. If there is something wrong

*Table 3.1* The Normal Processes Underlying Communication and Possible Abnormalities

| *False Negative (negative symptoms)* | *Normal Process* | *False Positives (positive symptoms)* |
|---|---|---|
| Failure to respond to ostensive stimuli | Recognition that communication is intended by other | Delusions of reference |
| No inference about mental states of other | Inferences about mental states of other | Paranoid delusions |
| Unable to represent mental states of others | Distinction between mental states of self and others | Incoherent speech, auditory hallucinations (3rd person) |

with the subject's ability to recognize an attempt to communicate (an ostensive stimulus) he might either see an attempt to communicate when there wasn't one (false positive), or he might fail to see an attempt to communicate which was in fact genuine (false negative). In both cases, there is misinterpretation and faulty communication of relevance. In the first case, too much relevance is attributed, in the second case, too little.

The false positive error in this case corresponds to a *delusion of reference,* where the subject erroneously believes that people are communicating with him. The false negative error would result in a lack of social responsiveness which is one aspect of *social withdrawal.* In general, we suggest that false positive errors lead to so-called "positive" symptoms, while false negative errors lead to "negative" symptoms.

*Paranoid delusions* can arise if the subject makes false but coherent inferences about the mental state of others.

If the subject confuses the mental states he might attribute to himself and to others, then it would follow that he apparently takes no account of the fact that he knows things that his hearers do not know. This could lead to certain kinds of *incoherence of speech* in which the subject fails to provide referents and introduces apparently unrelated topics without explanation (Rochester and Martin, 1979; Hoffman, 1986).

In extreme cases, the subject confuses his representations of the mental states of others with first-order representations of the real world. This could lead to certain auditory *hallucinations.* Auditory hallucinations have been explained as arising when the patient perceives his own thoughts as coming from an external source (e.g., Frith, 1987). However, it has always been difficult to explain why the "voices" are reported by patients to talk about them in the 3rd person, and why for the same patient there can be several different voices, male as well as female. It seems likely that what is most important to us in the beliefs of others is what they think about us. This content of their beliefs would be particularly important in determining the precise form of our communications. Therefore representations about the beliefs of others might take the form of 3rd person commentaries, for example, "he's not going to speak to me, he's too arrogant." Thus the common first rank symptom of hearing voices discussing the patient might be seen as a result of faulty interpretation of second-order representations. The mental states of others are still internally represented but misperceived as first-order representations of the real world. Hence the experience of hallucinations is created.

The false negative errors of the communication system all lead to varying degrees of *social withdrawal* and *lack of communication.* It is clear that all the examples of negative symptoms given in this column of the table apply very straightforwardly to autism.

## Negative and positive symptoms in willed action

Table 3.2 suggests the problems that might arise in the system for willed action. They would arise from the same fault in relevance computing processes. Hence, the arguments relating symptoms to abnormal processes are essentially the same as those we have outlined for Table 3.1. The failure to infer the appropriate actions leading to goals might lead to *incoherent speech* of a different kind from that associated with failures in the communication system. The patient meanders through a series of topics without ever reaching the point. Auditory hallucinations associated with failures in the action system would occur because the subject failed to distinguish between his own mental states and states in the real world. The patient might hear his thoughts as if they were coming from an external source. Likewise, the patient's own intentions might be perceived as having an external source, thus leading to *delusions of control.*

The false negative errors associated with the action system would lead to a general *lack of volition* and inability to achieve goals. In addition *flattening of affect* might occur if the subject was unable to represent his own mental states. For all three negative symptoms there are examples in relation to autistic individuals, most clearly documented in biographical accounts (e.g., Park, 1987).

The relations between symptoms and processing failures outlined in tables 3.1 and 3.2 are very tentative, but the tables imply interesting possibilities for classifying psychotic symptoms in terms of type and severity. First, there is the obvious distinction between symptoms associated with communication and those

*Table 3.2* The Normal Processes Underlying Action and Possible Abnormalities

| *False Negatives (negative symptoms)* | *Normal Process* | *False Positives (positive symptoms)* |
|---|---|---|
| Lack of volition | Recognition that a goal is achievable | Grandiose delusions |
| Unable to infer actions appropriate to goals | Inference of actions appropriate to goals | Delusions of causality, incoherent speech and acts |
| Unable to represent own mental states (flattening of affect) | Distinction between mental states and states of the world | Delusions of control, auditory hallucinations (thought broadcast) |

associated with action. If these systems are to some extent independent then we might expect the associated types of symptoms to be independent also.

Since the communication system is more complex, requiring the distinction between mental states of ourselves and others, we might expect this system to be more vulnerable, and thus symptoms associated with communication should reflect an earlier stage or a less severe form of the illness than those associated with action. Within both systems, the underlying processes are hierarchical. Thus if no distinction can be made between the mental states of the self and of others, the ability to infer the mental states of others is irrelevant. Likewise, if second-order representations cannot be formed at all, there are no mental states of self and others to be confused. Such a hierarchy indicates which symptoms are more or less severe. In this way, the present approach to the understanding of psychosis suggests the beginning of a rational and theoretically based scheme for classifying and relating symptoms.

For both tables the division into negative and positive symptoms reflects two types of processing error. For theoretical reasons, faults in the decision process have to allow for both false positives and false negatives. In practice, however, we see only false negatives in the case of autism, and only false positives in the case of acute phases of schizophrenia. Only some schizophrenic patients experience both positive and negative symptoms, while many chronic patients experience only negative symptoms.

How is this pattern to be explained? The key is the distinction between first- and second-order representations. Only if second-order representations are available and used can false positives occur. If second-order representations are not available at all, then false negatives are bound to occur, and only those. This would be the case in severe cases of autism, and might be the case in certain severe and late stages of schizophrenia where all vestiges of the formerly acquired second-order representation systems have disappeared.

It remains to be seen whether in mild cases of autism the ability to use second-order representation can be developed and practiced with time. If so, symptoms due to false positives would also occur. However, this has not been shown. Indeed, it might be very difficult to show, because the subjective experience of positive symptoms will depend on the patient's past experience. This past experience will be different for a person whose whole development took an abnormal course.

## Differences between schizophrenia and autism

Having drawn out the affinities between the two disorders, we must again turn to the vast differences between them. We have repeatedly stated that although similar cognitive dysfunction may underlie both schizophrenia and autism, this will not automatically mean that the signs and symptoms are similar. Nor does it exclude the possibility of additional cognitive deficits, which might well result in totally different additional impairments. To identify critical underlying cognitive differences is not an easy task. One initially striking difference, namely, the absence of positive symptoms in autistic individuals and their presence in schizophrenic patients, is less impressive now, because we can explain both presence and absence by the malfunctioning of one and the same cognitive process. We therefore think it could be misleading to stress the absence of delusions and hallucinations in autistic children. This absence might be of no greater significance than the absence of reading and spelling abnormalities in someone who has never been literate in the first place.

From their past experience schizophrenic patients know that people have mental states and what causes or changes them. We suggest, however, that when they are ill, these patients have great difficulty in inferring what these mental states are and how they are caused. Symptoms such as delusions of reference and delusions of persecution are a result of making incorrect inferences about the mental states of others. Autistic people do not make such attributions. They simply would not make the attempt to interpret the mental states of others, since they have never been sufficiently aware of their existence.

In addition to differences that might be explained by different age of onset, there are other differences that might be due to different causes. For instance, there is the characteristically uneven profile of abilities of autistic people of all levels of intelligence (Lincoln et al., 1988), and there are the peculiarly narrow interests, the occasional savant capabilities, the odd preoccupations and elaborate routines that are unique to classically autistic children. There are also characteristic odd movements, speech intonations, and sensory responses that are a frequent feature in autism, but rare in schizophrenia. None of these particular symptoms is universally present throughout the spectrum of autistic disorders, none is part of Wing's triad, and none can be explained by communication or monitoring of action failure. It remains to be seen whether these and other additional impairments can be explained as consequences of the early age of onset, or whether they are of separate origin.

## How can one study the neurophysiological basis of first- and second-order representations?

An entirely independent line of thinking leads us to believe that underlying the psychological deficit that we postulated for both autism and schizophrenia is some fairly specific damage to the brain. The existence of well adapted and able autistic and schizophrenic people suggests that the structures necessary for second-order representation can be damaged while leaving other cognitive structures intact. One would therefore assume that there are brain structures specifically concerned with the mechanisms necessary for second-order representation. In any case, we need to ask what these hypothetical structures are, and where they are located. We would also like to know what happens if these structures are damaged in the immature organism on the one hand, and the mature organism on the other. However, if we are properly to understand brain and behavior relationships we need to consider work with animals, since only here can true experiments be conducted.

The brain structures needed for second-order representation cannot have suddenly come into existence. They must have evolved, and thus animals must at least possess the precursors of such an ability. Before we can relate second-order representations to brain structures, we must attempt to delineate what this ability implies and what ability in animals might resemble it.

Leslie and Frith (1990) suggest that there are at least three components necessary for handling second-order representations: a decoupling mechanism, an inference mechanism, and a specific mechanism for relating first- and second-order representations. The decoupling mechanism is one component where one might look for a fault. According to Leslie (1987), the decoupling mechanism is designed to release a representation from its primary aim, namely to represent a real state of affairs. The primary representation is decoupled from this purpose and is now suspended from considerations of truth. There are three important consequences. First there is the detachment of the representation from its normal semantic associations. This means that other associations which we know to be incorrect can nevertheless be temporarily attached. The second feature is that it is not our perception that changes with decoupling. When pretending a banana is a telephone we still see that it is a banana, just as we still "know" it is a banana. Rather it is our responses that change. In other words, we behave as if the banana was a telephone (we put it to our ear, talk into it, etc.). Thus, while pretending we detach the responses appropriate to one object (which in some sense are the meaning of that object) and arbitrarily attach these responses to another object. The third feature of decoupling is that any rearrangement of stimuli and responses is temporary. When we have finished pretending we easily revert to our "normal" responses, eating bananas and not eating telephones.

It is these three consequences of decoupling that we can relate to phenomena reported in the literature on animal learning. In an extensive review of the kinds of tasks used to study learning and memory in monkeys, Ridley and Baker (submitted) suggest that there is a fundamental distinction between two kinds of learning. To us these two kinds of learning are reminiscent of the two types of knowledge. In one type the animal learns about the nature of the objects involved (i.e., their permanent properties). In particular it learns which objects to approach and which objects to avoid. For example food is placed always under the ballerina and never under the soldier. The monkey has to learn to approach the ballerina and avoid the soldier. Essentially, what is learned is the meaning of the object (e.g., the ballerina means food), and this is learned in terms of the appropriate response to be made to that object. This corresponds to first-order representations.

In contrast, according to Ridley and Baker, there is another type of learning where the animal learns to use the object as a sign. For example, if both food wells are covered by *green* plaques the food is in the left well, but if both are covered by *red* plaques then the food is in the right well. Here the animal has to learn to attach an arbitrary response to objects while the objects themselves remain neutral, neither to be generally approached nor avoided. Many more trials are needed to learn this task than are required to learn the ballerina vs. soldier task.

We suggest that the result of this type of learning is an analogue of the forming of second-order representations. In principle, the color plaques could be replaced by objects well known to the animal which, in the context of this particular task, would not represent their familiar meaning, but act as signs for something else. In an experiment reported by Gaffan and Bolton (1983; Experiment II, Stage 2) a monkey learned that a carrot meant "choose the black penny" and a sultana meant "choose the white penny." The black penny led to a food reward only when the carrot was there, but not the white penny, and vice versa. The cognitive requirements in this situation show certain similarities to those required for pretence. The representation of the object has to be detached from the representation of its normal meaning (e.g., eat) and has to be responded to in a new arbitrarily decided way (e.g., select a color). These responses apply only in the context of the experiment, and are thus temporary. Outside this context, carrot and sultana retain their semantic meaning and are eaten immediately.

Thus Ridley and Baker's distinction between two types of learning can be mapped readily onto Leslie's model of pretence (Figure 3.1). The first type of learning could be thought of as akin to forming first-order representations by which the permanent and real properties of objects are represented. The second and much more effortful type of learning might be akin to forming second-order representations, insofar as it is the context which determines which responses are to be (briefly and arbitrarily) attached to objects. Given that such a distinction can be made in animal learning, experiments could be conducted to find out which brain systems are involved. This is as far as we can go at present in suggesting ways of exploring the brain functions that underly the critical processes that we discussed in the main part of this essay.

The next step is to think about the kind of brain dysfunction that we might expect to give rise to a dysfunction in the formation of second-order representations. The justification for the distinction between the two kinds of learning in animals derives from studies of the effects of brain lesions. A great many experiments, reviewed by Ridley and Baker, have shown that "stimulus-reward association" (first-order) learning is impaired by lesions of the amygdala, while "arbitrary rule" (second-order) learning is impaired by lesions of the hippocampus. Here then a structural basis for the two types of processing is suggested. However, the results do not imply that the equivalent of first- and second-order representations in animals are stored respectively in the amygdala and hippocampus. Indeed, it has been shown that the hippocampus and amygdala are only necessary for the learning, not for the retention of the two types of tasks (Ridley et al., submitted; Jones and Mishkin, 1972). It remains quite open what other brain structures might be involved.

## Some ideas from neuropsychology

In current mainstream neuropsychology (Warrington and Weiskrantz, 1982), it is assumed that long term semantic memory is critically subserved by structures in the temporal lobe. This would be equivalent to first-order representations of the world. On the other hand, the central executive component of working memory is believed to be subserved by the frontal cortex (Goldman-Rakic, 1987). We would like to suggest that this component is responsible not only for temporary representations, but also for the arbitrary context-dependent meanings of objects. This demands second-order representations. Of course second-order representations do not exist on their own. In Leslie's (1987) model, a second-order representation is a "decoupled" first-order representation as indicated in his diagram (Figure 3.1). Warrington and Weiskrantz (1982) propose that there is a "cognitive mediational memory system" by which long term information from the posterior association cortex (i.e., temporal and parietal lobes) is additionally represented in a frontal system. We can therefore hypothesize that for second-order presentations both the frontal lobes and the connection from these to the temporal lobes need to be intact.

Bringing together these various ideas, we suggest that the processing of second-order representations is the job of the frontal cortex and its connections with various posterior structures. As yet, there is insufficient evidence for even the most tentative suggestions about which brain structures are involved in decoupling, and in keeping first-order and second-order representations distinct. However, a beginning is already made by elaborating the concepts of first- and second-order representations. On this basis, tasks can be designed that will permit the study of these issues in animals and in patients with known circumscribed lesions.

So far, neuropsychological tests have not been designed within the framework we are using in this chapter. All too often they are not designed within a cognitive framework at all, but rather in terms of brain areas (i.e., frontal tests, temporal tests, etc.). In these terms, we would expect that schizophrenic and autistic patients would be impaired on frontal tests rather than those concerned with more posterior regions. This need not mean, however, that the "lesion" is actually in the frontal cortex. In terms of our formulation, any difficulties with second-order representations might arise from malfunctioning connections between posterior regions and the frontal cortex.

There is currently considerable interest in the frontal lobes as a source of schizophrenic impairments (e.g., Weinberger, 1988). However, while many studies find that schizophrenic patients perform badly on frontal tests, they frequently perform badly on tests associated with other areas as well (e.g., Kolb and Wishaw, 1983). This is perhaps not surprising, since many patients show evidence of a general cognitive decline.

Since most neuropsychological tests presuppose a near normal general intellectual level, it is necessary to study autistic and schizophrenic patients of higher ability. A recent study adopted this strategy (Rumsey and Hamburger, 1988), and found that high IQ autistic patients are impaired only on frontal tests. As far as we are aware, this strategy has not yet been applied to schizophrenic patients. Tests derived specifically to examine the ability to form and use second-order representations should be used not only to study autistic and schizophrenic patients, but also neurological patients with various developmental or acquired disorders.

## Summary and conclusions

In this paper, we have put together the separate disorders of autism and schizophrenia and have drawn out the striking affinity between the negative signs of schizophrenia and the signs implied by Wing's triad. The affinity prompted us to propose that there is one and the same key abnormality that underlies the distinctive and profound communication failure in autism and the negative features of schizophrenia. This abnormality can be seen as a failure in the use of second-order representations. This failure leads to specific abnormalities of verbal and non-verbal communication, and of social interaction. It also leads to difficulties with the initiation of spontaneous willed action.

The positive symptoms of schizophrenia occur when erroneous representations of mental states are formed (through faulty inference), or when mental states and real states of the world are not properly distinguished. Such symptoms are not observed in autism because the awareness of mental states has never been fully developed. Hence misinterpretations do not arise.

The key abnormalities affect two systems: that concerned with communication (requiring representation of the mental states of others) and that concerning willed action (requiring representation of mental states of self). The representation of mental states as well as the representation of willed intentions require the ability to form second-order representation.

In order to look for a biological basis for the hypothesized cognitive processes, it is necessary to search for analogues in animal learning. Primates may have a capacity that is a precursor of the capacity to form second-order representations, and this could provide a useful tool for future investigations. Studies with animals and neurological patients suggest that while first-order representations (knowledge about the world) are processed in the posterior regions of the brain, especially the temporal lobes, objects may be "re-represented" in the frontal lobes. We can hypothesize that second-order representations depend on both the frontal lobes and connections from these to the temporal lobes.

In this brief account, we have done little more than to relate together psychotic symptoms, animal learning and brain function in terms of one cognitive process, namely the capacity to form and use second-order representation. The next step must be to develop techniques for studying this process in adults, children and animals.

## References

Allen, H.A. (1984) Positive and negative symptoms and the thematic organisation of schizophrenic speech. *British Journal of Psychiatry,* 144: 611–617.

American Psychiatric Association (1987) *Diagnostic and Statistical Manual for Mental Disorders.* Revised edition (DSM-III-R). American Psychiatric Association: Washington, D.C.

Asperger, H. (1944) Die "Autistischen Psychopathen" im Kindesalter. *Archiv für Psychiatrie und Nervenkrankheiten,* 117: 76–136.

Astington, J.W., Harris, P.L. and Olson, D.R. (eds.) (1988) *Developing Theories of Mind.* Cambridge: Cambridge University Press.

Attwood, A.H., Frith, U. and Hermelin, B. (1988) The understanding and use of interpersonal gestures by autistic and Down's syndrome children. *Journal of Autism and Developmental Disorders,* 18: 241–257.

Aylwood, E., Walker, E. and Bettes, B. (1984) Intelligence in schizophrenia: Meta-analysis of the research. *Schizophrenia Bulletin,* 10: 430–459.

Baron-Cohen, S., Leslie, A.M. and Frith, U. (1985) Does the autistic child have a "theory of mind"? *Cognition,* 21: 37–46.

Baron-Cohen, S., Leslie, A.M. and Frith, U. (1986) Mechanical, behavioural and intentional understanding of picture stories in autistic children. *British Journal of Development Psychology,* 4: 113–125.

Bleuler, E. (1911) Dementia praecox oder Gruppe der Schizophrenien. V. Aschaffenburg (ed.): *Handbuch der Psychiatrie,* Vol. 4., Chap. 1. Deuticke, Leipzig/Wien.

Bloom, L. and Lahey, M. (1978) *Language Development and Language Disorders.* New York: Wiley.

Crow, T.J. (1980) Molecular pathology of schizophrenia. More than one dimension of pathology? *British Medical Journal,* 280: 66–68.

Cutting, J. (1985) *The Psychology of Schizophrenia.* (Chapter 5) Churchill-Livingstone: Edinburgh.

Ellis, N.R. (1979) *Handbook of Mental Deficiency.* Hillsdale N.Y.: Erlbaum.

Frith, C.D. and Done, D.J. (1983) Stereotyped responding by schizophrenic patients in a two-choice guessing task. *Psychological Medicine,* 13: 779–786.

Frith, C.D. (1987) The positive and negative symptoms of schizophrenia reflect impairments in the perception and initiation of action. *Psychological Medicine,* 17: 631–648.

Frith, C.D. and Allen, H.A. (1988) Language disorders in schizophrenia and their implications for neuropsychology. In: P. Bebbington and P. McGuffin (Eds.) *Schizophrenia: The Major Issues.* Oxford: Heineman.

Frith, C.D. and Done, D.J. (1988) Towards a neuropsychology of schizophrenia. *British Journal of Psychiatry,* 153: 437–443.

Frith, C.D. and Done, D.J. (1989) Experience of alien control in schizophrenia reflect a disorder in the central monitoring of action. *Psychological Medicine,* 19, 359–364.

Frith, C.D. and Done, D.J. (1990) Stereotyped behavior in madness and in health. In: S.F. Cooper and C.T. Parish (Eds.) *The Neurobiology of Behavioural Stereotype.* Oxford: Oxford University Press.

Frith, U. (1989) *Autism: Explaining the Enigma.* Oxford: Blackwell.

Gaffan, D. and Bolton, J. (1983) Learning object – object associations by monkeys. *Quarterly Journal of Experimental Psychology,* 35B: 149–156.

Goldman-Rakic, P.S. (1987) Circuitry of primate prefrontal cortex and regulation of behaviour by representational memory. In: *Handbook of Physiology: The Nervous System.* Vol. 5 (Eds. F. Plum and V. Mountcastle) American Physiological Society, Bethesda, pp. 373–417.

Hemsley, D.R. (1977) What have cognitive deficits to do with schizophrenic symptoms? *British Journal of Psychiatry,* 130: 167–173.

Hermelin, B. and O'Connor, N. (1970) *Psychological Experiments with Autistic Children.* Oxford: Pergamon Press.

Hoffman, R.E. (1986) Verbal hallucinating and language production processes in schizophrenia. *The Behavioural and Brain Sciences,* 4: 503–548.

Johnstone, E.C., Owens, D.G.C., Frith, C.D. and Crow, T.J. (1986) The relative stability of positive and negative features in chronic schizophrenia. *British Journal of Psychiatry,* 150: 60–64.

Jones, B. and Mishkin, M. (1972) Limbic lesions and the problem of stimulus reinforcement associations. *Experimental Neurology,* 36: 362–377.

Kanner, L. (1943) Autistic disturbances of affective contact. *Nervous Child,* 2: 217–250.

Landry, S.H. and Loveland, K.A. (1988) Communication behaviours in autism and developmental language delay. *Journal of Child Psychology and Psychiatry,* 29: 621–634.

Leslie, A.M. (1987) Pretence and representation: the origins of 'theory of mind'. *Psychol. Review,* 94: 412–426.

Leslie, A.M. (1988a) Some implications of pretense for mechanisms underlying the child's theory of mind. In: Astington, J., Harris, P. and Olson, D. (eds.) *Developing Theories of Mind.* Cambridge: Cambridge University Press.

Leslie, A.M. (1988b) The necessity of illusion: perception and thought in infancy. In: Weiskrantz, L. (ed.) *Thought Without Language.* Oxford: Oxford University Press.

Leslie, A.M. and Frith, U. (1988) Autistic children's understanding of seeing, knowing and believing. *British Journal of Developmental Psychology,* 4: 315–324.

Leslie, A.M. and Frith, U. (1990) Prospects for a cognitive neuropsychology of autism: Hobson's choice. *Psychology Review 97,* 122–131.

Lincoln, A.J., Courchesne, E., Kilman, B.A., Elmasian, R. and Allen, M. (1988) A study of intellectual abilities in high-functioning people with autism. *Journal of Autism and Developmental Disorders,* 18: 505–524.

Lyon, N., Mejsholm, B. and Lyon, M. (1986) Stereotyped responding by schizophrenic out-patients. *Journal of Psychiatric Research,* 20: 137–150.

Kolb, B. and Wishaw, I.Q. (1983) Performance of schizophrenic patients in tests sensitive to left or right frontal, temporal or parietal function in neurological patients. *Journal of Nervous and Mental Disease,* 171: 435–443.

Morice, R.D. and Ingram, J.C.L. (1983) Language complexity and age of onset in schizophrenia. *Psychiatry Research,* 9: 233–242.

Mundy, P., Sigman, M., Ungerer, J. and Sherman, T. (1986) Defining the social deficit of autism: the contribution of non-verbal communication measures. *Journal of Child Psychology and Psychiatry,* 27: 657–669.

Myklebust, H. (1964) *The Psychology of Deafness: Sensory Deprivation, Learning, and Adjustment.* N.Y.: Grune and Stratton.

Owens, D.G.C. and Johnstone, E.C. (1980) The disabilities of chronic schizophrenia: their nature and the factors contributing to their development. *British Journal of Psychiatry,* 136: 384–395.

Owens, D.G.C., Johnstone, E.C., Crow, T.J., Frith, C.D., Jagoe, J.R. and Kreel, L. (1985) Lateral ventricular size in schizophrenia: relationship to the disease process and its clinical manifestations. *Psychological Medicine,* 15: 27–41.

Park, C.C. (1987) *The Seige: The First Eight Years of an Autistic Child.* 2nd Edition with epilogue "Fifteen Years After". Boston, Massachusetts: Atlantic-Little Brown.

Perner, J., Frith, U., Leslie, A., Leekham, S. (1989) Exploration of the autistic child's theory of mind: knowledge, belief and communication. *Child Development, 60,* 689–700.

Ridley, R.M., Aitken, D.M. and Baker, H.F. (1989) Learning about rules, but not about reward is impaired following lesions of the cholinergic projection to the hippocampus. *Brain Research 502,* 306–318.

Ridley, R.M. and Baker, H.F. A critical evaluation of primate models of amnesia and dementia. (Submitted to *Brain Research Reviews*).

Rochester, S.R. and Martin, J.R. (1979) *Crazy Talk: A Study of the Discourse of Schizophrenic Speakers.* New York, Plenum.

Rumsey, J.M., Andreasen, N.C. and Rapoport, J.L. (1986) Thought, language, communication and affective flattening in autistic adults. *Archives of General Psychiatry*, 43: 771–777.

Rumsey, J.M. and Hamburger, S.D. (1988) Neurophysiological findings in high functioning men with infantile autism, residual state. *Journal of Clinical and Experimental Neuropsychology*, 10: 201–221.

Sigman, M., Mundy, P., Sherman, T. and Ungerer, J. (1986) Social interactions of autistic mentally retarded and normal children and their caregivers. *Journal of Child Psychology and Psychiatry*, 27: 647–656.

Sigman, M. and Ungerer, J.A. (1984) Attachment behaviours in autistic children. *Journal of Autism and Developmental Disorders*, 14: 231–244.

Sperber, D. and Wilson, D. (1986) *Relevance: Communication and Cognition.* Oxford: Blackwell.

Venables, P.H. (1964) Input dysfunction in schizophrenia. In: B.A. Maher (Ed.) *Contributions to the Psychopathology of Schizophrenia.* New York, Academic Press.

Warrington, E.K. and Weiskrantz, L. (1982) Amnesia: a disconnection syndrome. *Neuropsychological*, 20: 233–248.

Weinberger, D.R. (1988) Schizophrenia and the frontal lobe. *Trends in the Neurosciences*, 11: 367–370.

Wing, J.K. and Freudenberg, R.K. (1961) The response of severely ill chronic schizophrenic patients to social stimulation. *American Journal of Psychiatry*, 118: 311.

Wing, J.K., Cooper, J.E. and Sartorius, N. (1974) *The Description and Classification of Psychiatric Symptoms: An Instruction Manual for the PSE and CATEGO Systems.* Cambridge University Press, Cambridge.

Wing, L. and Gould, J. (1979) Severe impairments of social interaction and associated abnormalities in children: epidemiology and classification. *Journal of Autism and Developmental Disorders*, 9: 11–79.

Wing, L. and Attwood, A. (1987) Syndromes of autism and atypical development. In: Cohen, D.J., Donnellan, A. and Paul, R. (eds.) *Handbook of Autism and Pervasive Developmental Disorders.* New York: Wiley.

Wing, L. (1988a) The continuum of autistic characteristics. In: Schopler, E. and Mesibov, E.B. (eds.) *Diagnosis and Assessment.* New York: Plenum.

Wing, L. (1988b) The autistic continuum. In: L. Wing (ed.) *Autism: Biological Aspects* London: Gaskill and Royal College of Psychiatrists.

# 4 Abnormalities in the awareness and control of action

*Christopher D. Frith, Sarah-Jayne Blakemore and Daniel M. Wolpert*

## 1 Introduction

In this review we will present a framework designed to provide a coherent account of a number of disparate observations concerning abnormalities in the awareness and control of action. Our framework is based on established models of normal motor learning and control (for a review, see Wolpert 1997). However, we are particularly concerned to explain abnormal experiences of motor control such as phantom limbs and the passivity phenomena associated with schizophrenia. In § 2 we will summarize the components of our model of motor control and learning. In § 3 we will outline the application of this model to a number of specific signs and symptoms of motor disorders.

## 2 An outline of the motor control system

A well-functioning motor system is an essential requirement if we are to move through our environment safely, reach and grasp objects and learn new skills. Making movements involves the production of an appropriate sequence of muscle contractions. At the same time sensory information is critical for deciding what movements to make and for observing the consequences of those movements. Motor control and motor learning can best be understood in terms of an engineering system (Craik 1948). In this system the motor commands emanate from controllers within the central nervous system (CNS). The brain also has access to the various kinds of sensory feedback that result from the movements generated by the motor commands. The basic task of the motor control system is to manage the relationships between motor commands and sensory feedback. This management is necessary for two reasons. First, it ensures that our movements achieve their goals. Second, it enables us to learn by experience to make more accurate and effective movements. Motor commands are transformed into sensory feedback every time our musculoskeletal system interacts with the environment, since every movement we make has immediate sensory consequences. Activity in the musculoskeletal system transforms efferent motor actions into reafferent sensory feedback. Once a sequence of motor commands has been issued it is possible to predict the subsequent behaviour of the motor system and the sensory consequences of that behaviour. However, these predictions cannot be made solely from knowledge of the sequence of motor commands. An additional set of variables, called state variables, also needs to be known. These are the configurations of parts of the body, such as joint angles and angular velocities and include the state of the system prior to the implementation of the motor commands. These state variables provide the basis for internal models of the motor system. On the basis of the motor commands and these state variables it is possible to determine the future behaviour of the system.

### *a Internal models of the motor system*

There is evidence that the CNS contains transformations, or internal models, which mimic aspects of one's own body and the external world (Wolpert *et al.* 1995; Wolpert 1997). Here we shall be concerned with two varieties of internal model, predictors and controllers (also known as forward and inverse models, respectively). Whenever a movement is made, a motor command is generated by the CNS and a predictor estimates the sensory consequences of that motor command. A controller, on the other hand, captures the relationship between the desired state and the motor command required to achieve that state. An important issue to stress in our discussion of such representations is that they do not need to be detailed or accurate models of the external world. Often an internal model need only provide a rough approximation of some external transformation in order to play a useful role. The function of predictors and controllers requires that at least three states of the motor system are represented: the current state of the system, the desired state of the system and the predicted state of the system.

#### *i Predictors (forward models)*

Predictors model aspects of the external world and of the motor system in order to capture the forward or causal relationship between actions and their outcomes (Ito 1970; Jordan 1996; Wolpert *et al.* 1995). Every time a motor command is issued to make a movement, an efference copy of the motor command is produced in parallel. Based on the efference copy, the predictor estimates the sensory consequences of the ensuing movement. This prediction can be used in several ways (Miall & Wolpert 1996; Wolpert 1997) and there is a substantial body of evidence that the CNS makes use of such prediction.

i Prediction is needed to anticipate and compensate for the sensory effects of movement. For example, during eye movements an efference copy of the motor command is used to predict the effects of the movement (Von Helmholtz 1886; Sperry 1950; Von Holst & Mittelstaedt 1950). In order to determine the location of an object relative to the head, its retinal location and the gaze direction must be known. As the eye muscles are thought to contain no sensory receptors used to determine the gaze direction, Von Helmholtz (1886) proposed that the gaze direction is determined by predicting the eye location based on the efference copy of the motor command going to the eye muscles. Using this estimate of eye position together with the object's retinal location, its true position in space can be determined. When the eye is moved without using the eye muscles (for example, by gently pressing on the eyelid with the finger), the retinal location of objects changes, but the predicted eye position is not updated, leading to the perception that the world is moving.

ii Prediction can also be used to filter sensory information, attenuating the component that is due to self-movement (reafference) from that due to changes in the outside world. The sensory consequences of self-generated movements are predicted from the efference copy produced in parallel with the motor command. Self-produced sensations can be correctly predicted from motor commands. As a result there will be little or no sensory discrepancy resulting from the comparison between the predicted and actual sensory feedback. In contrast, externally generated sensations are not associated with any efference copy and therefore cannot be predicted and will produce a higher level of sensory discrepancy. As the discrepancy between predicted and actual sensation increases, so does the likelihood that the sensation is externally produced. By using such a system it is possible to cancel out or attenuate sensations induced by self-generated movement and thereby distinguish sensory events due to self-produced motion from sensory feedback caused by the environment, such as contact with objects. Such a mechanism underlies the finding that the same tactile stimulus is perceived as much less intense when it is self-applied in comparison with when it is applied by another person (Weiskrantz *et al.* 1971). The perceived intensity of a self-applied tactile stimulus increases with the degree of discrepancy introduced between the predicted and actual sensory feedback (Blakemore *et al.* 1999).

iii Prediction can also be used to maintain accurate performance in the presence of feedback delays. In most sensorimotor loops the feedback delays between the issuing of a motor command and the perception of its sensory consequences are large. This is due to both neural transduction and processing delays, which can be as long as 250 ms. These delays can result in inaccuracy if the motor system compares the desired outcome with the perceived outcome to determine the performance error. As the perceived outcome is delayed relative to the actual outcome the motor system will respond to a perceived error which may no longer exist, thereby generating a potentially inappropriate response. A predictor can be used to estimate the actual outcome of the motor command without delay and compare this with the desired outcome. Such internal feedback of the estimated outcome of an action is available before the true sensory feedback (Miall *et al.* 1993).

iv Prediction also plays a critical role in a process that integrates sensory and motor information in order to estimate the current state of the system. The state of the motor system is not directly observable by the CNS, which has access only to the outgoing motor commands and the subsequent sensory feedback. Instead, the state has to be estimated by observing these signals. To produce optimal estimates, two processes can be used. The first uses a predictor to estimate the next state of the system. The second process uses sensory feedback to modify this estimate (Wolpert *et al.* 1995; Wolpert 1997). By using both sources of information the uncertainty of the state estimate can be reduced. The recognition that the representation of a limb position depends not only on current sensation but also on predictions based on motor commands can explain a number of the bizarre experiences associated with abnormalities of the motor system (see § 3(b)).

### *ii Controllers (inverse models)*

Controllers provide the motor commands necessary to achieve some desired outcome. For a simple reaching and grasping movement, the first step would be to plan the trajectory to be followed by the hand in order to reach the desired final position. The trajectory represents the desired configuration of the body at each point in time. The muscle activations necessary to achieve this trajectory depend on the dynamic parameters of the body such as the inertia and link lengths of the body segments. The controllers must learn to generate the appropriate motor commands such that the muscle activations achieve the desired trajectory. The controllers, therefore, receive a desired configuration of the body and produce motor commands which should achieve this configuration.

Recently it has been proposed that our ability to interact with many different objects in a variety of different environments relies on a 'divide-and-conquer' strategy. Complex tasks are decomposed into simpler subtasks, each learned by a separate controller (Ghahramani & Wolpert 1997; Wolpert & Kawato 1998; Blakemore *et al.* 1998*a*). Therefore, rather than having a single controller, multiple controllers develop, each tuned to a particular sensori-motor context. At any given time, one or a subset of these controllers contributes to the final motor command. The contribution each controller makes to the final motor command is determined by two distinct processes. The first uses sensory contextual information (affordances), such as the visual appearance of an object, to select controllers prior to movement initiation. For example, the apparent size and weight of an object would determine whether we try to pick it up with a precision grip or a power grip. The second process uses the errors in the predictions made by a set of predictors each tuned to a different context. As these predictors capture distinct dynamic behaviours of the motor system, their prediction errors can be used during movement to determine in which context the motor system is acting and thereby switch between controllers during a movement. For example, when we pick up a milk bottle which appears full, but is in fact empty, we select the inappropriate controller based on the visual information, but are able to switch controllers when the predicted outcome of our action does not match the actual outcome. This modular learning system, known as the multiple paired predictor-controller model (Wolpert & Kawato 1998), is capable of learning to produce appropriate motor commands under a variety of contexts and can switch rapidly between controllers as the context changes. These features are important for a full model of motor control and motor learning, as the human motor system is capable of very flexible, modular adaptation.

### *b Motor representations*

Our outline of the motor control system postulates several kinds of motor representation. These are listed below and shown graphically in figure 4.1.

- i Actual state of the system. The actual state of the system is not directly available to the CNS. Instead an estimated actual state of the system is inferred on the basis of the stream of motor commands and sensory feedback. For simplicity we will refer to the estimated state as the actual state as it represents the best estimate of the actual state available to the CNS.
- ii Desired state of the system. This representation holds the instantaneous goal of the system.
- iii Predicted next state of the system. This representation provides an estimate of the future state of the system derived from the predictors.
- iv Motor commands. These are derived from the controllers and are fine-tuned by sensory information (affordances) about the current state of the world

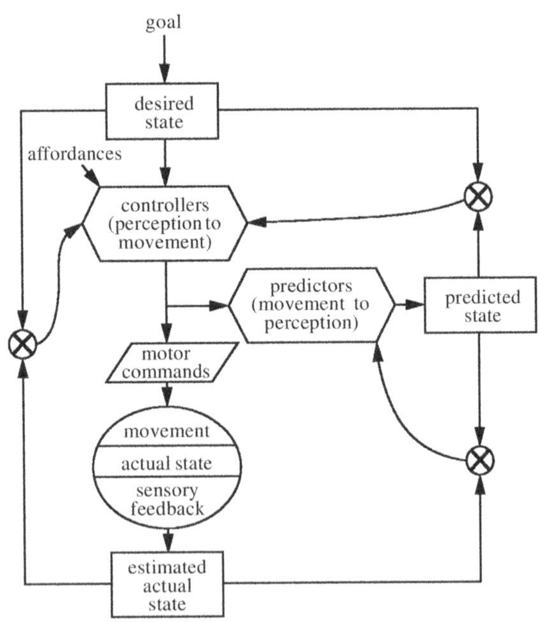


*Figure 4.1* The basic components of a motor control system based upon engineering principles.

(e.g. visual information about the position and shape of the object that is to be grasped).

v Sensory feedback. This is the consequence of the action performed, plus any environmental events.

Comparisons of these representations provides error signals that can be used to improve the functioning of the predictors and the controllers.

i Errors derived from differences between the desired and the actual state of the system can be used to improve the functioning of the controllers.

ii Errors derived from differences between the predicted and the actual state of the system can be used to improve the functioning of the predictors.

iii Errors derived from differences between the desired and the predicted state of the system can be used to improve the functioning of the controllers during mental practice.

In terms of this model the performance of a simple action involves the following stages. Current wishes and plans are used to formulate the desired state (instantaneous goal) of the system. The controllers generate appropriate motor commands on the basis of the difference between the actual state and the desired state. Computation by the controllers is 'fine-tuned' by the context in which the action is occurring. For example, if the action requires the grasping of an object, knowledge of the shape and position of the object provides 'affordances' which allow a more accurate computation of the appropriate motor commands (Greeno 1994). Once the motor commands have been computed the predictors calculate the expected state of the system. Subsequently, or in parallel with this process the action is performed. Once the movement has been made the new state of the system can be estimated on the basis of sensory feedback and knowledge of the motor commands that have been executed. If there are discrepancies between the new state and the desired and predicted states then modifications can be made to the predictors and controllers and further actions can be performed to correct the situation.

### *c Awareness of motor representations*

One major concern in this paper is to consider the extent to which we are aware of the functioning of some aspects of our motor control system (see also Jeannerod 1994). Here we shall review evidence indicating which components of the motor control system outlined in § 2(b) are available to consciousness and which are not.

#### *i Motor imagery and motor preparation*

The awareness of selecting and controlling our actions is a major component of consciousness. We can also readily imagine making movements in the absence of any overt behaviour. Furthermore this mental activity can have detectable consequences. First, mental practice of various tasks can lead to a significant improvement in subsequent performance (for a review, see Feltz & Landers 1983). Mental training affects several outcomes of motor performance such as muscular strength (Yue & Cole 1992), movement speed (Pascual-Leone *et al.* 1995) and temporal consistency (Vogt 1995). Second, prolonged performance of tasks in the imagination can lead to marked physiological changes. Subjects who performed or mentally simulated leg exercise increased heart rate and respiration rate in both conditions (Decety *et al.* 1991). Third, changes in brain activity associated with movements made in the imagination can readily be detected using brain imaging techniques such as positron emission tomography. Decety *et al.* (1994) asked subjects to imagine grasping three-dimensional objects presented to them. Stephan *et al.* (1995) compared execution of a sequence of joystick movements with imagining making such a sequence. These studies showed that the brain regions activated during motor imagery are a subset of those activated during motor execution. Jeannerod (1994) argued that motor imagery is closely related to motor preparation. Preparing a movement in advance and holding it in readiness while waiting for a signal to release the movement engages the same processes as those involved in imagining making that movement. Brain imaging studies of motor preparation and motor imagery highlight activity in the anterior cingulate cortex (ACC), the anterior supplementary motor cortex (SMA), inferior lateral premotor cortex and inferior parietal lobe (Decety *et al.* 1994; Stephan *et al.* 1995; Krams *et al.* 1998). Since these areas are engaged by motor preparation and motor imagery they are presumably involved with representations of intended and predicted movements. It has been argued that covert attention, that is attending to a particular object without actually moving the eyes or the hand towards it, is equivalent to mentally reaching for that object with the eyes (foveation) or the hand (e.g. Rizzolatti *et al.* 1987; Corbetta 1998). During the performance of covert attention tasks activity is observed in areas which overlap with those seen during motor imagery tasks: ACC, SMA, lateral premotor cortex (frontal eye fields) and intraparietal sulcus (IPS) (Corbetta *et al.* 1993; Nobre *et al.* 1997).

### *ii Limited awareness of affordances and motor commands*

These observations confirm that we can be aware of intended movements and can perform movement sequences in imagination. Furthermore, this motor imagery has specific neural correlates. There are a number of other observations, however, which demonstrate that the motor control system can also function in the absence of awareness. Goodale *et al.* (1986) (see also Bridgeman *et al.* 1981) report a pointing experiment in which the target occasionally jumped several degrees, unnoticed by the subjects. Nevertheless the subjects were able to adjust the trajectory of their moving hand to the target position. In this case the subjects were aware neither of the sensory information that elicited the movement correction nor of the change in the motor programme that was elicited. In another experiment involving reaching and grasping, Castiello *et al.* (1991) found that awareness of an unexpected target jump occurred more that 200 ms after the motor system had initiated an appropriate movement correction. Furthermore, appropriate grasping movements can be made even when conscious perception of the object to be grasped is incorrect. In the Ebbinghaus (Tichener) Circles Illusion two identical circles appear to be of different sizes because of the context in which they occur. The strength of this illusion can be measured by asking subjects to adjust the size of the circles until they appear to be identical. However, the size of this illusion is greatly reduced if it is measured in terms of the distance between the finger and thumb when grasping the central circles (Aglioti *et al.* 1995). The result from studies of this illusion and others (e.g. Gentilucci *et al.* 1996) suggests that there can be a dissociation between our perception of objects and the information which the sight of objects (their affordances) provides to fine-tune our reaching and grasping movements. An extreme example of this lack of awareness is provided by the case of D.F. described by Milner & Goodale (1995). D.F. was unaware of the shapes of objects and was unable to describe them or to discriminate between them, but she could nevertheless produce appropriate grasping actions based on the shapes of which she was unaware. A similar pattern of behaviour has been observed in another patient by Perenin & Rossetti (1996).

In terms of the model for motor control presented in § 2(b) these results suggest that we are not aware of the precise details of the motor commands that generate our actions, nor of the way in which immediate sensory information (affordances) is used to fine-tune these commands. Thus, it would appear that our awareness of our actions and of the sensory information on which these actions are based is derived from other sources. There are likely to be good reasons for this separation. For example, we have suggested (Frith 1995) that representations used for reaching an object need to be coded in egocentric coordinates, while representations for reporting the position of an object need to be in coordinates that are independent of a personal view. To reach for an object it is necessary to know where that object is in relation to our hand, not in relation to other objects in the environment. There are many different frames of reference that could be used for representing the position of an object (Andersen 1995). Some possibilities include the position of the object on the retina (retinotopic coordinates), the position of the object relative to the head (head-centred coordinates; Vetter *et al.* 1999), and the position of the object relative to the shoulder (shoulder-centred coordinates; Flanders *et al.* 1992). Animal studies suggest that cells exist which code in terms of each of these different coordinate systems. Cells of this type tend to be found in parietal cortex (Colby *et al.* 1995; Andersen *et al.* 1997). This brain region has a major role in the control of movements, including reaching and grasping with limbs and eyes (Rizzolatti *et al.* 1997). Evidence from the behaviour of cells in this region suggests that its role in motor control derives in part from an ability to translate from one coordinate system to another. For example, to use visual cues to make a limb movement necessitates a translation from retinotopic to body-centred coordinates (Jeannerod *et al.* 1995). The appropriate reach depends on where our arm is in relation to the target, and is independent of where we happen to be looking. Thus, in the region of parietal lobe concerned with reaching, objects are represented, not in terms of what they are, but in terms of how they may be reached (equivalent to the dorsal 'how' pathway of Milner & Goodale (1995)).

For such representations to be maintained the coordinates associated with each object must be altered, not only when the objects move, but also every time we move our eyes, limbs or body (Kalaska & Crammond 1992; Galletti *et al.* 1993). Consistent with this is the evidence that the receptive fields of cells in some regions of parietal cortex are 'remapped' prior to eye or limb movements (e.g. Duhamel *et al.* 1992). Awareness of these constant remappings would be confusing. In addition awareness of the remapping is unnecessary. The changes in representation that result from our own movements are entirely predictable on the basis of those movements and therefore do not require our attention. It seems plausible that to be aware of representations which changed every time we moved our bodies, or even our eyes, would be a positive disadvantage. Indeed, the mechanisms that underlie our conscious perception seem designed to maintain stability and to emphasize the unexpected.

### *iii Limited awareness of the actual state of the motor system*

In the outline of the motor control system presented in § 2 (b) a major role is played by representations of the predicted state of the system that will result from intended acts. In most situations, especially those that are routine, the actual state of the motor system will correspond closely to the state predicted before the action was performed. If awareness puts an emphasis on the unexpected, then we would predict that there would be only limited awareness of the actual state of the motor system whenever this has been successfully predicted in advance. We may only be aware of the actual sensory consequences of our movements when they deviate from what we expect.

An extreme example of a lack of awareness of action resulting from predictability comes from overlearned tasks. With sufficient practice many tasks can become 'automatic' and can performed without any need to think about the actions required to perform the task. This automaticity can be proved by showing that a second, attention-demanding task can be carried out at the same time as the overlearned task without impairing performance (e.g. Passingham 1996). While performing such tasks we are not aware of the actual state of our motor system, nor are we aware of our intended actions or their predicted consequences.

A more specific example of a reduced awareness of the actual state of the system, or at least of the sensory feedback that indicates the actual state of the system comes from studies of tickling. It is well known that the intensity of the tactile experience when we tickle ourselves is greatly reduced in comparison with the sensation when someone else tickles us (Weiskrantz *et al.* 1971). Corresponding to this reduction in tactile sensation is a reduction of activity in somatosensory cortex (Blakemore *et al.* 1998*b*). This phenomenon occurs because self-generated tactile sensation can be predicted from the motor commands that generated the movements that created the sensations. This prediction is based on a rather precise specification. Thus, the perceived intensity of a self-generated tactile sensation is markedly affected by small deviations in the timing or trajectory of the tactile stimulus from the movement that generated it (Blakemore *et al.* 1999). For example, if there is a delay of 100 ms between the movement and the tactile stimulation, then the perceived intensity of the tactile stimulation increases even though the subject is unaware of the delay.

In some circumstances we are unaware of even quite large deviations of actual movements from those expected. This seems to happen as long as the desired state is successfully achieved. For example, Fourneret & Jeannerod (1998) gave false feedback about the trajectory of an arm movement so that subjects, who could not see their arm or hand, had to make considerable deviations from a straight movement in order to generate a straight line on a computer screen. The subjects could achieve the desired result of drawing a straight line by making deviant movements. However, verbal reports indicated that they were unaware that they were making deviant movements. It seems then that we are largely unaware of sensory feedback about the actual state of our motor system as long as our intentions have been achieved. In most cases successful achievement implies that sensory feedback has been correctly predicted, but in some circumstances we remain unaware even of unexpected sensory feedback. When we come to consider abnormalities in the control of action (§ 3(a,b)) we shall see that a major insight derived from the engineering model is that estimates of the current state of the system are not only derived from sensory inputs, but also from the preceding stream of motor commands. In many situations information from this latter stream seems to be more important in determining the experience of the patient.

### *iv The timing of awareness*

In addition to examining which aspects of the motor control system are accessible to awareness attempts have also been made to investigate the time at which awareness emerges during the generation of an action. Libet *et al.* (1983) and McCloskey *et al.* (1983) asked normal volunteers to estimate the time at which they initiated a finger movement (i.e. the time at which the finger started to move). This reported time of awareness consistently anticipated the actual starting time of the movement by 50–80 ms. If transcranial magnetic stimulation is applied to the motor cortex then there is a substantial delay in the initiation of a movement, but there is a far smaller delay in the perceived time of initiating the movement (Haggard & Magno 1999). These observations imply that our awareness of initiating a movement is not derived from sensory signals arising in the moving limb. This information will not be available until after the limb has started moving. In terms of the model of motor control we are formulating here, the most likely representation relating to awareness of movement initiation is the predicted state of the system (e.g. the predicted position of the limb and associated sensations; see also Haggard *et al.* 1999). This can be formed as soon as the predictors have calculated the expected sensory consequences of making the intended movement.

More controversial are studies in which volunteers try to indicate the time at which they are aware of having the 'urge' to make a movement (Libet *et al.* 1983). This can precede the production of the movement by *ca.* 300 ms and might correspond to the formation of the representation of the intended position of the limb that precedes motor preparation. Haggard & Eimer (1999) asked subjects to indicate the time at which 'they first began to prepare the movement' and related this to various components of the motor readiness potential. In this study subjects moved either their left or their right index finger. Haggard & Eimer (1999) found that the onset of the lateralized readiness potential, rather than earlier components of the readiness potential, covaried with the perceived time at which preparation of the movement began. This observation suggests that the awareness of preparing to move is associated with the exact specification of the movement (i.e. which finger will be moved) rather than some more abstract representation of action. In terms of our framework of the motor system, specification of the goal of the movement seems not to be sufficient for awareness of preparing to move. Awareness of preparing to move requires that the controllers have completed the specification of the sequence of motor commands needed to make the movement. Awareness of initiation of the movement, on the other hand, has to wait further until the predictors have specified the sensory consequences of the movement. It is these predicted consequences that form our awareness of initiating the movement.

In this brief review we have presented evidence that some, but not all aspects of the motor control system are accessible to awareness. In the remainder of this paper we will discuss a variety of human movement abnormalities and attempt to convince the reader that the model of the motor system illustrated in figure 4.1 provides a useful and unifying framework for understanding these various disorders. We shall also suggest that to understand these disorders it is important to consider the patient's awareness of different aspects of the motor control system. In some cases the problem resides principally in an abnormality of awareness rather than an abnormality of control.

## 3 Abnormalities of the perception and control of action

### *a Abnormalities in the control of action while awareness remains unimpaired*

#### *i Optic ataxia and other forms of apraxia*

Patients with optic ataxia (Bálint's syndrome) (Bálint 1909, translated by Harvey 1995; Perenin & Vighetto 1988) have difficulty grasping objects which they can see quite clearly. Their difficulty has at least three components: the arm fails to extend correctly in space, the wrist fails to rotate to match the orientation of the object to be grasped, and the hand fails to open in anticipation of gripping the object (Jeannerod *et al.* 1994). However, although clumsy, the attempted movement matches the patient's intentions and the patient is aware of having a problem with reaching, although this is often attributed to a problem with vision rather than a problem with movement. In terms of our characterization of the motor system the problem in optic ataxia occurs because the controllers are not properly finely 'tuned' by the immediate context (i.e. the affordances offered by the shape of the object to be grasped). All other aspects of the control of movement and the awareness of that control remain intact (figure 4.2).

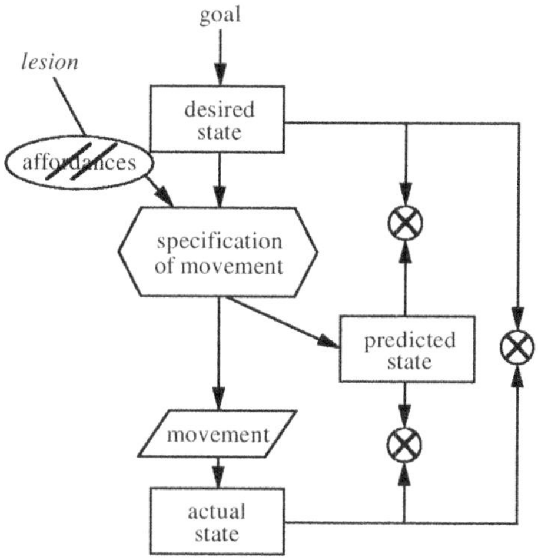


*Figure 4.2* The underlying disorder leading to optic ataxia. The fine tuning of grasping actions afforded by the precise shape and position of objects is no longer available to the patient. The patient is aware that actions are clumsy.

However, the controllers do not rely solely on the immediate affordances provided by the sight of the object that is to be grasped in order to derive an appropriate sequence of motor commands. Relevant information is also available from memory and can be used in the absence of affordances. As a result some patients can grasp a well-known object such as a lipstick more accurately than an unknown object of exactly the same shape (Jeannerod *et al.* 1994). In this example the information used by the controllers comes from long-term knowledge about objects. Relevant information is also available from short-term memory, although this is not as useful as actual sight of the object. If vision of the object to be grasped is removed for only a few seconds then the reaching and grasping of normal subjects is impaired (Goodale *et al.* 1994; Rossetti 1998). The information available in short-term memory in this situation may be derived from representations about the position and nature of the object rather than representations specifically tailored for grasping the object. Patient D.F., who could grasp objects without being able to recognize them, completely lost her ability to grasp objects after a short delay during which the object was not visible. In contrast, the reaching behaviour of a patient with optic ataxia can improve after a short delay in the dark (Milner *et al.* 1999). Presumably this is because, for this patient, information about the object in short-term memory, although not ideal for grasping, is better than the faulty information provided by the sight of the object.

Optic ataxia is one of many forms of apraxia: difficulties in making voluntary movements in the absence of a primary motor defect. In terms of our model, apraxia occurs when there is insufficient information for the controllers to construct an appropriate sequence of motor commands. This suggestion relates closely to the suggestion of Pause *et al.* (1989, p. 1599) that 'the motor disability . . . does not lie in the loss of kinetic memory to perform movements, but in the loss of their evocation by appropriate sensory stimuli'. Because relevant information comes from many different sources there can be many different forms of apraxia. We have already mentioned patients who can grasp a lipstick (information derived from long-term knowledge), but not a neutral cylinder of the same shape (information derived from immediate sight of the object). Other patients are unable to produce an action to command, e.g. they cannot obey the command 'to blow', but, when presented with a lit candle will blow it out. In these cases information can be used from the sight of the object, but not from verbal commands. De Renzi *et al.* (1982) have formally demonstrated other such dissociations, finding patients who can mime the use of an object to verbal instruction, but cannot imitate the same gesture when performed by someone else, and also finding patients with the opposite pattern of disorder.

In § 2(c)(ii) we discussed the need to translate between different coordinate frames in order to use visual information to generate movements (Andersen 1995). Patients with apraxia seem to have lost the ability to translate certain kinds of information into coordinates appropriate for constructing actions. We also mentioned the evidence from animal studies that the parietal cortex may have a major role in translating from one coordinate frame to another (Colby & Duhamel 1996). Apraxia can occur after damage to many brain regions, but is particularly associated with damage to the parietal lobe (De Renzi & Lucchelli 1988). With regard to optic ataxia, lesions in the superior parietal cortex (or more precisely in the IPS between BA7 and 39) impair the ability to make accurate reaching and grasping movements in both man (Perenin & Vighetto 1988) and monkey (Gallese *et al.* 1997; Rushworth *et al.* 1997) (for a discussion of the precise location of the critical area in parietal cortex see Passingham (1998)). Imaging studies of grasping in healthy volunteers also implicated the IPS in the control of visually guided reaching (Clower *et al.* 1996). There is as yet little evidence that other forms of apraxia can be related to specific lesions, largely because there is so little agreement as to how to classify the different forms of apraxia.

### *ii The 'anarchic hand' sign*

Patients showing the anarchic hand sign (sometimes known as the alien hand sign, see Marchetti & Della Salla (1998)) have a hand that moves 'of its own accord' without the will of the patient. In one case it was noted that the patient had picked up a pencil and 'had been scribbling with the [affected] right hand . . . She then indicated that she had not herself initiated the original action of the right arm . . . She experienced a feeling of dissociation from the actions of the right arm, stating . . . that "it will not do what I want it to do" ' (Goldberg *et al.* 1981, p. 685). In another case the patient's 'left hand would tenaciously grope for and grasp any nearby object, pick and pull at her clothes, and even grasp her throat during sleep. . . . She slept with the arm tied to prevent nocturnal misbehaviour. She never denied that her left arm and hand belonged to her, although she did refer to her limb as though it were an autonomous entity' (Banks *et al.*

1989, p. 456). Typically the anarchic hand grasps objects in its vicinity in an inappropriate manner; it will grasp doorknobs or pick up a pencil and scribble with it. Patients clearly recognize that there is a discrepancy between what the hand is doing and their desired actions. The patients are upset by the actions of the hand and will often try to prevent it from moving by grasping it firmly with the other hand.

In many ways the patient with an anarchic hand shows the converse problem to the patient with optic ataxia. We have just reviewed (§ 3(a)(i)) the evidence that the parietal cortex contains representations of the various objects in our immediate environment in terms of the appropriate movements needed to reach and grasp them. The patient with optic ataxia fails to form these representations and therefore has difficulties with reaching and grasping. In the patient with an anarchic hand these representations are activated inappropriately. The sight of an object is sufficient to elicit the movement even though this does not fit with the patient's current goals. In terms of our characterization of the motor system, the movements of the anarchic hand occur because the effects of the affordances supplied by the immediate visual environment are no longer inhibited by the currently intended action (figure 4.3). However, the rest of the system is intact. Representations of the intended and actual positions of the hand are available, so that patients know that the behaviour of the hand does not conform with their intentions.

What is the brain mechanism which prevents us from responding to every graspable object in our environment? The anarchic hand sign is often associated

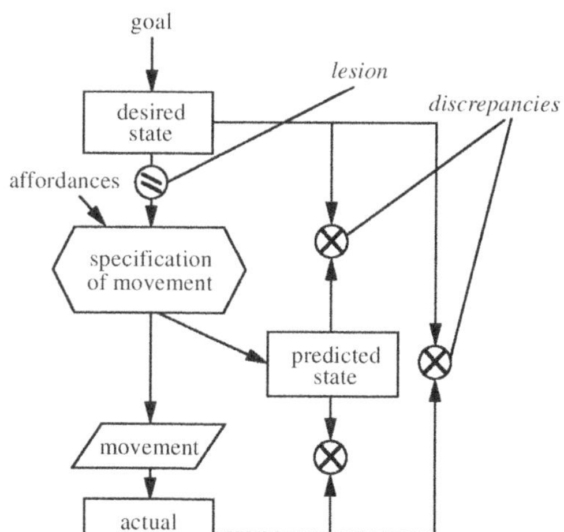


*Figure 4.3* The underlying disorder leading to an anarchic hand. The actions of the hand are no longer controlled by the intentions of the patient. Instead the hand makes stereotyped responses to objects in the environment. The patient is aware of the discrepancies between intentions and the actions of the hand.

with unilateral damage to the SMA contralateral to the anarchic hand (Goldberg *et al.* 1981). The anterior part of the SMA is considered to be one of a number of 'higher-order' motor areas in contrast to areas, such as the primary motor cortex, which are directly concerned with execution (Pickard & Strick 1996). In contrast to executive motor regions, the anterior SMA does not show increasing activation with increasing force (Dettmers *et al.* 1995). On the other hand, unlike executive motor regions the anterior SMA is activated specifically in tasks requiring selection between different movements (Deiber *et al.* 1991), especially when these movements have to be made only in the imagination and not actually executed (Stephan *et al.* 1995). When the precise timing of events is investigated there is evidence that some neurons in the anterior SMA are active during movement preparation, but not during movement execution (Rizzolatti *et al.* 1990). Ball *et al.* (1999) using combined electroencephalography and functional magnetic resonance imaging observed a sharp drop in activity in an area referred to as intermediate SMA that coincided with a sharp increase in activity in primary motor cortex just before execution of a movement. They suggest that the function of this region of the SMA may be essentially inhibitory, so that a movement can only be initiated by primary motor cortex when activity in the anterior SMA drops. This would account for the preferential activation of the anterior SMA when movements are imagined because in such cases execution must be inhibited. Such a role for the anterior SMA could explain why an 'anarchic hand' should be released when this region is damaged.

The major projections to motor cortex (area 4) come from lateral and medial premotor areas (area 6, including the SMA) and from parietal cortex (areas 5 and 7b in the monkey, probably equivalent to areas 5 and 40 in man; see Passingham 1993). This pattern of projections is consistent with the idea that signals arising in parietal cortex enable motor cortex to generate appropriate reaching and grasping movements to any object in the immediate environment, while signals arising in the SMA permit selection of the one movement appropriate to current intentions. Unilateral damage to what is probably a rather circumscribed region of the SMA releases inappropriate reaching and grasping in the contralateral hand, creating an anarchic hand.

(There is some evidence that the anarchic hand is often associated with damage to the anterior corpus callosum as well as the SMA (Parkin 1996). In these cases the unwanted actions of the anarchic hand often consist of interference with the actions of the other hand, rather than unintended grasping behaviour. For example, the anarchic left hand might undo buttons that the right hand had just done up. This behaviour would also be explained in terms of a failure of inhibition. However, in these cases the inhibition arises from signals concerning the behaviour of the hand selected for performing the action. These inhibitory signals fail to be transmitted through the corpus callosum.)

We have argued that patients with optic ataxia and the anarchic hand have disorders of motor control, but no associated disorder in their awareness of the motor system. This is because the impairment concerns the mechanisms by which the controller constructs and selects the precise movements required for an action. These processes are not available to consciousness. In § 3(b) we shall consider syndromes in which motor impairments are associated with abnormalities of awareness.

### *b Abnormalities of motor control and awareness*

#### *i Phantom limbs*

After amputation of all or part of a limb many patients report that they experience a phantom limb. Although they know that there is no limb they still feel the presence of it (Ramachandran & Hirstein 1998). Some patients report being able to move their phantoms voluntarily, while others experience their phantom as paralysed and cannot move it even with intense effort. If the limb was paralysed before amputation the phantom normally remains paralysed. If not, then typically immediately after amputation patients can generate movement in the phantom. However, with time they often lose this ability (Ramachandran 1993). Some finger amputees experience their phantom fingers only when they flex the fingers in the intact hand as when making a fist or grabbing a cup. There is frequently a latency of 2–3 s before the phantom emerges and when the normal fingers are extended again the phantom takes 2–3 s to disappear (Ramachandran 1993). In these cases the position of the phantom is determined by the actions of the contralateral limb and there is a marked delay in the formation of the phantom.

The existence of phantom limbs has long seemed deeply mysterious. How is it possible to experience a limb in a particular position in space when there is no limb and, as a result, the brain is no longer receiving any relevant somatosensory or proprioceptive information? There is now substantial evidence for neural plasticity in the mature human brain. After amputation of a limb there is reorganization of the deafferented region of cortex. As a result stimulation of the skin of distant areas such as the face or the chest can elicit sensation in a phantom arm (Ramachandran *et al.* 1992; Aglioti *et al.* 1994; Kew *et al.* 1997). Thus the experience of the presence of a phantom limb can be supported by somatosensory signals coming from other parts of the body. The presence of proprioceptive signals from other limbs can also explain how a patient can experience a phantom in the positions occupied by the intact contralateral limb. However, these mechanisms cannot explain cases in which the position of the phantom is not determined by the positions of other limbs or cases in which the patient can voluntarily move the phantom. Our explanation of these phenomena is that the estimated position of a limb is not solely based on sensory information, but also on the stream of motor commands issued to the limb muscles. On the basis of these commands the predictor can estimate the new position of the limb before any sensory feedback has been received. Indeed, as we have already argued, the normal experience of the limb is often based on this predicted state, rather than the actual state. Even in the absence of a limb, streams of motor commands can still be issued. If these commands lead to the prediction of movement then the phantom will be experienced as moving.

However, the motor control system is designed to adapt to changing circumstances. Since the limb does not actually move there is a discrepancy between the predicted and the actual consequences of the motor commands. With time the predictors will be modified to reduce these discrepancies. At this point the issuing of a stream of motor commands will not lead to the prediction of a change in limb position. Such adaptation in the predictors could explain why patients eventually lose the ability to move their phantoms.

Such adaptation of the predictors would also explain how Ramachandran & Rogers Ramachandran (1996) were able to reinstate voluntary movement of the phantom by providing false visual feedback of a moving limb corresponding to the phantom. This was achieved by placing a mirror in the midsaggital plain. With the head in the appropriate position it was possible for the patient to see the intact limb at the same time as the mirror reflection of this limb. This reflection so closely resembles the missing limb that the patient has the strong illusion of seeing the missing limb. If the intact limb is moved then the patient receives from the mirror visual feedback of movement in the missing limb. For most patients moving their hand in this mirror box rapidly leads to the perception that they are now able to move the phantom limb again. In some cases this perception continues even when the mirror box is no longer being used.

In a reformulation of the proposals of Ramachandran & Rogers Ramachandran (1996), we suggest that the false visual feedback supplied by the mirror box allowed the predictors to be updated. In consequence the efference copies produced in parallel with the motor commands now generated changes in the predicted position of the missing limb corresponding to what the patient had seen in the mirror.

Ramachandran & Hirstein (1998) proposed that dynamic images of the body are formed in the parietal lobes and provide the basis for the experience of phantom limbs. This formulation resembles our suggestion that parietal cortex is involved in the representation of predicted limb positions. However, as we have seen, the parietal lobe contains representations of limb positions in terms of many different coordinate systems. Which of these particular coordinate systems relates to the experience of phantoms and the precise locations for such representations remains to be determined. Evidence that phantom limbs are represented in the parietal cortex comes from the observation that a phantom limb patient lost his phantom after a right parietal stroke (Sunderland 1978). Unfortunately the precise location of the lesion in this case was not specified.

### *ii Missing limbs*

After peripheral deafferentation of a limb the patient will often develop a phantom even though the deafferented limb is still present. This phantom may be contained within the real limb, but, in some circumstances, may become separated from the limb and become supernumerary (e.g. Kew *et al.* 1997, subject 2). However, in other cases patients do not develop phantoms, but rather are unaware of the existing limb unless it can be seen. We are not aware of any systematic comparison of deafferented patients who develop phantoms with those in whom the limb fades. However, a study of cases reported in the literature suggests that the critical difference lies in whether or not the deafferented limb is also paralysed. The cases described by Kew *et al.* (1997) who developed phantoms had limbs that were deafferented and paralysed. In contrast the patient described by Cole (1991) was completely deafferented for touch, but was not paralysed and achieved a remarkable degree of motor control which was largely based on visual feedback. This patient never developed a phantom, but for him and his body it was literally 'out of sight, out of mind' (Cole 1991).

Most deafferented patients in whom the motor output system remains intact are unwilling to attempt movements because they are so inaccurate. Rothwell *et al.* (1982) demonstrated that a patient with peripheral deafferentation was unable to make automatic reflex corrections to movements and was unable to sustain constant levels of muscular contraction or maintain long action sequences in the absence of visual feedback. The lack of a sensation of the current position of the limb is not only a problem for checking the success of movement through feedback. It also creates a problem because the computation by the controllers of the appropriate movement requires that the starting position of the limb must be known.

Similar problems can occur after brain damage in somatosensory areas as a result of which the patient can no longer experience the limb contralateral to the lesion. Jeannerod *et al.* (1986) described a patient with hemianaesthesia after damage involving the right inferior parietal lobe. The patient could initiate simple single-component movements, but could not make complex multicomponent movements with his left hand in the absence of visual feedback. Wolpert *et al.* (1998) describe an interesting variant of this phenomenon. Patient P.J. had a large cyst in the left parietal lobe and reported the experience of the position and presence of her right limbs fading away over seconds if she could not see them. Her experience of a constant tactile stimulus or a weight also faded away, but changes in such sensations could be detected. Slow reaching movements to peripheral targets with the right hand were inaccurate, but reaching movements made at a normal pace were unimpaired. In this case there seemed to be a circumscribed problem with the representation of the current limb position in that it could not be maintained in the absence of changing stimulation.

In all these cases of deafferentation without paralysis, visual signals provide the only sensory information for making accurate movements. They provide information about the position of a limb prior to movement and provide feedback about the accuracy of the movement. As a result the motor control system will learn to ignore somatosensory and proprioceptive signals when predicting the outcome of movements or estimating the current state of the system. It will learn to base such estimates solely on the stream of motor commands and upon visual information. In the absence of visual signals the estimates cannot be made and the experience of the limb fades away.

In patients with deafferentation and paralysis no movements can be made and so the system has no chance to learn to attend to one modality of sensation rather than another. The experience of a phantom can therefore be driven by sensations from other limbs that have been remapped into the deafferented cortical region.

### *iii Supernumerary limbs*

Patients sometimes report experiencing one or more supernumerary limbs in addition to their real ones (Vuilleumier *et al.* 1997). Of particular interest is the patient described by Hari *et al.* (1998) who reported experiencing an additional left arm. The extra arm occupied the position vacated by the real left arm a minute or so previously. The felt position of the phantom extra arm mirrored the voluntary (but not passive) movements of the right arm. Experience of the extra arm ceased if the patient moved her left arm or looked at it or had it touched.

The estimated position of a limb is based on integrating information from motor commands and sensory feedback. Failure to integrate these two sources of information could lead to the experience of two limbs rather than one. At the time of initiating action the patient of Hari *et al.* (1998) has the normal awareness of movement based on the representation of the predicted position of the arm. However, the representation of the estimated actual position of the arm fails to get updated on the basis of the motor commands. This discrepant representation of the estimated position of the arm emerges into awareness some time after the movement has been completed leading to the experience of an extra arm. Correct updating of this representation occurs on the basis of signals from the somatosensory or visual system. However, false updating can also occur based on motor commands controlling the right limb. This false updating must be based on motor commands rather than sensory feedback since passive movements of the right arm do not affect the phantom. Presumably the effect of signals concerning movements of the right limb are normally suppressed when they are discrepant from the motor commands driving the left limb. We are suggesting that movement of the phantom in this case derives from motor signals relating to the contralateral limb. This is different from the mechanism underlying the phenomenon described by some amputees in which the fingers of the phantom follow the movements of fingers on the contralateral hand. In these cases it is assumed that the experience is driven by somatosensory and proprioceptive signals from the contralateral fingers. If this is so, then movements of the phantom in amputees should be experienced whether the contralateral finger movements are active or passive.

The extra phantom limb experienced by the patient of Hari *et al.* (1998) emerged after a subarachnoid haemorrhage leading to an infarction in the right frontal lobe including damage to the most anterior region of the right SMA. However, brain scans suggested that there was also a congenital abnormality in the corpus callosum.

In our discussion of the anarchic hand sign (§ 3(a)(ii)) we suggested that the SMA, in particular the anterior part, has a major role in initiating movements and interacts with the parietal cortex in order to ensure that the movement initiated corresponds to the desired action. The case described by Hari *et al.* (1998) in which damage to the anterior SMA was associated with an extra phantom left arm suggests that this interaction between SMA and parietal cortex may also ensure integration between representations of predicted and actual limb positions. Damage to the anterior SMA can result in a failure of this integration.

### *iv Anosognosia*

A patient with anosognosia is unaware of some impairment that has resulted from brain damage (Babinsky 1914). Here we shall be concerned only with those patients in whom the impairment concerns the motor control of a limb. Such patients typically have right-hemisphere damage leading to paralysis (or weakness) on the left side usually associated with hemianaesthesia. In § 3(b)(ii) we argued that this combination provides the appropriate circumstances for the development of a phantom limb. However, these patients, rather than developing a phantom limb, develop the false belief that there is nothing wrong with the paralysed limb. For example, the left side of Mrs F.D.'s body was completely paralysed as the result of a stroke.

*Doctor:* 'Mrs F.D., can you walk?'
*F.D.:* 'Yes.'
*Doctor:* 'Can you move your hands?'
*F.D.:* 'Yes.'
*Doctor:* 'Are both hands equally strong?'
*F.D.:* 'Yes, of course they are.'

(Ramachandran 1996, p. 124)

Sometimes patients will attempt to 'explain away' the lack of movement in the paralysed limb.

*Doctor:* 'Mrs L.R., why aren't you using your left arm.'
*L.R.:* 'Doctor, these medical students have been prodding me all day and I'm sick of it. I don't want to use my left arm.'

(Ramachandran 1996, p. 125)

In some cases the patient will claim to have moved a limb to command even though no movement has occurred.

*Doctor:* 'Can you clap?'
*F.D.:* 'Of course I can clap.'
*Doctor:* 'Will you clap for me?'

The patient proceeded to make clapping movements with her right hand as if clapping with an imaginary hand near the midline.

*Doctor:* 'Are you clapping?'
*F.D.:* 'Yes, I am clapping.'

(Ramachandran 1996, p. 124)

This disorder is often associated with unilateral neglect for the left side of space. Geschwind (1965) suggested that anosognosia arises from a disconnection such that sensory feedback (both somatosensory and visual), indicating that the limb is not working, is no longer available to a left-hemisphere monitoring system. However, making sure that the paralysed left arm can be seen in the right visual field does not alter the denial of impairment. Heilman *et al.* (1998) have proposed a 'feed-forward' theory of anosognosia. According to this account anosognosic patients receive no signals indicating movement failure because the comparator which contrasts intended and actual movements receives no signal that a movement has been intended. Because patients do not try to move the paralysed limb they never discover that it is paralysed. While this account can explain denial of impairment, it is not clear how it can explain cases, such as the one described above, in which the patient apparently experiences having made a movement when none has actually occurred.

How is it possible to experience a limb movement when none has actually occurred? On the basis of our review of evidence concerning the normal awareness of motor control we suggested that awareness of initiating a movement was based on a representation of the predicted consequences of making that movement, rather than its actual consequences. A representation of the predicted consequences of a movement can be formed as long as the controllers can compute the appropriate motor commands and the predictors can derive from these the expected consequences. Thus, a patient with a paralysed limb would have the normal experience of initiating a movement with that limb as long as the controller and predictor were functioning normally. However, to continue to believe that he or she had initiated that movement would require further abnormalities in the system. First, there would have to be a failure to register the discrepancy between the predicted consequences and the actual consequences of the movement that was initiated. We have already quoted the work of Fourneret & Jeannerod (1998) demonstrating that normal people can have a remarkably limited awareness of the actual form of the movements they have made. Thus, the patient with anosognosia is showing, in exaggerated form, a tendency already present in the normal state. The exaggeration of this tendency could be related to the neglect of the left side of space often shown by such patients. Second, there would have to be a failure to update the operations of the predictor. With experience the predictor should learn that the motor commands issued by the controller result in minimal movements of the paralysed limb. In the patient with anosognosia this updating does not occur.

We suggest, then, that the false experience of movement reported by patients with anosognosia occurs because, while representations of the desired and predicted positions of the limb are appropriate, the patient is not aware of the discrepant representation of the actual position of the limb. The controllers issue the appropriate motor commands, but, due to paralysis, do not generate a limb movement. However, the predictors have estimated, on the basis of these commands

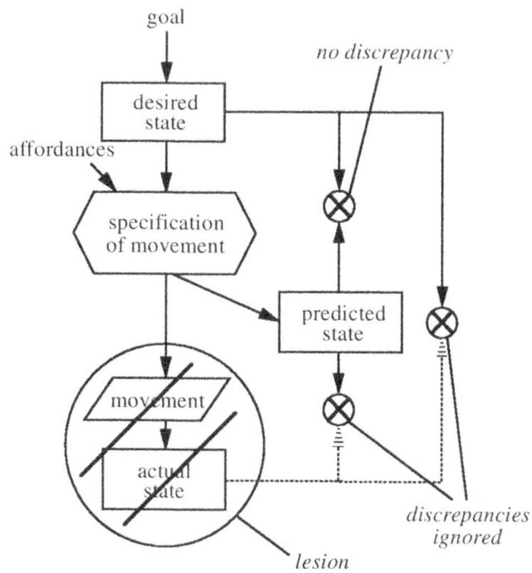


*Figure 4.4* The underlying disorder leading to anosognosia. The patient formulates the action needed to fulfil his intention and is aware that the action initiated is appropriate. No information about the actual position of the limb is available to indicate that no action has actually occurred.

and from past experience prior to brain damage, the new position of the limb. The lack of a discrepancy between intended and predicted positions indicates success. Contrary information derived from sensory feedback concerning actual limb positions is not available, since the relevant brain regions have been damaged or else this contrary information is neglected (figure 4.4). As a result the estimated position of the limb is based on sequences of motor commands and not upon sensory feedback.

Anosognosia is usually associated with damage to the right hemisphere, especially the parietal lobe. However, there is, as yet, no information about the precise location of the lesions that lead to the illusion that a paralysed limb is being moved normally. Damage to the parietal lobe is most frequently associated with apraxia rather than anosognosia and apraxic patients can sometimes show features of anosognosia. For example, Sirigu *et al.* (1999) studied three patients with apraxia while they performed gestures to command (e.g. extend index and little finger). On some trials the patients saw their own hand performing the gesture, but on other trials they saw the hand of an experimenter performing the same or a different gesture. On nearly 90% of trials in which the patients saw the experimenter making accurately the gesture that they were trying to make they believed that they were observing their own hand even though they had actually made a very clumsy gesture. In these cases false visual feedback elicited a form of anosognosia. However, the patients were not generally anosognosic. When they saw their own hand they recognized and were distressed by the clumsiness of their gestures. Furthermore, the lesions in these cases were in the left parietal cortex, which is typical for apraxia, rather than the right parietal cortex, which is typical for anosognosia.

In another experiment Sirigu *et al.* (1996) investigated the effects of parietal lobe lesions (both left- and right-sided) on the time needed to make imaginary movements. How long we take to make movements in the imagination depends upon the functioning of the predictor, not upon the actual state of the system. Sirigu *et al.* (1996) showed that a patient with unilateral damage to the motor cortex showed strong correlations between the time to make actual movements and the time to make imaginary movements with both the intact and the impaired hand. For the impaired hand the times for actual and imagined movements were much slower. In this case the predictor had been updated to take account of the changed abilities of the impaired hand. In contrast patients with parietal lesions did not show this close link between actual and imagined movements in the limb contralateral to the lesion. In these cases the discrepancies between predicted and actual movements have not been used to update the estimates made by the predictors.

Clearly damage to parietal cortex can impair awareness of the actual state of the motor system and also lead to failure to take note of discrepancies between the actual and predicted states of the system. However, though these problems may be necessary for anosognosia they do not seem to be sufficient. Another consequence of parietal lesions is unilateral spatial neglect. This syndrome, especially in its perceptual form, is usually associated with lesions in the right inferior parietal lobe (Vallar & Perani 1986) and is often associated with anosognosia. Patients with neglect fail to notice or respond to objects and events in their left hemifield. Neglect of this kind would allow even visual evidence that a movement had not been made to be ignored.

Ramachandran (1996) considered that the accounts of anosognosia of the kind outlined above are not sufficient to explain the extent to which anosognosic patients can ignore the wealth of evidence indicating that they are paralysed. He proposes that there are additional factors at work which enable patients to ignore sensory anomalies. These factors have parallels with those associated with delusions and confabulations. Confabulations are more usually associated with memory impairments. The patient recollects past events which did not and, indeed, could not have happened. The patient seems to be unaware of the impossibility of what he or she is reporting. Such problems are typically associated with damage to the right frontal cortex (Burgess & Shallice 1996), which is believed to have a role in monitoring the consequences of action at a high level. There is evidence that this role also applies to the motor system. For example, if a normal volunteer is performing a task with two hands, but one hand is hidden behind a mirror, then the illusion is created that both hands are seen, when, in fact, the subject is viewing a single hand and its mirror image. In this case, if the task is to move the hands out of phase, the visual feedback falsely indicates that the hands are moving in phase.

Performance of this somewhat disturbing task in which there is a discrepancy between expectations derived from intended movements and what is actually seen, elicits activity in right dorsolateral prefrontal cortex (Fink *et al.* 1999). It is plausible that damage to this region might result in failure to respond to such discrepancies.

### *v Utilization behaviour*

Some patients with damage to the frontal lobes show 'utilization behaviour' (Lhermitte 1983) in which the patient uses objects inappropriately. The sight of an object elicits a stereotyped action which is inappropriate in the wider context. For example, if there is a glass within reach of the patient, he will grasp it. If a bottle of water is placed on the desk he will grasp this too and then pour water into the glass and drink it. Such behaviour is not shown by normal subjects put in the same situation or by patients with posterior lesions.

> 'If the examiner asks the patient why he grasped the objects and used them, then the answer is always the same, "You held them out to me, I thought I had to use them."
>
> The examiner then . . . gives the instruction, "You are mistaken; from now on don't grasp any of the objects I will show you, and in no case must you use them."
>
> After about 20–30s, during which time the patient's attention has to be distracted . . . the behaviour remains unchanged. If the examiner asks if the patient remembers the instruction, the latter replies, most of the time, "It's true, I remember."
>
> "Then why [did you grasp the objects]?"
>
> "Because you held out the objects to me and I thought I had to reach and grasp them." '
>
> (Lhermitte 1983, p. 246)

Much more complex actions can also be elicited by the environment in which the patient finds himself. 'Patient 1 . . . came to see me at my apartment. . . . We returned to the bedroom. The bedspread had been taken off and the top sheet turned back in the usual way. When the patient saw this he immediately began to get undressed [including taking off his wig]. He got into bed, pulled the sheet up to his neck and prepared to go to sleep' (Lhermitte 1986, p. 338).

On the surface this behaviour is very similar to that associated with the anarchic hand. Actions are elicited by objects in the environment even though such actions are not appropriate. However, there is an additional problem which is reflected in the patient's experience of this disorder of control. The patient showing utilization behaviour does not perceive a discrepancy between his actions and his intentions. He is not upset by the actions and he does not develop strategies to prevent the actions occurring. On being asked why he performed the actions the patient will 'rationalize', saying that he performed the action because he thought that is what the examiner wanted him to do. Our formulation of utilization behaviour is that the patient's actions are involuntarily elicited by objects in the environment, but that the patient erroneously experiences these actions as intended.

Problems with the experience of intention are not unique to these patients. Normal three-year-old children do not distinguish between an intentional movement and a knee-jerk reflex. Only at five years do children state that the knee-jerk reflex was unintended (Schultz *et al.* 1980). Three-year-old children, however, do state that their movement was unintended in the interlaced finger game. In this task the child can see that the designated finger remains stationary while the wrong finger moves. The child has a clear goal which has not been achieved. The lack of success is taken to indicate a lack of intention. In the case of the knee-jerk reflex there is no simple prior goal, and thus a judgement cannot be made as to whether or not the movement was successful. Smith (1978) suggested that, without an explicitly stated goal, the default judgement is that actions are intended. Only by the age of five can the child form the much more abstract goal of 'not moving' in order to interpret the knee-jerk reflex correctly.

A corollary of this argument is that, if an explicit goal is formed just prior to an action which achieves that goal, then the action will be perceived as intended. Wegner & Wheatley (1999) have used just this technique to elicit the erroneous perception of intended action in normal adults. A subject and a confederate simultaneously used a single mouse to control the position of a pointer on a screen. If the attention of the subject was drawn to an object on the screen shortly before the pointer stopped near that object, then the subject frequently believed that he had intentionally moved towards the object even though in reality his arm had been moved passively by the confederate. As long as the action did not conflict with some explicitly formed goal then the action was perceived as intended.

These results suggest that the experience of an action as intended depends on the relationship between the action and a prior goal. If the action does not match the goal then the action is unintended. If, however, there is no prior goal then, by default the action is perceived as intended. In these terms utilization behaviour can be explained as resulting from a failure to represent goals. We suggest that the problem causing utilization behaviour occurs at an earlier stage in the development of an action than that causing the anarchic hand. The problem has two components. First, there is no awareness of goals and intended actions (figure 4.5). The patient is not aware of what he is going to do until after he has done it. Second, inappropriate responses elicited by objects in the environment are not inhibited. These components can be related if we assume that a lack of awareness of intentions reflects a failure to develop such intentions. Responses to objects in the environment are normally inhibited until an intention has been developed. The system that develops intentions also inhibits inappropriate responses.

The high-level control system we are describing here is based on the supervisory attentional system developed by Shallice (1988, pp. 328–352) to explain the

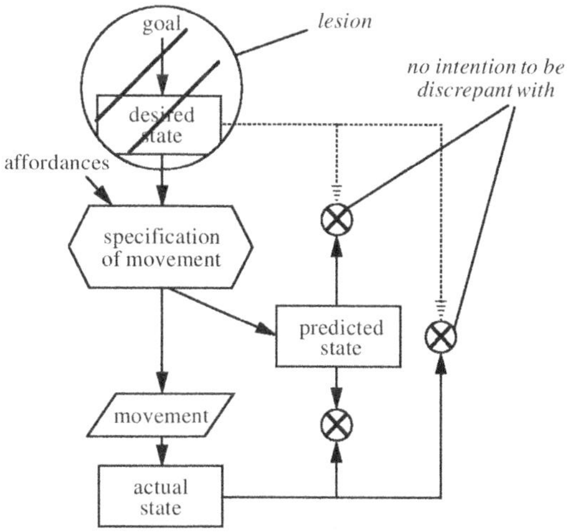


*Figure 4.5* The underlying disorder leading to utilization behaviour. The patient does not form any intentions and so makes stereotyped responses to objects in the environment. The patient is not aware that these responses are inappropriate.

behaviour of patients with frontal lobe lesions. These patients have no problems in routine situations, but have difficulty coping with novel tasks. With such tasks they may make inappropriate routine responses (a form of utilization behaviour) or they may fail to respond. This response failure occurs because, in novel situations it is not only necessary to inhibit inappropriate responses elicited by objects in the environment, but also to initiate responses when there is no external stimulus to elicit them.

While there is good evidence that this high-level control system is instantiated in prefrontal cortex (Shallice 1988), it has proved more difficult to relate particular components of this system to specific regions within prefrontal cortex. Imaging studies suggest that dorsolateral prefrontal cortex (BA46 and 9) is particularly involved in selection between alternative actions when there are no external cues to indicate which action is the most appropriate (Jahanshahi & Frith 1998). However, utilization behaviour seems to be more concerned with failure to inhibit inappropriate movements rather than a failure select appropriate ones. There is some evidence that the lesions that produce utilization behaviour are more likely to involve the ACC (Degos *et al.* 1993). Such lesions are also associated with difficulties in inhibiting routine responses, for example, inhibiting saccades to peripheral stimuli (Paus *et al.* 1991).

There is also, as yet, little evidence concerning brain areas concerned with awareness of intended actions. In one of the few relevant imaging studies Jueptner *et al.* (1997) trained volunteers until they could perform a paced sequence of button presses routinely and without thought. The volunteers were then scanned, either while performing this task in routine mode, or when deliberately thinking of which button had to be pressed next in the sequence. The requirement to be aware of their intended action increased activity in dorsolateral prefrontal cortex and in the ACC (BA32). There are no direct connections between these regions and motor cortex, so that their influence on movement is mediated via their connections with premotor regions including the SMA (Lu *et al.* 1994). On the basis of their study of patients with medial frontal lesions, Paus *et al.* (1991) concluded that the ability to inhibit routine responses depends upon input from the ACC to the SMA. Thus, the same system has been implicated both in the awareness of intended actions and in the inhibition of routine actions. These proposals are also in accord with our suggestion that utilization behaviour is caused by damage to an earlier stage in the system that generates actions than that associated with the anarchic hand.

### *c Abnormalities in the perception of action while the control of action is largely intact*

#### *i Delusions of control; passivity experiences associated with schizophrenia*

Many patients with schizophrenia describe 'passivity' experiences in which actions, thoughts or emotions are made for them by some external agent rather than by their own will. 'My fingers pick up the pen, but I don't control them. What they do is nothing to do with me.' 'The force moved my lips. I began to speak. The words were made for me' (Mellors 1970, p. 18). In most cases the actions made when the patient 'feels' that he is being controlled by alien forces are not discrepant with his intentions. Thus the patient may be correctly performing the task set by the experimenter (e.g. making random movements of a joystick) at the same time as having the experience of passivity (see Spence *et al.* 1997). The patient does not try to correct these 'controlled' actions or prevent them from occurring. Clearly actions are being correctly selected and irrelevant affordances are being suppressed.

We have previously suggested that these abnormal experiences arise through a lack of awareness of intended actions (Frith 1987). However, this formulation is inconsistent with the patients' ability to follow the commands of the experimenter, to avoid showing utilization behaviour, and to correct errors on the basis of sensory feedback about limb positions (which requires comparison of intended actions and their consequences). Instead we suggest that the experience of alien control arises from a lack of awareness of the predicted limb position (figure 4.6). As a result the patient is not aware of the exact specification of the movement. He is aware of his goal, of the intention to move and of the movement having occurred, but he is not aware of having initiated the movement. It is as if the movement, although intended, has been initiated by some external force. In a variation on this theme Spence (1996) suggested that the problem is to do with the timing of awareness. Normally we are aware of initiating a movement *ca.* 80

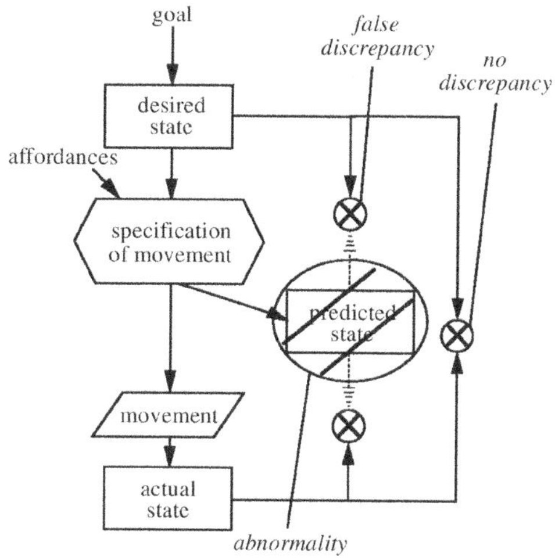


*Figure 4.6* The underlying disorder leading to delusions of control. The patient formulates the action appropriate to his intention and the action is successfully performed. The patient is aware that the action matches the intention, but has no awareness of initiating the action or of its predicted consequences. The patient feels as if his intentions are being monitored and his actions made for him by some external force.

ms before the movement actually begins and, therefore well before any sensory feedback resulting from the movement (Libet *et al.* 1983). Spence suggested that, in the presence of delusions of control, the awareness of the sensory consequences of the movement precedes the awareness of initiating the movement, which is in the opposite order to the normal experience of our own agency. We suggest that, in the presence of delusions of control, the patient is not aware of the predicted consequences of a movement and is therefore not aware of initiating a movement.

There is nothing obviously abnormal in the motor control of these patients. This suggests that accurate representations of predicted states are available and used by the motor system. However, these representations are not available to awareness. A number of experiments confirm that there are subtle problems consistent with a lack of awareness of predicted actions. These patients fail to make rapid error corrections based on awareness of discrepancies between intended and predicted limb positions, although they have no difficulty correcting errors based on visual feedback about actual limb positions (Malenka *et al.* 1982; Frith & Done 1989). These patients have difficulty remembering the precise details of actions made in the absence of visual feedback (Mlakar *et al.* 1994; Stirling *et al.* 1998). They also have difficulty distinguishing between correct visual feedback about the position of their hand and false feedback when the image of the hand they see is in fact that of another person attempting to make the same movements as the patient (Daprati *et al.* 1997).

Jeannerod (1999) suggested that conscious judgement about a movement requires a different form of representation from that needed for comparisons of predictions and outcomes within the motor system. Following Barresi & Moore (1996) (see also Frith 1995) he suggests that conscious judgements about movements require 'third-person' information while control of movement depends upon private 'first-person' information. In terms of this formulation he suggests that schizophrenic patients fail to monitor the third-person signals that enable them to make judgements about their own actions. We would suggest, rather, that, in schizophrenia, something goes wrong with the mechanism that translates the first-person representations that are involved in motor control into the third-person representations that are needed for conscious monitoring of the motor control system. This is part of a more general problem that these patients have in escaping from a first-person, egocentric view of the world.

Spence *et al.* (1997) used brain imaging to identify brain regions associated with the experience of delusions of control. They scanned schizophrenic patients with and without such delusions while they performed a response selection task. The presence of delusions of control was associated with overactivity in right inferior parietal cortex. We suggest that this overactivity reflected a heightened response to the sensory consequences of the movements the patients were making during scanning. Normally activity associated with sensory stimulation is much reduced if this stimulation is the direct consequence of our own movements (Blakemore *et al.* 1998*b*). This is because the sensory consequences of our movements can be predicted. In the presence of delusions of control, modulation of sensory areas based on such predictions fails, and the regions are overactive. Although the patient is making an active movement, the brain activity and the associated experience resembles that seen with passive arm movements (Weiller *et al.* 1996).

We have already discussed (§ 2(c)(ii)) the evidence that the parietal cortex has a major role in the control of action which depends upon forming representations in many different coordinate systems (e.g. retinotopic, head centred, body centred, etc.). As yet, however, we have not considered in any detail the nature and location of the subset of these representations that are available to consciousness. Such consideration is crucial for understanding abnormalities in the awareness of the motor system as observed in anosognosia and delusions of control. Frith (1995) and Jeannerod (1999) theorized that representations suitable for awareness need to be in viewer-independent or 'third-person' coordinates, and not in the private, egocentric coordinates that are more suited for the direct control of movement. Is there any evidence for segregation of these kinds of representation in parietal cortex? We have already presented evidence that there is a general lack of awareness of the details of motor commands and their fine-tuning by affordances as in reaching and grasping. The IPS seems to have a major role in this activity as revealed by single-cell neurophysiology, imaging studies and the effects of lesions. Of particular interest is the observation that optic ataxia, which is caused by lesions to the IPS, is defined by problems with reaching and grasping, but is not associated with any disorder of awareness. In contrast, imaging studies of motor preparation and motor imagery, which emphasize awareness of motor representations, tend to activate the inferior parietal lobe (supramarginal gyrus, BA40; Stephan *et al.* 1995; Krams *et al.* 1998). Lesions in this region, particularly in the right hemisphere, are associated with disorders of awareness such as neglect and anosognosia (Vallar & Perani 1986). This is also the region that is overactive when patients with schizophrenia are experiencing delusions of control.

Given that schizophrenic patients do not have fundamental problems with the control of action it seems unlikely that the brain abnormality associated with delusions of control is located in parietal cortex where the overactivity is observed. It is more likely that the damage involves the system that normally modulates activity at this site. Fletcher *et al.* (1999), for example, provide evidence of abnormal modulation of long-range corticocortical connections in patients with schizophrenia and suggest that the anterior cingulate has a key role in this modulatory system. We have already mentioned evidence from imaging that the ACC is involved in attention to future actions (Jueptner *et al.* 1997) and may have a role in suppressing inappropriate actions via its connections with the SMA (Paus *et al.* 1991). We speculate that it may also have a role in modulating representations in the inferior parietal cortex which underpin awareness of the current and future states of the motor system.

## 4 Conclusions

In this paper we have attempted to develop a framework based upon well-established principles of motor control in such a way that the components of the system can be related first to the subjective experience of motor control, and second to the underlying physiology upon which motor control depends. We have devoted much attention to the abnormalities of control associated with various neurological and psychiatric disorders. Careful consideration of these abnormalities provides important evidence linking awareness of control to the underlying components of the system. Indeed, we consider that these abnormalities cannot be properly understood without taking into account the subjective experience of the patients. As yet the physiological underpinnings of the motor control system are understood only in the broadest terms. However, there is a rapidly increasing body of evidence from studies of patients with circumscribed lesions and from functional brain imaging studies to aid in generating a more detailed account. On the basis of this evidence it is now possible to explore the brain systems concerned specifically with awareness of the different aspects of the motor control system.

In this paper we have only considered relatively simple motor functions such as reaching and grasping or learning sequences of movements. However, the control system we have described, involving representations of desired and predicted states and models for generating these states, could apply equally well to much more difficult problems. It is simple, in principle, to extend the concept of internal models of the motor system to internal models of the external world, of other people's mental processes, or of states of one's own mind. For example, rather than changing the position of an arm, one might wish to change someone else's belief about the world. Of course, we have no direct knowledge of their belief, we have to estimate this just as we have to estimate the current position of our own limbs. Given an estimate of a person's current belief, a controller could used to compute the behaviour (or speech) we need to adopt in order to produce the required change. A predictor could be run to check whether this behaviour would indeed produce the desired change in the belief of the other person. Similar analysis could be applied to the control of many aspects of the external world.

This work was funded by the Wellcome Trust. We are grateful to Richard Passingham, Patrick Haggard and Richard Frackowiak for their comments on earlier drafts of this paper.

## References

Aglioti, S., Bonazzi, A. & Cortese, F. 1994 Phantom lower limb as a perceptual marker of neural plasticity in the human brain. *Proc. R. Soc. Lond.* B **255,** 273–278.

Aglioti, S., DeSouza, J.-F.-X. & Goodale, M.-A. 1995 Size-contrast illusions deceive the eye, but not the hand. *Curr. Biol.* **5,** 679–685.

Andersen, R. A. 1995 Encoding of intention and spatial location in the posterior parietal cortex. *Cerebr. Cortex* **5,** 111–122.

Andersen, R. A., Snyder, L. H., Bradley, D.C. & Xing, J. 1997 Multimodal representation of space in the posterior parietal cortex and its use in planning movements. *A. Rev. Neurosci.* **20,** 303–330.

Babinsky, M. J. 1914 Contribution a l'etude des troubles mentaux dans l'hemiplegie organique cerebrale (agnosognosie). *Revue Neurologique* **1,** 845–847.

Bálint, R. 1909 Seelenlämung des 'Schauens', optisches Ataxie, räumliche Störung der Aufmerksamkeit. *Monatsschift für Psychiatrie und Neuologie* **25,** 51–81.

Ball, T., Schreiber, A., Feige, B., Wagner, M., Lücking, C. H. & Kristeva-Feige, R. 1999 The role of higher-order motor areas in voluntary movements as revealed by high-resolution EEG and fMRI. *NeuroImage* **10,** 682–694.

Banks, G., Short, P., Martinez, A. J., Latchaw, R., Ratcliff, G. & Boller, F. 1989 The alien hand syndrome; clinical and postmortem findings. *Arch. Neurol.* **46,** 456–459.

Barresi, J. & Moore, C. 1996 Intentional relations and social understanding. *Behav. Brain Sci.* **19,** 107–154.

Blakemore, S.-J., Goodbody, S. J. & Wolpert, D. M. 1998*a* Predicting the consequences of our own actions: the role of sensorimotor context estimation. *J. Neurosci.* **18,** 7511–7518.

Blakemore, S.-J., Wolpert, D. M. & Frith, C. D. 1998*b* Central cancellation of self-produced tickle sensation. *Nature Neurosci.* **1,** 635–640.

Blakemore, S.-J., Frith, C. D. & Wolpert, D. W. 1999 Spatiotemporal prediction modulates the perception of self-produced stimuli. *J. Cogn. Neurosci.* **11,** 551–559.

Bridgeman, B., Kirch, M. & Sperling, A. 1981 Segregation of cognitive and motor aspects of visual function using induced motion. *Percept. Psychophysiol.* **29,** 336–342.

Burgess, P. W. & Shallice, T. 1996 Confabulation and the control of recollection. *Memory* **4,** 1–53.

Castiello, U., Paulignan, Y. & Jeannerod, M. 1991 Temporal dissociation of motor responses and subjective awareness. A study in normal subjects. *Brain* **114,** 2639–2655.

Clower, D. M., Hoffman, J. M., Votaw, J. R., Faber, T. L., Woods, R. P. & Alexander, G. E. 1996 Role of posterior parietal cortex in the recalibration of visually guided reaching. *Nature* **383,** 618–621.

Colby, C. L. & Duhamel, J.-R. 1996 Spatial representations in parietal cortex. *Cerebr. Cortex* **5,** 105–115.

Colby, C. L., Duhamel, J. R. & Goldberg, M. E. 1995 Oculocentric spatial representation in parietal cortex. *Cerebr. Cortex* **5,** 470–481.

Cole, J. D. 1991 *Pride and a daily marathon.* London: Duckworth.

Corbetta, M. 1998 Frontoparietal cortical networks for directing attention and the eye to visual locations; identical, independent, or overlapping neural systems? *Proc. Natl Acad. Sci. USA* **95,** 831–838.

Corbetta, M., Miezin, F., Shulman, G. & Petersen, S. E. 1993 A PET study of visuospatial attention. *J. Neurosci.* **13,** 1202–1226.

Craik, K. J. W. 1948 Theory of the human operator in control systems. II. Man as an element in a control system. *Br. J. Psychol.* **38,** 142–148.

Daprati, E., Franck, N., Georgieff, N., Proust, J., Pacherie, E., Dalery, J. & Jeannerod, M. 1997 Looking for the agent: an investigation into consciousness of action and self-consciousness in schizophrenic patients. *Cognition* **65,** 71–86.

Decety, J., Jeannerod, M., Germain, M. & Pastene, J. 1991 Vegetative response during imagined movement is proportional to mental effort. *Behav. Brain Res.* **42,** 1–5.

Decety, J., Perani, D., Jeannerod, M., Bettinardi, V., Tadary, B., Woods, R., Mazziotta, J. C. & Fazio, F. 1994 Mapping motor representations with PET. *Nature* **371,** 600–602.

Deiber, M.-P., Passingham, R. E., Colebatch, J. G., Friston, K. J., Nixon, P. D. & Frackowiak, R. S. J. 1991 Cortical areas and the selection of movement. *Exp. Brain Res.* **84,** 393–402.

Degos, J. D., Dafonseca, N., Grey, F. & Cesaro, P. 1983 Sever frontal syndrome associated with infarcts of the left anterior cingulate gyrus and the head of the right caudate nucleus – a clinicopathological case. *Brain* **116,** 1541–1548.

De Renzi, E. & Lucchelli, F. 1988 Ideational apraxia. *Brain* **113,** 1173–1188.

De Renzi, E., Faglioni, P. & Sergato, P. 1982 Modality-specific and supramodal mechanisms of apraxia. *Brain* **105,** 301–312.

Dettmers, C., Fink, G. R., Lemon, R. N., Stephan, K. M., Passingham, R. E., Silbersweig, D. A., Holmes, A., Ridding, M. C., Brookes, D. J. & Frackowiak, R. S. J. 1995 Relation between cerebral activity and force in the motor areas of the human brain. *J. Neurophysiol.* **74,** 802–815.

Duhamel, J. R., Colby, C. L. & Goldberg, M. E. 1992 The updating of the representation of visual space in parietal cortex by intended eye movements. *Science* **255,** 90–92.

Feltz, D. L. & Landers, D. M. 1983 The effects of mental practice on motor skill learning and performance. A meta-analysis. *J. Sport Psychol.* **5,** 27–57.

Fink, G. R., Marshall, J. C., Halligan, P. W., Frith, C. D., Driver, J., Frackowiak, R. S. J. & Dolan, R. J. 1999 The neural consequences of conflict between intention and the senses. *Brain* **122,** 497–512.

Flanders, M., Helms-Tillery, S. I. H. & Soechting, A. J. F. 1992 Early stages in a sensorimotor transform. *Behav. Brain Sci.* **15,** 309–362.

Fletcher, P., McKenna, P. J., Friston, K. J., Frith, C. D. & Dolan, R. J. 1999 Abnormal cingulate modulation of fronto-temporal connectivity in schizophrenia. *NeuroImage* **9,** 337–342.

Fourneret, P. & Jeannerod, M. 1998 Limited conscious monitoring of motor performance in normal subjects. *Neuropsychologia* **36,** 1133–1140.

Frith, C. D. 1987 The positive and negative symptoms of schizophrenia reflect impairments in the perception and initiation of action. *Psychol. Med.* **17,** 631–648.

Frith, C. D. 1995 Consciousness is for other people. *Behav. Brain Sci.* **18,** 682–683.

Frith, C. D. & Done, D. J. 1989 Experiences of alien control in schizophrenia reflect a disorder in the central monitoring of action. *Psychol. Med.* **19,** 359–363.

Gallese, V., Fadiga, L., Fogassi, L., Luppino, G. & Murata, A. 1997 A parieto-frontal circuit for hand grasping movements in the monkey: evidence from reversible inactivation experiments. In *Parietal lobe contributions to orientation in 3-D space* (ed. P. Thier & H. O. Karnath), pp. 255–269. Heidelberg, Germany: Springer.

Galletti, C., Battaglini, P. P. & Fattori, P. 1993 Parietal neurons encoding spatial locations in craniotopic coordinates. *Exp. Brain Res.* **96,** 221–229.

Gentilucci, M., Chieffi, S., Daprati, E., Saetti, M. C. & Toni, I. 1996 Visual illusion and action. *Neuropsychologia* **34,** 369–376.

Geschwind, N. 1965 Disconnexion syndromes in animals and man. *Brain* **88,** 237–294.

Ghahramani, Z. & Wolpert, D. M. 1997 Modular decomposition in visuomotor learning. *Nature* **386,** 392–395.

Goldberg, G., Mayer, N. H. & Toglia, J. U. 1981 Medial frontal cortex and the alien hand sign. *Arch. Neurol.* **38,** 683–686.

Goodale, M. A., Pélisson, D. & Prablanc, C. 1986 Large adjustments in visually guided reaching do not depend on vision of the hand or detection of target displacement. *Nature* **320,** 748–750.

Goodale, M. A., Jacobson, L. S., Milner, A.D., Perrett, D. I., Benson, P. J. & Hietanen, J. K. 1994 The nature and limits of orientation and pattern processing visuomotor control in a visual form agnosic. *J. Cogn. Neurosci.* **6,** 46–56.

Greeno, J. G. 1994 Gibson's affordances. *Psychol. Rev.* **101,** 336–342.

Haggard, P. & Eimer, M. 1999 On the relation between brain potentials and awareness of voluntary movements. *Exp. Brain Res.* **126,** 128–133.

Haggard, P. & Magno, E. 1999 Localising awareness of action with transcranial magnetic stimulation. *Exp. Brain Res.* **127,** 102–107.

Haggard, P., Newman, C. & Magno, E. 1999 On the perceived time of voluntary actions. *Br. J. Psychol.* **90,** 291–303.

Hari, R., Hanninen, R., Makinen, T., Jousmaki, V., Forss, N., Seppa, M. & Salonen, O. 1998 Three hands: fragmentation of bodily awareness. *Neurosci. Lett.* **240,** 131–134.

Harvey, M. 1995 Psychic paralysis of gaze, optic ataxia, spatial disorder of attention. Translated from Bálint 1909. *Cogn. Neuropsychol.* **12,** 266–282.

Heilman, K. M., Barrett, A.M. & Adair, J. C. 1998 Possible mechanisms of anosognosia: a defect in self-awareness. *Phil. Trans. R. Soc. Lond.* B **353,** 1903–1909.

Ito, M. 1970 Neurophysiological aspects of the cerebellar motor control system. *Int. J. Neurol.* **7,** 162–176.

Jahanshahi, M. & Frith, C. D. 1998 Willed action and its impairments. *Cogn. Neuropsychol.* **15,** 483–533.

Jeannerod, M. 1994 The representing brain – neural correlates of motor intention and imagery. *Behav. Brain Sci.* **17,** 187–202.

Jeannerod, M. 1999 To act or not to act: perspectives on the representation of actions. *Q. J. Exp. Psychol.* A **52,** 981–1020.

Jeannerod, M., Michel, F. & Prablanc, C. 1986 The control of hand movements in case of hemianaesthesia following a parietal lesion. *Brain* **107,** 899–920.

Jeannerod, M., Decety, J. & Michel, F. 1994 Impairment of grasping movements following bilateral posterior parietal lesions. *Neuropsychologia* **32,** 369–380.

Jeannerod, M., Arbib, M. A., Rizzolatti, G. & Sakata, H. 1995 Grasping objects: the cortical mechanisms of visuomotor transformation. *Trends Neurosci.* **18,** 314–320.

Jordan, M. I. 1996 Computational aspects of motor control and motor learning. In *Handbook of perception and action: motor skills* (ed. E. H. Heuer & E. S. Keele), pp. 71–118. New York: Academic Press.

Jueptner, M., Stephan, K. M., Frith, C. D., Brooks, D. J., Frackowiak, R. S. & Passingham, R. E. 1997 Anatomy of motor learning. I. Frontal cortex and attention to action. *J. Neurophysiol.* **77,** 1313–1324.

Kalaska, J. F. & Crammond, D. J. 1992 Cerebral cortical mechanisms of reaching movements. *Science* **255,** 1517–1525.

Kew, J. J. M., Halligan, P. W., Marshall, J. C., Passingham, R. E., Rothwell, J. C., Ridding, M. C., Marsden, C. D. & Brooks, D. J. 1997 Abnormal access of axial vibrotactile input to deafferented somatosensory cortex in human upper limb amputees. *J. Neurophysiol.* **77,** 2753–2764.

Krams, M., Rushworth, M. F. S., Deiber, M.-P., Frackowiak, R. S. J. & Passingham, R. E. 1998 The preparation, execution and suppression of copied movements in the human brain. *Exp. Brain Res.* **120,** 386–398.

Lhermitte, F. 1983 'Utilisation behaviour' and its relation to lesions of the frontal lobes. *Brain* **106,** 237–255.

Lhermitte, F. 1986 Human autonomy and the frontal lobes. II. Patient behavior in complex and social situations: the 'environmental dependency syndrome'. *Annls Neurol.* **19,** 335–343.

Libet, B., Gleason, C. A., Wright, E. W. & Pearl, D. K. 1983 Time of conscious intention to act in relation to onset of cerebral activity (readiness potential): the unconscious initiation of a freely voluntary act. *Brain* **106,** 623–642.

Lu, M.-T., Preston, J. R. & Strick, P. L. 1994 Interconnections between prefrontal cortex and the premotor areas in the frontal lobe. *J. Comp. Neurol.* **341,** 375–392.

McCloskey, D. I., Colebatch, J. G., Potter, E. K. & Burke, D. 1983 Judgements about the onset of rapid voluntary movements in man. *J. Neurophysiol.* **49,** 851–863.

Malenka, R. C., Angel, R. W., Hamptom, B. & Berger, P. A. 1982 Impaired central error correcting behaviour in schizophrenia. *Arch. Gen. Psychiat.* **39,** 101–107.

Marchetti, C. & Della Salla, S. 1998 Disentangling the alien and anarchic hand. *Cogn. Neuropsychiat.* **3,** 191–208.

Mellors, C. S. 1970 First-rank symptoms of schizophrenia. *Br. J. Psychiat.* **117,** 15–23.

Miall, R. C. & Wolpert, D. M. 1996 Forward models for physiological motor control. *Neural Net.* **9,** 1265–1279.

Miall, R. C., Weir, D. J., Wolpert, D. M. & Stein, J. F. 1993 Is the cerebellum a Smith predictor? *J. Mot. Behav.* **25,** 203–216.

Milner, A.D. & Goodale, M. A. 1995 *The visual brain in action.* Oxford University Press.

Milner, A.D., Paulignan, Y., Dijkerman, H. C., Michel, F. & Jeannerod, M. 1999 A paradoxical improvement of misreaching in optic ataxia: new evidence for two separate neural systems for visual localization. *Proc. R. Soc. Lond.* B **266,** 2225–2229.

Mlakar, J., Jensterle, J. & Frith, C. D. 1994 Central monitoring deficiency and schizophrenic symptoms. *Psychol. Med.* **24,** 557–564.

Nobre, A. C., Gitelman, D. R., Sebestyen, G. N., Meyer, J., Frackowiak, R. S. J., Frith, C. D. & Mesulam, M.-M. 1997 Functional localisation of the system for visuospatial attention using positron emission tomography. *Brain* **120,** 515–533.

Parkin, A. J. 1996 The alien hand. In *Methods in madness: case studies in cognitive neuropsychiatry* (ed. P. W. Halligan & J. C. Marshall), pp. 173–183. Hove, UK: Psychology Press.

Pascual-Leone, A., Dang, N., Cohen, L. G., Brasil-Neto, J., Cammarota, A. & Hallett, M. 1995 Modulation of motor responses evoked by transcranial magnetic stimulation during the acquisition of new fine motor skills. *J. Neurophysiol.* **74,** 1037–1045.

Passingham, R. E. 1993 *The frontal lobes and voluntary action.* Oxford University Press.

Passingham, R. E. 1996 Attention to action. *Phil. Trans. R. Soc. Lond.* B **351,** 1423–1432.

Passingham, R. E. 1998 The specialisation of the human neocortex. In *Comparative neuropsychology* (ed. A.D. Milner), pp. 271–298. Oxford University Press.

Paus, T., Kalina, M., Patockova, L., Angerova, Y., Cerny, R., Mecir, P., Bauer, J. & Krabec, P. 1991 Medial vs lateral frontal lobe lesions and differential impairment of central-gaze fixation maintenance in man. *Brain* **114,** 2051–2067.

Pause, M., Kunesch, E., Binkovski, F. & Freund, H.-J. 1989 Sensorimotor disturbances in patients with lesions of the parietal cortex. *Brain* **112,** 1599–1625.

Perenin, M.-T. & Rossetti, Y. 1996 Grasping without form discrimination in an hemianopic field. *Neuro Report* **7,** 793–797.

Perenin, M.-T. & Vighetto, A. 1988 Optic ataxia: a specific disruption in visuo-motor mechanisms. I. Different aspects of the deficit in reaching for objects. *Brain* **111,** 643–674.

Pickard, N. & Strick, P. L. 1996 Motor areas of the medial wall: a review of their location and functional activation. *Cerebr. Cortex* **6,** 342–353.

Ramachandran, V. S. 1993 Behavioural and magnetoencephalographic correlates of plasticity in the adult human brain. *Proc. Natl Acad. Sci. USA* **90,** 10413–10420.

Ramachandran, V. S. 1996 What neurological syndromes can tell us about human nature: some lessons from phantom limbs, Capgras syndrome, and anosognosia. *Cold Spring Harb. Symp. Quant. Biol.* **61,** 115–134.

Ramachandran, V. S. & Hirstein, W. 1998 The perception of phantom limbs. *Brain* **121,** 1603–1630.

Ramachandran, V. S. & Rogers-Ramachandran, D. 1996 Synaesthesia in phantom limbs induced with mirrors. *Proc. R. Soc. Lond.* B **263,** 377–386.

Ramachandran, V. S., Rogers-Ramachandran, D. & Stewart, M. 1992 Perceptual correlates of massive cortical reorganization. *Science* **258,** 1159–1160.

Rizzolatti, G., Riggio, L., Dascola, I. & Umilta, C. 1987 Reorienting attention across the horizontal and vertical meridians – evidence in favour of a premotor theory of attention. *Neuropsychologia* **25,** 31–40.

Rizzolatti, G., Gentilucci, M., Camarda, R. M., Gallese, V., Luppino, G., Matelli, M. & Fogassi, L. 1990 Neurons relating to reaching–grasping arm movements in the rostral part of area 6 (area 6a beta). *Exp. Brain Res.* **82,** 337–350.

Rizzolatti, G., Fogassi, L. & Gallese, V. 1997 Parietal cortex: from sight to action. *Curr. Opin. Neurobiol.* **7,** 562–567.

Rossetti, Y. 1998 Implicit short-lived motor representations of space in brain damaged and healthy subjects. *Conscious. Cogn.* **7,** 520–558.

Rothwell, J. C., Traub, M. M., Day, B. L., Obeso, J. A., Thomas, P. K. & Marsden, C. D. 1982 Manual motor performance in a deafferented man. *Brain* **105,** 515–542.

Rushworth, M., Nixon, P. D. & Passingham, R. E. 1997 Parietal cortex and movement. I. Movement selection and reaching. *Exp. Brain Res.* **117,** 292–310.

Schultz, T. R., Wells, D. & Sarda, M. 1980 The development of the ability to distinguish intended actions from mistakes, reflexes and passive movements. *Br. J. Soc. Clin. Psychol.* **19,** 301–310.

Shallice, T. 1988 *From neuropsychology to mental structure.* Cambridge University Press.

Sirigu, A., Duhamel, J. R., Cohen, L., Pillon, B., Dubois, B. & Agid, Y. 1996 The mental representation of hand movements after parietal cortex damage. *Science* **273,** 1564–1568.

Sirigu, A., Daprati, E., Pradat-Diehl, P., Franck, N. & Jeannerod, M. 1999 Perception of self-generated movement following left parietal lesion. *Brain* **122,** 1867–1874.

Smith, M. C. 1978 Cognizing the behavior stream: the recognition of intentional action. *Child Dev.* **49,** 736–743.

Spence, S. A. 1996 Free will in the light of neuropsychiatry. *Philosoph. Psychiat. Psychol.* **3,** 75–90.

Spence, S. A., Brooks, D. J., Hirsch, S. R., Liddle, P. F., Meehan, J. & Grasby, P.M. 1997 A PET study of voluntary movement in schizophrenic patients experiencing passivity phenomena (delusions of alien control). *Brain* **120,** 1997–2011.

Sperry, R. W. 1950 Neural basis of the spontaneous optokinetic response produced by visual inversion. *J. Comp. Physiol. Psychol.* **43,** 482–489.

Stephan, K. M., Fink, G. R., Passingham, R. E., Silbersweig, D., Ceballos-Baumann, A. O., Frith, C. D. & Frackowiak, R. S. J. 1995 Functional anatomy of mental representation of upper extremity movements in healthy subjects. *J. Neurophysiol.* **73,** 373–386.

Stirling, J. D., Hellewell, J. S. E. & Quraishi, N. 1998 Self-monitoring dysfunction and the schizophrenic symptoms of alien control. *Psychol. Med.* **28,** 675–683.

Sunderland, S. 1978 *Nerves and nerve injuries,* 2nd edn. Edinburgh, UK: Churchill Livingstone.

Vallar, G. & Perani, D. 1986 The anatomy of unilateral neglect after right hemisphere stroke lesions. A clinical/CT-scan correlation study in man. *Neuropsychologia* **24,** 609–622.

Vetter, P., Goodbody, S. J. & Wolpert, D. M. 1999 Evidence for an eye-centred representation of the visuomotor map. *J. Neurophysiol.* **81,** 935–939.

Vogt, S. 1995 On relations between perceiving, imagining and performing in the learning of cyclical movement sequences. *Br. J. Psychol.* **86,** 191–216.

Von Helmholtz, H. 1886 *Handbuch der Physiologischen Optik.* Leipzig: Voss.

Von Holst, E. & Mittelstaedt, H. 1950 Das Reafferenzprincip (Wechselwirkungen zwischen Zentralnervensystem und Periferie). *Naturwissenschaften* **37,** 464–476.

Vuilleumier, P., Reverdin, A. & Landis, T. 1997 Four legs – illusory reduplication of the lower limbs after bilateral parietal lobe damage. *Arch. Neurol.* **54,** 1543–1547.

Weiller, C., Juptner, M., Fellows, S., Rijntjes, M., Leonhardt, G., Kiebel, S., Muller, S., Diener, H. C. & Thilmann, A. F. 1996 Brain representation of active and passive movement. *NeuroImage* **4,** 105–110.

Weiskrantz, L., Elliot, J. & Darlington, C. 1971 Preliminary observations of tickling oneself. *Nature* **230,** 598–599.

Wegner, D. M. & Wheatley, T. 1999 Apparent mental causation – sources of the experience of will. *Am. Psychol.* **54,** 480–492.

Wolpert, D. M. 1997 Computational approaches to motor control. *Trends Cogn. Sci.* **1,** 209–216.

Wolpert, D. M. & Kawato M. 1998 Multiple paired forward and inverse models for motor control. *Neural Net.* **11,** 1317–1329.

Wolpert, D. M., Ghahramani, Z. & Jordan, M. I. 1995 An internal model for sensorimotor integration. *Science* **269,** 1880–1882.

Wolpert, D. M., Goodbody, S. J. & Husain, M. 1998 Maintaining internal representations: the role of the human superior parietal lobe. *Nature Neurosci.* **1,** 529–533.

Yue, G. & Cole, K. J. 1992 Strength increases from the motor program. Comparison of training with maximal voluntary and imagined muscle contractions. *J. Neurophysiol.* **67,** 1114–1123.

# 5 Explaining delusions of control

## The comparator model 20 years on

*Chris Frith*

Many of the symptoms of schizophrenia, particularly those described by Schneider (Schneider, 1957) as first rank, seem to reflect a confusion between changes in sensation caused by actions of the self and changes with external causes. Examples include, *hearing thoughts spoken aloud, thought echo, made emotions, somatic passivity experiences,* and *delusions of control.* In all these cases the patient is attributing effects generated by the self to external forces.

Perhaps we should experience surprise, not at the strange ideas of the patients, but at the ease with which the rest of us make the distinction between self and other generated sensation. This was Helmholtz' concern (Helmholtz, 1866): When an image moves across our retina, how do we know whether this is the world moving across our eyes, or our eyes moving across the world? His answer was that an active movement, moving the eyes across the world, will be preceded by a motor command, which does not occur when the world moves in front of our eyes. Information about this motor command, subsequently termed *corollary discharge* or *reafference copy,* can be used to predict the sensory consequences of the eye movement. The predicted and observed outcomes of the movement can be compared. If they match, then the changes were self generated.

Given this account, it seems plausible that first rank symptoms, such as delusions of control, might occur because something goes wrong with this comparator mechanism (Feinberg, 1978; Frith, 1987). Since this first suggestion, the comparator model has become far more sophisticated and has been supported by empirical studies (e.g. Frith & Done, 1989).

The first increase in the sophistication of the model came from the development of engineering approaches to the study of motor control (e.g. Miall & Wolpert, 1996). In order to overcome the inherent delays in feedback signals associated with movement, the system needs to generate a *forward model.* The forward model predicts the consequences of implementing motor commands in terms of both kinematics (where and when our hand will arrive) and in terms of sensations (what it will feel like). If we can predict where our hand is going to be after the motor command has been implemented, then we can check whether we have chosen the correct command before we actually make the movement. If we can predict the sensations we are going to feel, then they are unimportant and can be attenuated.

Experiments suggest that patients with delusions of control have problems with both the kinematic and sensory aspects of the forward model (Blakemore, Smith, Steel, Johnstone, & Frith, 2000; Franck et al., 2001; Lindner, Thier, Kircher, Haarmeier, & Leube, 2005). But the precise nature of these problems remain to be specified. Recently Synofzik, Thier, Leube, Schlotterbeck, and Lindner (2010) have shown that the problem lies in the precision of the prediction of the sensory consequences of action: the less the precision the greater the severity of delusions of control. As a result of this lack of precision, patients rely more strongly on external cues for agency, leading to better than normal adaptation to external feedback.

One problem with the proposal that patients with delusions of control fail to compute a forward model is that such a failure would be associated with major problems in motor control. This is clearly not evident in the every-day behaviour of patients with delusions of control. Indeed, there is evidence that the automatic predictions that occur well below awareness are intact in patients with delusions of control (Delevoye-Turrell, Giersch, & Danion, 2002). The problems arise at a higher level, in particular in relation to agency: the conscious experience of motor control. For example, the motor problems revealed in the experiment by Synofzik et al. (2010) were relatively subtle. The major problem related to the patients' subjective experience of movement as indicated by their report of the discrepancy between their actual movement and what they saw in the virtual reality setup. A much more specific account is required linking the function of the comparator with the experience of agency (Synofzik, Vosgerau, & Newen, 2008). Another problem with the proposal is that observations of a number of disorders, including schizophrenia, show that a mere failure of prediction is not sufficient to generate a delusion (Davies, Coltheart, Langdon, & Breen, 2001). Unlike healthy subjects, delusional patients are prepared to explain anomalous perception in terms of beliefs that are highly implausible.

Our understanding of the cognitive basis of the sense of agency has been greatly enhanced by the discovery of the phenomenon of *intentional binding* (Haggard, Clark, & Kalogeras, 2002). The experience of agency is associated with binding, such that actions and their consequences are experienced as closer together in time as long as the action is experienced as the cause of the outcome. Studies of binding have shown that the experience of agency depends upon two components, first an advance prediction of the effects of the action and, second, a retrospective component whereby the nature of the outcome changes the experience of the action (Moore, Lagnado, Deal, & Haggard, 2009). Voss et al. (2010) have demonstrated that delusions and hallucinations are associated with a failure of the predictive component, while the retrospective component remains intact. Thus, the patients' experience of agency relies excessively on the sensory outcomes of their actions, confirming, from a very different perspective, the results of Synofzik et al. (2010).

The series of studies I have outlined above have considerably advanced our understanding of the control and experience of action in the normal case as well as in patients with first rank symptoms. While the essence of Helmholtz' original idea remains intact, the new models emphasise prediction rather than monitoring. This emphasis provides an interesting link to the role of dopamine. We have known for many years that dopamine blocking drugs can reduce the severity of symptoms such as delusions of control (e.g. Johnstone, Crow, Frith, Carney, & Price, 1978), but it is only more recently that evidence has emerged that dopamine has a critical role in prediction, or, more precisely, that dopamine release is a signal of reward prediction error (Schultz & Dickinson, 2000). So far dopamine's role in prediction has been explored mainly in classical learning paradigms concerned with which stimulus or which action will be rewarded. However, we should now examine whether dopamine has an equivalent role in the predictions associated with the control of action.

The framework in which prediction plays such an important role in the experience of action is essentially Bayesian. The prediction is the prior expectation and the sensory feedback is the new evidence on the basis of which the prior should be updated. Bayes' theorem indicates the extent to which such updating should occur. This framework is relevant for understanding the normal experience of agency, as well as all kinds of delusions and hallucinations, including symptoms of first rank such as delusions of control. Indeed, within this framework there is no real distinction between hallucinations (perceptions) and delusions (beliefs). Both depend upon appropriate combination of prior expectations and new evidence. This raises the possibility that an account could be developed, within this framework, that would apply to all the positive symptoms associated with schizophrenia (Fletcher & Frith, 2009). The comparator model would be seen as a special case within this framework and it is also possible that the two-factor account of delusions would be consistent with a Bayesian account.

There are two remaining problems. First, while a general theory of symptoms seems appropriate since some commonality between symptoms is required to justify the persistence of the idea of a unitary diagnosis of schizophrenia, there also needs to some account of why specific symptoms differ so markedly from one patient to another. Second, even a general, Bayesian approach does not provide a plausible account for the most striking of all first rank symptoms, *thought insertion.* This is ironic given that it was to explain this symptom that the comparator theory was first proposed (Feinberg, 1978). The problem is both theoretical and practical (see e.g. Vosgerau & Newen, 2007). Can we treat a thought like an action? In what sense can we predict the consequences of thought, since thinking seems to generate neither kinematics nor sensations? We need to develop objective measures of thinking analogous to all the ingenious measures of action and the experience of action that have so successfully been applied to the study of delusions of control.

## References

Blakemore, S. J., Smith, J., Steel, R., Johnstone, C. E., & Frith, C. D. (2000). The perception of self-produced sensory stimuli in patients with auditory hallucinations and passivity experiences: Evidence for a breakdown in self-monitoring. *Psychological Medicine, 30*(5), 1131–1139.

Davies, M., Coltheart, M., Langdon, R., & Breen, N. (2001). Monothematic delusions: Towards a two-factor account. *Philosophy, Psychiatry & Psychology, 8*(2/3), 133–158.

Delevoye-Turrell, Y., Giersch, A., & Danion, J. M. (2002). A deficit in the adjustment of grip force responses in schizophrenia. *Neuroreport, 13*(12), 1537–1539.

Feinberg, I. (1978). Efference copy and corollary discharge: Implications for thinking and its disorders. *Schizophrenia Bulletin, 4,* 636–640.

Fletcher, P. C., & Frith, C. D. (2009). Perceiving is believing: A Bayesian approach to explaining the positive symptoms of schizophrenia. *Nature Reviews Neuroscience, 10*(1), 48–58.

Franck, N., Farrer, C., Georgieff, N., Marie-Cardine, M., Dalery, J., d'Amato, T., et al (2001). Defective recognition of one's own actions in patients with schizophrenia. *The American Journal of Psychiatry, 158*(3), 454–459.

Frith, C. D. (1987). The positive and negative symptoms of schizophrenia reflect impairments in the perception and initiation of action. *Psychological Medicine, 17*(3), 631–648.

Frith, C. D., & Done, D. J. (1989). Experiences of alien control in schizophrenia reflect a disorder in the central monitoring of action. *Psychological Medicine, 19*(2), 359–363.

Haggard, P., Clark, S., & Kalogeras, J. (2002). Voluntary action and conscious awareness. *Nature Neuroscience, 5*(4), 382–385.

Helmholtz, H. v. (1866). *Handbuch der Physiologischen Optik.* Leipzig: Voss.

Johnstone, E. C., Crow, T. J., Frith, C. D., Carney, M. W., & Price, J. S. (1978). Mechanism of the antipsychotic effect in the treatment of acute schizophrenia. *Lancet, 1*(8069), 848–851.

Lindner, A., Thier, P., Kircher, T. T., Haarmeier, T., & Leube, D. T. (2005). Disorders of agency in schizophrenia correlate with an inability to compensate for the sensory consequences of actions. *Current Biology, 15*(12), 1119–1124.

Miall, R. C., & Wolpert, D. M. (1996). Forward models for physiological motor control. *Neural Networks, 9*(8), 1265–1279.

Moore, J. W., Lagnado, D., Deal, D.C., & Haggard, P. (2009). Feelings of control: Contingency determines experience of action. *Cognition, 110*(2), 279–283.

Schneider, K. (1957). Primary & secondary symptoms in schizophrenia. *Fortschritte der Neurologie – Psychiatrie, 25*(9), 487–490.

Schultz, W., & Dickinson, A. (2000). Neuronal coding of prediction errors. *Annual Review of Neuroscience, 23,* 473–500.

Synofzik, M., Thier, P., Leube, D. T., Schlotterbeck, P., & Lindner, A. (2010). Misattributions of agency in schizophrenia are based on imprecise predictions about the sensory consequences of one's actions. *Brain, 133*(Pt 1), 262–271.

Synofzik, M., Vosgerau, G., & Newen, A. (2008). Beyond the comparator model: A multifactorial two-step account of agency. *Consciousness and Cognition, 17*(1), 219–239.

Vosgerau, G., & Newen, A. (2007). Thoughts, motor actions, and the self. *Mind & Language, 22*(1), 22–43.

Voss, M., Moore, J., Hauser, M., Gallinat, J., Heinz, A., & Haggard, P. (2010). Altered awareness of action in schizophrenia: A specific deficit in predicting action consequences. *Brain, 133*(10), 3104–3112.

## Section 2

# Will & consciousness

# 6 Willed action and the prefrontal cortex in man

## A study with PET

*C. D. Frith, K. J. Friston, P. F. Liddle and R. S. J. Frackowiak*

## 1 Introduction

Positron emission tomography (PET) allows experiments to be done which relate localized brain activity to higher mental functions, such as action (Roland, 1985), language (Ingvar 1983) and thought (Roland & Friberg 1985). We have taken this approach one stage further and related localized brain activity to one specific cognitive component, namely the generation of willed acts. For this purpose we have used the technique pioneered by Petersen *et al.* (1988) and designed tasks that differ only in whether or not the act performed is willed. Differences in rCBFs elicited by the tasks must therefore show the location of brain activity associated with willed action.

An action is willed when we consciously pay attention to its selection (James 1890). Such a deliberate selection is subjectively experienced as willed and occurs when we have a choice of action. Spontaneous or self-generated actions are not specified by an external trigger stimulus, but are internally driven. They may be contrasted with automatic acts where the appropriate response is fully specified by an external stimulus (Norman & Shallice 1985). Goldberg (1985) and Passingham *et al.* (1989) have proposed that internally driven and stimulus driven responses are associated with different brain systems. For example, lesions in the supplementary motor area (SMA) impair internally generated responses, but not those elicited by external stimuli (Passingham *et al.* 1989). Goldman-Rakic (1987) proposed that, for monkeys to succeed in the delayed performance test, an area of dorsolateral prefrontal cortex (the monkey equivalent of Brodmann area 46) is required to be intact. In this test the response is not sufficiently specified by the currently available stimulus and has to be determined by a representation held in memory. Shallice (1988) suggested that the frontal cortex in man subserves a 'supervisory attentional system' (SAS) that is critically needed for the performance of novel tasks, but not for the performance of routine tasks in which actions are specified by the current situation. In novel situations, the SAS takes over control of action by using routine stimulus analysis and response production mechanisms in novel combinations.

On the basis of these proposals we contrasted novel and routine tasks that used the same stimulus and response mechanisms. In the routine tasks, each response was specified by a stimulus. In the novel tasks, the response was not fully specified and had to be selected by willed action. Thus, differences in rCBF between routine and novel tasks would reflect – not stimulus analysis or response production which were common to both – but differences between systems associated with external and internal response determination. In other words, rCBF would point us to the system responsible for willed acts. We expected that the brain activity associated with this particular component of higher mental function would be in the prefrontal cortex. In order to show that this mental process is a process in its own right and independent of stimulus and response modality we examined two different systems. In study 1 the input was auditory (heard words), and the response was verbal (spoken words). In study 2 the input was somato-sensory (touched fingers) and the response was motor (lifted fingers).

## 2 Task design

The design of the tasks is shown in table 6.1. In both studies the stimuli were presented at the rate of 1 per 2 s, and six measurements of rCBF (scans) were taken from each volunteer. Each of the three tasks was performed twice, in the order 1–2–3–3–2–1 controlling for any simple learning or habituation effects.

In study 1 the stimulus words were taken from the MRC Psycholinguistics Database. Ninety-six frequent words were chosen which all had unambiguous opposites (e.g. boy–girl, hot–cold). In task 1 these words were spoken by the experimenter in random order and had simply to be repeated by the volunteer. In task 2 the words were again presented in random order and the volunteer had to respond with the 'opposite' word (e.g. hot–cold). All volunteers practised

*Table 6.1* Tasks Used for Cognitive Activation

| | | *task 1* | *task 2* | *task 3* |
|---|---|---|---|---|
| study 1 verbal | **stimulus** hear words | **random words** man . . . hot . . . | **random words** man . . . hot . . . | **fixed words** next . . . next . . . |
| | **response** say words | **repeat words** man . . . hot . . . | **say opposite** woman . . . cold . . . | **generate words beginning with 'F'** e.g. fox . . . first . . . |
| study 2 sensorimotor | **stimulus** touch 1st or 2nd finger | **random touch** 1.1.2.1.2.2 | **random touch** 1.1.2.1.2.2 | **random touch** 1.1.2.1.2.2 |
| | **response** lift 1st or 2nd finger | **move touched finger** 1.1.2.1.2.2 | **move other finger** 2.2.1.2.1.1 | **move fingers at will** e.g. 2.1.2.2.1.1 |

producing opposite words beforehand. This was to ensure that they knew exactly what the appropriate opposite response was and thus to exclude any element of choice. In task 3 the volunteer heard the word 'next' every 2 s and had to respond with *any* word beginning with 'S' on the first occasion and 'F' on the second. In task 2 semantic analysis of the stimulus word was required, but this was not the case in tasks 1 and 3. In tasks 1 and 2 the response was fully specified, while in task 3 it was left open.

Performance was recorded during scanning and hesitations were counted. These occurred on less than 1% of the trials in tasks 1 and 2, confirming that these responses were fully specified by the stimuli. In the open ended word generation task (task 3) more hesitations occurred, but all volunteers produced a response to every stimulus ('next') for about the first 90 s. Thereafter the occasional response was omitted; however, this change in the rate of production was too small to have any detectable effect on the scan.

In study 2 either the first or second finger of the right hand was touched in a random sequence with a metal spatula. In task 1 the volunteer lifted the finger that was touched, in task 2 he lifted the other finger and in task 3 the touch acted as a signal indicating that the volunteer should lift *either* one of his fingers at will. To achieve this, volunteers were instructed to move their fingers in a random sequence that was different from the sequence of touches.

For both studies, in task 1 the stimulus routinely specified the response, in task 2 the stimulus also specified the exact response, but in a less obvious manner, and in task 3 the exact response was left open and not specified by the stimulus.

## 3 Volunteers

Six volunteers took part in study 1 and another six in study 2. All were male and right-handed. They were aged between 25 and 45 years.

## 4 Measurement of rCBF

Scans were obtained with a high resolution PET scanner (CTI model 931–08/12, Knoxville, U.S.A.) whose physical characteristics have been described elsewhere (Spinks *et al.* 1988). Scans were reconstructed using a Hanning filter with a cut-off frequency of 0.5 giving a transaxial resolution of 8.5 mm full width at half maximum. The reconstructed images contained 128 × 128 pixels, each of 2.05 × 2.05 mm.

Volunteers inhaled $C^{15}O_2$ at a concentration of 6 MBq ml$^{-1}$ and a flow rate of 500 ml min$^{-1}$ through a standard oxygen face mask for a period of 2 min. Dynamic PET scans were collected for a period of 3.5 min starting 0.5 min before $C^{15}O_2$ delivery, according to a protocol described elsewhere (Lammertsma *et al.* 1990). Integrated counts during the build-up phase of the scan were used as indices of rCBF. Each task was commenced 30 s before the start of inhalation of $C^{15}O_2$ and continued for 3 min.

## 5 Statistical analysis

The 15 original scan slices (6.75 mm interplane distance) were interpolated to 43 planes to render the voxels approximately cubic. The AC–PC line was identified directly from the PET image (Friston *et al.* 1989) and the data transformed into a standard stereotactic space. In this space 1 pixel represents 2 mm in the $x$ and $y$ dimensions according to the atlas of Talairach & Tournoux (1988). The stereotactically normalized image had 26 planes with an effective interplanar distance of 4 mm. To increase signal to noise ratio and accommodate variability in functional anatomy each image was smoothed with a Gaussian filter 10 pixels wide.

Differences in global activity were removed after an analysis of covariance (Friston *et al.* 1990) with global counts as covariate and activation condition as treatment. The differences between one condition and another were assessed with the appropriate contrast (weighting of the six condition means) using the $t$-statistic (Wildt & Ahtola 1978). This analysis was done for each pixel and the resulting set of $t$ values constituted the $t$-statistical parametric map (SPM{t}).

With so many comparisons being made, many $t$-values will reach conventional levels of significance by chance. Therefore the 'omnibus' significance of these SPMS was assessed by comparing the observed and expected number of pixels above $p < 0.001$ using the $\chi^2$ test of proportions (Friston *et al.* 1991 *a*). Thus, if we observed in a certain comparison that 10% of the pixels were significant at this level (instead of the 0.1% expected) then this would be strong evidence against the hypothesis that the differences in RCBF were simply due to chance. In this study, only the comparisons that were highly significant (at $p < 0.001$ or better) in this omnibus sense are reported.

Having established that there was an overall difference between two conditions, the regional distribution of $t$-values (shown in figure 6.1) indicates the qualitative nature of this difference. Only pixels with $t$-values at $p < 0.001$ or better are shown, rendered on drawings of the brain outline and major sulci derived from the atlas of Talairach & Tournoux (1988). This statistical methodology has been validated by applying the same analysis (smoothing, ANCOVA and pixel–by–pixel $t$-tests) to scans obtained from 'phantoms' containing pockets of radioactivity of known location and extent (Bailey *et al.* 1991). The SPMS derived from these phantoms (also using a cut-off of $p < 0.001$) correctly located 5% changes in activity in 21 mm radius cylinders (and larger changes spread over smaller areas), while displaying no false positives.

We choose to represent differences between conditions in terms of $t$-values rather than absolute differences in RCBF because variability in RCBF is systematically different across brain regions (being higher in grey than in white matter, for example). Thus a small change in one region may be significant, whereas a large change in another region is not. These differences in variability necessitate the pixel–by–pixel approach that we have adopted (Friston *et al.* 1990).

Differences between conditions include both increases and decreases in RCBF. As a result of the normalization of each set of data by total activity, local increases in

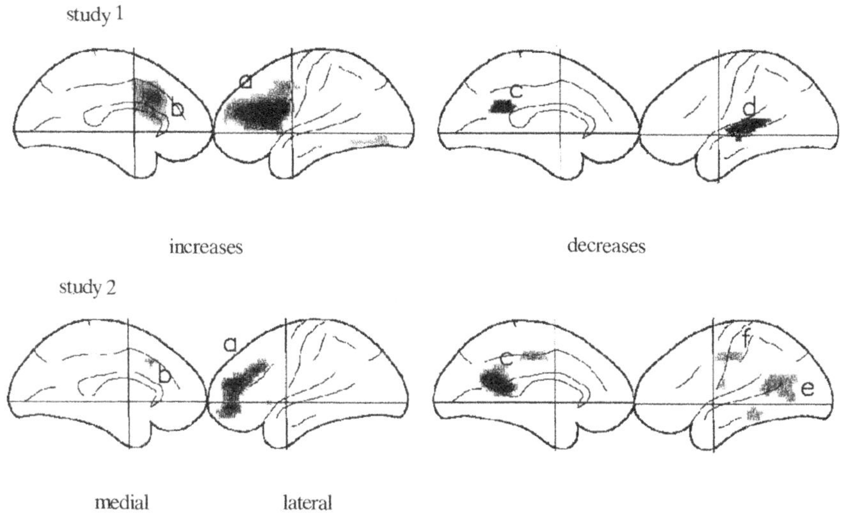


*Figure 6.1* Statistical parametric maps (SPMS) of the *t*-statistic used to make comparisons between the routine response and the internally generated response (tasks 1 and 3). Top: study 1. Bottom: study 2. Left: increases in RCBF. Right: decreases in RCBF. Only the left hemisphere is shown. Each pair of drawings represents a medial and a lateral view of the brain. The SPMS are images of the *t*-value associated with each pixel. Only pixels with a *t*-value corresponding to $p < 0.001$ are shown. The volume SPM was divided into four sagittal blocks (lateral and medial for each hemisphere) and the highest *t*-value displayed on the appropriate brain outline. The colour scale is arbitrary and the outline and sulci are based on the atlas of Talairach & Tournoux (1988).

Cortices that contribute to these profiles of significant change include a, dorsolateral prefrontal cortex (area 46); b, anterior cingulate (area 32); c, posterior cingulate (area 23); d, superior temporal gyrus (area 22); e, angular gyrus (area 39); and f, sensori-motor cortex.

RCBF must be offset by decreases elsewhere. However, these decreases should be randomly distributed across the rest of the brain. Any localized patterns of decrease represent real effects.

## 6 Results

No differences in cortical RCBF were revealed in comparisons of tasks 1 and 2.

For both studies, brain activity associated with willed action was identified by contrasting RCBF in task 3 with RCBF in task 1. These contrasts revealed increased activity, during performance of tasks involving willed action (task 3), in the dorsolateral prefrontal cortex (DLPFC) and the anterior cingulate cortex. Cortical renderings of these areas of activation are shown in figure 6.1. The coordinates of the location of maximum significance within these areas of activation are shown in table 6.2. Representing these areas by a single point is somewhat misleading as

*Table 6.2* Anatomical Location of Areas Shown in Figure 6.1

(Distances are in mm relative to the AC–PC line in the stereotactic space defined by Talairach & Tournoux (1988). The coordinates are the means of the coordinates of highest significance across the three slices with the most significant change. Coordinates in square brackets define areas of increased RCBF observed in previous studies of routine tasks.)

| *Area* | *study 1 verbal* | | | *study 2 sensori-motor* | | |
|---|---|---|---|---|---|---|
| increases | x | y | z | x | y | z |
| dlpfc area 46 left | −43 | 29 | 20 | −35 | 39 | 21 |
| dlpfc area 46 right | | | | 35 | 26 | 24 |
| anterior cingulate area 32 | 4 | 23 | 36 | −3 | 16 | 34 |
| decreases | | | | | | |
| posterior cingulate area 23 | 0 | −50 | 24 | −4 | −49 | 20 |
| sensori-motor cortex left | | | | −20 | −18 | 44 |
| | | | | [−29 | −22 | 52][c] |
| angular gyrus area 39 left | | | | −34 | −61 | 16 |
| superior temporal area 22 left | −46 | −23 | 4 | | | |
| | [−50 | −10 | −4][w] | | | |
| | [−46 | −22 | 14][p] | | | |
| superior temporal area 42 right | 44 | −15 | 10 | | | |
| | [50 | −10 | −4][w] | | | |
| | [42 | −24 | 12][p] | | | |

c Moving index finger (Colebatch *et al.* 1991).
p Listening to words (Petersen *et al.* 1988).
w Listening to words (Wise *et al.* 1991).

the areas of activation are large. Nevertheless there is a marked similarity in the coordinates for the two studies. A major difference was that (willed) word generation was associated with increases in left DLPFC only, whereas (willed) movement generation was associated with bilateral increases. In addition, the area activated in the verbal task extended backwards into Broca's area (area 44) whereas that associated with the sensori-motor task extended downward into area 10. The pattern of decreases associated with willed action revealed only one area in common to the two studies: the posterior cingulate cortex. In addition, the verbal task was associated with bilateral decreases in posterior superior temporal cortex (auditory association areas). In contrast, the sensori-motor task was associated with decreases in sensori-motor cortex on the left and in the posterior temporo-parietal area (area 39), also on the left.

## 7 Discussion

In two very different modalities we have found that the generation of responses that were not fully specified by immediately available stimuli (willed actions) was associated with increased activity in DLPFC in the region of Brodmann area 46. This result is consistent with Goldman–Rakic's analysis of the effects of lesions in this area in monkeys. Our word generation task (task 3 of study 1) is a paced version of the verbal fluency task which is widely used in neuropsychological assessments. Milner (1964) has shown that performance of this task is impaired by frontal lobe lesions especially when these are on the left.

Petersen *et al.* (1988) studied a word generation task in which subjects had to respond with a use for the word presented (e.g. cake–eat). In comparison to a control task (word reading) this task activated areas of prefrontal cortex, including a location in DLPFC close to that observed in the present study and also the anterior cingulate cortex. Petersen *et al.* proposed that, in contrast to their control task, their word generation task required semantic association and selection for action. They suggested that prefrontal activation was related to semantic association whereas anterior cingulate activation was associated with selection for action. We suggest that the word generation task used by Petersen *et al.* also differed from their control task in that the word to be generated was not completely specified by the stimulus word and thus required willed action. In our critical word generation task (words starting with 'F' or 'S') no semantic analysis of the stimuli was required. Furthermore, in our task 2 (opposites), where semantic associations were required, no prefrontal activation was observed. We therefore suggest that the prefrontal activity observed by Petersen *et al.* should be reinterpreted as being specifically associated with the requirement to generate responses by willed action.

A recent study by Deiber *et al.* (1991) on movement control included a task in which subjects had to generate a random sequence of movements by repeatedly putting a joystick into one of four different positions. This task was associated with bilateral prefrontal activation, very similar to that observed in our random finger movement task. Thus, an association between response generation (willed action) and activity in DLPFC has been consistently observed in four different PET studies.

In both our critical response generation tasks increased activity was also observed in the anterior cingulate cortex. We follow Petersen *et al.* (1988) in suggesting that this activity was associated with selection for action (i.e. attention to response selection) rather than internal response generation. A recent PET study (Pardo *et al.* 1990) has reported that performance of the Stroop colour/word interference task is associated with increased blood flow in the anterior cingulate cortex, but no increase in DLPFC. This is a very effortful task in which the subject must name the incongruent 'ink' colour of a colour word (e.g. the word 'red' written in green). However, although the task requires much effort, the response is entirely specified by the stimulus. Taken in conjunction with our own result, this again confirms that the DLPFC is specifically concerned with internal response generation, whereas the anterior cingulate (possibly in reciprocal relation with posterior cingulate) is concerned with response selection and attention.

The pattern of decreased blood flow associated with willed action was different in the two studies. The verbal task was associated with bilateral decreases in posterior superior temporal cortex (auditory association areas). Previous studies have observed increased blood flow in these areas when hearing words (Nishizawa *et al.* 1982; Petersen *et al.* 1988; Wise *et al.* 1991). Random finger movement was associated with decreased blood flow in sensori-motor cortex and in inferior parietal cortex. A very similar area of sensori-motor cortex was activated in a study in which volunteers had to move their right index finger at regular intervals (Colebatch *et al.* 1991). Random finger movement was also associated with decreases in a left inferior parietal area lying along the superior temporal sulcus in the boundary between Brodmann areas 37 and 39 (angular gyrus). Lesions in this area are associated with finger agnosia (Mazzoni *et al.* 1990).

Thus, in both studies, decreases were observed in cortical areas concerned with the modalities specific to the study: word identification in study 1, and finger identification in study 2. At present we can only speculate as to why the changes in these areas were decreases. One possibility is that there was a suppression of stimulus analysis relative to task 1, because stimulus analysis would interfere with internal response generation. Another possibility is that the same neural network is used to generate responses internally as is used to identify stimuli, but that responses are generated more efficiently when the overall activity of this network is low (Friston *et al.* 1991 *b*). In either case, our results show that PET can be used to study the interaction between prefrontal cortex and other parts of the brain.

PET studies of prefrontal function are of particular importance for our understanding of the 'functional' psychoses, such as schizophrenia. Weinberger *et al.* (1986) have shown that the Wisconsin card sorting task activates DLPFC in normal volunteers, but not in schizophrenic patients. Warkentin *et al.* (1989) have obtained a similar result using the verbal fluency task. Our results suggest that the critical cognitive component of these tasks is internal response generation – willed action. Future PET activation studies using the task described here should make it possible to elucidate the pathophysiology of certain of the 'negative' features of schizophrenia (poverty of action, lack of will) which are so especially devastating.

We are grateful to Dr Philip Quinlan of the Psychology Department, RHBNC, for giving us access to the MRC Psycholinguistics Database. We thank Miss C. Taylor and Mr G. Lewington for their help in scanning the volunteers. We are grateful to our colleagues in the MRC Cyclotron Unit Chemistry and PET Methods sections for making these studies possible. Karl Friston is supported by the Wellcome Trust.

## References

Bailey, D. L., Jones, T., Friston, K. J., Colebatch, J. G. & Frackowiak, R. S. J. 1991 Physical validation of statistical parametric mapping. *J. Cereb. Blood Flow Metab.* (suppl.) **11**, S150.

Colebatch, J. G., Deiber, M.-P., Passingham, R. E., Friston, K. J. & Frackowiak, R. S. J. 1991 Regional cerebral blood flow during arm and hand movements in human subjects. *J. Neurophysiol.* **65(6)**, 1392–1401.

Deiber, M.-P., Passingham, R. E., Colebatch, J. G., Friston, K. J., Nixon, P. D., & Frackowiak, R. S. J. 1991 Cortical areas and the selection of movement: a study with PET. *Expl Brain Res.* **84,** 393–402.

Friston, K. J., Passingham, R. E., Nutt, J. G., Heather, J. D., Sawle, G. V. & Frackowiak, R. S. J. 1990 Localisation in PET images: direct fitting of the intercomissurial (AC-PC) line. *J. Cereb. Blood Flow Metab.* **9,** 690–695.

Friston, K. J., Frith, C. D., Liddle, P. F., Dolan, R. J., Lammertsma, A. A. & Frackowiak, R. S. J. 1990 The relationship between global and local changes in PET scans. *J. Cereb. Blood Flow Metab.* **10,** 458–466.

Friston, K. J., Frith, C. D., Liddle, P. F. & Frackowiak, R. S. J. 1991 *a* Comparing functional PET images: the assessment of significant change. *J. Cereb. Blood Flow Metab.* **11,** 690–699.

Friston, K. J., Frith, C. D., Liddle, P. F. & Frackowiak, R. S. J. 1991 *b* Investigating a network model of word generation with positron emission tomography. *Proc. R. Soc. Lond.* B **244,** 101–106.

Goldberg, G. 1985 Supplementary motor area structure and function: review and hypothesis. *Behav. Brain Sci.* **8,** 567–616.

Goldman-Rakic, P. S. 1987 Circuitry of primate prefrontal cortex and regulation of behaviour by representational memory. In *Handbook of physiology: the nervous system volume 5* (ed. F. Plum & V. Mountcastle), pp. 373–417. Bethesda: American Physiology Society.

Ingvar, D. H. 1983 Serial aspects of language and speech related to prefrontal cortical activity. *Hum. Neurobiol.* **2,** 177–189.

James, W. 1890 *Principles of psychology.* New York: Holt.

Lammertsma, A. A., Cunningham, V. J., Deiber, M.-P., Heather, J. D., Bloomfield, P.M., Nutt, J. G., Frackowiak, R. S. J. & Jones, T. 1990 Combination of dynamic and integral methods for generating reproducible functional rCBF images. *J. Cereb. Blood Flow Metab.* **10,** 675–686.

Mazzoni, M., Pardossi, L., Cantini, R., Giorgetti, V. & Arena, R. 1990 Gerstmann syndrome: a case report. *Cortex* **26,** 459–467.

Milner, B. 1964 Some effects of frontal lobectomy in man. In *The frontal granular cortex and behaviour* (ed. J. M. Warren & K. Akert), pp. 313–334. New York: McGraw Hill.

Nishizawa, Y., Skyhöj-Oelsen, T., Larsen, B. & Lassen, N. A. 1982 Left-right cortical asymmetries of regional cerebral blood flow during listening to words. *J. Neurophysiol.* **48,** 458–466.

Norman, D. A. & Shallice, T. 1985 Attention to action: willed and automatic control of behaviour. In *Consciousness and self regulation* (ed. R. J. Davidson, G. E. Schwartz & D. Shapiro), pp. 1–18. New York: Plenum.

Pardo, J. V., Pardo, P. J., Janer, K. W. & Raichle, M. E. 1990 The anterior cingulate cortex mediates processing selection in the Stroop attentional conflict paradigm. *Proc. Natn. Acad. Sci. U.S.A.* **87,** 256–259.

Passingham, R. E., Chen, Y. C. & Thaler, D. 1989 Supplementary motor cortex and self-initiated movement. In *Neural programming* (ed. M. Ito), pp. 13–24. Basel: Karger.

Petersen, S. E., Fox, P. T., Posner, M. I., Mintun, M. & Raichle, M. E. 1988 Positron emission tomographic studies of the cortical anatomy of single word processing. *Nature, Lond.* **331,** 585–589.

Roland, P. E. 1985 Cortical organisation of voluntary behaviour in man. *Hum. Neurobiol.* **4,** 155–167.

Roland, P. E. & Friberg, L. 1985 Localisation of cortical areas activated by thinking. *J. Neurophysiol.* **53,** 1219–1243.

Shallice, T. 1988 *From neuropsychology to mental structure,* Chapter 14. Cambridge University Press.

Spinks, T. J., Jones, T., Gilardi, M. C. & Heather, J. D. 1988 Physical performance of the latest generation of commercial positron scanners. *IEEE Trans. Nucl. Med.* **35,** 721–725.

Talairach, J. & Tournoux, P. 1988 *Co-Planar stereotaxic atlas of the human brain.* Stuttgart: Thieme.

Warkentin, S., Nilsson, A., Risberg, J. & Carlson, S. 1989 Absence of frontal lobe activation in schizophrenia. *J. Cereb. Blood Flow Metab.* (suppl. 1) **9,** S354.

Weinberger, D. R., Berman, K. F. & Zec, R. F. 1986 Physiological dysfunction of the dorsolateral prefrontal cortex in schizophrenia. I. Regional cerebral blood flow (rCBF) evidence. *Arch. of Gen. Psychiat.* **43,** 114–125.

Wildt, D. R. & Ahtola, O. T. 1978 *Analysis of covariance.* London: Sage.

Wise, R., Chollet, F., Hadar, U., Friston, K., Hoffner, E. & Frackowiak, R. 1991 Distribution of cortical neural networks involved in word comprehension and word retrieval. *Brain* **114** (Pt. 4), 1803–1817.

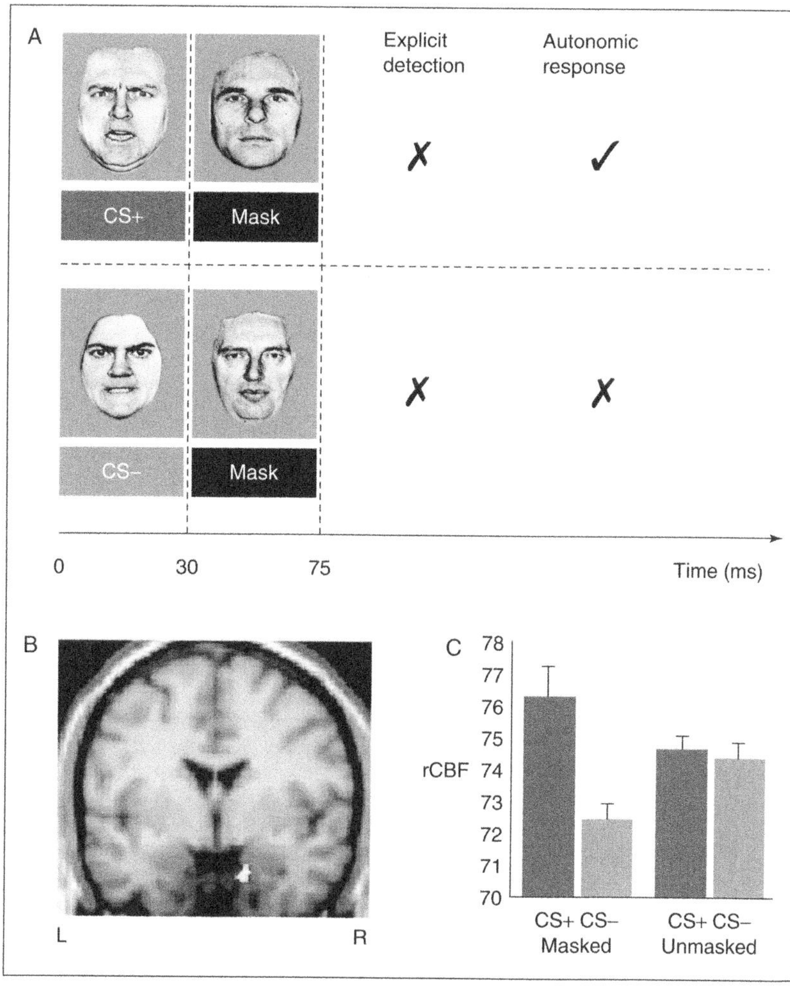


*Figure 7.2* Activity in the amygdala elicited by aversive stimuli of which the subject is not aware. **(A)** Right amygdala response to masked conditioned faces. Prior to PET scanning, healthy subjects were repeatedly shown an angry face (the CS+) paired with a 100dB noise. Another angry face (the CS−) was also shown repeatedly but never paired with noise. During scanning, the CS+ and CS− faces were presented for 30 ms, and immediately followed by a 45 ms masking stimulus (a neutral face). This masking procedure prevented subjects from explicitly reporting any awareness of the CS+ or CS− faces. Despite being 'unseen', masked CS+ presentations elicited greater autonomic responses (changes in skin conductance) than masked presentations of the CS− face. A mediobasal region of the right amygdaloid complex responded more to the masked CS+ than to the masked CS− face, shown on a coronal MRI section **(B)**. The mean adjusted regional cerebral blood flow (rCBF) for the different experimental conditions is also shown **(C).** Although the right amygdala responded differentially to the masked conditioned faces, this differential activity was not seen when the same stimuli were shown unmasked and explicitly reported via a button press (unmasked). Modified from Ref. 22.

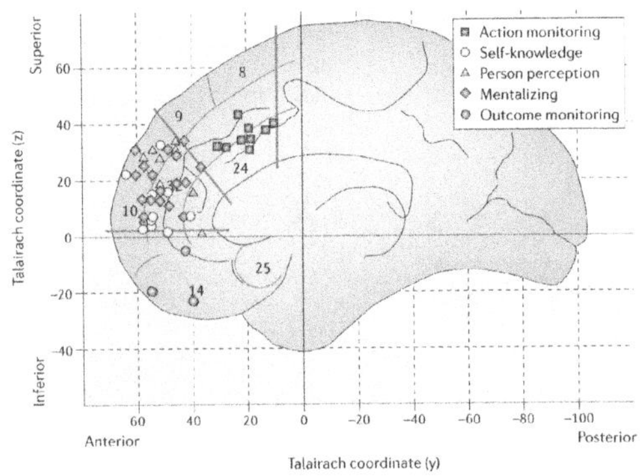


*Figure 10.3* Mapping of medial frontal cortex activations observed during action monitoring, social cognition and outcome monitoring. A meta-analysis of medial frontal cortex (MFC) activations suggests that social cognition tasks, which involve self-knowledge,[52,53,55–58,96,97,120,121] person perception[61–65,69,122,123] and mentalizing,[55,72,73,77–79,109,111,112,118,124-131] activate areas in the anterior rostral MFC (arMFC). By contrast, activations from action-monitoring tasks[28,29,83,99,132-136] occur in the posterior rostral region of the MFC (prMFC), and activations from tasks involving the monitoring of outcomes[40,39,41] occur in the orbital MFC (oMFC).

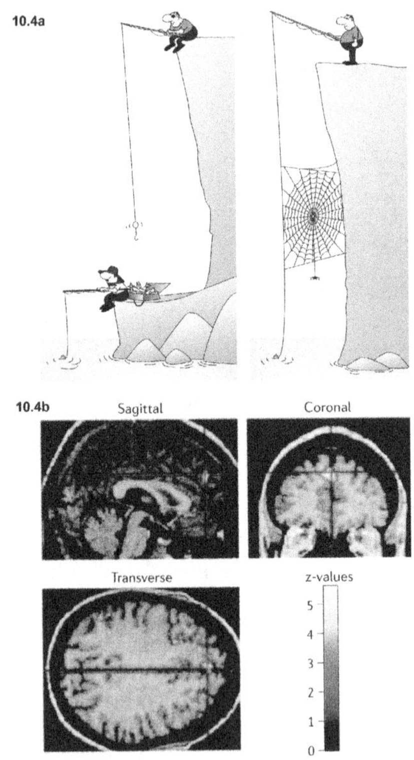


*Figure 10.4* The cartoon (panel **a**) illustrates the idea of theory of mind[113,114]. The joke on the left depends on the deceit of the man who is stealing the fish. The joke on the right does not involve theory of mind. Comparison of the two types of joke shows activation in the medial prefrontal cortex, which is shown in a single subject in panel **b**.

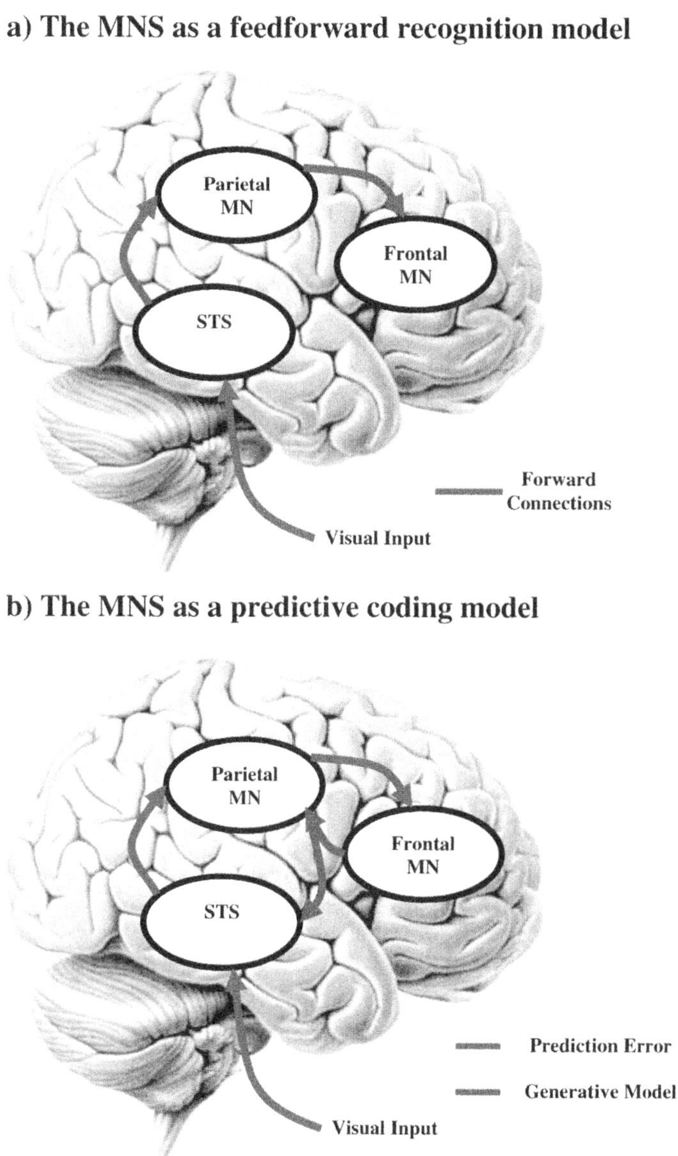


*Figure 12.1* Schemas of the mirror-neuron system.

Hierarchical architecture for predictive coding with empirical BayeS

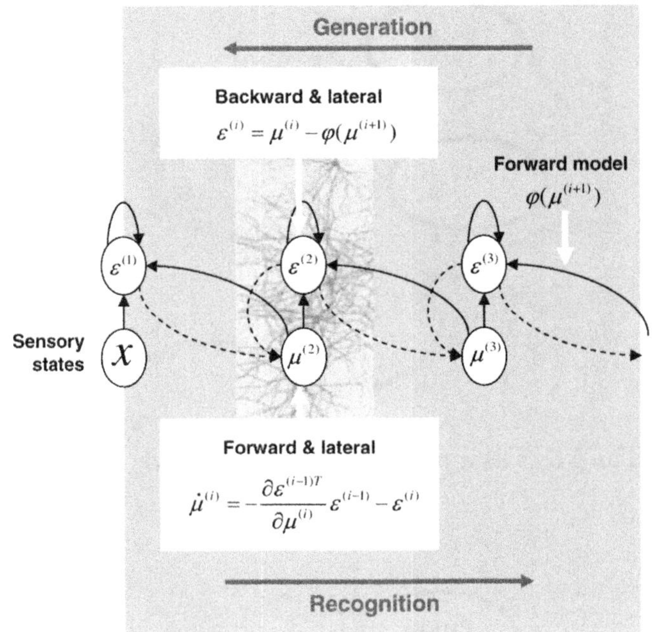


*Figure 12.2* Hierarchical architecture for predictive coding with empirical BayeS.

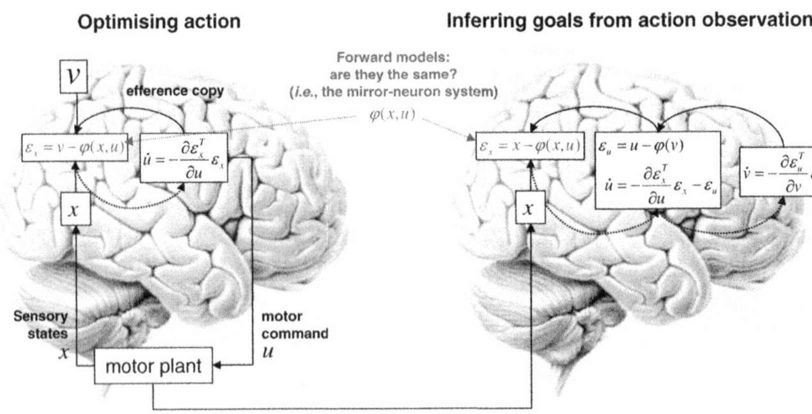


*Figure 12.3*

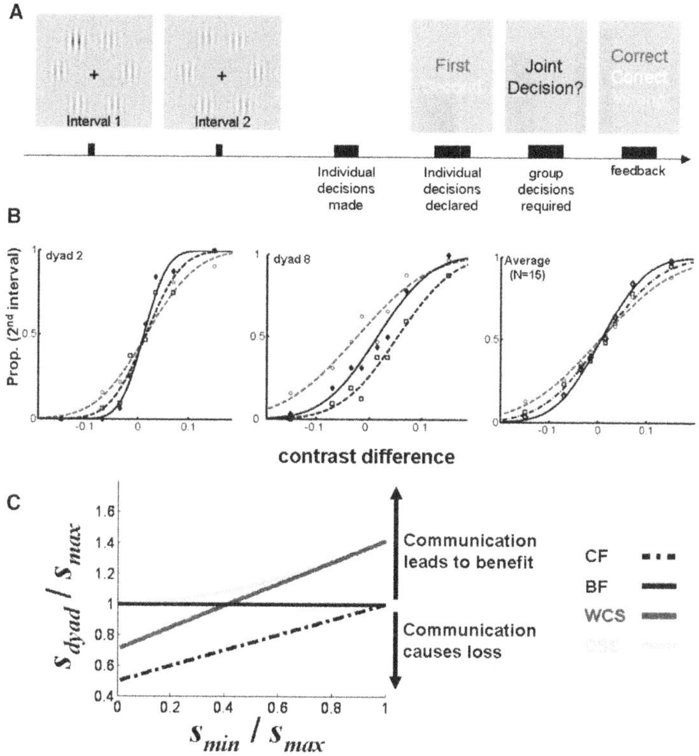


*Figure 13.1* (**A**) Experimental paradigm. Each trial consisted of two observation intervals. In each interval, six vertically oriented Gabor patches were displayed equidistantly around an imaginary circle (duration: 85 ms). In either the first or second interval, there was one oddball target that had slightly higher contrast than all of the others (in this example, upper-left target in interval 1). (**B**) Two example psychometric functions and the group average in experiment 1. The proportion of trials in which the oddball was reported to be in the second interval is plotted against the contrast difference at the oddball location (i.e., contrast in the second interval minus contrast in the first). A highly sensitive observer would produce a steeply rising psychometric function with a large slope. Blue circles, performance of the less sensitive observer ($s_{min}$) of the dyad; red squares, performance of the more sensitive observer ($s_{max}$); and black diamonds, performance of the dyad ($s_{dyad}$). The blue and red dashed curves are the best fit to a cumulative Gaussian function[9]; the solid black curve is the prediction of the WCS. $N =$ 15 dyads. (**C**) Predictions of the four models (see Eqs. 1 to 4). The $x$ axis shows the ratio of individual sensitivities ($s_{min}/s_{max}$), with values near one corresponding to dyad members with similar sensitivities and values near zero to dyad members with very different sensitivities. The $y$ axis shows the ratio of dyad sensitivity to the more sensitive member ($s_{dyad}/s_{max}$). Values above the horizontal line indicate communication benefit; in this range the dyad is better than the more sensitive observer. The red curve, which corresponds to the WCS model, is above the horizontal line only if $s_{min}/s_{max}$ is larger than ~0.4, reflecting the prediction that communication by WCS is beneficial only if dyad members have approximately the same competence. The green curve, which corresponds to the DSS model, never crosses the black horizontal line, so for this model, communication will invariably be beneficial. The dot-dashed and solid black lines indicate the CF and BF models, respectively.

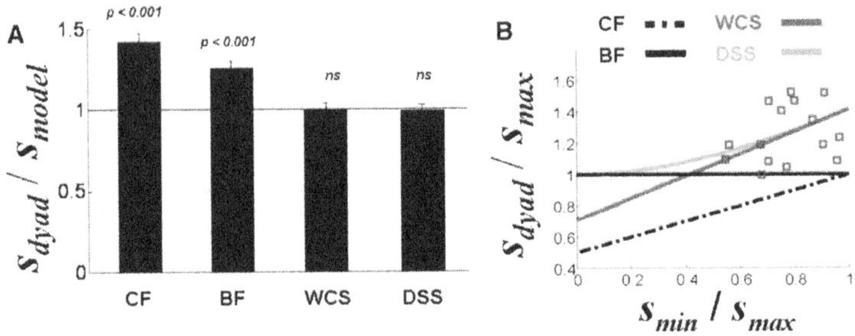


*Figure 13.2* Results of experiments 1. (**A**) Plot of the ratio of the dyad slope to the slope predicted by each model. The BF model comparison also depicts collective benefit over the more sensitive observer. Error bars indicate SEM ($N = 15$). (**B**) Distribution of data points and model predictions. Collective benefit ($s_{dyad}/s_{max}$) is plotted against relative sensitivity ($s_{min}/s_{max}$). Each blue square represents one dyad.

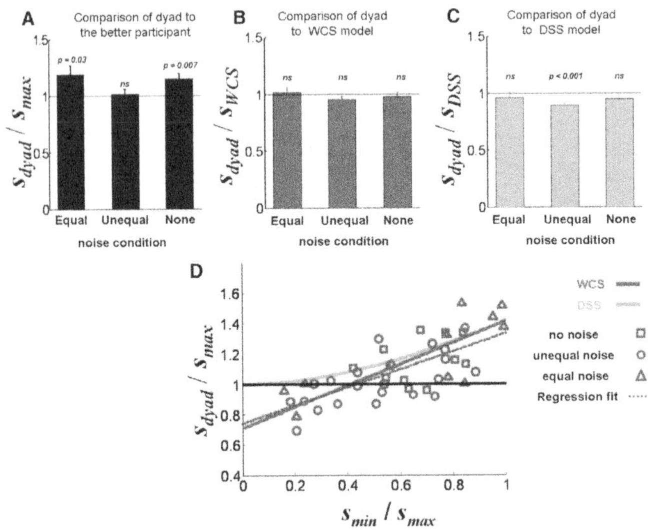


*Figure 13.3* Results of experiment 2. (**A**) Ratio of the dyad slope to the maximum individual slope for the three noise conditions (equal, unequal, and none; see main text). The line at $s_{dyad}/s_{max} = 1$ corresponds to the case in which the dyad is performing exactly as well as the more sensitive member. Values above and below the line correspond to benefit and loss due to communication, respectively. ns, not significant. (**B**) Ratio of the dyad slope to the slope predicted by the WCS model, the latter denoted $s_{WCS}$. This ratio was not significantly different from zero for any of the noise conditions. (**C**) Ratio of the dyad slope to the slope of the DSS model. For the unequal noise condition, this ratio was significantly smaller than 1 ($p < 10^{-4}$). (**D**) Distribution of data points and model predictions (the latter taken from Fig. 1C). Collective benefit ($s_{dyad}/s_{max}$) is plotted against relative sensitivity ($s_{min}/s_{max}$). Each dyad contributed four sets of data points (one triangle for equal, one square for none, and two circles for unequal conditions). The solid black line indicates the boundary of collective benefit (see Fig. 1C). In (A) to (C), error bars denote SEM ($N = 11$ data points for equal and none conditions; $N = 22$ for unequal condition).

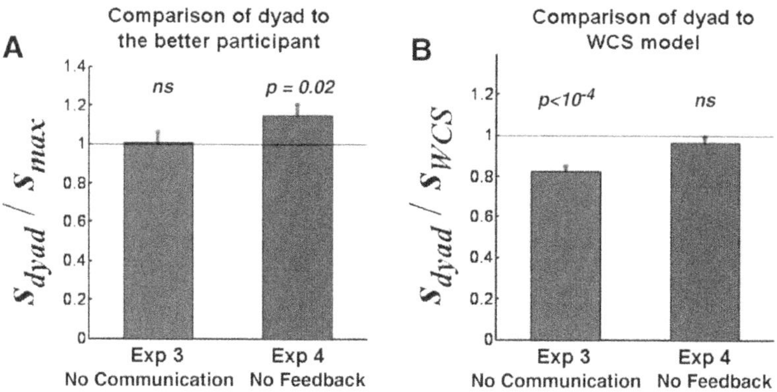


*Figure 13.4* Results of experiments 3 and 4. *y*-axis conventions are the same as in Fig. 3, A and B. (**A**) Collective benefit ($s_{dyad}/s_{max}$) is plotted for experiment 3 (red, without communication) and for experiment 4 (blue, without feedback). (**B**) Ratio of the dyad slope to the slope predicted by the WCS model for experiment 3 (red, without communication), and experiment 4 (blue; without feedback). In all panels, error bars denote SEM ($N = 14$ for experiment 3; $N = 11$ for experiment 4).

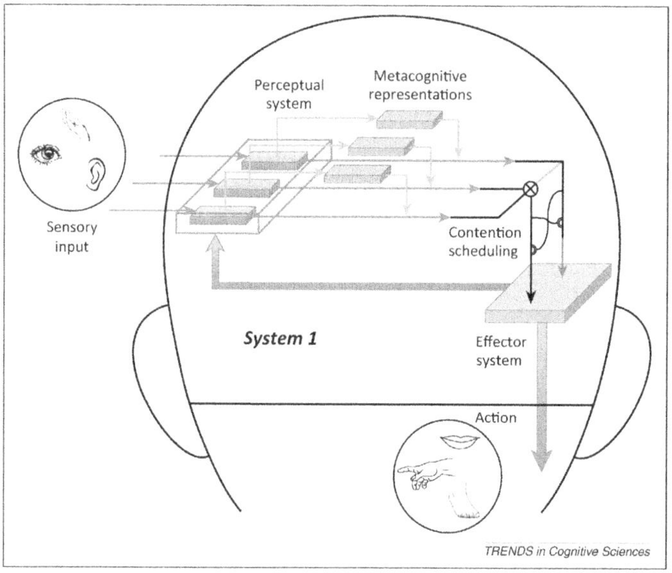


*Figure 14.1* System 1 metacognition with a single agent. The control of cognitive processes in an individual's system 1 occurs automatically and at a sub-personal level[3]. Contention scheduling, a term introduced by Norman and Shallice[18], refers to a mechanism for resolving competition between processes that overlap in their effector system requirements. Metacognitive representations reflect the properties of the functioning of these cognitive processes. System 1 uses metacognitive representations to improve control. An example of such representations would be the reliability of sensory signals. Cognitive processes estimated to be more reliable can be given greater weight[12].

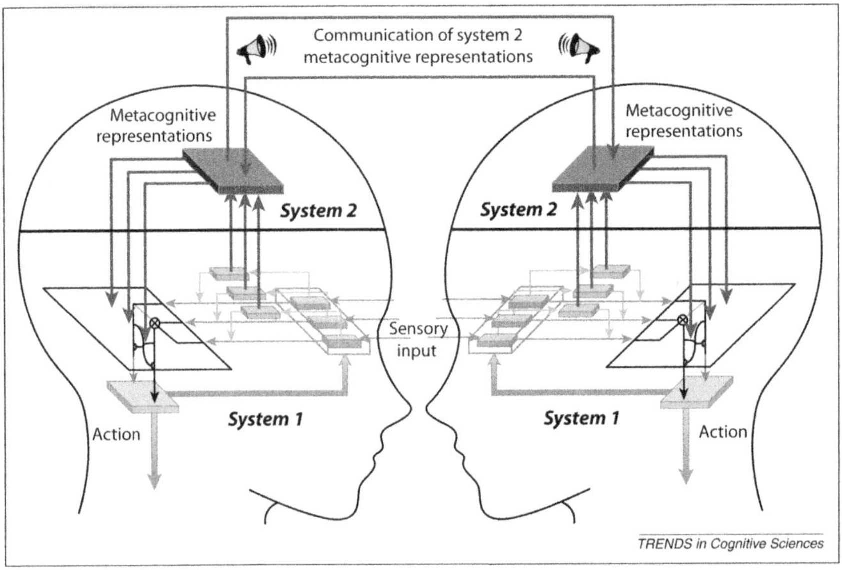


*Figure 14.2* System 2 metacognition for cognitive control across two agents. System 2 metacognitive representations are derived from information in system 1, but they are in a form available for verbal report. For example, the reliability of a sensory signal can be reported in terms of confidence. When agents are cooperating, these reports can be used to optimise control by, for example, giving more weight to the more confident observer[32]. Via system 2, verbal reports can also have long-term effects on the functioning of system 1[57].

# 7 The neural correlates of conscious experience

## An experimental framework

*Chris Frith, Richard Perry and Erik Lumer*

In the last few years there has been a dramatic increase in the willingness of neuroscientists to speculate about the biological basis of consciousness[1,2]. At the same time philosophers increasingly refer to neuropsychological data when discussing the nature of consciousness[3,4]. From both sides of the debate we are told that questions about the neural basis of consciousness can now be answered through experimentation. In this article we shall try to make as clear as possible the assumptions that underlie such experiments and indicate the areas where progress is likely to be made. We shall consider only the problem of the *association* between consciousness and neural activity. We believe that systematic exploration of the neural correlates of consciousness will increase our understanding of the nature and purpose of consciousness.

A fundamental assumption is that for every mental state (state of consciousness) there is an associated neural state; it is impossible for there to be a change of mental state without a corresponding change in neural state. Questions about the neural correlates of consciousness are essentially questions about the relationships between mental states and neural states.

### Levels versus contents of consciousness

A useful distinction can be made between factors influencing the overall level of consciousness and those determining its content. The former are generally associated with arousal, which is controlled at least in part by the ascending reticular activating system of the pons. Other structures implicated in arousal include the locus coeruleus, involved in vigilance, and the intralaminar nuclei of the thalamus, where lesions can lead to coma and vegetative states[5]. The level of consciousness can also be altered by exogenous substances, such as anaesthetics and psychoactive drugs[6].

A second aspect of consciousness concerns the content of subjective experience, that is, what one is conscious of. This is determined by the interaction between exogenous factors derived from our environment and endogenous factors, such as attention. The contents of consciousness include percepts of the objects around us, memories of past events and intentions concerning future actions. The contents of consciousness are associated with activity in specific cortical areas. Awareness of visual movement, for example, is associated with activity in visual area V5 (also called MT) at the parietal-occipital-temporal junction[7], while conscious recollection of events requires that the medial temporal lobe and its inputs are intact[8].

The relationship between level of arousal and contents of consciousness is complex and yet to be determined. Both very low and very high levels of arousal are generally associated with impoverished contents of consciousness[9]. Of particular interest is the dream state in which a low level of arousal (sleep) is associated with vivid sensory imagery[10]. As suggested by Llinas and Pare[11], insights into the nature of consciousness might be gained by analysis of the similarities and differences between wakefulness and dreaming, and between these states and slow-wave sleep. Both dreaming and wakefulness are endowed with subjective experience, although dreaming is dissociated from awareness of external (and internal) sensory events in the rapid-eye-movement sleep phases during which dreams mostly occur. These two states are characterized by a similar complex pattern of activation in the thalamo–cortical system (see Box 7.1). Another potential route to link states of consciousness to brain function is based on a careful examination of the physiological effects of anaesthesia. For example, barbiturates greatly depress spontaneous neuronal activity; they also produce a decrease in excitability of brainstem reticular networks. Moreover, the EEG remains uniformly synchronous under barbiturate anaesthesia, in contrast with scalp potentials recorded during wakefulness[12]. Which of these physiological changes is critically associated with the altered state of arousal under general anaesthesia remains to be determined. In the rest of this paper, however, our discussion of the neural correlates of consciousness will largely be concerned with subjective awareness and the contents of consciousness. To aid this discussion we shall make frequent use of the term 'representation', which in this context refers to a mental entity that stands for something in the external world.

### Box 7.1 Do animals dream?

#### *Inferring consciousness in the absence of a verbal report*

While there continues to be argument about whether animals other than man are conscious and what they are conscious of, we are confident that animals (at least mammals) dream. What is the basis of this confidence? Essentially it is that we have a very reliable and specific physiological marker for dreaming.

On the basis of measures of electroencephalography (EEG) and electromyography (EMG), sleep can be divided into several clear stages. In one of these stages the EEG shows the low-voltage, fast activity characteristic of waking, but muscle tone is actively inhibited and behavioural sleep persists. Stereotypic bursts of saccadic eye movements called rapid eye movements occur, giving this state the name REM sleep. In 90–95%

of cases, arousal from REM sleep yields reports of dreaming when the person is asked to report immediately. Dreams are characterized by vivid hallucinatory imagery, usually in the visual domain, and illusions of self-motion. Although thought-like mentation can occur in other stages of sleep this does not have the vivid quality of dreams. Awakening during non-REM sleep yields reports of sensation and motion in only 5–10% of cases and these reports are of considerably reduced intensity. Dreaming resembles waking consciousness in that both involve mental representations. Dreaming differs from waking consciousness in that the dreamer has no insight (except at the moment of waking) and regards the dream events as completely real. Dreaming also differs from waking consciousness in that memory of the dream fades rapidly and is lost unless rehearsed immediately upon waking. Within five minutes of the termination of a period of REM sleep, awakening yields no report of dreaming and it is estimated that there is amnesia (in the sense of a lack of episodic memory) for over 95% of dreams. What we do remember of our dreams derives from those fragments dwelt upon immediately after waking (Ref. a).

Mammals show the same stages of sleep as are observed in humans. In particular they show REM sleep characterized by a 'waking' pattern of EEG, rapid eye movements and inhibited muscle tone. Observing the twitches and growls of a dog during REM sleep, one is strongly inclined to conclude that it is having dream experiences similar to our own. While we cannot obtain a report of an animal's dream experiences, it is possible to make lesions that remove the paralysis normally associated with REM sleep (Ref. b). Cats with such lesions get up during REM sleep and appear to the observer to be acting out dreams. These results strongly suggest that, during dreams, animals are having experiences the same as those humans have. Because, in intact animals, these experiences are not expressed in overt behaviour, it would seem reasonable to conclude these experiences are occurring in a mental domain. During dreams, at least, it is likely that animals form mental representations and have conscious experiences very similar to those of humans. The same is likely to be true in the waking state. The problem is that we have, as yet, no physiological marker analogous to REM that indicates that a mental representation has been formed.

The neural correlates of the different stages of sleep have been studied extensively in mammals. Acetylcholine levels are at a minimum during slow wave sleep (SWS) and maximal during REM. In contrast, noradrenaline and serotonin levels are high during SWS and near zero during REM. Associated with these neuromodulatory changes there are shifts in the direction of flow of neural information between the neocortex and the hippocampus. During REM sleep (and during active exploration in the waking state) information flows from neocortex to hippocampus. During SWS (and quiet rest) information flows in the opposite direction. These patterns of neural activity seem to be associated with different aspects of the consolidation and updating of long-term memories (Ref. c). It has been possible to acquire this extensive body of knowledge about the neural correlates of a form of consciousness (dreaming) because there is a very reliable physiological marker (REM) for this state in humans, which can also be observed in other mammals.

It has often been stated that when we dream we experience insanity. This is because we have no insight into the hallucinatory nature of our dreams and because we accept the improbabilities and impossibilities of dream sequences without question. However, it is the insanity associated with delirium rather than psychosis that dreams most resemble (Ref. d). While the hallucinations and delusions associated with psychosis represent a similar deviation from reality, the patient does not simply accept them, but reflects upon them and develops coherent and complex explanations to explain their occurrence. We would suggest that the form of consciousness associated with dreams is consciousness without reflection; that is, it is consciousness but not self-consciousness; experience but without reflection upon that experience. In consequence we have no insight and no episodic memory. During dreams do we discover what it is like to be a dog or a cat?

**References**

**a** Hobson. J.A. (1988) *The Dreaming Brain,* Basic Books

**b** Jouvet, M. (1979). What does a cat dream about? *Trends Neurosci.* 2, 15–16

**c** Stickgold, R. (1998) Sleep: off-line memory reprocessing *Trends Cognit. Sci.* 2, 484–492

**d** Hobson, J.A. (1997) Dreaming as delirium: a mental status analysis of our nightly madness *Semin. Neurol.* 17, 121–128

## Mental representations

Cognitive neuroscientists persistently talk about neural representations. For example, a recent paper stated that 'the role of the prefrontal cortex in visual attention is to provide neural representations of to-be-attended information'[13]. We prefer to use more neutral terms, such as 'patterns of neural activity', for neurophysiological states. However, we suggest that it might be convenient to refer to the contents of consciousness (that is, phenomenal consciousness) as mental representations; mental entities that can stand for things in the outside world, and can usually be reported. When I remember something I have a mental representation of a past event. When I imagine something I have a mental representation of something that could occur in the outside world. When I perceive something I have a mental representation of something currently in the outside world. To say that we are conscious of something (or aware of something) is equivalent to saying that we have a mental representation of something. When we speak of the neural correlates of mental representations it is clear that we are referring to the contents of consciousness rather than to the level of consciousness.

Given that all mental activity derives from brain activity, it follows that all mental representations have corresponding neural activities. However, not all neural activities have corresponding mental representations. This is the crucial lesson taught us by phenomena such as blindsight[14]; behaviour can be guided by neural responses to visual stimuli in the absence of any awareness. In some cases, highly processed information can be used unconsciously, as evidenced in masked priming experiments[15]. A major part of the programme for studying the neural correlates of consciousness must be to investigate the difference between neural activities that are associated with awareness and those that are not.

The closely related lesson learnt from phenomena like blindsight is that goal-directed behaviour is not a reliable indicator of mental representation or subjective experience. To discover what someone is conscious of we need them to give us some form of report about their subjective experience. Such reports are qualitatively different from behaviour; reports, like consciousness, have content. They are about something. Behaviour simply occurs.

## Verbal reports

How do we know about the contents of consciousness? The most direct way is by verbal report. I learn about your current mental representations from what you tell me about your perceptions, memories and intentions. You can describe the colour of an object, rate the intensity of a sensation, report whether one experience is the same or different from another. Such reports depend upon a shared communication system, such as language. Obviously there will be occasions where such reporting is not perfect (see Box 7.2), but, in general, this system works well. After all, outside the laboratory, such reporting is the basis of most of human communication. This communication system is constantly tuned to maintain the successful sharing of experience. I validate my understanding of your report by matching your description to my experience.

### Box 7.2 Why should I believe what you tell me about your mental states?

#### *When verbal reports are inadequate*

There is a fundamental distinction between reports (whether verbal or behavioural) and behaviour. Reports are about something, are intended to convey meaning and can be true or false. Behaviour, on the other hand, simply occurs. Behaviour is not about anything. We might wrongly interpret its significance, but ideas of truth and falsity do not apply. This objectivity makes behaviour an attractive subject for scientific study, but such study tells us nothing about consciousness. To study consciousness we depend upon reports about mental states, but what if these reports cannot be relied upon? In psychophysical studies with normal volunteers we take it for granted that their reports are accurate. However, if we study patients with obvious brain damage, or psychosis or 'psychogenic' disorders, we have to be very wary about our reliance upon reports about mental states. If an abnormal mental state is reported does this mean: (a) the patient is experiencing an abnormal mental state?; (b) the patient is not able to report certain mental states correctly?; (c) the patient is trying to deceive us?

A large and controversial industry has grown up around the use of physiological and behavioural markers of lying. In one version of 'lie detecting' the subject might be shown a series of pictures and asked if he recognizes them. For the critical item, the subject denies having seen it, but shows a large increase in skin conductance and characteristic evoked potentials in the EEG. Clearly he has guilty knowledge about this item, but is trying to make us believe he knows nothing about it (Ref. a). The same procedure has been applied to patients with obvious brain damage. For example, a patient with prosopagnosia might be unable to recognize the faces of familiar people. If, however, we measure skin conductance when the faces are presented, then we will see an enhanced response to familiar, but unrecognized, faces (Ref. b). Similar effects can be observed in patients with amnesia (Ref. c). Nevertheless, we do not conclude that these patients are lying. Rather, we use these observations as evidence that, in these cases, as in blindsight, there are two neural pathways concerned with recognition; one conscious and the other unconscious. In these cases of organic damage we conclude that the conscious pathway has been damaged while the other remains intact. Why do we not conclude that these patients are lying? Because, firstly, they have obvious brain damage, and secondly, they do not gain anything by lying. There is nothing intrinsic to the physiological measures so far developed to indicate whether or not they are lying.

Our situation becomes even more uncertain when examining patients with 'functional' blindness or 'psychogenic' amnesia (Ref. d). These are patients in whom no obvious organic damage can be found. Sometimes they seem to obtain short-term gains from their symptoms. When asked to guess they might perform worse than chance. This could be the sign of a naive liar who avoids giving what he knows to be the correct answer. Yet these patients seem distinctly different from malingerers who are faking injury in order to obtain compensation and can be caught out, for instance, by using a 'damaged' limb when they think they are unobserved. If their symptoms are indeed faked, then hysterical patients seem abnormally devoted to keeping up the pretence. The long-term disadvantages resulting from the symptom more than outweighs the short-term gains. What is the neural concomitant of the dissociations present in hysteria in which it seems as if the patient does not know that he is 'lying'? If a specific physiological marker for the presence of mental representations can be found, then our understanding of disorders like hysteria will be greatly increased.

**References**

**a** Farwell, L.A. and Donchin, E. (1991) The truth will out: interrogative polygraphy ('lie detection') with event-related brain potentials *Psychophysiology* 28, 531–547

**b** Bauer, R.M. (1994) Autonomic recognition of names and faces in prosopagnosia: a neuropsychological application of the guilty knowledge test *Neuropsychologia* 22, 457–469

**c** Diamond, B.J., Mayes, A.R. and Meudell, P.R. (1996) Autonomic and recognition indices of memory in amnesic and healthy control subjects *Cortex* 32, 439–459

**d** Fukuda, M. *et al.* (1996) Event-related potential correlates of functional hearing loss: reduced P3 amplitude with preserved N1 and N2 components in a unilateral case *Psychiatry Clin. Neurosci.* 50, 85–87

## Behavioural reports

However, we do not need to use language to report our mental experiences. Gestures and movements can be made with a deliberate communicative intent. In many experiments the observer will indicate that he sees something by pressing a button. In this case a behavioural response (the button press) is a report in the sense that it means something: observer and experimenter have agreed, prior to the experiment, that a button press will mean that the stimulus has been perceived. More complex behavioural reports can be agreed. For example, in an experiment on binocular rivalry (see below) the observer can press the left button for one percept and the right button for the other. The advantage of a behavioural report is that it can be used in situations where a verbal report is not possible. A patient in the 'locked-in' state can indicate his or her wishes by minimal finger movements or eyeblinks[16]. The same procedure can be used in studies of animals. In a binocular rivalry experiment, a monkey can be trained to press the left button for one percept and the right button for the other[17]. The disadvantage of the behavioural report is that it can all too easily be confused with mere behaviour. Is that man who is violently waving his arm around swatting a wasp or hailing a taxi? Furthermore, appropriate behaviour can occur in the absence of any awareness of what is guiding the behaviour. This phenomenon is most obvious in neurological cases such as blindsight and the agnosias that follow lesions in the ventral visual pathways[18].

With human observers we know about the discrepancy between behaviour and awareness because verbal reports are available – the observer tells us that he was guessing – but how do we know that a monkey is not guessing? One solution is to use parameters that are well outside the guessing range in humans and to demonstrate that the performance of the monkey closely resembles that of the human in terms of response times and their distribution. In this way the experimenter uses the verbal report of the human in an attempt to validate the behavioural report of the monkey[17]. Another solution is to develop tasks in which the monkey learns to report the presence of a stimulus rather than making a forced choice about the nature of a stimulus[19].

## Identifying the neural correlates of mental representations

In our search for the neural correlates of consciousness we aim to identify that kind of neural activity which has a formal relationship with reports about mental representations. There are two parts to this aim. The first part is to identify neural activity that is related to mental representations. We are searching for situations in which changes in neural activity predict changes in mental representation and the converse. We can predict either the direction of the change or the time at which the change occurs. For example, in a study of threshold determination, the presence (or absence) of a certain pattern of neural activity would predict the presence (or absence) of a particular mental representation. The time at which the change in neural activity occurred would also predict the time of the change of mental representation. It should be noted, however, that for this prediction it is not necessary for the changes in the two domains to occur precisely at the same time. It is merely necessary that an early change in the neural activity is associated with an early change in the mental representation. Prediction is still possible if there is systematic time difference between the changes in the two domains.

It is also necessary to show that these relationships are not simply the concomitant consequence of changes in stimulation or changes in behaviour. The most direct way of 'partialling out' these unwanted effects is to keep them constant. Hence the emphasis on paradigms in which, for example, subjective experience changes while stimulation remains constant (e.g. binocular rivalry).

The second part of our aim is to show that neural activity associated with mental representations is qualitatively different from other kinds of neural activity. To achieve this aim it is necessary to identify neural correlates of changing stimulation and changing behaviour that occur in the absence of changes in mental representations. Comparison of these different kinds of neural activity will demonstrate that there is a certain pattern or type of neural activity that is uniquely associated with mental representations: the neural 'signature' of consciousness (see Box 7.3).

### Box 7.3 Neural correlates and signatures of consciousness

A systematic investigation of the brain bases of consciousness is predicated on the assumption that at any moment subjective experience is associated with a corresponding pattern of neuronal activity. This basic tenet underlies current research programs on consciousness, in which the first objective is to characterize the neural correlates of consciousness (NCC) (Ref. a). Key questions that must be addressed empirically include: in which areas are such correlates present (or absent)? Are the neurons involved of a particular type? Do they fire in a particular way, either by themselves or with respect to other neurons?

An issue of current focus concerns the localization of brain activity correlated with phenomenal awareness. For example, Schacter and co-workers have proposed that there is a specific brain system, separate from the structures involved in perception and action, that mediates conscious awareness (Ref. b). Conversely, it has been suggested that certain brain regions and pathways do not contribute directly to conscious experience. Thus, Crick and Koch have suggested that activity in the primary visual cortex (V1) is not directly linked to visual awareness (Ref. c). In a variant of this 'eliminative' view, Milner and Goodale suggest that the occipito-parietal pathway subserves an on-line system for visually guided actions that operates in the absence of awareness (Ref. d). One difficulty in testing these hypotheses is that in any given area, the NCCs could in principle take many forms. Possibilities that have been considered include a modulation of firing rates, neuronal synchronization, and activity of cells in specific layers or with particular spike trains (e.g. bursting cells). When assessing whether activity in a given area reflects conscious experience, caution must therefore be taken in drawing conclusions from restricted measures of neuronal activity, such as those pertaining to mean firing rates. For instance, neuronal synchronization in V1 has been shown to reflect the functional dominance of one eye in amblyopia in cats, whereas no dominance-related modulation of firing rate was observed in this area (Ref. e); such synchronization might contribute to the formation of perceptual states.

In contrast with accounts of consciousness based on particular brain systems, integrative theories of brain function propose that subjective experience emerges as the result of interactions among widely distributed brain regions that mediate perception, attention, memory and action (Ref. f). Accordingly, the NCCs should be expressed in terms of patterns of correlation among separate and distant brain areas.

In exploring these possibilities, it will be important to guard against spurious correlates of conscious experience – neuronal activity that, although correlated with a particular subjective state, does not account for its emergence. To discover bona fide neural correlates of conscious experience, brain activity must be measured under various experimental conditions and with a range of measurement techniques, in the search for patterns of activity that consistently correlate with conscious experience across multiple conditions. We refer to these patterns as neural signatures of consciousness (NSC). The identification of such robust neural signatures will be essential for the formulation of hypotheses regarding the neural mechanisms that give rise to consciousness, and for the design of experiments aimed at interfering with such mechanisms.

### *Measuring neural activity*

Direct measures of neural activity can be made at the level of the single cell, but this work is largely restricted to animals. Changes in electrical activity occurring at the scalp (EEG and MEG) can be recorded in humans. These measures reflect post-synaptic potentials in large populations of cells (Ref. g). Indirect measures of neural activity at the level of large populations of cells can be made in humans by measuring blood flow (PET) or blood oxygenation level (fMRI). These indirect measures largely reflect pre-synaptic activity (Ref. h). Functional MRI and PET are good measures for localizing activity, while EEG and MEG are good for revealing the precise timing of activity. All these techniques can also be used to examine the interactions between distant brain areas using measures of effective connectivity (Ref. i) and structural equation modelling (Ref. j).

Our emphasis on the need for verbal report to identify the contents of consciousness implies that the search for the neural correlates of consciousness will largely be restricted to humans. At present, studies of neural activity in the human brain are restricted to techniques that measure activity in large populations of cells. However, if the neural signature of consciousness relates to activity in certain cortical layers or to the precise timing of spike trains, then consideration of activity at the level of the single cell will be critical. It will therefore be very important to show how activity in large populations of neurons relates to activity at the single-cell level. This is likely to be achieved through computational modelling (Ref. k) and also through application of fMRI to the monkey brain.

### References


**a** Crick, F. and Koch, C. (1998) Consciousness and neuroscience *Cereb. Cortex* 8, 97–107

**b** Schacter, D.L., McAndrews, M.P. and Moscovitch, M. (1988) Access to consciousness: dissociations between implicit and explicit knowledge in neuropsychological syndromes, in *Thought Without Language* (Weiskrantz, L, ed.) pp. 242–278, Oxford University Press

**c** Crick, F. and Koch, C. (1995) Are we aware of neural activity in primary visual cortex? *Nature* 373, 121–123

**d** Milner, A.D. and Goodale, M.A. (1995) *The Visual Brain in Action,* Oxford University Press

**e** Roelfsema, P.R. *et al.* (1994) Reduced synchronization in the visual cortex of cats with strabismic amplyopia *Eur. J. Neurosci.* 6, 1645–1655

**f** Kinsbourne, M. (1988) Integrated field theory of consciousness, in *Consciousness in Contemporary Science* (Marcel, A.J. and Bisiach, E., eds), pp. 239–256, Oxford University Press

**g** Lopes da Silva, F. (1991) Neuronal mechanisms underlying brainwaves: from neural membranes to networks *Electroencephalogr. Clin. Neurophysiol.* 90, 81–93

**h** Jueptner, M. and Weiller, C. (1995) Review: does measurement of regional cerebral blood flow reflect synaptic activity? – implications for PET and fMRI *NeuroImage* 2, 148–156

**i** Gerstein, G.L., Bedenbaugh, P. and Aertsen, A. (1989) Neuronal assemblies *IEEE Trans. Biomed. Eng.* 36, 4–14

**j** McIntosh, A.R. and Gonzalez-Lima, F. (1991) Structural equation modelling of functional neural pathways mapped with 2-deoxyglucose: effects of acoustic startle habituation on the auditory system *Brain Res.* 546, 295–302

**k** Lumer, E.D., Edelman, G.M. and Tononi, G. (1997) Neural dynamics in a model of the thalamocortical system: II. The role of neural synchrony tested through perturbations of spike timing *Cereb. Cortex* 7, 228–236

We suggest that it will be useful to distinguish three kinds of neural activity: (1) neural activity associated with mental representations; (2) neural activity associated with changes in a sensory stimulus, in the absence of changes in mental representations; and (3) neural activity associated with behaviour in the absence of mental representations (see Fig. 7.1). Each of these three kinds of activity can be identified using specific experimental paradigms.

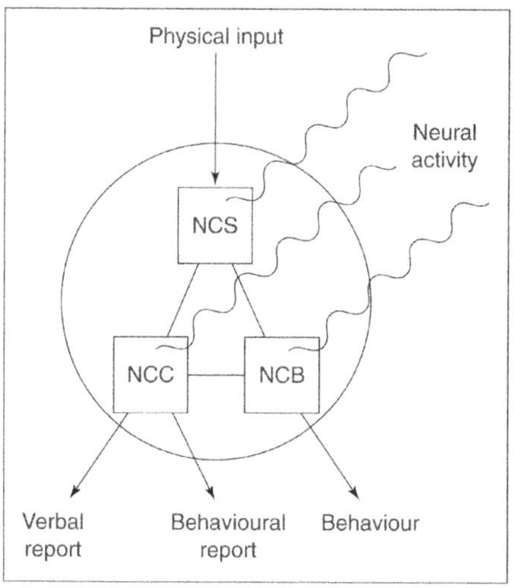


*Figure 7.1* Schematic illustration of the three neural correlates that must be contrasted in order to specify the neural correlates of consciousness. NCS: neural correlates of sensory stimulation. NCB: neural correlates of behaviour. NCC: neural correlates of consciousness. The three different classes of activity need not be spatially segregated in discrete brain regions.

## A taxonomy of experimental paradigms for studying consciousness

In Tables 7.1 and 7.2 we have made an attempt to systematize the experimental paradigms relevant to the three hypothetical types of neural activity. We have associated these with three kinds of psychological processes; those concerned with the present (perception and imagery), those concerned with the past (memory) and those concerned with the future (intentions and actions). These tables provide a basis of a programme for the development of experimental studies of the neural correlates of consciousness. Because studies of neurological cases and other disorders associated with abnormal mental states continue to play such a major role in the identification of the neural correlates of consciousness, we have included a

*Table 7.1* Experimental Paradigms for Studying the Neural Correlates of Consciousness in Normal States

| | *Perception* | *Memory* | *Action* |
|---|---|---|---|
| Subjective experience changes, stimulation and/or behaviour remains constant | Neural correlates of binocular rivalry[23] | Neural correlates of episodic recall[43] | Neural correlates of the awareness of intention[30] |
| Stimulation changes, subjective experience remains constant | Neural correlates of changes in stimulation without awareness[41] | Neural correlates of unrecognised old items[43] | Neural correlates of stimuli eliciting action without awareness[15] |
| Behaviour changes, subjective experience remains constant | Neural correlates of correct guessing without awareness[42] | Neural correlates of implicit learning[44] | Neural correlates of implicit motor behaviour[45] |

In each category one example is given of an experimental paradigm that has been or could be used to identify neural correlates of consciousness, sensory stimulation or behaviour.

*Table 7.2* Experimental Paradigms for Studying the Neural Correlates of Consciousness in Abnormal States

| | *Perception* | *Memory* | *Action* |
|---|---|---|---|
| Subjective experience changes, stimulation and/or behaviour remains constant | Neural correlates of hallucinations[24] | Neural correlates of confabulation[40] | Neural correlates of abnormal intentions (delusions of control)[49] |
| Stimulation changes, subjective experience remains constant | Neural correlates of stimulation of the blind field in blindsight[14] | Neural correlates of unrecognised items in amnesia[47] | Neural correlates of stimuli eliciting unintended actions[50] |
| Behaviour changes, subjective experience remains constant | Neural correlates of correct reaching in form agnosia[46] | Implicit learning in amnesia[48] | Neural correlates of unintended actions[33] |

In each category one example is given of an experimental paradigm that has been or could be used to identify neural correlates of consciousness, sensory stimulation or behaviour.

table specifically for such studies (Table 7.2). We discuss some of the paradigms listed in these tables below.

### *Perception and attention*

Many authors have suggested that the study of visual awareness is likely to provide a good starting point for investigating the neural correlates of consciousness. This notion is based on the wealth of data available on the neuroanatomy and physiology of the visual system in monkeys. Under the often implicit assumption of strong homology between the visual systems of human and monkeys, this information can be brought to bear in the design and interpretation of experimental studies. Whether we can study the neural correlates of consciousness in the monkey directly is less clear. Much important work has been reported in which the verbal reports of a human observer were correlated with activity in the brain of an anaesthetised monkey exposed to the same stimulus[20]. This approach might well identify activity that is necessary for consciousness, but it seems unlikely to identify activity that is sufficient. However, even studies of awake, behaving monkeys are problematic. We believe that monkeys do have mental representations, but it is very difficult to prove this supposition. We can train monkeys to report their perceptions behaviourally, but we cannot validate these behavioural reports with verbal ones. This situation would change dramatically if reliable neural signatures of mental representations could be found in humans (see Box 7.3). The observation of the same patterns of neural activity in monkeys would provide a validation of behavioural reports.

Meanwhile in the last decade, there has been a surge of experimentation on the neural basis of conscious vision in humans. Two experimental paradigms have emerged in which visually guided performance takes place in the absence of conscious perception of the stimulus.

Instances of the first category are given by the phenomenology of patients with lesions in the occipito-temporal pathway. Injury to the earliest stage of this pathway, in the striate cortex (V1), can lead to blindsight, in which subjects report being unaware of stimuli in the contralateral visual field but produce goal-directed behaviour that is contingent on these sensory cues[14]. Another example of a dissociation between conscious perception and behaviour is provided by a patient, D.F., who has form agnosia and is unable to report the orientation of a mail slot but can nevertheless post a letter in it. These observations have led Milner and Goodale to propose the existence of a rapid response system that is mainly unconscious, and depends on processing in the dorsal pathway, and of an object recognition system that is conscious and results from ventral stream processing[18]. This formulation implies what is perhaps the simplest possible neural signature for consciousness: activity in some brain regions is associated with mental representations, while activity in other regions is not. However, we think this is unlikely to be a general principle for the specification of the neural signature of consciousness (see Box 7.3).

In normal subjects, appropriate behaviour in the absence of conscious perception can be observed in masking experiments. The introduction of a mask a few tens to hundreds of milliseconds after presentation of a stimulus (such as a face) can abolish the subjective perception of the stimulus; yet, autonomic and motor responses to aspects of the stimulus may still be elicited[21]. In this paradigm the aim is to show that the presence of a certain kind of neural activity predicts autonomic and motor responses. Using masking it has been shown, for example, that activity in the amygdala changes with changes in facial expression of which the subject is unaware[22] (see Fig. 7.2). By studying effects close to the masking threshold it should be possible to identify a different kind of activity that predicts conscious perception of the stimulus. In particular, it should be possible to identify some pattern of neural activity that predicts whether or not the masked object will be consciously perceived.

One of the best available experimental paradigms with which to study the neural correlates of subjective visual perception is provided by the bistable perception that arises when the physical stimulus readily allows two alternative perceptual interpretations. Perceptual instability arises, for example, when dissimilar images are shown to each eye, the instability in this case is called binocular rivalry. Because the changes in perception occur despite a constant visual input, neural responses associated with perception can be distinguished from those entirely dependent on stimulus characteristics. In this example the aim is to show that the timing of the change in perception correlates with the timing of certain changes in neural activity. Recent studies with awake monkeys trained to report their percepts during rivalry have revealed that, whereas the firing of most neurons in the primary visual cortex correlates with the stimulus and not the percept, activity of neurons at higher stages of the visual pathway, such as the inferotemporal cortex, mainly reflect the percept[17]. This result has now been confirmed in human volunteers using functional MRI[23]. However, because activity throughout the brain could be monitored using this technique it was additionally shown that changes in parietal and frontal activity were also correlated with changes in perception.

In patients with blindsight, changes in stimulation or behaviour can occur in the absence of changes in perception (as discussed above). In contrast, there are various hallucinatory experiences in which perception occurs in the absence of sensation. For example, patients with schizophrenia frequently hear voices speaking to them or about them. If such patients can be persuaded to indicate when these experiences occur then the associated neural activity can be identified. One such study suggests that activity associated with hallucinations occurs in sensory association areas, but not in primary sensory areas[24]. Similar investigations could be applied to patients with phantom limbs[25].

The studies of perception reviewed above demonstrate that stimuli can be highly processed and yet not enter awareness. Attention might be the critical mechanism by which preprocessed stimuli are selected for awareness. In consequence, studies of selective attention will continue to be of major interest in the investigation of the neural correlates of consciousness. In particular, we need to find out whether there is a characteristic difference in the neural activity associated with attended

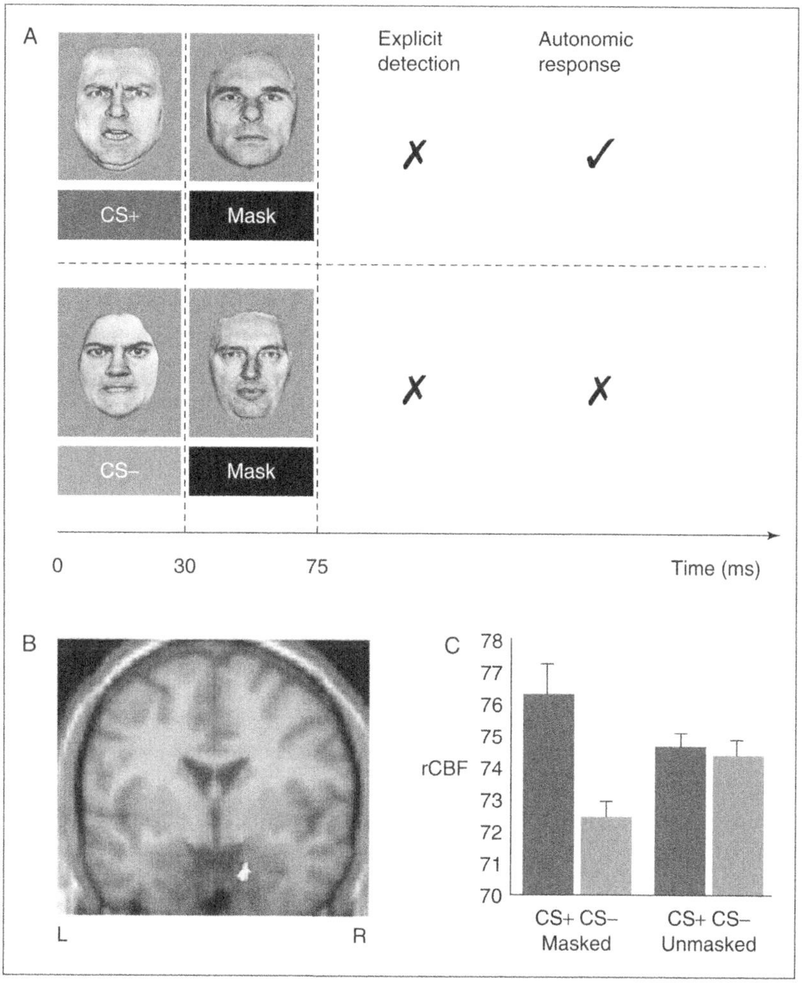


*Figure 7.2* Activity in the amygdala elicited by aversive stimuli of which the subject is not aware. **(A)** Right amygdala response to masked conditioned faces. Prior to PET scanning, healthy subjects were repeatedly shown an angry face (the CS+) paired with a 100dB noise. Another angry face (the CS−) was also shown repeatedly but never paired with noise. During scanning, the CS+ and CS− faces were presented for 30 ms, and immediately followed by a 45 ms masking stimulus (a neutral face). This masking procedure prevented subjects from explicitly reporting any awareness of the CS+ or CS− faces. Despite being 'unseen', masked CS+ presentations elicited greater autonomic responses (changes in skin conductance) than masked presentations of the CS− face. A mediobasal region of the right amygdaloid complex responded more to the masked CS+ than to the masked CS− face, shown on a coronal MRI section **(B).** The mean adjusted regional cerebral blood flow (rCBF) for the different experimental conditions is also shown **(C).** Although the right amygdala responded differentially to the masked conditioned faces, this differential activity was not seen when the same stimuli were shown unmasked and explicitly reported via a button press (unmasked). Modified from Ref. 22. (See figure in colour plate section.)

and unattended stimuli. However, the precise relationship between attention and awareness remains unclear. It is not necessarily the case that unattended stimuli do not reach awareness. The extent to which unattended stimuli are processed depends on the perceptual 'load' imposed by the task requiring attention[26]. Study of the neural activity associated with unattended stimuli has advantages over behavioural studies because the degree to which the unattended stimuli are processed can be studied without alerting subjects to their presence[27]. Lack of any detectable physiological response to unattended stimuli would be good evidence that they did not reach awareness.

Disorders of attention can result from lesions to the inferior parietal and frontal cortex. Such lesions can lead to unilateral neglect, in which the patient is unable to attend to objects in the visual field contralateral to the lesion. Neglect differs from occipitally related blindsight in that extensive visual processing of neglected stimuli is preserved[28]. One problem in interpreting the pathological basis of this disorder, though, is that the extent and nature of the lesions (e.g. grey- versus white-matter damage) are often poorly specified. Thus, it is not clear whether right inferior parietal cortex, where lesions associated with unilateral neglect are often located, has a special role in the direction of attention, or whether damage to underlying white matter is critical owing to the disconnection of visual and motor regions[29].

### *Action and intention*

The relationship of neural activity in the motor system to the awareness of intentions has also been studied extensively. Libet[30] has shown that brain activity that precedes a voluntary movement can be detected (in the EEG) well in advance of reports of awareness of the intention to move. This pioneering study illustrates the advantages of studying the motor system, as correlations can be explored between the times at which mental and physical events occur. Haggard and Eimer[31] present data suggesting that the time of awareness of initiating a movement correlates with the time at which the late, lateralized component of the readiness potential begins (probably reflecting the time at which the exact movement is specified), but not with the beginning of the early phase of the readiness potential. Studies that combine the high spatial resolution of fMRI and the high temporal resolution of EEG should be able to locate the brain regions associated with these various potentials.

A series of experiments from Jeannerod's group has demonstrated dissociations between behaviour and awareness in normal volunteers making rapid grasping movements. Corrections to the trajectory of a movement made in response to target movements occur several hundred milliseconds in advance of reported awareness of target movement[32] (see Fig. 7.3). In this respect, the distinction we have made in Tables 7.1 and 7.2 between perception and action is somewhat artificial. As Milner and Goodale have pointed out, perception and action are intimately linked[18]. In most cases the purpose of perception is to permit action. Studies of patients with blindsight or form agnosia should be particularly informative

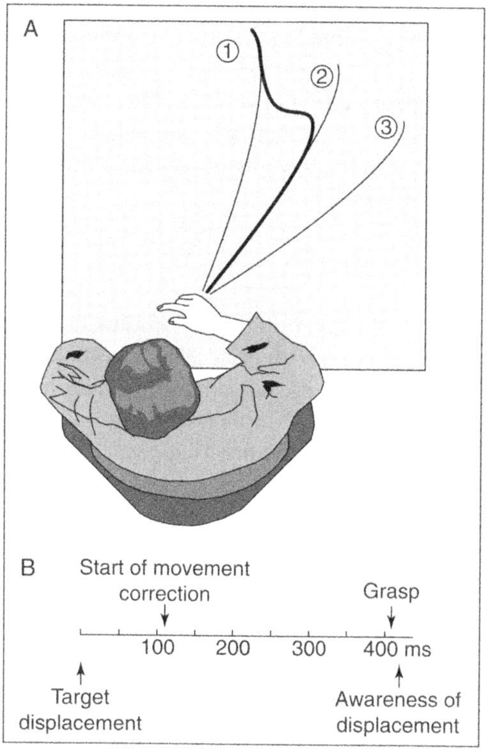


*Figure 7.3* Dissociation of behaviour and awareness in the actions of normal subjects. **(A)** When one of three rods (1, 2 and 3) was illuminated the subject moved his right hand and grasped the target rod with finger and thumb as quickly as possible. The paths followed by the subject's forefinger are indicated by the thin lines. On 20% of trials, as soon as the subject started to move, the target indicator light switched from the centre rod to one of the outer rods (perturbed trials). This switch elicited a smooth and rapid movement correction shown by the bold line. In addition to grasping the target rod, subjects gave a vocal response (saying 'tah') as soon as they perceived that the target was illuminated. On the perturbed trials they gave a second vocal response to indicate when they were aware of the target switch. **(B)** The mean times at which the various events occurred for the perturbed trials. The first signs of movement correction occurred approximately 100 ms after the target switch. However, the vocal response indicating awareness of the target switch did not occur until 300 ms later. The authors of the original paper reported that: 'on some occasions, the dissociation between motor and vocal responses was such that subjects, to their own surprise, were already lifting the target rod when they emitted the vocal response'. (Modified from data reported in Ref. 32, Figs 2 and 3 and Table 2.)

in revealing the neural activity associated with reaching and grasping in the absence of awareness of the object of the action. It is likely that the same system is involved as operates in the rapid, 'unconscious' error correction observed in normal volunteers.

Other examples of motor behaviour in the absence of awareness are provided by patients with an 'anarchic' hand or with utilization behaviour in whom goal-directed behaviour can be observed in the absence of awareness of an intention to act[33].

In contrast, mental representation of action in the absence of behaviour is present during motor imagery, or in patients who are able to 'move' a phantom limb. During motor imagery neural activity is observed in most of the motor system excluding primary motor cortex[34].

### *Memory and learning*

Studies of memory have close parallels with studies of perception and action. Patients with amnesia, like those with blindsight, can show behaviour influenced by past experience of which they are not conscious[35]. Normal volunteers can also show such behaviour via priming or implicit learning[36]. Studies of the neural correlates of these phenomena are beginning to appear[37]. Mental representations of past events are involved in episodic memory and explicit learning. The neural activity associated with such mental representations can be identified by contrast with that associated with the various forms of implicit memory[38]. It is also possible to study neural activity associated with false memories (analogous to hallucinations) that can be elicited in normal people in certain experimental paradigms[39] and can be observed in patients who confabulate[40].

## Conclusions

It is clear from this brief summary that there are already a number of studies in the literature that address questions concerning the neural correlates of conscious experience. The purpose of this article has been to develop a framework in which such studies can be linked to one another, and to make explicit the fundamental significance of such studies for our understanding of the neural correlates of conscious experience. As the amount of evidence on this topic increases we shall be in a much better position to identify the characteristic neural signatures of consciousness (if there are any) and to address more difficult questions concerning the function of consciousness and the mechanisms by which mental representations emerge from neural activity.

## Acknowledgements

This article is written on behalf of, and based on a series of discussions in, the Consciousness Club, an informal group of scientists and clinicians from the Wellcome Department of Cognitive Neurology and the Institute of Cognitive Neuroscience, University College London. Its members include Sarah-Jayne Blakemore, Raymond Dolan, Paul Fletcher, Richard Frackowiak, Karl Friston, Chris Frith, Andreas Kleinschmidt, Erik Lumer, Emiliano Macaluso, Ludovica Marini, Dave McGonigle, John Morris, Richard Perry, Chiara Portas, Geraint Rees, Mick Rugg and Bob Turner. We are grateful to Mike Martin for his comments on philosophical aspects. Preparation of this article was supported by the Wellcome Trust.

## Outstanding questions

- Does the pattern of neural activity associated with conscious perception have some common feature across different sensory modalities?
- Can measurement of neural activity be used to infer the existence of mental representations in the absence of a verbal (or a non-verbal) report?
- Does the apparent unity of conscious experience require the convergence of disparate streams of neural activity into a few 'convergence zones' within the brain, or might the neural correlates of consciousness be found in multiple, independent brain areas?
- Is there evidence, at the neural level, for an intimate relationship between phenomenal consciousness and language?
- What is the minimum set of brain regions that is sufficient for the existence of mental representations?

## References

1 Crick, F. (1994) *The Astonishing Hypothesis,* Macmillan
2 Edelman, G.M. (1989) *The Remembered Present,* Basic Books
3 Dennett, D. (1991) *Consciousness Explained,* Penguin Books
4 Churchland, P.S. (1993) *Neurophilosophy: Towards a Unified Science of the Mind–Brain,* MIT Press
5 Purpura, K.P. and Schiff, N.D. (1997) The thalamic intralaminar nuclei: a role in visual awareness *The Neuroscientist* 3, 314–321
6 Kihlstrom, J.F. *et al.* (1990) Implicit and explicit memory following surgical anaesthesia *Psychol. Sci.* 1, 303–306
7 Barbur, J.L. *et al.* (1993) Conscious visual perception without V1. *Brain* 116, 1293–1302
8 Schacter, D.L. (1989) On the relation between memory and consciousness: dissociable interactions and conscious experience, in *Varieties of Memory and Consciousness: Essays in Honour of Endel Tulving* (Roediger, H.L. and Craik, F.I.M., eds), pp. 355–389, Erlbaum
9 Easterbrook, J.A. (1959) The effect of emotion on cue utilisation and the organisation of behaviour *Psychol. Rev.* 66, 183–201
10 Hobson, J.A. (1988) *The Dreaming Brain,* Basic Books
11 Llinas, R.R. and Pare, D. (1991) On dreaming and wakefulness *Neuroscience* 44, 521–535
12 Contreras, D. *et al.* (1997) Spatiotemporal patterns of spindle oscillations in cortex and thalamus *J. Neurosci.* 17, 1179–1196
13 Miller, E.K. and Desimone, R. (2000) The prefrontal and visual cortices: the neural basis of top-down control of visual attention, in *Attention and Performance* (Vol. XVIII) (Monsell, S. and Driver, J., eds), pp. 515–534, MIT Press

14 Weiskrantz, L. (1986) *Blindsight: A Case Study and Implications,* Oxford University Press
15 Dehaene, S. *et al.* (1998) Imaging unconscious semantic priming *Nature* 395, 597–600
16 Gallo, U.E. and Fontanarosa, P.B. (1989) Locked-in syndrome: report of a case *Am. J. Emerg. Med.* 6, 581–583
17 Leopold, D. and Logothetis, N. (1996) Activity changes in early visual cortex reflect monkeys' percepts during binocular rivalry *Nature* 379, 549–553
18 Milner, A.D. (1998) Streams and consciousness: visual awareness and the brain *Trends Cognit. Sci.* 2, 25–30
19 Cowey, A. and Stoerig, P. (1995) Blindsight in monkeys *Nature* 373, 247–249
20 Zeki, S. (1993) The physiology of the colour pathways, in *A Vision of the Brain,* pp. 256–263, Blackwell Science
21 Ohman, A. and Soares, J.J.F. (1994) 'Unconscious anxiety': phobic responses to masked stimuli *J. Abnorm. Psychol.* 103, 231–240
22 Morris, J., Ohman, A. and Dolan, R.J. (1998) Conscious and unconscious emotional learning in the human amygdala *Nature* 393, 467–470
23 Lumer, E.D., Friston, K.J. and Rees, G. (1998) Neural correlates of perceptual rivalry in the human brain *Science* 280, 1930–1934
24 Silbersweig, D.A. *et al.* (1995) A functional neuroanatomy of hallucinations in schizophrenia *Nature* 378, 176–179
25 Hari, R. *et al.* (1998) Three hands: fragmentation of bodily awareness *Neurosci. Lett.* 240, 13113–13114
26 Lavie, N. (1995) Perceptual load as a necessary condition for selective attention *J. Exp. Psychol. Hum. Percept. Perform.* 21, 451–468
27 Rees, G., Frith, C.D. and Lavie, N. (1997) Modulating irrelevant motion perception by varying attentional load in an unrelated task *Science* 278, 1616–1619
28 Driver, J. and Mattingley, J.B. (1998) Parietal neglect and visual awareness *Nat. Neurosci.* 1, 17–22
29 Gaffan, D. and Hornak, J. (1997) Visual neglect in the monkey: representation and disconnection *Brain* 120, 1647–1657
30 Libet, B. (1993) The neural time factor in conscious and unconscious events, in *Experimental and Theoretical Studies of Consciousness* (Ciba Foundation Symposium 174), pp. 123–137, John Wiley & Sons
31 Haggard, P. and Eimer, M. (1999) On the relation between brain potentials and the awareness of voluntary movements *Exp. Brain Res.* 126.1, 128–133
32 Castiello, U., Paulignan, Y. and Jeannerod, M. (1991) Temporal dissociation of motor responses and subjective awareness *Brain* 114, 2639–2655
33 Marchetti, C. and Della Salla, S. (1998) Disentangling the alien and anarchic hand *Cognit. Neuropsychiatry* 3, 191–208
34 Stephan, K.M. *et al.* (1995) Functional anatomy of the mental representation of upper extremity movements in healthy subjects *J. Neurophysiol.* 73, 373–386
35 Schacter, D.L. (1992) Consciousness and awareness in memory and amnesia: critical issues, in *The Neuropsychology of Consciousness* (Milner, A.D. and Rugg, M.D., eds), pp. 180–200, Academic Press
36 Kunst-Wilson, W.R. and Zajonc, R.B. (1980) Affective discrimination of stimuli that cannot be recognised *Science* 207, 557–558
37 Buckner, R.L. and Koutstaal, W. (1998) Functional neuroimaging studies of encoding, priming, and explicit memory retrieval *Proc. Natl. Acad. Sci. U.S. A.* 95, 891–898

38 Clark, R.E. and Squire, L.R. (1998) Classical conditioning and brain systems: the role of awareness *Science* 280, 77–81
39 Schacter, D.L. *et al.* (1996) Neuroanatomical correlates of veridical and illusory recognition memory: evidence from positron emission tomography *Neuron* 17, 267–274
40 Burgess, P.W. and Shallice, T. (1996) Confabulation and the control of recollection *Memory* 4, 1–53
41 He, S., Cavanagh, P. and Intriligator, J. (1996) Attentional resolution and the locus of visual awareness *Nature* 383, 334–337
42 Pierce, C.S. and Jastrow, J. (1885) On small differences in sensation *Memoirs of the National Academy of Sciences* 3, 75–83
43 Rugg, M.D. *et al.* (1998) Dissociation of the neural correlates of implicit and explicit memory *Nature* 392, 595–598
44 Hazeltine, E., Grafton, S.T. and Ivry, R. (1997) Attention and stimulus characteristics determine the locus of motor-sequence encoding: a PET study *Brain* 120, 123–140
45 Rossetti, Y. (1998) Implicit short-lived motor representations of space in brain damaged and healthy subjects *Conscious. Cognit.* 7.3, 520–558
46 Milner, A.D. and Goodale, M.A. (1995) *The Visual Brain in Action,* Oxford University Press
47 Diamond, B.J., Mayes, A.R. and Meudell, P.R. (1996) Autonomic and recognition indices of memory in amnesic and healthy control subjects *Cortex* 32, 439–459
48 Knowlton, B.J., Ramus, S.J. and Squire, L.R. (1992) Intact artificial-grammar learning in amnesia: dissociation of abstract knowledge and memory for specific instances *Psychol. Sci.* 3, 172–179
49 Spence, S.A. *et al.* (1997) A PET study of voluntary movement in schizophrenic patients experiencing passivity phenomena (delusions of alien control) *Brain* 120, 1997–2011
50 Lhermitte, F. (1983) 'Utilization behaviour' and its relation to lesions of the frontal lobes *Brain* 106, 237–255

# 8 What's at the top in the top-down control of action?

## Script-sharing and 'top-top' control of action in cognitive experiments

*Andreas Roepstorff and Chris Frith*

### Metaphors of up and down in the brain

The distinction between 'top-down' and 'bottom-up' processes is one of the more important conceptual models in cognitive psychology. This organization of neuronal and cognitive processes along a vertical axis appears very straightforward, indeed almost intuitive, but on second thoughts, things may get more complicated. Along which kind of dimension does this movement occur?

On the one hand, there appears to be a purely anatomical distinction between 'lower' and 'higher' parts of the brain, where 'the top' of this axis is to be understood, somewhat loosely, as the anterior frontal regions such as the prefrontal cortex, and the bottom are the more posterior and 'deeper' structures terminating at the brain stem. In these terms, the model also carries evolutionary connotations, as the axis distinguishes the 'lower' reptile brain from the higher, more advanced mammalian – and ultimately human – brain.

The model also refers to a relationship between the organism and the environment. In this sense, 'bottom' is that which comes to the organism 'from the outside.' This is usually taken to be the sensory inputs, while 'the top' is all that understanding and knowledge that the organism has on its own (Frith & Dolan, 1997). Finally, 'top' and 'down' also evoke semantic resonances of power and control, as in the colloquial distinctions between 'the top executive' and 'the man on the floor' (Lakoff & Johnson, 1980).

Perhaps the beauty, and indeed also effectiveness, of the top-bottom model for describing both brain organization and cognitive function is precisely that it brings together these very different levels of organization: An anatomical organization, an evolutionary perspective and notions of control and governance. However, as with most other metaphorical relationships that serve to structure how thoughts are expressed and how they are set to work with each other (Lakoff & Johnson, 1980), there comes a point where the reality described seems to resist the apparent simplicity of the metaphorical model. We believe that this becomes apparent once one considers how the notions become implemented in the design and interpretation of cognitive experiments.

## Where is the top in top-down control?

The distinction between 'bottom-up' and 'top-down' control of action is nicely illustrated in response selection tasks. In a choice reaction time task (CRT) where participants have to move a finger as soon as that finger is touched the control of response selection is bottom-up since the imperative signal (in the environment) indicates which response should be selected in each trial. In contrast to other CRTs in which the relationship between stimulus and response has to be learned, the responses in this tactile version are automatic and reaction time does not increase with the number of possible choices from 2 to 8 (Leonard, 1959). In a willed action task the control of response selection is top-down since, in each trial, it is the participant who has to decide which response to select. The imperative signal merely indicates when the response should be made. The flow of information that controls response selection in these two cases is illustrated in Fig. 8.1.

By using functional brain imaging it has been possible to assign brain regions to some of the boxes in these diagrams. In particular, top-down response selection is consistently associated with activity in the prefrontal cortex (Deiber et al., 1991; Frith, Friston, Liddle, & Frackowiak, 1991).

There are several problems with this diagram of top-down control. First of all, if we take the box-and-arrow diagram seriously as a model of what happens at the neural level it tells us that there should be a region in the brain (the top) in which there are only outputs and no inputs. There is no evidence that such a

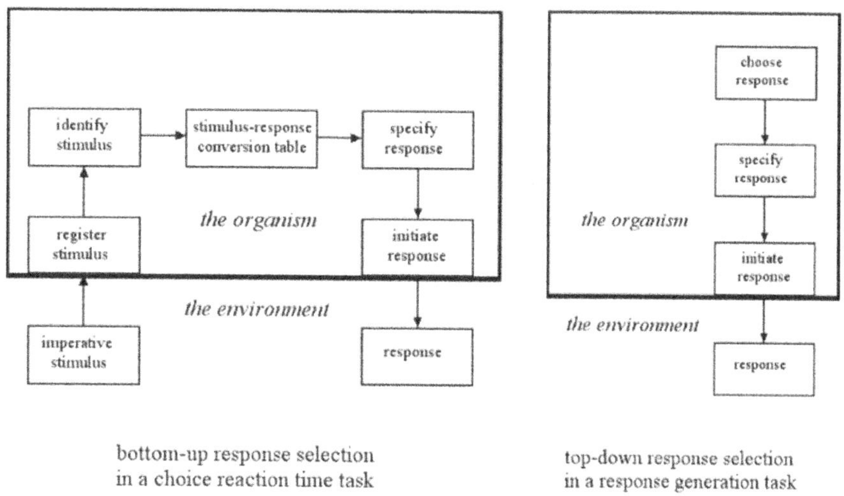


*Figure 8.1* Bottom-up and top-down processes in cognitive tasks.

region exists (S. Zeki, personal communication). Secondly, if we think about what is at the top in cognitive terms we are confronted with the problem of what or who makes the response selection. Presumably it is the much-maligned homunculus. Hence, the logical consequence of the representation in Fig. 8.1 is that the homunculus must be located in a place in the brain that has only output and no inputs. This place is a bit like the country east of the Sun and west of the Moon. It is therefore no wonder that the dominant trend within cognitive science has been to declare the homunculus as real as the hobbit or other fairy tale creatures.

We believe, however, that the problem with the homunculus may be conceptual rather than ontological, i.e., the blame may be on idealized models of cognitive function such as those depicted in Fig. 8.1 rather than on that unreal homunculus arising from it. In the following we will examine in some detail recent brain imaging experiments on top-down control of action. We shall argue that models such as that depicted in Fig. 8.1 will not suffice to account for how the observed pattern of action is installed in the first place. We will suggest that a notion of 'shared scripts for action' may remedy some of these shortcomings. This will allow us to create a space of asylum for a homunculus that is, at the same time, more stupid, and somewhat less omnipotent and consistent than the one implicated in Fig. 8.1.

## Cross-species neural correlates of action

In a recent article in *Science,* Nakahara, Hayashi, Konishi, and Miyashita (2002) described a remarkable experiment. Not only had the authors succeeded in training two macaque monkeys to perform a simplified version of the Wisconsin card sorting task (WCST), they had also managed to familiarize the animals with all the unpleasantness of a running MR scanner – the noise, the fixation of the head, the limited field of view etc. – to such a degree that the monkeys could perform the task while undergoing a fMRI examination.

As is probably well known, the experimental participant in a WCST is presented with cards that display symbols in specific shapes, colors, numbers, etc., such as three green circles, or four yellow triangles. The task of the participant is to sort the cards into different piles without knowing the criteria for a correct sorting. They are given feed-back about the correctness of their sort after each card has been placed, and once they have discovered the sorting rule, e.g., that the cards should be sorted by color, the sorting dimension is changed by the experimenter, and the participant then has to discover the new rule, e.g., that the cards are to be sorted by shape. Throughout decades of research (Milner, 1963; Monchi, Petrides, Petre, Worsley, & Dagher, 2001; Stuss et al., 2000), the WCST has been established as a standard cognitive test that targets participants' abilities to switch between cognitive sets, and a poor performance in the test can be a key neuropsychological indicator of a putative prefrontal lesion. The control of action needed in this task is clearly top-down.

Nakahara et al. trained monkeys to perform a computerized version of the WCST where a target card was displayed on the computer screen, followed by three cards that differed on two dimensions (color and shape of symbols). The monkeys were then supposed to select one of the three cards that reflected the current sorting criteria (color or shape). Feedback was provided by a visual display on the screen and a liquid reward for the correct choice.

The main effect of the set-shifting component of the WCST was found in the ventrolateral prefrontal cortex bilaterally, (see Fig. 8.2A) at the ventral end of the inferior ramus of the arcuate sulcus. Subsequently, the same experiment was conducted on 10 human volunteers – the only difference being that they were not given a liquid reward following a correct answer. In these participants, the main activation was found in the posterior part of the bilateral inferior frontal sulcus (Brodmann's area 44/45, see Fig. 8.2B). This activation site has also been found in other studies on the WCST. Nakahara et al. argue that the main sites of activation in the two species, the Brodmann area 44/45 in humans and the Petrides and Pandya area 44/45 in macaque monkeys have a similar cytoarchitecture. The authors, hence, suggest that they may be considered both functional and anatomical homologues.

We think that the experiment demonstrates two highly interesting findings. The first, and perhaps most obvious, is the elegant demonstration of inter-species functional and anatomical homologues in higher cognitive function. In order to perform

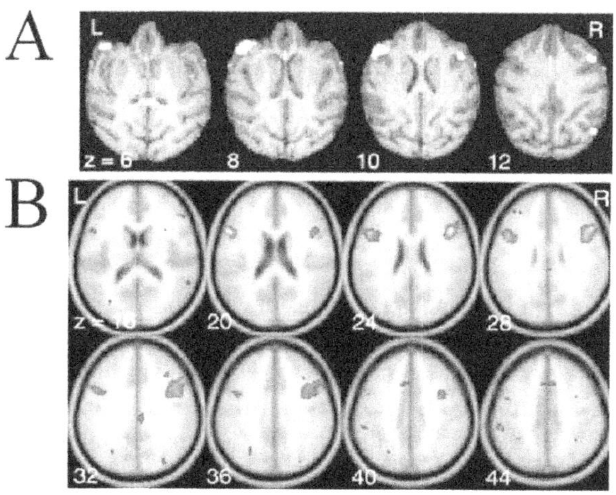


*Figure 8.2* Shift related activations elicited by the Wisconsin card sorting task (WCST) in **A** macaque monkeys and **B** humans. **A** Statistical parametric map (SPM) overlaid on a transverse section of a normalized, structural MR image. The main activations are in the posterior part of the ventrolateral prefrontal cortex bilaterally, approximately at the Petrides and Pandya area 44/45. **B** Main activations are bilaterally in the posterior part of the ventrolateral prefrontal cortex.

Reproduced from (Nakahara et al. 2002)

well in a WCST, the experimental participant – be that human or monkey – must be able to establish, maintain, and alter a particular cognitive set, which can be used as a template for acting in the world. For that they appear to draw on activity in anatomically, ontogenetically, and functionally similar brain regions in the prefrontal cortex. This seems to be a clear case of a 'top-down' control of action in two senses of the metaphor discussed above. It is an 'executive top' that establishes a model for acting in the world, the efficacy of which is continuously monitored, and it is an 'anatomical top', since the main areas of activations seem to take place in very 'top-like' frontal regions of the brain. In this respect, the brain scans reveal no apparent differences between the two species.

The details of the experiment reveal another equally interesting aspect of action control, but this one is not visible from the images depicting activated brains. Although both monkey and man managed to perform very well in the WCST at the time of testing, they had learned it in very different ways. Getting the macaque monkeys to do the trick proficiently in the MRI scanner involved about 1 year of operant training. Compared with this very arduous process, the human volunteers simply did the task according to the verbal instruction, with a relatively short (30–60 min) period of familiarization training before the MRI scan (Yashushi Miyashita, personal information). These differences are noteworthy in that they point to two very different ways of establishing similar – in terms of behavior and brain activation – patterns of control of action.

The human case may appear trivial. As a task, WCST is interesting because the important rule is a meta-rule, i.e., a rule about a rule (cf. Bateson's 1972 concept of meta-communication as 'communication about communication'). This meta-rule, which the participant has to understand in order to act correctly, says that 'the (meta-) rule of the game is that the rules (of sorting) keep changing.' In later versions of the task the participant gets this meta-rule from the verbal instructions. Once he has understood it, he knows how to interpret that stream of stimulus-response-feedback, which the actual experiment consists of, as instances of the underlying rule. This is clearly a case of top-down control, since this understanding of the situation allows the participant to act correctly – ideally even on the first experimental run.

Aspects of the 'top-down' metaphor break down at this point. As shown in Fig. 8.1, bottom-up processes are usually considered to be driven 'from the outside' by the sensory inputs, while top-down processes are driven 'from the inside' by mental processes. However, the 'verbal instructions' that enable the human volunteers to perform well in the task, fail to fit this scheme. The instructions are clearly coming 'from the outside' and are mediated via the senses, i.e., bottom-up, and yet their main purpose is to allow for the very rapid establishment of a consistent model for how the participants are to interpret and respond in the situation, i.e., top-down. We suggest that the solution to this conceptual problem is to factor the experimenter into the model of the control of action in the experiment.

The purpose of the instructions in this experiment and in general is that the experimental participant and the experimenter come to share a common understanding of the nature of the experiment and of the intended stimulus-response

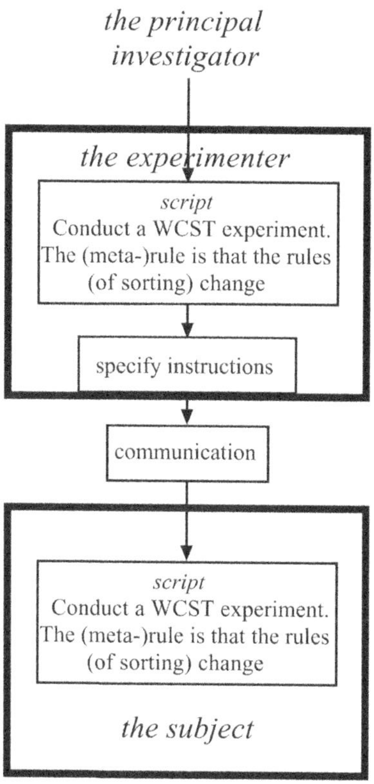


*Figure 8.3* Communicating the WCST script through a 'top-top' exchange.

relationship (Roepstorff, 2001). We have suggested elsewhere (Jack & Roepstorff, 2002) that this process can be described as a 'sharing of scripts' between the experimenter and the participant (Fig. 8.3). In this model, the 'top' of the 'top-down' process is no longer a hypothetical place of outputs, without inputs (Fig. 8.1). Instead, the origin of the 'executive top' employed in the WCST is outside the brain of the participant, namely in the mind of the experimenter. We call this interaction between experimenter and experimental participant a 'top-top' exchange of scripts. Of course, the sharing of scripts depends upon instructions communicated through visual or acoustic signals. However, once this communication is successfully accomplished participant and experimenter have common, shared representations about the nature of the task (see Pickering & Garrod, 2004 for a similar argument about aligned representations in successful dialogue). These shared representations largely concern top-level aspects of control, i.e., the goals of the task rather than low-level aspects specifying precisely how movements should be made.

At this level of analysis, the contrast with the monkey, which must go through 1 year of operant training, is dramatic. We don't know much about what goes on in the monkey's mind during that period. Judging from the amount of training needed, it seems reasonable to believe that establishing an understanding of the experimental situation, which allows the monkey to act proficiently and to be rewarded at an 'acceptable' level – whatever that means for a monkey – must be a tough process. However, judging from the performance at the time of scanning, which was comparable to that of the human participants, it seems likely that the end-result is that the monkey comes to enact a script with strong affinities to the experimenter's script of the WCST: The (meta-) rule is that the rule (of sorting) constantly changes. The finding by Nakahara et al., that there were anatomically similar brain activations in humans and monkeys, supports this interpretation. In this respect, the two experimental scenarios are similar. But whereas the human participant receives this script directly from the experimenter in a 'top-top' exchange, the monkey has to reconstruct this script solely via the concrete stimuli and rewards offered to it. It happens as the monkey, based on the previous understandings of the situation, reacts to the reward responses that the experimenter dispenses. We propose to call this set of interactions a top-down–bottom-up process of synchronizing scripts (Fig. 8.4).

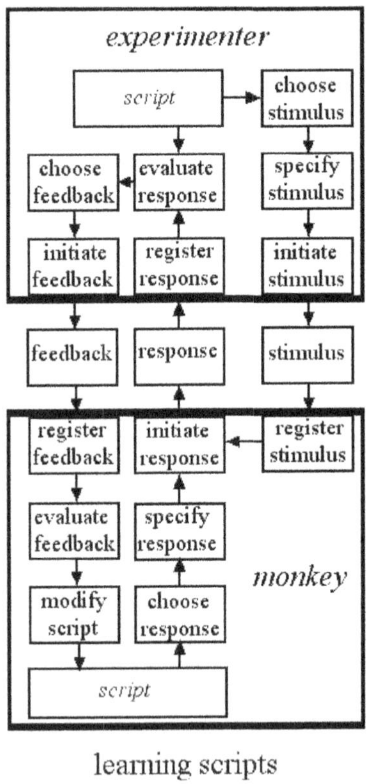


*Figure 8.4* Learning the WCST script via top-down-bottom-up feedback.

In our use of the 'script' metaphor, we have been inspired by the world of theatre; by the relation between the performance of an actor enacting a particular role on a stage and the underlying script (Jack & Roepstorff, 2002). It seems likely to us that both monkeys and humans in the experiment by Nakahara et al. came to share aspects of the experimenter's script for the experimental situation. However, the details of the experimental setup suggest that there are also important differences in the scripts enacted by the two species. The human participant knows that he is taking part in an experiment and that this requires that he should expose himself to the somewhat unpleasant environment of an MR scanner without complaining and without moving (Roepstorff, 2002). This contrasts with the experimental procedure for the monkey where the head is fixed with an implanted head holder. The feed-back structure in the experiment is also very different between the species, the monkeys are provided with liquid rewards when they sort correctly, while the human participants do not need rewards, but only visual cues indicating whether they are right or wrong.

As with the differences between the 'top-top' and the 'top-down-bottom-up' exchange of scripts, this suggests that there is a much greater overlap between the script of the experimenter and that of the human participant than between the script of the experimenter and that of the monkey. The differences can be summarized by saying that in the human case, it is expected that experimenter and participant come to share an interpretive frame for the context of the experiment, for the interpretation of the stimuli, and for the proper plans for action. Based on the article by Nakahara et al., we have no way of estimating the actual degree of script sharing between the experimenter and the monkey. But we may hypothesize that the ease with which an experimental set up with humans can be established points to one of the most interesting aspects of human perception, cognition and control of action: The almost automatic sharing of contexts, interpretive frames, and schemes for action.

## The script in 'willed action' tasks

We have discussed the role of scripts in the 'top-down' control of experiments, demonstrating that what is at the 'top' of most experiments is an interaction between the participant and the experimenter. Often it is the experimenter who is at the top in the sense that it is he who determines what the participant will do. We shall now return to a consideration of 'willed action' tasks and see whether the concept of scripts can also help us to understand top-down control in these tasks.

We believe that willed action tasks are extreme examples of top-down control. This is because the instructions are inadequate to determine what the participant should do. In effect the experimenter is saying to the participant, 'I am not going to tell you what to do. You must decide for yourself.' This is why we characterize such tasks as depending upon will. But by characterizing them in this way we seem unavoidably to introduce a homunculus into our cognitive model. At some point in the model an action has to be selected (see Fig. 8.1) without any input from the external environment. So something, a homunculus, has to be doing the choosing.

This idea of something that selects actions of its own will is fundamental to our concept of agency. If we observe that the actions of some creature are entirely predetermined by forces or signals in the environment then we do not consider that creature to be an agent. On the other hand, if we see behavior that is not simply responsive to changes in the environment we classify the creature as an agent. This applies to something as simple as a dot moving on a screen. If unexpected changes in speed or direction are observed we rate the dot as being more like an agent (Tremoulet & Feldman, 2000). A fundamental feature of our world is that it contains a class of things (agents) that can choose actions for themselves. It is also fundamental that each of us is one of those kinds of things. Beyond the consideration of motives in everyday life we do not concern ourselves too much with the precise mechanisms by which these agents can freely select actions.

So when we instruct a someone to perform a willed action task we are effectively saying, 'Be an agent. Choose the responses for yourself.' But, of course, this instruction has to be unpacked and a script generated. To be like an agent we have to select our responses in such a way that an observer cannot easily predict what our next response will be. And the best way to do this is to choose the next response at random. In random number generation tasks, this instruction is made explicit, 'generate a series of random numbers as if you are taking them out of a hat.' The pattern of brain activity associated with explicit random number generation and willed action tasks is strikingly similar (Frith et al., 1991; Jahanshahi, Dirnberger, Fuller, & Frith, 2000). We believe it likely that, when participants are asked to select responses 'at will' they assume a script that requires them to respond randomly. This analysis seems to imply that the participant in a willed action experiment is not being a free agent, but is simulating being an agent by choosing responses at random.

But how do we generate a sequence of random responses? We could put numbers into a hat, shake it, pick out one number without looking and then repeat the process. Indeed, this is how the task was explained to participants in the random number generation experiment by Jahanshahi et al. (2000). Unfortunately, we can't do this mentally. We may have a mental image of the hat with the numbers in it, but it is hard to imagine picking out a piece of paper without knowing what number we are going to find on it and then being surprised by the result. So a different strategy has to be used based on a more complex script concerned with what we believe random sequences are like. Some of these beliefs are correct: Each number should occur equally often. Others are false (the gamblers fallacy): The same number won't occur twice in succession, numbers will not come in sequential order (3 after 4 or 4 after 3). These rules for randomness are used to constrain response selection in each trial. If I have chosen 1, 4, and 7 so far, in the next trial I must choose a different number that isn't 6 or 8. Also I had better break away from the upward trend and not choose 9. This leaves me with just 2, 3, or 5. Thus, even in a willed action task, most of the work in selecting responses is not made by the participant (i.e., the homunculus), but by the implicit script imposed by the experimenter. Furthermore, once the acceptable responses have been narrowed down to a few possibilities, it doesn't really matter which of those remaining possibilities are chosen. Environmental triggers could be used to make this final choice, leaving nothing for the homunculus to do. If a choice must still be made, whatever does the choosing does not have to be smart.

We have argued elsewhere (Nathaniel-James & Frith, 2002) that the activity observed in the dorsolateral prefrontal cortex (DLPFC) during willed action and random number generation tasks is not associated with will (i.e., endogenous selection), but with the specification of which responses are acceptable and which are inappropriate given the script associated with the task (Fig. 8.5). When the cognitive load becomes too high, as in dual task situations, activity in the DLPFC is reduced and inappropriate responses are produced. Damage to the DLPFC has similar effects. Thus, this region of the frontal cortex that has long been associated with top-down control, would better characterized as having a role in the implementation of scripts.

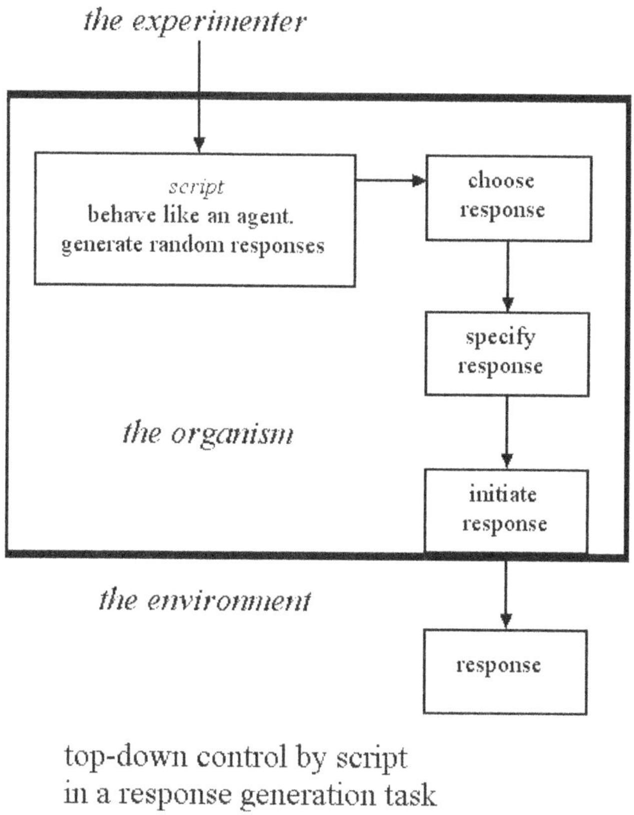


*Figure 8.5* Top-down control by script of a willed action task.

We have analyzed willed action tasks in some detail in order to demonstrate that even for these tasks, top-down control is better thought of in terms of control by the experimenter who in turn is controlled by scientific knowledge provided by his predecessors and peers. The difficulty with these tasks is that this control is very indirect. A lot of work has to be done by the participant to unpack the script implicit in the instruction to 'select the response for yourself.' The participant has to work out what the experimenter means by this instruction. The instruction, 'press the left button when you see the green light' is much more straightforward. It takes a long time to train monkeys to perform top-down tasks like the WCST precisely because monkeys cannot be told – and do not have the capacity to work out quickly – what the experimenter has in mind. Once the script has been understood through verbal instruction or trial and error learning, similar brain areas appear to be used by monkeys and humans to implement the script. But these are probably not the areas that are needed for understanding the script in the first place.

Performance of top-down tasks depends on an intimate interaction between experimenter and participant in which they successfully share a script for the performance of the task. Performance of the task is a joint enterprise, but it is only rarely described as such in the cognitive literature. Outside the laboratory this strange distinction between participant and experimenter no longer holds and the shared nature of our endeavors is much more obvious. Once the analytical attention is shifted from the actual performance of the participant during the experiment to the 'setting up' of the experiment, the inherently shared aspects of the cognitive experiment become very apparent (Roepstorff, 2002, 2003, 2004). This approach marks a change of focus from the classical object of cognitive neuroscience, the enacting of the experimental script, to the standard object of analysis of ethnography and anthropology, the construction and framing of the performance (Jack & Roepstorff, 2002; Roepstorff, 2001). In a sense, it is – like the WCST discussed above – a shift from a primary level to a secondary or meta-level.

We have recently conducted a script-based brain imaging experiment into the ascription of agency that may serve to pinpoint this distinction.

## Mentalizing and the experience of agency

Gallagher, Jack, Roepstorff, and Frith (2002) report a PET experiment where the effective contrast was established by a computerized version of the game rock-paper-scissors (RPS). In the two main conditions, participants were led to believe that they played against either a human opponent or a computer that followed simple rules. In fact, apart from two short lead-in and lead-out sequences before and after the actual scanning window, they played against a random sequence.

Two types of data were collected from the experiment. Analysis of the cerebral blood-flow using PET showed a single area in the paracingulate cortex that was more strongly activated when participants believed they were playing against a person. No brain regions were differentially activated when participants believed they were playing against the computer. Retrospective reports, obtained by semi-structured interviews after the experiment, all described phenomenal differences between the two conditions. Briefly, in the conditions where participants believed they were playing against a person, they all described experiences of an intentional interaction with the opponent using words like guessing, double-bluffing, discovering individual strategies, and seeing the opponent's moves as 'something you can go along with.' In other words, all participants mentalized the imaginary opponent (Gallagher & Frith, 2003). In contrast, the computer was mainly described by participants as either random or rule-bound. We have argued (Jack & Roepstorff, 2002) that as the stimuli during the scanning window were identical in the two conditions, the significant contrast in the objective brain scanning measurements and the coherent differences in the phenomenal subjective reports were driven by differences in the script. These were mainly established via the instructions for the experiment and the prior knowledge the participants had of playing the game and of interacting with persons and computers.

We believe that the RPS experiment is a somewhat extreme case of top-top control of action in a cognitive experiment. As with the experiments on random number generation and the WCST, discussed above, the brain activation elicited is a result of the implementation of a particular script. In this experiment we take the observed brain activation to be related to that particular attitude or stance that the participant assumes in interpreting the stimuli and in determining his responses, rather than to the actual execution of the response. Adopting the script of playing against a person rather than the script of playing against a computer requires that the participant adopts an intentional stance towards his opponent. In other words, in this condition, not only must the participant share the script proposed by the experimenter, he must also think about the script adopted by his opponent.

In the post-experiment interviews, none of our participants expressed doubts that they had played a person or a computer. In a very interesting comment, one of our participants even reflected on the understanding of the experiment in the following way: "I clearly felt someone was there [when playing the person]. It is very difficult to see from the pattern [of the opponent's responses]. I [am] not sure that I would have had that sense, had I not known that I was not playing the computer." This suggests that once a particular stance has been taken, both the perceptual qualities and the actual button presses followed, in a sense without reflection (Fig. 8.6). There is nothing in the post-experiment interviews that speaks against this interpretation. Perhaps more anecdotally, it is also in accordance with the post-hoc reflections of the first experimental participant, who happens to be one of the authors of this article.

We consider that this experiment shows two interesting aspects of 'control of action.' Firstly, participants are in an almost trivial sense in control of their own actions during the experiment, nobody tells them which button to press when playing the computer or when playing the person. Yet their understanding of the

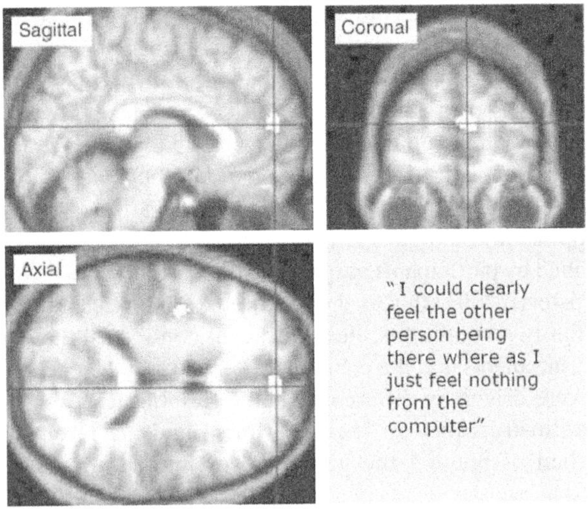


*Figure 8.6* Typical phenomenal report and region of maximum activation in the paracingulate cortex elicited when participants 'take the intentional stance' in the RPS experiment.

Redrawn from (Gallagher & Frith, 2003), images display group data mapped onto a template brain

situation, which motivates their actions, is largely governed by the frame of interpretation provided by the experimenter. If the participant distrusts this, the experiment is likely to fail. In other words, the experiment only works because the framing of it is not made explicit. Had the participants been involved in a meta-communication about the experiment prior to the examination: *We tell you that you play a person, but in fact, you play a random sequence,* we would have been surprised to find any activations.

Secondly, the experience of agency in the participant is closely linked to his understanding of agency in the opponent. Judging from the interviews, interacting with a person seems to invoke almost prototypical understanding of human agency as something that is neither rule-bound nor random. The actions of the other is something you may go along with and, during the interaction, you may develop an understanding of their particular characteristics. It is uncertain whether it is actually possible to learn to identify these psychological traits, or whether they really exist. Computer simulations of RPS interactions suggest that they may develop into Hamiltonian chaos situations, where the trajectory may be simple or complex, depending on the initial conditions (Sato, Akiyama, & Farmer, 2002). However, as argued by Sato et al. (2002), nothing indicates that actual players choose the 'rational' strategy, i.e., to play each move randomly. Theoretically, this strategy has the advantage that there is no strategy that can beat it, but the disadvantage that it cannot beat any strategy. Furthermore, as discussed above, it is probably impossible to implement random choices in a human mind anyway. Instead, the default option seems to be to assume that the opponent, like oneself, is an agent with all that entails in terms of drives, motives, strategies, and aspirations. And it is this 'homunculus' that forms the template for action in the game.

## 'Top-top' interactions, parallel processes, and consciousness

The problem about standard representations of top-down functions such as depicted in Fig. 8.1 was that the ultimate source of control, 'the top,' becomes a free-floating independent homunculus. We believe that one important lesson to be drawn from the studies on 'willed action' and on 'mentalizing' discussed in this paper is that although the experimental participants in both situations report that they are in control of their actions, further analysis demonstrates that, in fact, both the actual patterns of behavior and the phenomenal experiences are influenced by top-top interactions on one hand, and by underlying, unattended processes on the other. This understanding does not go down very well with a notion of executive control by an omnipotent homunculus, but it may open up another interpretation.

Even when actions are determined by some shared script we still have the experience that there is something in us that makes endogenous choices and thus we continue to be an agent. Even when brain events run so fast that they cannot be attended to in real time, we still have the experience that they are ours. In contrast with the homunculus assumed in representations such as Fig. 8.1, it seems that the actual capacities of the homunculus are, in fact, very limited. It is constantly left unaware of the actual links between perception and action, and it is constantly being overwhelmed by clever tricks imposed by other people. And yet it may be in relation to an entity like this that basic understandings of agency, of self, and of other are being linked. Instead of explaining the little man away, we propose to grant him some mental asylum. Perhaps we need this little virtual person not only to preserve the idea that we are in control of our own actions, but also to preserve the idea that we are stable selves, unchanged by all the influences thrust upon us by others.

We suggest that a useful conceptual space for a notion of the homunculus may be located at the nexus between those many parallel processes that the brain is constantly engaged in, and the input from other people, of top-top interactions. In this understanding, the role of a putative homunculus becomes one of a dual gate keeper: On one hand, between those many parallel processes and the attended few, on the other hand between one mind and another.

Wegner (2002) has claimed that the sense of being an autonomous self is an illusion. As we have argued above, the feeling of control and consistency may indeed seem illusionary from an outside perspective. However, from the inside perspective of the individual, it appears to be a very important anchor point both for action and perception. If we did not have the experience of this inner homunculus that is in control of our actions, our sense of self would dissolve into the culture that surrounds us.

A more important feature of this awareness is that it puts us in touch with other agents. It is this aspect that has been largely ignored in discussions of the neural correlates of consciousness. This is perhaps the most important message of the experiment reported by Nakahara et al. (2002). Being in touch with others, sharing frames of interpretations and models for action through 'top-top' interactions, is a prerequisite for setting up cognitive experiments fast and efficiently. Indeed, this ability appears to be piggybacking on a much more general human cognitive competence. We believe that humans differ from other animals most in the possession of a complex of abilities that allow for 'top-top' interactions. Within social anthropology, it is old hat that culture, understood as that which can be shared and exchanged, is an integral part of human nature. This implies that it may be difficult to separate 'social cognition' from 'nonsocial cognition' since so much of human attention and cognition is directed to, and informed by other people, and the cognitive experiment is but one interesting special case of this general condition (Roepstorff, 2001). It is, however, only recently that models of human cognition within a biological and evolutionary framework appear to converge on similar understandings (e.g., Deacon, 1997, Tomasello & Rakoczy 2003).

We are arguing that top-down control is not, after all, only control by the 'self,' but instead it is control mediated by other minds and more generally by culture. In the case of the experimenter the script is provided by the community of scientists who publish in his field (Fleck, 1979; Roepstorff, 2002). While bottom-up control is exerted by the physical world, top-down control is exerted by the mental world. Typically actions under top-down control are determined by considerations like, 'what does he want me to do?' Or 'what is the appropriate thing to do in this situation?' An important feature of top-down control is that we are aware of selecting our actions, whereas bottom-up control can often be achieved without awareness. This is where the self comes in; because we are aware of selecting an action we feel that we are acting as an autonomous agent. Even in an experimental setting, we could have chosen to do something different such as playing tricks with the experimenter (Roepstorff, 2001).

Although we believe there are good reasons to maintain a 'weak' analytical notion of a homunculus, we do not know exactly in which part of the brain to grant it physical asylum. It has been argued that an 'attentional homunculus' should be conceived of as a parietal-frontal system rather than of one particular place (Nobre, 2001). We do not disagree with this. However, it is tempting to suggest that one putative anchor point for a homunculus, which serves as reference for the experience, ascription and detection of agency, is somewhere between the anterior part of the cingulate gyrus and the paracingulate gyrus. This area constantly turns up in a large variety of brain imaging studies related to attention to action, to the self, and to others (Frith, 2002; Gallagher & Frith, 2003; McCabe, Houser, Ryan, Smith, & Trouard, 2001; Vogeley et al., 2001). We have argued above that attention to action, to the self and to others can be thought of in terms of sharing scripts. One component of script sharing seems to be the ability to take the perspective of another person. Indeed, in a recent brain imaging study, which studied the contrast between simulating the perspective of another person and the self perspective, this region was activated (Ruby & Decety, 2001). There is furthermore some evidence that damage to this area can create a disorder known as 'environmental dependency syndrome' (Lhermitte, 1986). Actions of patients suffering from this condition appear to be determined by highly stereotyped and common scripts, which, almost bypassing 'free will', appear to be triggered by objects present in the immediate environment, e.g., seeing a bed in the neurologist's flat prompts the patient to take off his clothes and go to sleep.

These findings all appear in accordance with a model of action control where neuronal activity in the anterior cingulate/paracingulate may serve as one anchor point for the ascription of agency and script both in the self and in others. For those who fancy evolutionary 'just so' stories it may, furthermore, be relevant that certain parts of the anterior cingulate appear to have undergone major morphological changes in the recent evolution of pongids and homids, including the development of an unusual type of large spindle shaped projection neurons (Nimchinsky et al., 1999). Whether these have anything to do with the asylum of the homunculus is, however, highly speculative.

## Acknowledgements

The authors acknowledge helpful suggestions from Jakob Hohwy, Anthony Jack, and two anonymous reviewers. Andreas Roepstorff was supported by a grant from the Danish National Research Foundation to the Center for Functionally Integrative Neuroscience. Chris Frith is supported by the Wellcome Trust and the James S McDonnell Foundation.

## References

Bateson, G. (1972). *Steps to an ecology of mind.* New York: Ballantine.

Deacon, T. W. (1997). *The symbolic species. The co-evolution of language and brain.* New York: Norton.

Deiber, M.-P., Passingham, R. E., Colebatch, J. G., Friston, K. J., Nixon, P. D., & Frackowiak, R. S. J. (1991). Cortical areas and the selection of movement. *Experimental Brain Research, 84,* 393–402.

Fleck, L. (1979). *Genesis and development of a scientific fact.* Chicago: Chicago University Press.

Frith, C. (2002). Attention to action and awareness of other minds. *Consciousness and Cognition, 11,* 481–487.

Frith, C., & Dolan, R. J. (1997). Brain mechanisms associated with top-down processes in perception. *Philosophical Transactions of the Royal Society in London Biological Sciences, 352,* 1221–1230.

Frith, C. D., Friston, K. J., Liddle, P. F., & Frackowiak, R. S. J. (1991). Willed action and the prefrontal cortex in man: a study with PET. *Proceedings of the Royal Society of London, Series B, 244,* 241–246.

Gallagher, H., Jack, A. I., Roepstorff, A., & Frith, C. D. (2002). Imagining the intentional stance in a competitive game. *NeuroImage, 16,* 814–821.

Gallagher, H. L., & Frith, C. D. (2003). Functional imaging of 'theory of mind'. *Trends in Cognitive Science, 7,* 77–83.

Jack, A. I., & Roepstorff, A. (2002). Introspection and cognitive brain mapping: from stimulus-response to script-report. *Trends in Cognitive Sciences, 6,* 333–339.

Jahanshahi, M., Dirnberger, G., Fuller, R., & Frith, C. D. (2000). The role of the dorsolateral prefrontal cortex in random number generation: a study with positron emission tomography. *NeuroImage, 12,* 713–725.

Lakoff, G., & Johnson, M. (1980). *Metaphors we live by.* Chicago: Chicago University Press.

Leonard, J. A. (1959). Tactual choice reactions. I. *Quarterly Journal of Experimental Psychology, 11,* 76–83.

Lhermitte, F. (1986). Human autonomy and the frontal lobes. II. Patient behavior in complex and social situations: the 'environmental dependency syndrome'. *Annals of Neurology, 19,* 335–343.

McCabe, K., Houser, D., Ryan, L., Smith, V., & Trouard, T. (2001). A functional imaging study of cooperation in two-person reciprocal exchange. *Proceedings of the National Academy of Sciences USA, 98,* 11832–11835.

Milner, B. (1963). Effects of brain lessons on card sorting. *Archives of Neurology, 9,* 90–100.

Monchi, O., Petrides, M., Petre, V., Worsley, K., & Dagher, A. (2001). Wisconsin card sorting revisited: distinct neural circuits participating in different stages of the task identified by event-related functional magnetic resonance imaging. *Journal of Neuroscience, 21,* 7733–7741.

Nakahara, K., Hayashi, T., Konishi, S., & Miyashita, Y. (2002). Functional MRI of macaque monkeys performing a cognitive set-shifting task. *Science, 295,* 1532–1536.

Nathaniel-James, D. A., & Frith, C. D. (2002). The role of the dorsolateral prefrontal cortex: evidence from the effects of contextual constraint in a sentence completion task. *NeuroImage, 16,* 1094–1102.

Nimchinsky, E. A., Gilissen, E., Allman, J. M., Perl, D. P., Erwin, J. M., & Hof, P. R. (1999). A neuronal morphologic type unique to humans and great apes. *Proceedings of the National Academy of Sciences USA, 96,* 5268–5273.

Nobre, A. C. (2001). The attentive homunculus: now you see it, now you don't. *Neuroscience and Biobehavioral Reviews, 25,* 477–496.

Pickering, M., & Garrod, S. (2004). Toward a mechanistic psychology of dialogue. *Behavioral Brain Sciences, 27.02,* 169–190.

Roepstorff, A. (2001). Brains in scanners: an Umwelt of cognitive neuroscience. *Semiotica, 134,* 747–765.

Roepstorff, A. (2002). Transforming subjects into objectivity. An ethnography of knowledge in a brain imaging laboratory. *FOLK, Journal of the Danish Ethnographic Society, 44,* 145–170.

Roepstorff, A. (2003). A double dissociation in twentieth century psychology? *Journal of Consciousness Studies, 10,* 62–67.

Roepstorff, A. (2004). Mapping brain mappers: An Ethnographic Coda. In R. S. Frackowiak et al. (Eds.), *Human brain function* (2nd ed.), 1105–1117. Amsterdam: Elsevier.

Ruby, P., & Decety, J. (2001) Effect of subjective perspective taking during simulation of action: a PET investigation of agency. *Nature Neuroscience, 4,* 546–550.

Sato, Y., Akiyama, E., & Farmer, J. D. (2002). Chaos in learning a simple two-person game. *Proceedings of the National Academy of Sciences USA, 99,* 4748–4751.

Stuss, D. T., Levine, B., Alexander, M. P., Hong, J., Palumbo, C., Hamer, L., Murphy, K. J., & Izukawa, D. (2000). Wisconsin card sorting test performance in patients with focal frontal and posterior brain damage: effects of lesion location and test structure on separable cognitive processes. *Neuropsychologia, 38*, 388–402.

Tomasello, M., & Rakoczy, H. (2003). What makes human cognition unique? From individual to shared individuality. *Mind & Language*, 18, 121–147.

Tremoulet, P. D., & Feldman, J. (2000). Perception of animacy from the motion of a single object. *Perception, 29*, 943–951.

Vogeley, K., Bussfeld, P., Newen, A., Herrmann, S., Happe, F., Falkai, P., et al. (2001). Mind reading: neural mechanisms of theory of mind and self-perspective. *NeuroImage, 14*, 170–181.

Wegner, D. M. (2002). *The illusion of conscious will.* Cambridge, MA: MIT Press.

# 9 Action, agency and responsibility

*Chris D. Frith*

## 1 Introduction

Marc Jeannerod was a master in the design of experiments. In particular he had the ability to devise paradigms that seem on the surface very simple, but have the power to address deep problems about the mind. I am thinking, in particular, of his studies of reaching and grasping (e.g., Castiello, Paulignan, & Jeannerod, 1991) and motor imagery (e.g., Jeannerod & Decety, 1995). In this essay I will consider just one of these elegant experiments and draw out some of its implications for our understanding of agency. I will also explore the relevance of our understanding of agency for the problem of free will. The problem of will was one of Marc's major concerns throughout his career. The French subtitle of one of his early books was 'The physiology of will' (Jeannerod, 1983).

The particular problem I will address arises from the conflict between the vivid experience of being in control of our actions and the doctrine of determinism which concludes that this experience must be an illusion. I will explore the cultural origins of our experience of responsibility and suggest that the mechanisms that underlie this experience are compatible with determinism. Furthermore, our experience of responsibility plays a vital role in the maintenance of social cohesion.

## 2 The experience of action

The study reported by Fourneret and Jeannerod (1998) was the culmination of a decade long series of studies on the visual control of action (e.g., Pelisson, Prablanc, Goodale, & Jeannerod, 1986 see also O'Shea, et al., 2014). In this study volunteers had to use their arm to move a stylus across a horizontal graphics tablet from a position close to the body to a target about 20 cm away. They could not see their arm, but only a cursor that was controlled by their arm movement. The trick in this study was that the movement of the cursor was sometimes distorted. When the stylus was moved straight ahead the cursor on the screen might deviate 10° to the right. Thus, in order to make the cursor move straight ahead, the volunteer had to make an arm movement that deviated 10° to the left. The striking result was that subjects seemed to be unaware of these distortions. They corrected their movements to allow for the distortions, but seemed unaware that they were making these corrections. For example, if they were asked to repeat the movement they had just made, then they made a straight-ahead movement and not the deviating movement they had just made, even in the absence of distracting visual feedback. The authors conclude, 'These results suggest that normal subjects are not aware of signals generated by their own movements'.

Many other experiments have confirmed this observation and shown that movements can occur, not only without awareness, but also without intentional control (e.g., Pisella et al., 2000). Such results led the philosopher Metzinger (2006) to say that the phenomenology of volition, 'is thin and it is evasive'. So what is it about our actions that we are aware of?

While we are not aware of the details of our actions or the sensations associated with them, we are vividly aware of being in control. The doctrine of determinism, however, states that every event is necessitated by past history and conditions according to the laws of nature. From this point of view all our actions are also predetermined and so our experience of being in control is an illusion. The implication is that our belief in free will is also an illusion, a supposition supported by many, from Hume (1758) to Wegner (2003). Why then is our belief in free will so strong?

Some believe that it is our experience of being an agent that leads to a belief in free will. Spinoza (1677) said, 'Experience teaches us no less clearly than reason, that men believe themselves to be free, simply because they are conscious of their actions, and unconscious of the causes whereby those actions are determined'. Recent experimental studies are beginning to reveal, firstly, the cognitive basis of the experience of being an agent and, secondly, to hint as to why the belief that we are control of our actions may be important, even if it is an illusion.

However, before I consider these developments, I suggest that it might be more helpful to think about our actions in terms of responsibility rather than free will. Our culture makes an important distinction between voluntary and involuntary behaviour and also between outcomes that are intended and those that are not intended. We are not usually held responsible for acts that were involuntary or outcomes that were unintended. Free will and responsibility are closely related and many legal systems require that we can only be held fully responsible for those actions we have freely chosen. This is sometimes referred to as moral responsibility. However, the relationship between the moral and the legal is never perfect. Actions can be legal, while still being widely considered to be immoral. Nevertheless, the attribution of responsibility has an important function in society and has a major impact on our lives.

So what is it about our experience that makes us feel responsible for our actions? This is not a new question. Hellenistic philosophers, such as Epicurus, picked out two critical components. The first is the feeling of being an agent; it was I that caused the outcome (Τήν ἐξ ἑαυτοῦ αἰ τίαν; the cause from me), rather than someone or something else (Bobzien, 2006). The second is the feeling that I could have chosen otherwise. This is also the basis for the experience of regret. 'For it is on the grounds that it was possible for us also not to have chosen and not to have done this that we feel regret' (On Fate: Alexander of Aphrodisias, see Bobzien, 1998).

## *2.1 The feeling of agency*

In a series of elegant experiments, Patrick Haggard and colleagues have demonstrated the phenomenon of *intentional binding,* which is probably fundamental to the experience of agency (Haggard, Clark, & Kalogeras, 2002). In a typical experiment, participants press a button with a tone being heard 250 ms later. Using the paradigm introduce by Libet, Gleason, Wright, and Pearl (1983) participants are asked after each trial to indicate either when they pressed the button, or when they heard the tone. The times reported, which we might call *mental times,* are systematically shifted from the associated physical times. The time of pressing the button is perceived to be later, and the time of hearing the tone is perceived to be earlier. In other words, the interval between pressing the button and hearing the tone is smaller in mental time than in physical time. The action is bound closer to its outcome.

The critical result, however, is that this binding of action to outcome only occurs when the action is voluntary and deliberate. When the same finger movement is involuntary, having been caused by magnetic stimulation to the motor cortex, then the experienced times of the movement and the tone are pulled apart.

Timing is an example of a strong cue for causation. We perceive causation when an effect occurs shortly after a likely cause. And this perception can be an illusion. If we think of an outcome and then it occurs shortly afterwards we are likely to believe that we caused it even when we did not (Wegner & Wheatley, 1999). On the basis of our expectation before the action and on what occurs after the action the brain creates a perception of agency; of me causing the action. Intentional binding is an objective marker of this experience.

If responsibility is important for our sense of agency we would expect this experience to be enhanced when the outcome of our action has moral consequences. This expectation was confirmed in an experiment by Moretto, Walsh, and Haggard (2011) who found enhanced intentional binding when an action was followed by a moral rather than a merely economic outcome.

The other strong experience associated with agency is regret. Regret has to be distinguished from disappointment. We feel disappointment when the outcome of our action is worse than we expected. We feel regret when we learn that we would have achieved a better outcome if only we had chosen the other action. Regret is strongly linked to agency because, to feel regret, we have to believe that we could have chosen the other action. We feel much less regret if the action was chosen by the majority decision of a group, even though our decision was the same as the majority (Nicolle, Bach, Frith, & Dolan, 2011). We also feel less regret if we chose a habitual action rather than a novel one (Guttentag & Ferrell, 2004). In both the cases the degree of regret goes with the degree of agency.

Of particular interest is the observation that our decisions are affected by the anticipation of regret. We make our choice, not only on the basis of the anticipated outcomes associated with potential actions, but also on the regret we would expect to feel if it turns out that the option not chosen would have been better. This effect can be demonstrated by comparing situations in which the outcomes associated with the unchosen options will be known with situations where they will not be known. For example, when bidding in an auction we might be told that we had lost and also the amount of the winning bid or we might simply be told that we had lost. The former situation has much more potential for regret, if, for example, it turns out that the winning bid was only a little higher than our own. To avoid this anticipated regret people make higher bids when they expect to be told the winning bid (Filiz-Ozbay & Ozbay, 2007).

### *2.2 The experience of agency has social consequences*

The success of social groups depends upon reciprocity and trust. We help others in the expectation that others will help us in the future. The maintenance of cooperation has been studied in the laboratory using trust games. Participants in these games can invest money in the group. The nature of the investment is such that, while each individual loses slightly from such investment, the group as a whole gains. So, if everyone invests, then everyone gains. There is, however, a strong temptation to get a free ride. That is, gaining more by benefitting from the investments of others while not investing oneself. Over time, the appearance of free riders lowers cooperation and everyone in the group suffers (Fehr and Gachter, 2002, #1026). Cooperation can be maintained and even enhanced, however, by allowing sanctions. Participants can pay small amounts to punish, through fines, other members of the group. This punishment is typically applied to free riders. As a result free riding decreases, cooperation is maintained and everyone in the group benefits (Fehr and Gachter, 2002). Furthermore, in the long run, people will choose to be in a group where such sanctions are applied rather than in a group without sanctions (Gürerk, Irlenbusch, & Rockenbach, 2006).

The relevance of all this to the study of agency is the observation that such punishments are only applied to participants who are considered responsible for their actions. Singer et al. (2006) asked participants to award reward and punishments points to players in a trust game. As would be expected people who invested a majority of their stake were rewarded, while those who only invested a very small proportion were punished. However, the participants were told that some of the players were not freely deciding how much to invest, but were simply following written instructions. These players were neither punished, nor rewarded, even though their behaviour was identical to that of the players who made their decisions freely.

This result suggests that the concepts of agency and responsibility are important for determining whether people should be punished or rewarded for their behaviour, which, in turn, has a critical role in maintaining group cooperation and social cohesion. Of course, this idea is not new. The distinction between deliberate, intentional acts and outcomes that are unintended and accidental is at the basis of most legal systems. Furthermore, these systems assume that responsibility is something that emerges during childhood and is uniquely human. Non-human animals are no longer tried in court (Humphrey, 2002) and, below a certain age, children are not considered to be responsible for their actions. However, this minimum age of criminal responsibility varies widely from one legal system to another, even within Europe. For example, in Switzerland it is 7 years, while in Luxembourg it is 18 years (see Hazel, 2008). Some believe that even 18 is too young for full responsibility. The argument here is that the frontal lobes are still not fully mature in adolescence (see e.g., Mackintosh, 2011).

### *2.3 Responsibility and the brain*

What are the neural mechanisms that underlie our experience of action? Why do we need mature frontal lobes to be considered fully responsible for our actions? I have suggested that there are two aspects of the experience of agency. The first is the feeling that I am the cause of some outcome. The second is that I could have done something else. Both of these experiences are critical to the concept of responsibility.

The feeling that I am the cause of an outcome allows us to distinguish between deliberately intended and accidental outcomes. This experience is a form of perception created by binding together expectations, based on intentions and prior beliefs, with sensations associated with the outcome (Moore & Haggard, 2008). But, in addition to the binding together of intention and outcome, we need to make a metacognitive reflection upon the extent to which we are in control of our actions (i.e. a judgement of agency). When people are asked to make judgements about their degree of agency, activity is seen in frontopolar cortex (BA 10, Miele, Wager, Mitchell, & Metcalfe, 2011). Other aspects of metacognition, such as reflecting on the accuracy of our perceptual judgements (confidence), have also been associated with processes associated with frontopolar cortex (Fleming, Weil, Nagy, Dolan, & Rees, 2010).

The feeling that I could have done something different, associated with regret, has also been associated with processes occurring in prefrontal cortex. Patients with lesions to orbital frontal cortex do not seem to experience regret and their behaviour is not influenced by anticipated regret (Camille et al., 2004). In an imaging study anticipation of regret was associated with activity in medial orbitofrontal cortex (Coricelli et al., 2005).

The feeling that I could have done something different is an example of counterfactual thinking. The most basic example of the influence of a counterfactual process on behaviour occurs when we learn from the actions we could have performed and not just from the ones we did perform. Consider the game stone–paper–scissors. I play *rock* and I am beaten by *paper.* If I am a simple reinforcement learning device, then I will lower my estimate of the value of playing *rock.* But I learn nothing new about the value of playing *paper* or *scissors.* However, if I use counterfactual thinking, then I can note that I would have won if I had played *scissors* and can increase my estimate of the value of playing this move. Updating of values on the basis of actions that could have been made has been observed in the behaviour of monkeys (Abe & Lee, 2011), as well as humans (Boorman, Behrens, Woolrich, & Rushworth, 2009), and is particularly associated with processes instantiated in frontopolar cortex (Platt & Hayden, 2011).

### *2.4 Responsibility, free will and determinism*

Many neuroscientists (e.g., Greene & Cohen, 2004; Roth, 2010) believe that free will is incompatible with determinism and, therefore conclude that free will is an illusion. I have argued here that, even if it is an illusion, this feeling is critical for the acceptance that we are responsible for our actions and can be held to account for them. Thus this feeling of responsibility has a very important role in creating social cohesion. I suggest that the cognitive basis for the feeling of responsibility is, first, a mechanism that binds intentions to outcomes. This makes a distinction between expected and unexpected outcomes. Second, is the process that enables us to think about what would have happened if we had performed a different action, an example of counterfactual thinking? Both of these processes could occur in a fully determined manner, while still leading to the experiences relevant to the feeling of responsibility.

## 3 The cultural creation of responsibility

### *3.1 Stories about experience*

I highlighted the experiment by Fourneret and Jeannerod (1998) because it suggests how little awareness we have of our own actions. There is another important lesson to be learned from this experiment. This is that we are not aware of how little insight we have into our own actions. We think we know all about our actions and are eager to explain and justify them. This practice applies, not only to the rather limited kinds of action we study in the lab, but also to the more important decisions that we make in real life.

In the Fourneret and Jeannerod experiment, participants were asked to repeat the action they had just made, without being given any visual feedback. Even though they had just moved their arm 10° to the left, they believed they had moved their arm straight ahead and it was the movement that they believed they had made that they reproduced. There are many more realistic examples of such failures of insight. Indeed, it has become a basic tenet of cognitive psychology that we have little or no knowledge of the cognitive processes that underlie our behaviour (Kihlstrom, 1987). Nevertheless, we are happy to give reports on these processes, which are based on intuitive theories about the causes of behaviour, sometimes called folk psychology (Nisbett & Wilson, 1977). Nisbett and Wilson report many cases of where these explanations of behaviour are erroneous. A widely quoted example concerns a position bias in choice behaviour (but see Kühberger, Kogler, Hug, & Mösl, 2006; Wilson & Nisbett, 1978). There was a pronounced bias to choose the rightmost item in an array of identical nylon stockings, but subjects never gave this as a reason for their choice and, when the possibility was raised, denied that there was an effect of position.

A particularly striking example of our willingness to make up erroneous *post facto* justifications for behaviour is found in the phenomenon of change blindness (Hall, Johansson, Tarning, Sikstrom, & Deutgen, 2010; Johansson, Hall, Sikstrom, & Olsson, 2005). In one experiment participants were shown a series of pairs of faces and asked which one they preferred. They were then immediately shown again the face they had just chosen and asked to explain why they preferred it. On a small number of trials, by the use of sleight of hand, they were actually shown the face they had just rejected. Nevertheless, most of the time, participants would proceed to justify and explain this choice that they had not actually made.

That we are not aware of cognitive processes underlying choice behaviour is, perhaps, not so surprising. We would not expect to be aware of the neural activity that underlies these processes, so what is it that we could become aware of through introspection? Presumably the cognitive processes will generate some conscious experiences. For example, we seem to be aware of the time taken by a process to complete. This leads to the experiences such as *perceptual fluency* (the time taken to recognise something, Bornstein & D'Agostino, 1994) and *action selection fluency* (the time taken to choose an action, Chambon & Haggard, 2012). However, these experiences do not give us direct access to the underlying cognitive processes that generate them. We can use such experiences to make inferences about the processes, but these inferences can sometimes be wrong.

Consider the experience of perceptual fluency. This experience seems to have a role in the *mere exposure effect.* In this paradigm people are presented with a series of pictures, each presented very briefly. Afterwards they are unable to distinguish the pictures they have seen before from novel pictures. However, if asked which pictures they prefer, they tend to choose the ones they have seen before (Kunst-Wilson & Zajonc, 1980). This result shows that people have access to cues indicating which pictures have been seen before, but misinterpret these cues as indicating liking for a stimulus. One possible cue is perceptual fluency (Bornstein & D'Agostino, 1994). We can perceive a picture more quickly when we have seen it before and we are aware of differences in this perceptual fluency (Forster, Leder, & Ansorge, 2012). For reasons that need to be explored further we associate perceptual fluency with liking (Reber, Schwarz, & Winkielman, 2004).

A similar story can be told about the experience of emotion. In the well known experiment of Schachter and Singer (1962) subjects experienced an increase in physiological arousal caused by an injection of adrenaline. However, how they interpreted this experience in terms of emotion (euphoria or anger) depended on instructions and context. On the basis of these and other studies I agree with Schwitzgebel (2008) that our insight into our own experiences may be highly unreliable and provides very limited and inaccurate access to the underlying cognitive processes.

### 3.2 *How discussion and instruction can change our experiences and behaviour*

Although we have so little insight into the causes of our actions and the nature of our experiences, we are very happy to make up stories about them. In turn these stories will influence how others understand and experience the causes of action. Ultimately these stories are derived from beliefs about actions and experiences that we learn from others and which are part of our culture. And, of course, these beliefs can change. Even a brief discussion can change the way we describe our experiences and also change our behaviour. I suggest that it is precisely because our introspection is so unreliable that we can adopt new stories about the causes of our experiences and behaviour.

A striking example of how stories about the causes of action can affect our behaviour, comes from a study of will power. If people have to sit next to a plate of nice food, but have been told not to eat any, then much mental effort is exerted in the attempt to resist temptation. After such exertion, people show less persistence. For example, they will give up more quickly when given impossible puzzles to solve (Baumeister, Bratslavsky, Muraven, & Tice, 1998). It seems that will power is a cognitive resource that can be depleted by exertion (ego depletion). More recently this idea has been questioned. Ego depletion experiments were repeated, but this time, participants were given different stories about the effects of exerting will power. One group was told, 'Working on a strenuous mental task can make you feel tired such that you need a break before accomplishing a new task', while the other group was told, 'Sometimes, working on a strenuous mental task can make you feel energised for further challenging activities'. The behaviour of the people in these groups corresponded to their instructions, with the 'energised' group making fewer errors on a STROOP task after their strenuous mental activity, while the 'depleted' group made more errors (Job, Dweck, & Walton, 2010).

Much further work is needed to explore the mechanisms underlying these effects. One possibility is that, through discussion, people learn to reinterpret the fragile cues associated with the experience of decision-making and action. I already discussed the *mere exposure effect* in which people mistake the experience of perceptual fluency as a cue of liking rather than of prior exposure. My prediction would be that it should be possible to teach people to use the feeling of perceptual fluency as a cue that they have seen the picture before, thus making their story about their experience closer to reality.

Discussion of *post facto* justifications of choice can also affect our perception at a much more basic level. Bahador Bahrami and colleagues have reported a series of experiments in social psychophysics. In these studies, two participants work together to detect signals in standard psychophysical paradigms. After making individual decisions, the pair discussed disagreements about the signal and came up with a consensus through discussion. As long as their perpetual abilities are roughly similar, then the pair achieves better performance than the better partner working alone (Bahrami et al., 2010). This advantage occurs over and above any individual learning. The group advantage can be modelled on the assumption that people share with each other their confidence in their decision about the signal and choose the answer of the more confident member on a trial by trial basis. This was confirmed when a detailed analysis was performed on what was actually said during the discussion (Fusaroli et al., 2012). Pairs developed, from scratch, linguistic tools for communicating and calibrating levels of confidence. Of particular relevance here is the observation that the individual performance of someone involved in such an interaction improved to a significantly greater extent than people who had just as much practice with the signal detection task, but worked on their own (Olsen et al., in preparation). Discussion of perceptual decision making with others can improve individual perception.

### *3.3 The emergence of responsibility and the experience of volition*

I suggest that our experiences of volition and responsibility are also influenced by instruction and discussion. For example, the phenomenon of intentional binding can be influenced by instructions about the effects of action. Dogge, Schaap, Custers, Wegner, and Aarts (2012) increased the binding between an *involuntary* key press and a tone by encouraging participants 'to perceive themselves as the cause for producing the tone'.

Instructions can also decrease the influence of the subtle cues available in our experience of action. In difficult choice reaction time tasks people typically slow down after they have made an error (post-error slowing). This is an example of metacognitive or intentional control. Performance is monitored and, when there is evidence of an error, behaviour is adjusted to prevent its reoccurrence. Rigoni, Wilquin, Brass, and Burle (2013) gave people text to read claiming that 'scientists now recognise that free will is an illusion' or control texts in which free will was not mentioned. The people in the group who had been primed to have a weaker belief in free will showed reduced post-error slowing in a reaction time task. In cognitive terms free will is equated with intentional control, so that a loss in the belief in free will leads to a weakening of the motivation to apply intentional control.

There are now several experiments demonstrating how beliefs about free will can alter volitional behaviour (e.g., Baumeister, Masicampo, & Dewall, 2009; Vohs & Schooler, 2008). I suggest, however, that the response to such instructions will depend on what people believe to be the effects of a loss of intentional control. For example, I suspect that most people believe that intentional control is needed to overcome our selfish impulses. However, it may well be that, in many circumstances, our basic impulse is to be prosocial (see for example Valdesolo & DeSteno, 2008). The effects of instructions are likely to depend upon what people believe about the relevant cognitive processes, rather than the actual nature of those cognitive processes.

Given the increasing evidence of how readily volitional behaviour and experience can be altered by instructions and beliefs, it would be surprising if there were no effects of upbringing and culture. Epicurus believed that we acquire the idea that we are causal agents through the observation that human beings, including ourselves, are praised and blamed for their actions (Bobzien, 2006). It is certainly the case that experiences of volition and responsibility arise rather slowly during the course of childhood.

I have suggested that the idea and experience of responsibility depend upon two factors. The first is the experience of being an agent and causing things to happen. The second is the counter-factual thought that I could have acted differently. It is this second factor that leads to the experience of regret. It is only by the age of 5 that children can report a mature experience of agency, distinguishing between a voluntary movement of the leg and a knee jerk reflex (Shultz, Wells, & Sarda, 1980). A true experience of regret seems to arise much later, at around the age of 9 (Rafetseder & Perner, 2012). Prior to this age children base their judgments solely on what they got without taking into account what they could have got. Finally there is some preliminary evidence that the excessive risk taking behaviour seen in adolescence may be related to a lack of, or failure to take account of, anticipated regret (Gerrard, Gibbons, Benthin, & Hessling, 1996). Thus it seems that the ability to take regret into consideration, when making choices, continues to develop during adolescence (Habib et al., 2012).

Are there cultural differences in the experience of agency? Among the Mopan Mayas of Central America punishment is applied equally if the outcome is accidental, rather than deliberate. Saying a falsehood is not excused even if, at the time, the speaker believes it to be true. Children who indulge in pretend play are reproved. It seems that, for this cultural group, the intention behind the action has no importance. It is only the outcome that counts in applying praise or blame (Danziger, 2006). It would be interesting and informative to study intentional binding and post-error slowing in such a group.

## 4 Conclusions

The studies of action that Marc Jeannerod pioneered concern behaviour that is far more restricted than actions occurring outside the laboratory. Nevertheless, I believe that what these studies reveal about our experience of action have important implications for behaviour in 'real life'. They reveal that our introspection is a very unreliable method for uncovering the cognitive basis of our actions. However, we like to reflect upon our behaviour and experiences and to discuss these reflections with others. Through these discussions we develop explicit accounts of the world and ourselves. It is the history of these discussions that largely determine individual and cultural differences.

The effects of culture on experience need not necessarily lead to a more accurate understanding of our actions. For example, our experience of being a causal agent may not accurately reflect the cognitive and neural processes underlying our actions. The important aspect of this story about agency is that we have a social consensus about the causes of our actions (Proust, 2012). Our experience of being responsible for our actions is extremely important for generating social cohesion and benefitting the members of the group. We all benefit from reciprocal altruism and, to the extent to which we can exert intentional control, from deliberately following explicit advice from other members of our group.

However, once social cohesion is established, it will enhance the effects of the various unconscious mechanisms I have discussed. Our desire to be part of the group increases our tendency to imitate others (e.g., Over & Carpenter, 2009) and to behave in a prosocial, rather than a selfish manner (e.g., Bateson, Nettle, & Roberts, 2006). Furthermore, this unconscious imitation of the behaviour of others takes advantage of all that dangerous trial and error learning undertaken by previous generations (see Frith & Frith, 2012).

These powerful effects indicate the importance of our experience of being responsible agents with intentional control. But is this experience merely a necessary illusion or do we really have some degree of intentional control over our actions? Reflecting on the regret we might feel, if it turns out that we have chosen the wrong option, can affect our behaviour (e.g., Filiz-Ozbay & Ozbay, 2007). Furthermore, the reflection on our actions engendered by discussions with others, and by instructions, can also change our behaviour (e.g., Rigoni et al., 2013). I believe these are demonstrations that we do sometimes have intentional control over our behaviour. We are not merely automatons in a deterministic world. Through counter-factual thinking we can create what might have been and what might be. We are not limited to reacting to the world. We can also change it (Friston, Daunizeau, Kilner, & Kiebel, 2010).

These reflections on responsibility reveal Marc Jeannerod's legacy to me in relation to my understanding of the nature of volition. As revealed by the study of Fourneret and Jeannerod (1998) and many of Marc's other studies, our awareness of our actions is very limited and very fragile. This fragility can lead to incorrect interpretations. But these interpretations can be altered by discussion.

Marc's discoveries about the nature of action have opened a window onto the mechanisms underlying human interactions and the emergence of culture.

## Acknowledgements

This work was supported by the Wellcome Centre for Neuroimaging at UCL and All Souls College, Oxford. I am grateful to Uta Frith & Rosalind Ridley for their comments on earlier drafts of this paper and to Panagiotis Mitkidis for checking my Greek. The paper has, I hope, been much improved by revisions in response to the comments of two anonymous referees.

## References

Abe, H., & Lee, D. (2011). Distributed coding of actual and hypothetical outcomes in the orbital and dorsolateral prefrontal cortex. *Neuron, 70,* 731–741.

Bahrami, B., Olsen, K., Latham, P. E., Roepstorff, A., Rees, G., & Frith, C. D. (2010). Optimally interacting minds. *Science, 329,* 1081–1085.

Bateson, M., Nettle, D., & Roberts, G. (2006). Cues of being watched enhance cooperation in a real-world setting. *Biology Letters, 2,* 412–414.

Baumeister, R. F., Bratslavsky, E., Muraven, M., & Tice, D. M. (1998). Ego depletion: Is the active self a limited resource? *Journal of Personality and Social Psychology, 74,* 1252–1265.

Baumeister, R. F., Masicampo, E. J., & Dewall, C. N. (2009). Prosocial benefits of feeling free: Disbelief in free will increases aggression and reduces helpfulness. *Personality and Social Psychology Bulletin, 35,* 260–268.

Bobzien, S. (1998). *Determinism and freedom in stoic philosophy.* Oxford: Clarendon Press.

Bobzien, S. (2006). Moral responsibility and moral development in epicurus' philosophy. In: B. Reis (Ed.), *The virtuous life in Greek ethics* (pp. 206–299). New York: Cambridge University Press.

Boorman, E. D., Behrens, T. E., Woolrich, M. W., & Rushworth, M. F. (2009). How green is the grass on the other side? Frontopolar cortex and the evidence in favor of alternative courses of action. *Neuron, 62,* 733–743.

Bornstein, R. F., & D'Agostino, P. R. (1994). The Attribution and discounting of perceptual fluency: Preliminary tests of a perceptual fluency/attributional model of the mere exposure effect. *Social Cognition, 12,* 103–128.

Camille, N., Coricelli, G., Sallet, J., Pradat-Diehl, P., Duhamel, J. R., & Sirigu, A. (2004). The involvement of the orbitofrontal cortex in the experience of regret. *Science, 304,* 1167–1170.

Castiello, U., Paulignan, Y., & Jeannerod, M. (1991). Temporal dissociation of motor responses and subjective awareness. A study in normal subjects. *Brain, 114*(Pt 6), 2639–2655.

Chambon, V., & Haggard, P. (2012). Sense of control depends on fluency of action selection, not motor performance. *Cognition, 125,* 441–451.

Coricelli, G., Critchley, H. D., Joffily, M., O'Doherty, J. P., Sirigu, A., & Dolan, R. J. (2005). Regret and its avoidance: A neuroimaging study of choice behavior. *Nature Neuroscience, 8,* 1255–1262.

Danziger, E. (2006). The thought that counts: Interactional consequences of variation in cultural theories of meaning. In: S. Levinson, & N. Enfield (Eds.), *The roots of human sociality: Culture, cognition and human interaction* (pp. 259–278). New York: Berg Press (Wenner-Gren Foundation for Anthropological Research).

Dogge, M., Schaap, M., Custers, R., Wegner, D. M., & Aarts, H. (2012). When moving without volition: Implied self-causation enhances binding strength between involuntary actions and effects. *Consciousness and Cognition, 21,* 501–506.

Fehr, E., & Gachter, S. (2002). Altruistic punishment in humans. *Nature, 415,* 137–140.

Filiz-Ozbay, E., & Ozbay, E. Y. (2007). Auctions with anticipated regret: Theory and experiment. *American Economic Review, 97,* 1407–1418.

Fleming, S. M., Weil, R. S., Nagy, Z., Dolan, R. J., & Rees, G. (2010). Relating introspective accuracy to individual differences in brain structure. *Science, 329,* 1541–1543.

Forster, M., Leder, H., & Ansorge, U. (2012). It felt fluent, and I liked it: Subjective feeling of fluency rather than objective fluency determines liking. *Emotion, 13,* 280–289.

Fourneret, P., & Jeannerod, M. (1998). Limited conscious monitoring of motor performance in normal subjects. *Neuropsychologia, 36,* 1133–1140.

Friston, K. J., Daunizeau, J., Kilner, J., & Kiebel, S. J. (2010). Action and behavior: A free-energy formulation. *Biology Cybernatics, 102,* 227–260.

Frith, C. D., & Frith, U. (2012). Mechanisms of social cognition. *Annual Review of Psychology, 63,* 287–313.

Fusaroli, R., Bahrami, B., Olsen, K., Roepstorff, A., Rees, G., Frith, C., & Tylen, K. (2012). Coming to terms: Quantifying the benefits of linguistic coordination. *Psychological Science, 23,* 931–939.

Gerrard, M., Gibbons, F. X., Benthin, A. C., & Hessling, R. M. (1996). A longitudinal study of the reciprocal nature of risk behaviors and cognitions in adolescents: What you do shapes what you think, and vice versa. *Health Psychology, 15,* 344–354.

Greene, J., & Cohen, J. (2004). For the law, neuroscience changes nothing and everything. *Philosophical Transactions of the Royal Society of London B Biological Sciences, 359,* 1775–1785.

Guttentag, R., & Ferrell, J. (2004). Reality compared with its alternatives: Age differences in judgments of regret and relief. *Developmental Psychology, 40,* 764–775.

Gürerk, O., Irlenbusch, B., & Rockenbach, B. (2006). The competitive advantage of sanctioning institutions. *Science, 312,* 108–111.

Habib, M., Cassotti, M., Borst, G., Simon, G., Pineau, A., Houde, O., & Moutier, S. (2012). Counterfactually mediated emotions: A developmental study of regret and relief in a probabilistic gambling task. *Journal of Experimental Child Psychology, 112,* 265–274.

Haggard, P., Clark, S., & Kalogeras, J. (2002). Voluntary action and conscious awareness. *Nature Neuroscience, 5,* 382–385.

Hall, L., Johansson, P., Tarning, B., Sikstrom, S., & Deutgen, T. (2010). Magic at the marketplace: Choice blindness for the taste of jam and the smell of tea. *Cognition, 117,* 54–61.

Hazel, N. (2008). *Cross-national comparison of youth justice* (p. 74). London: Youth Justice Board 74.

Hume, D. (1758). *An enquiry concerning human understanding* (p. 2005) Oxford: Oxford University Press 2005.

Humphrey, N. (2002). *Bugs and beast before the law. The mind made flesh* (pp. 235–254) Oxford: Oxford University Press 235–254.

Jeannerod, M. (1983). *Le cerveau–machine. Physiologie de la volonté.* Paris: Librarie Arthème Fayard.

Jeannerod, M., & Decety, J. (1995). Mental motor imagery: A window into the representational stages of action. *Current Opinion in Neurobiology, 5,* 727–732.

Job, V., Dweck, C. S., & Walton, G. M. (2010). Ego depletion – is it all in your head?: Implicit theories about willpower affect self-regulation. *Psychological Science*

Johansson, P., Hall, L., Sikstrom, S., & Olsson, A. (2005). Failure to detect mismatches between intention and outcome in a simple decision task. *Science, 310,* 116–119.

Kihlstrom, J. F. (1987). The cognitive unconscious. *Science, 237,* 1445–1452.

Kunst-Wilson, W. R., & Zajonc, R. B. (1980). Affective discrimination of stimuli that cannot be recognized. *Science, 207,* 557–558.

Kühberger, A., Kogler, C., Hug, A., & Mösl, E. (2006). The role of the position effect in theory and simulation. *Mind and Language, 21,* 610–625.

Libet, B., Gleason, C. A., Wright, E. W., & Pearl, D. K. (1983). Time of conscious intention to act in relation to onset of cerebral activity (readiness-potential). The unconscious initiation of a freely voluntary act. *Brain, 106*(Pt 3), 623–642.

Mackintosh, N. (2011). *Brain waves module 4: Neuroscience and the law* (p. 35) London: Royal Society 35.

Metzinger, T. (2006). Conscious volition and mental representation: Toward a more fine-grained analysis. In: N. Sebanz, & W. Prinz (Eds.), *Disorders of volition* (pp. 19–48). Cambridge, Mass: Bradford Books, MIT Press.

Miele, D. B., Wager, T. D., Mitchell, J. P., & Metcalfe, J. (2011). Dissociating neural correlates of action monitoring and metacognition of agency. *Journal of Cognitive Neuroscience, 23,* 3620–3636.

Moore, J., & Haggard, P. (2008). Awareness of action: Inference and prediction. *Conscious and Cognition, 17,* 136–144.

Moretto, G., Walsh, E., & Haggard, P. (2011). Experience of agency and sense of responsibility. *Conscious and Cognition, 20,* 1847–1854.

Nicolle, A., Bach, D. R., Frith, C., & Dolan, R. J. (2011). Amygdala involvement in self-blame regret. *Society for Neuroscience, 6,* 178–189.

Nisbett, R. E., & Wilson, T. D. (1977). Telling more than we can know – verbal reports on mental processes. *Psychological Review, 84,* 231–259.

Olsen, K., Bahrami, B., Christensen, P., Rees, G., Roepstorff, A., & Frith, C. D. (2013). Human interaction accelerates visual perceptual learning in individuals, (in preparation).

O'Shea, J., Gaveau, V., Kandel, M., Koga, K., Susami, K., Prablanc, C., & Rossetti, Y. (2014). Kinematic markers dissociate error correction from sensorimotor realignment during prism adaptation. *Neuropsychologia, 55,* 15–24.

Over, H., & Carpenter, M. (2009). Priming third-party ostracism increases affiliative imitation in children. *Developmental Science, 12,* F1–F8.

Pelisson, D., Prablanc, C., Goodale, M. A., & Jeannerod, M. (1986). Visual control of reaching movements without vision of the limb. II. Evidence of fast unconscious processes correcting the trajectory of the hand to the final position of a double-step stimulus. *Experimental Brain Research, 62,* 303–311.

Pisella, L., Grea, H., Tilikete, C., Vighetto, A., Desmurget, M., Rode, G., Boisson, D., & Rossetti, Y. (2000). An 'automatic pilot' for the hand in human posterior parietal cortex: Toward reinterpreting optic ataxia. *Nature Neuroscience, 3,* 729–736.

Platt, M. L., & Hayden, B. (2011). Learning: Not just the facts, ma'am, but the counterfactuals as well. *PLoS Biology, 9,* e1001092.

Rafetseder, E., & Perner, J. (2012). When the alternative would have been better: Counterfactual reasoning and the emergence of regret. *Cognition and Emotion, 26,* 800–819.

Reber, R., Schwarz, N., & Winkielman, P. (2004). Processing fluency and aesthetic pleasure: Is beauty in the perceiver's processing experience? *Personality and Social Psychology Review, 8,* 364–382.

Rigoni, D., Wilquin, H., Brass, M., & Burle, B. (2013). When errors do not matter: Weakening belief in intentional control impairs cognitive reaction to errors. *Cognition, 127,* 264–269.

Roth, G. (2010). Free will – insights from neurobiology. In: U. J. Frey, C. Stormer, & K. P. Willfuhr (Eds.), *Homo novus – a human without illusions* (pp. 231–245). New York: Springer.

Schachter, S., & Singer, J. E. (1962). Cognitive, social, and physiological determinants of emotional state. *Psychological Review, 69,* 379–399.

Schwitzgebel, E. (2008). The unreliability of naive introspection. *Philosophical Review, 117,* 245–273.

Shultz, T. R., Wells, D., & Sarda, M. (1980). Development of the ability to distinguish intended actions from mistakes, reflexes, and passive movements. *British Journal of Social and Clinical Psychology, 19,* 301–310.

Singer, T., Seymour, B., O'Doherty, J. P., Stephan, K. E., Dolan, R. J., & Frith, C. D. (2006). Empathic neural responses are modulated by the perceived fairness of others. *Nature, 439,* 466–469.

Spinoza, B. (1677). Part III: Of the affects. In *Ethics* (translation 1994) (p. 73). Penguin: London.

Valdesolo, P., & DeSteno, D. (2008). The duality of virtue: Deconstructing the moral hypocrite. *Journal of Experimental Social Psychology, 44,* 1334–1338.

Vohs, K. D., & Schooler, J. W. (2008). The value of believing in free will: Encouraging a belief in determinism increases cheating. *Psychological Science, 19,* 49–54.

Wegner, D. M. (2003). *The illusion of conscious will.* Cambridge, Mass.: The MIT Press.

Wegner, D. M., & Wheatley, T. (1999). Apparent mental causation – Sources of the experience of will. *American Psychologist, 54,* 480–492.

Wilson, T. d. C., & Nisbett, R. E. (1978). The accuracy of verbal reports about the effects of stimuli on evaluations and behavior. *Social Psychology, 41,* 118–131.

## Section 3

# Social cognition

# 10 Meeting of minds

## The medial frontal cortex and social cognition

*David M. Amodio and Chris D. Frith*

For humans, like many animal species, survival depends on effective social functioning. Social skills facilitate our access to sustenance, protection and mates, and socially adept individuals tend to be healthier and live longer[1,2]. However, social interaction in humans is exceedingly complex compared with that in other animal species: representations of internal somatic states, knowledge about the self, perceptions of others and interpersonal motivations are carefully orchestrated to support skilled social functioning. This complex set of processes, which is broadly referred to as social cognition[3], has recently been associated with activity in a network of brain regions, including the medial frontal cortex (MFC, in which, for convenience, we include the anterior cingulate cortex, ACC), the temporoparietal junction, the superior temporal sulcus and the temporal poles. This research suggests that the MFC has a special role in social cognition, whereas other regions in the network serve more general functions. However, so far, the functional significance of this activity is not well understood.

Social cognition has been studied from various theoretical and methodological perspectives. In the behavioural sciences, social psychologists have investigated how the self interacts dynamically with the social environment, and how knowledge structures of social groups (such as stereotypes) might influence behaviour through both conscious and unconscious mechanisms[4–6]. Although social psychologists have developed a rich theoretical and methodological framework for examining and understanding social cognition, they have only recently begun to consider its neural substrates. Neuroscientists, meanwhile, have investigated how underlying neural structures support unique yet coordinated roles in various aspects of social cognition. Initially, neuroscientific explorations of social cognition arose from neuropsychological studies of patients[7,8]. More recently, non-invasive neuroimaging methods such as functional MRI (fMRI) have permitted neuroscientists to explore the neural correlates of social cognitive phenomena in normally-functioning humans. As a result of these evolving fields, social psychologists and cognitive neuroscientists have begun to cross paths in the domain of social cognitive neuroscience[9]. Although they have arrived from different theoretical and methodological origins and often speak different scientific languages, they share a common goal: to understand the relationship between the brain and the social mind. In this review, we seek to integrate theory and research from neuroscience and social psychology in order to place this work in a broader conceptual framework and promote synergy across fields.

In proposing a theoretical framework for understanding the role of the MFC in social cognition, we consider evidence from three broad categories of tasks suggested by recent studies of functional divisions in the MFC[10]. The first category concerns control and monitoring of action, which is typically associated with activity in the dorsal ACC, although some have also proposed that the pre-supplementary motor area (preSMA) has a role[11]. The second category concerns the monitoring of outcomes that relate to punishments and rewards, which is linked to activity in the orbital cortex. Finally, we focus on the category of primary interest: social cognition. Social cognitive processes, such as self-reflection, person perception, and making inferences about others' thoughts, have been associated with activity extending from the ACC to the anterior frontal poles, most typically located in the transitional area between these two regions, the paracingulate cortex. Throughout this review we use the MFC as a designation that subsumes all these regions. We begin by outlining the anatomical subregions of the human MFC and their respective connections with other brain regions, primarily on the basis of anatomical studies of the monkey brain. Next, we review research reporting selective MFC activation in tasks associated with action monitoring, outcome monitoring, self-knowledge, person-knowledge and mentalizing – restricting included research to studies of normal adults using common neuroimaging methods such as fMRI, positron emission tomography (PET) and electroencephalography (EEG). We then propose a theoretical framework to account for the observed activation patterns, whereby the MFC supports a general mechanism for the integration of complex representations of possible actions and anticipated outcomes, and suggest that such integration is particularly relevant to the domain of social cognition.

### Talairach coordinates

Talairach coordinates provide a standardized method for describing the location of activations in the brain in three-dimensional space. Talairach space comprises x, y and z coordinates (represented as x,y,z): x denotes left versus right, y denotes rostral (anterior) versus caudal (posterior), and z denotes dorsal (superior) versus ventral (inferior). The Montreal Neurological Institute's system uses the same metric space, but their coordinates are based on a slightly larger and more representative brain.

## Connectivity of the MFC

The MFC consists of Brodmann areas (BAs) 9 and 10 (medial regions), 24, 25 and 32, with 11 and 14 in the medial orbital cortex (FIG. 10.1). Most MFC projections are intrinsic or involve neighbouring prefrontal areas[12]. With regard to more distal connections, the medial and lateral regions of orbitofrontal cortex

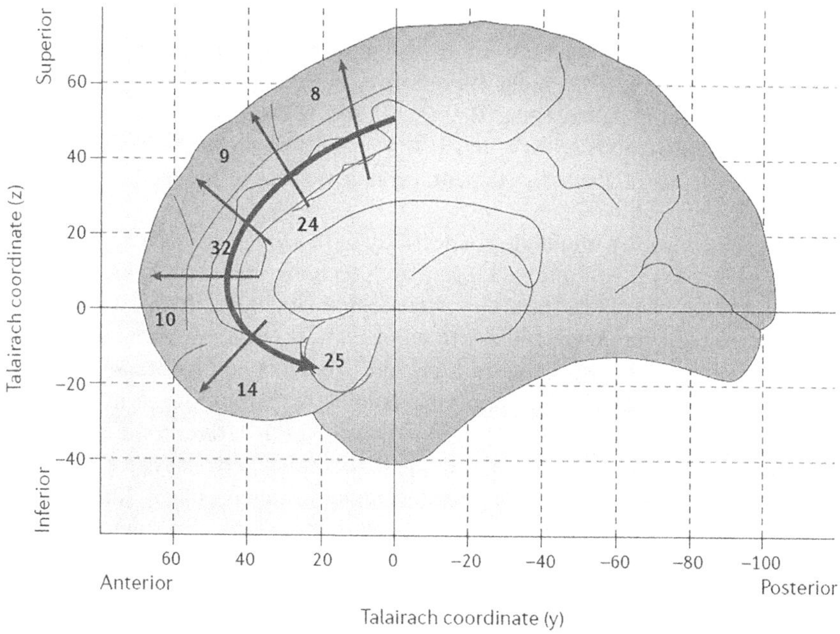


*Figure 10.1* Anatomical studies of the medial frontal cortex reveal two major axes of connectivity. The first axis, illustrated by the thick arrow, bends around the genu of the corpus callosum. Along this axis, the more superior regions (Brodmann areas 8 and 9) and the more superior parts of the anterior cingulate cortex have strong connections with lateral premotor, supplemental motor and cingulate motor areas, whereas the most inferior areas have strong connections with the rhinal cortex. The second axis of connectivity runs at right angles to the first, as illustrated by the thin arrows. Along this axis, cingulate regions have stronger connections with the amygdala than do more dorsal and frontopolar regions. The approximate demarcation of the Brodmann areas is taken from REF. 18.

(OFC) are part of distinct networks. Medial regions of the OFC receive few direct sensory-related inputs, in contrast to lateral regions[13]. Rather, major afferents to the medial regions come from the dorsolateral prefrontal cortex, temporal pole, anterior superior temporal gyrus, parietotemporal cortex and posterior cingulate cortex[12,13].

There are two distinct axes within the medial prefrontal region, along which patterns of connectivity vary (FIG. 10.1). The first axis bends around the genu of the corpus callosum (thick arrow in FIG. 10.1), along which the most inferior caudal areas (BAs 25, 24 and 32) have strong connections with the rhinal cortex, compared with the adjacent, more rostral areas (BAs 14, 32 and 10). The most superior part of the medial prefrontal cortex (BA 9) has few, if any, connections with the rhinal cortex, but instead has robust connections with the lateral premotor cortex, the supplementary motor area and the cingulate motor area[12]. The more superior and caudal parts of the ACC (BAs 24 and 32) are also connected with the premotor cortex[14]. A second axis runs at right angles to the first, distinguishing cingulate regions from frontopolar regions (thin arrows in FIG. 10.1). The amygdala has strong inputs to cingulate regions (BAs 24, 25 and 32), but only weak connections with frontopolar regions (BAs 9 and 10)[15,16]. Evidence for these distinct axes of connectivity is also reflected in thalamic connections with the medial prefrontal cortex[17].

What little is known about the connectivity of the MFC has been derived from studies of monkeys. Although the same architectonic areas can be identified in humans and monkeys[18,19], the frontopolar region (including BAs 10 and 32) is greatly expanded in humans relative to monkeys[19]. However, whether this region is expanded in humans relative to great apes remains controversial[20]. Clearly some caution is warranted in applying connectivity findings in monkeys to humans. Nevertheless, a recent meta-analysis of PET-derived functional connectivity in the human brain supports the distinctions between these superior–inferior and caudal–rostral axes in human medial frontal regions[21]. Results from the recently developed technique of diffusion tractography also suggest considerable similarity between connectivity in human and monkey prefrontal cortices[22].

## Functional divisions of the MFC

In human studies, functional divisions may be determined by the nature of various tasks found to activate medial frontal regions. The most caudal region of the MFC contains one or more cingulate motor areas, which are differentially involved in movements of the hand, eye and mouth[23,24], and activity in this region has been related directly to behavioural response rates[25]. Koski & Paus[21] suggest that the division between the caudal and rostral ACC can be made at the vertical plane defined by the Talairach coordinate $y = 10$ (line a in FIG. 10.2). The more posterior region of the rostral ACC (prACC, using the nomenclature of Picard and Strick[24] but sometimes called the dorsal ACC) has been associated with 'cognitive' tasks (for example, attention and error monitoring), whereas the more anterior region of the rostral ACC (arACC) has been associated with 'emotional' tasks (for example, rating the pleasantness of pictures)[10]. On the basis of a detailed meta-analysis of studies in which activation of the MFC was observed, Steele & Lawrie[26] confirmed this distinction between cognitive and emotional regions, and defined a boundary providing maximum discrimination (line b in FIG. 10.2). Koski and Paus[21] suggest that there is a fourth, subcallosal region, which is defined by the horizontal plane at Talairach coordinate $z = 2$, approximating the split in the ACC between supracallosal BAs 24 and 32, and subcallosal BAs 24 and 14. A meta-analysis of PET studies suggests that subcallosal activations are related to autonomic and visceral aspects of emotional responses[21]. In the following sections we examine more closely the wide range of experimental

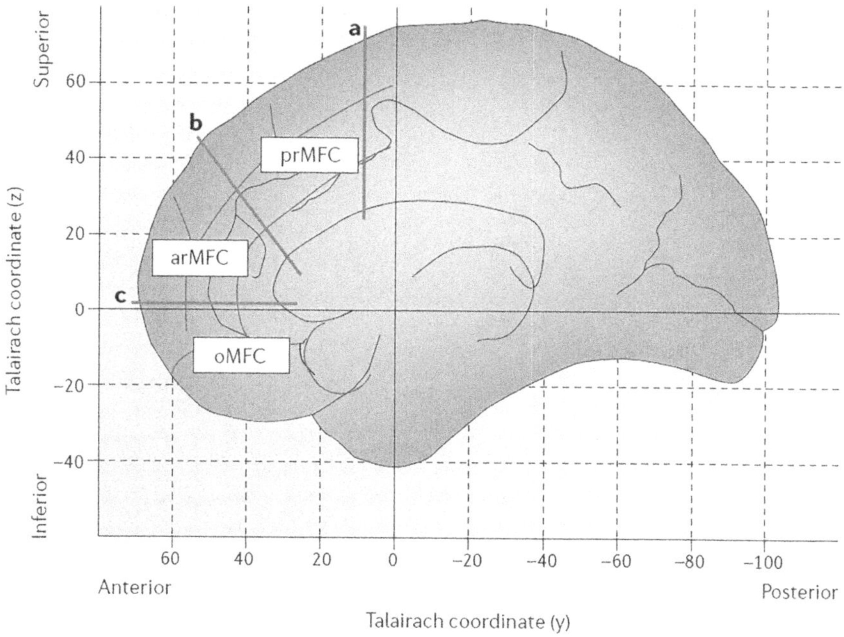


*Figure 10.2* Functional divisions of the medial prefrontal cortex. Meta-analyses of task-related neural activations observed in the medial frontal cortex (MFC) have revealed functional divisions associated with cognitive versus emotional processes[10,25,26]. The more posterior region of the rostral MFC (prMFC) is activated by cognitive tasks, such as those designed to engage action monitoring and attention. By contrast, the more anterior region of the rostral MFC (arMFC) is activated by emotional tasks, such as rating one's emotions in response to pictures of varying valence. Line **a** denotes the division between the prMFC and caudal MFC, and line **b** divides the prMFC and arMFC. Line **c** marks the boundary between the arMFC and orbital MFC (oMFC). The oMFC has been linked to the monitoring of task outcomes associated with punishment or reward. For the purposes of this diagram, the MFC includes the anterior cingulate cortex.

tasks that have been found to activate different divisions of the medial wall of the frontal cortex. On the basis of these findings, we speculate on the processes instantiated in these regions. Before focusing on the uniquely social cognitive functions ascribed to the anterior rostral MFC (arMFC), which includes the paracingulate cortex, we characterize the processes associated with the regions that flank the arMFC along the caudal–rostral axis noted above to provide a theoretical and anatomical context for our final discussion of arMFC function. The location of the activity elicited by the various studies discussed below is shown in FIG. 10.3.

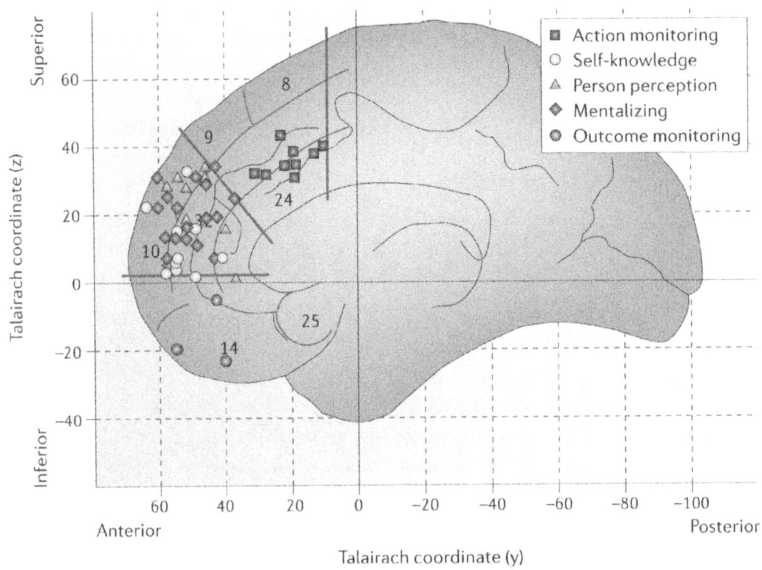


*Figure 10.3* Mapping of medial frontal cortex activations observed during action monitoring, social cognition and outcome monitoring. A meta-analysis of medial frontal cortex (MFC) activations suggests that social cognition tasks, which involve self-knowledge,[52,53,55–58,96,97,120,121] person perception[61–65,69,122,123] and mentalizing,[55,72,73,77–79,109,111,112,118,124–131] activate areas in the anterior rostral MFC (arMFC). By contrast, activations from action-monitoring tasks[28,29,83,99,132–136] occur in the posterior rostral region of the MFC (prMFC), and activations from tasks involving the monitoring of outcomes[40,39,41] occur in the orbital MFC (oMFC). (See figure in colour plate section.)

## Stroop colour-naming task

The Stroop task is commonly used to investigate response conflict. Participants view words presented in colours (for example, red and blue) that are either compatible (red written in red) or incompatible (red written in blue) with the word meaning. On incompatible trials, participants must inhibit the prepotent tendency to read the word's text in order to correctly report the colour of the word.

## Response inhibition

Response inhibition refers to the process of withholding a habitual response when changing task demands require an alternative response. Response inhibition is a crucial component of behavioural regulation that has been ascribed as a function of the posterior rostral ACC by much research, although it probably involves the coordination of several neural systems.

## Posterior region of the rostral MFC

The posterior rostral MFC (prMFC) has been implicated in the continuous internal monitoring of action across several studies[27]. Humans continuously monitor their actions to ensure that they are consistent with intentions and the current situational context. Action monitoring is particularly important in situations involving response conflicts, as in the Stroop colour-naming task, or requiring response inhibition. Such conflicts typically elicit increased response errors and engage slower, more controlled patterns of response[28–30]. Neuroimaging and event-related potential (ERP) research has linked the process of action monitoring to MFC activity. Barch *et al.*[31] report an extensive meta-analysis of functional imaging studies that included data from three different tasks involving action monitoring: those in which prepotent responses must be inhibited; responses are not fully determined by the task context; or errors are committed. Activity observed in these studies generally clusters in the prACC (mean Talairach coordinates: 3,19,35). In a study by Gerhing *et al.*[32], participants categorized target stimuli that were sometimes flanked by distractor stimuli associated with an erroneous response, which caused conflict and elicited errors. Response errors on this task, which reflect a conflict between intention and behaviour, evoked an ERP component that has been localized to the ACC[33–35]. Subsequent research has shown that this component, the error-related negativity (ERN), is larger when stimulus conflict is high versus low[36], when errors lead to large versus small monetary losses[37], and when errors indicate the undesired application of social stereotypes[38].

These findings suggest that conflict monitoring, error monitoring and response selection might depend on a single underlying process instantiated in the prMFC (but for an alternative view, see REFS 10,37). For example, recent studies have emphasized the role of decision making in action selection – that is, a mechanism for choosing one action rather than another (for an example, see REF. 39). Given a choice, we select actions expected to lead to better outcomes. Such selection requires a representation of expected values of different actions, as well as the continuous monitoring of outcomes in order to update these expected values. Several studies have investigated prediction and monitoring processes associated with selection of action. Walton *et al.*[39] observed activity in the prMFC (0,18,36) when participants monitored the outcome of actions that were self-selected, but not when they monitored the outcome of externally-guided actions. Knutson *et al.*[40] reported that the activity in the prMFC (0,22,42) was correlated with trial-by-trial variations in the anticipated probability of monetary gain. In research by Coricelli *et al.*, a similar region of prMFC activity (0,24,33) was associated with regret, that is, discovering that an unselected action would have led to a better outcome[41]. Finally, Brown & Braver reported that prMFC activation (8,33,33) was associated with prediction of the probability of error[42]. This set of findings is also consistent with the suggestion that the prMFC is involved in the processing of ambiguous response feedback[11].

**Event-related potential**

(ERP). An electrical signal produced by summated postsynaptic potentials of cortical neurons in response to a discrete event, such as a stimulus or response in an experimental task. Typically recorded from the scalp in humans, ERPs can be measured with extremely high temporal resolution and can be used to track rapid, real-time changes in neural activity.

Considered as a whole, the literature suggests that the prMFC is involved in representing and continuously updating the value of possible future actions in order to regulate behaviour[43].

## Orbital region of the MFC

Traditionally, the orbitofrontal cortex (OFC) has been implicated in processing information concerning rewards and punishments (for an example, see REF. 44). Elliott *et al.*[45] proposed distinct roles for the lateral and medial OFC on the basis of neuroimaging studies of learning and gambling tasks. They concluded that the OFC is involved in monitoring the reward value of stimuli and responses, with the lateral OFC having a special role in situations in which responses to previously-rewarded stimuli must be suppressed. This characterization is complementary to our description of the posterior rostral MFC as being involved in monitoring the value of different possible actions. Rather than guiding behaviour in terms of the value of possible actions (as with the prMFC), we propose that the oMFC guides behaviour in terms of the value of possible outcomes. Supporting this characterization, Knutson *et al.* reported that an area of the orbital region of the MFC (oMFC; mean Talairach coordinates −4,52,−6), in addition to the prMFC, was associated with anticipated gain probability[40]. Walton *et al.*[39] found that the activity in the oMFC (12,54,−22), but not the prMFC, was elicited by the need to monitor the outcomes of externally guided actions. They conjectured that, as the actions did not need to be chosen by the participants, the values of these actions were not relevant and therefore the prMFC was not activated. Furthermore, Coricelli *et al.* found that activity in the oMFC (−10,40,−24) correlated with the amount of anticipated regret associated with a decision[41]. Studies of patients with lesions to the oMFC support this characterization of the role of this region[46,47].

Taken together, these results are consistent with the idea that the oMFC represents and updates the value of possible future outcomes, just as the prMFC represents and updates the value of possible future actions[39,48]. These characterizations are consistent with the anatomical connectivity of these regions, with the oMFC being primarily connected to sensory association areas, and the prMFC being primarily connected to the motor system. These characterizations are also consistent with similar functional distinctions in the striatum regarding action versus reward, which have topographical connections to posterior versus anterior regions of the frontal cortex[49,50].

## Anterior region of the rostral MFC

The location of the anterior rostral region of the MFC (arMFC) between the two regions discussed so far – the prMFC and oMFC – suggests it has access to information about both actions and outcomes. However, this characterization does not sufficiently explain the wide range of tasks shown to activate the arMFC, which comprise roughly three different categories: self-knowledge, person knowledge and mentalizing (BOX 10.1).

### Box 10.1 Mentalizing tasks

***The story of Max and the chocolate***

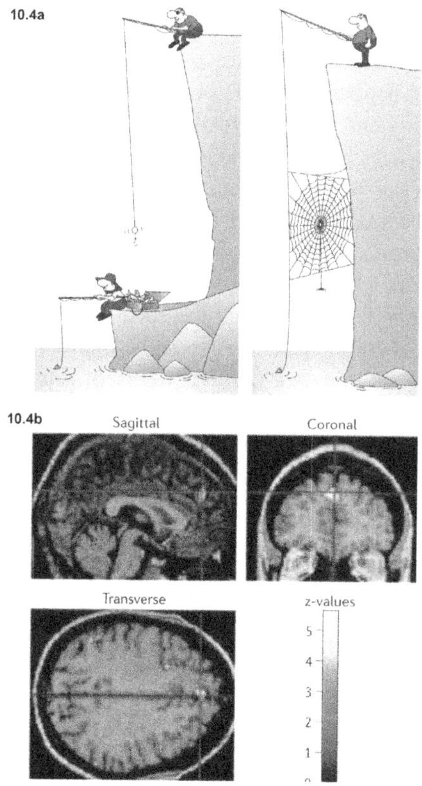


*Max eats half his chocolate bar and puts the rest away in the kitchen cupboard. He then goes out to play in the sun. Meanwhile, Max's mother comes into the kitchen, opens the cupboard and sees the chocolate bar. She puts it in the fridge.*

*When Max comes back into the kitchen, where does he look for his chocolate bar: in the cupboard, or in the fridge?*[108]

Mentalizing is the cognitive process that needs to be engaged to answer this question. We have to recognize that Max's behaviour will be determined by the current contents of his mind and what he believes about the world, not by the actual state of the world. We must recognize that he doesn't know his mother has moved the chocolate, and therefore falsely believes that it is still in the cupboard. This story is an example of a first-order false belief. If Max had peeped back into the kitchen when his mother was moving the chocolate, his mother would have had a second-order false belief. She would have falsely believed that Max believed the chocolate was in the cupboard. Mentalizing is relevant for thinking about other peoples' intentions and desires as well as their beliefs.

Brain imaging studies of mentalizing (or theory of mind) have used many different tasks. For example, stories – as in the example above – or strip cartoons illustrating similar stories without words are presented, and the subject is asked to explain the behaviour of the characters or choose the appropriate ending to the narrative (for examples, see REFS 72, 109). In other studies, subjects passively view animations of simple objects that move and interact in a way that automatically elicits attributions of mental states[110,111]. In yet other studies, the subject engages in a real-time interaction with another person during a competitive or cooperative game (for example, rock–paper–scissors) in which success requires the 'reading' of the intentions of the other person (for example, see REF. 112). It is striking that these different paradigms all elicit activity in the medial frontal cortex when contrasted with appropriate control tasks[70].

The cartoon (panel **a**) illustrates the idea of theory of mind[113,114]. The joke on the left depends on the deceit of the man who is stealing the fish. The joke on the right does not involve theory of mind. Comparison of the two types of joke shows activation in the medial prefrontal cortex, which is shown in a single subject in panel **b**. (See figure in colour plate section.)



### *Self-knowledge*

Socrates famously urged his followers to 'know thyself'. Modern psychology suggests this is much easier said than done. The self is a complex and dynamic phenomenon that is often difficult to operationalize for scientific study[51]. At its most basic level, self-knowledge involves the ability to differentiate the self from other objects and to recognize attributes and preferences related to oneself. Initial neuroimaging investigations of the self have asked participants to determine whether a series of trait words apply to themselves. Evaluation of self-related traits has been shown to elicit activity in the arMFC in several studies[52–56] (but see BOX 10.2). Extending this basic finding, Macrae *et al.* gave their subjects a surprise recognition test of trait words, some of which subjects previously judged according to their self-relevance[57]. Words associated with increased arMFC activity during initial viewing were more likely to be remembered.

**Box 10.2 The meaning of resting state activation in the MFC**

In experimental tasks involving self-judgments, reductions in the blood oxygen level dependent (BOLD) responses from a baseline condition are often observed. For example, Mitchell *et al.*[61] showed that self-related judgments elicited greater activity in the medial frontal cortex (MFC) than other-related judgments. However, self-related judgments did not elicit more activity than a baseline condition involving passive fixation on a cross-hair; rather, other-related judgments were associated with a significant reduction relative to baseline activity. Reduction of the BOLD signal in the medial prefrontal cortex is also observed in comparison to a resting base line with a number of cognitive tasks, such as working memory[116]. This curious but commonly observed pattern raises questions about the nature of the baseline condition. What cognitive processes are engaged when subjects are simply instructed to rest? Some theorists have suggested that a resting baseline promotes self-reflective thought[96,117] or social 'day dreaming'[118]. D'Argembeau *et al.* provided direct evidence for these speculations[119]. They confirmed that self-referential thoughts did occur during rest and that activity in the MFC (measured with positron emission tomography) correlated with the amount of self-referential processing.

It seems plausible, therefore, that a baseline of unconstrained rest is likely to elicit some of the same cognitive processes and associated neural activity as are engaged by explicit social tasks. It is also likely that the cognitive activity that occurs during rest might depend on the context in which this condition occurs. In order to interpret the results of studies concerned with activity in the MFC, high level comparison tasks are essential[67]. We suggest that if unconstrained rest is used as an additional baseline condition, then the experimenter should make some attempt to discover what cognitive processes are occurring under this condition.

Activation of the arMFC has also been associated with the monitoring of one's own emotional state. For example, Ochsner *et al.*[58] monitored neural activity while participants viewed images depicting a person in a positive, negative or neutral scene. On each trial, participants were asked to judge their own affective response, the affective response of the person in the picture, or whether the picture depicted an indoor or outdoor scene. Judgements of one's own affective response, relative to judging whether the scene was indoors or outdoors, activated the arMFC. On the basis of previous studies[10,59] and their own research[26], Steele and Laurie have suggested that this region (mean Talairach coordinates: 5,46,18) is concerned with emotion, in contrast to the adjacent more posterior and superior region that is concerned with cognition. However, this conclusion is based largely on research involving emotion induction, in which participants are asked to report their emotional experience. Such commonly-used 'emotion' tasks overlap significantly with tasks assessing self-knowledge – that is, being asked to report one's emotional response is essentially a question about self-knowledge. Given the observation that many other studies activating the same region did not involve strong emotions, we suggest that its characterization as an emotional sector of the MFC is not appropriate. However, direct comparisons of introspection about 'hot' and 'cold' mental states might well reveal systematic differences.

### *Person perception*

Much research investigating the neural activity associated with the perception and judgments of other people has implicated the arMFC[60]. Participants in a study performed by Mitchell *et al.*[61] judged whether adjectives 'could ever be true' of preceding nouns that referred to people or inanimate objects. Judgments about people activated regions of the arMFC (for example, 3,39,0), whereas judgments about inanimate objects activated regions associated with semantic memory. Similar activations were found when participants decided whether behaviours were appropriate for people versus dogs (10,48,32)[62], formed impressions about people as opposed to objects (−9,54,36)[63], observed social interactions (2,52,26)[64], and viewed personally familiar faces (−4,53,19)[65]. It is not clear from these studies whether the observed arMFC activity is associated with thinking about people *per se* or with the mental states ascribed to them. Supporting the latter interpretation, Mitchell *et al.* found that activity in the arMFC (9,54,36) was associated with thinking about the mental states of dogs as well as those of people[66].

**Blood oxygen level dependent signal**

(BOLD signal). fMRI measures local changes in the proportion of oxygenated blood in the brain; the blood oxygen level dependent, or BOLD, signal. This proportion changes in response to neural activity. Therefore, the BOLD signal, or haemodynamic response, indicates the location and magnitude of neural activity.

**Working memory**

Working memory refers to a set of processes involved in rehearsing and manipulating information that has either just been experienced or just been retrieved from long-term memory, often in the service of goal-directed behaviour. Working memory functions are typically associated with activity in the dorsolateral prefrontal cortex.

Observations from self-knowledge studies raise the possibility that activations elicited during the judgment of self-attributes (discussed above) might actually represent a more general process of thinking about 'social' attributes, regardless of whether they pertain to the self. Although several studies have directly contrasted thinking about one attribute of the self versus another, the results are equivocal. For example, Kelley *et al.* observed more activity in the arMFC (10,52,2) of participants when they were thinking about attributes of the self versus George W. Bush[53]. However, Schmitz *et al.*[55] observed activity in a similar region (6,56,4) when participants thought about either the self or a close friend (see also REF. 67). The key difference between these studies might lie in the degree of similarity between the self and the other person. This possibility has been investigated explicitly by Mitchell *et al.*[68] In their study, participants viewed a series of faces and judged them for similarity to themselves. Thinking about more similar others led to greater arMFC activity (9,57,3) in an area very close to the peak activity associated with self-description reported by Kelley *et al.*[53]. Indeed, there seems to be some evidence for a spatial separation between activity elicited when thinking about the self and a similar or familiar other versus unknown others (for examples, see REFS 67,69). The region activated by the self and others close to the self is in the most inferior portion of the region we have labelled the arMFC, whereas the region activated by unknown others is in the most superior portion (FIG. 10.3).

## *Mentalizing*

To engage in successful social interaction, one must recognize that others have independent experiences and intentions, and perhaps even ulterior motives. The ability to represent another person's psychological perspective is referred to as mentalizing[70] and requires theory of mind[71] (BOX 10.1). Mentalizing allows us to predict the behaviour of others. Initial investigations into the neural correlates of mentalizing observed a characteristic network of activations when participants read stories about social interaction, which included the temporoparietal junction, the superior temporal sulcus, the temporal poles, the posterior cingulate cortex and the MFC[72,73]. Various mentalizing tasks have been studied, including story and cartoon comprehension, and the viewing of real-time interactions, which consistently activate the MFC, primarily in the arMFC region[70,74].

In the social psychological literature, the process of determining the causes of a person's behaviour (for example, their beliefs, perceptions or goals) is known as attribution[75,76]. Attribution research asks how we know when a person's behaviour reflects their disposition or their situation. Although attribution is more about the interaction of personality and the situation in determining a person's behaviour, whereas mentalizing is more about inferring another's current knowledge and intentions, a recent fMRI investigation of attribution processes found that judgments made on the basis of clear attributional information are associated with activation of the arMFC (5,50,0), as when typical mentalizing tasks are used[77].

Walter *et al.*[78] make an interesting distinction between reading the private intentions of a person (for example, replacing a light bulb in order to read) and the communicative intentions that are involved in social interactions (for example, showing a map to request directions). They claim that only the reading of communicative intentions is associated with activity in the paracingulate cortex, whereas reading private intentions activates the ACC proper. The same distinction was observed by Grèzes *et al.* using a very different paradigm[79,80]. In these studies, participants observed a video of someone lifting a box. In the first study, the person in the video had sometimes been deceived about the weight of the box. When the subjects judged, from the lifting movements, that the person in the video had a false belief (leading to a private intention about how to lift the box), greater activity was seen in the prMFC (−2,26,56). In the second study, the person in the video sometimes tried to deceive the observer by pretending that the box was heavier or lighter than it really was. When judging that the person in the video was being deceptive (a communicative intention), greater activity was seen in the arMFC (−8,42,20). Therefore, consistent with the subdivisions outlined above, thinking about private intentions elicits activity in the prMFC, whereas thinking about communicative intentions elicits activity in the arMFC.

Each of the tasks reviewed here that elicited activity in the arMFC involved thinking about the psychological attributes of people regardless of whether the person was the self or another person, or whether judgments pertained to dispositions or mental states. However, there are hints of further divisions within this area. Thinking about unfamiliar others and thinking about the simple actions of others activates the lower border of the prMFC and the most superior area of the arMFC. By contrast, thinking about familiar others activates the most inferior area of the arMFC and the upper border of the oMFC. Does this separation relate to the distinction between outcomes and actions? People may have ideas about how unfamiliar others might act. We can often predict actions on the basis of the situation a person is in without needing to know what sort of a person they are. By contrast, predicting how people will feel might depend more on having some familiarity with them. So, we can speculate that the more superior part of the region is more involved with actions, whereas the inferior part is more involved with feelings and outcomes. This division is, of course, commensurate with the likely function of the adjacent regions: the prMFC pertaining to actions, the oMFC pertaining to outcomes.

## Value, pain and self-reflection

We have proposed a functional characterization of more posterior MFC regions, but the functional significance of the arMFC remains less clear. In the remainder of this review, we address this problem by trying to define a trajectory of cognitive processing in the MFC. Our proposal is that representations become more complex and abstract as we move forward through the MFC. A similar proposal has previously been made by Ochsner and Gross in relation to the representation of reinforcement contingencies[81]. Studies of pain provide clues to the form taken by this increasing degree of abstraction. For example, on the basis of pain research, Craig[82] has proposed that high-resolution, modality-specific sensory representation of the physiological condition of the body in the posterior insula is re-represented in the anterior insula. This second-order re-representation in the right anterior insula is believed to subserve subjective feelings and the awareness of a physical self. We propose that a similar progression, which is involved in the broader process of social cognition, occurs in the MFC.

Pain controls our behaviour through a particularly primitive form of value, but even the negative value of pain is subject to top-down control. Rainville *et al.* studied changes in neural activity associated with the analgesic effects of hypnosis in different segments of the ACC[83,84]. In the most caudal region (1,5,56/−1,3,39), activity elicited by a painful stimulus was unaffected by hypnosis. However, the reduced subjective experience of pain resulting from hypnosis was associated with decreased activity in the prACC (3,20,30/0,29,35). Similar results were reported by Wager *et al.*[85], such that treatment with placebo analgesia did not affect the caudal ACC (0,−4,50) and inferior ACC (0,54,−18) activity in response to pain, whereas placebo treatment was associated with reduced prACC activity (4,23,27/3,18,34). Furthermore, the change in prACC activity was correlated with the change in subjective ratings of pain (see also REF. 86). These studies suggest that the caudal region of the ACC represents more objective aspects of pain (for example, the temperature of the stimulus), whereas the prACC represents subjective properties of pain.

This distinction between objective and subjective aspects of pain has also been suggested by research on empathy by Singer *et al.*[87] Activity in the caudal ACC (6,6,42) was elicited only by pain felt by the self. Activity in the prACC (−3,24,33) was elicited by pain to the self and also by the knowledge that a significant other was in pain (see also REFS 88,89). Here again, the response to pain in this more anterior region was independent of sensory input, suggesting a more abstract form of representation. The results of EEG studies show that this region is also involved when we observe the actions of others. A negative ERP component arising from the MFC is seen not only when we make an error, but also when we receive delayed error feedback[90–92] or observe someone else making an error[93,94]. How can we link these results with our characterization of the prACC as being about the value of possible actions? An important facet of pain is our strong desire for action to escape or reduce it. Similarly, we also have strong drives to take action when we know that a significant other is in pain. Top-down influences that devalue the pain, such as hypnosis and placebo analgesia, should also devalue our drive to take action.

The stimuli used in studies of negative emotion induction can also be viewed as the application of painful stimuli. Typically, subjects are shown photographs of unknown people in painful or dangerous situations. Whether or not these stimuli elicit activity in the arMFC depends on the task participants are given. A stimulus with strong emotional valence[95,96] activates the caudal ACC (14,6,30/−5,3,48) even when participants are simply reporting whether the scene is indoors or outdoors, but the arMFC is only activated by such stimuli when participants are asked to rate their emotional arousal in response to the stimuli; the activated regions are located at Talairach coordinates 0,50,16 (REF. 97) and −3,41,8 (REF. 96). As with pain, the caudal region of the ACC is activated by unpleasant stimuli across tasks, whereas a more anterior region is activated only when participants report how unpleasant the picture makes them feel. Again, we find that more anterior regions of the MFC seem to be concerned with subjective, more abstract representations of experience.

But why does the subjective experience of pain activate the prMFC, whereas reporting the subjective experience of emotionally arousing pictures activates the arMFC? The primary difference is that pain is intrinsically unpleasant, whereas a picture is only unpleasant when we think about the experiences of the people depicted in it. In the study of Singer *et al.*, the arMFC was not activated by application of pain to the participant[87]. However, activity in this region (−6,45,21) was elicited by the knowledge that a loved one was in pain, with greater activity associated with higher self-ratings of empathy. Therefore, it is not the subjective unpleasantness of the pain itself that activates this region, but rather thinking about the subjective unpleasantness of the pain. Thinking about pain is the same meta-cognitive process that is involved in thinking about the unpleasantness of emotionally-arousing pictures.

Recent evidence reported in the ERP literature also suggests that the more anterior regions of the MFC are involved in more complex social cognitive processing. ERP research on error processing and cognitive control has revealed two important neural components. The ERN, which occurs within milliseconds of a response, reflects an early, pre-conscious stage of conflict monitoring that is associated with dorsal regions of the ACC, whereas the error-positivity ($P_e$), which occurs ~200 ms post response, is associated with the awareness of error commission and has been linked to activity in the rostral anterior cingulate and paracingulate cortices[98,99]. This distinction is consistent with functional organizations suggested by Eisenberger and Lieberman[100], and by Ochsner and his colleagues[58,67]. In a study by Amodio *et al.*[101] that capitalized on this distinction, participants performed a cognitive task purporting to measure their level of racial bias either confidentially (in private) or while being observed by an ostensibly non-prejudiced experimenter (in public). When in private, participants presumably regulated their response according to their internal motives for accuracy on the task, whereas in public they additionally regulated behaviour according to the perceived social demand to appear non-prejudiced. Amodio *et al.* found that better response control in private was predicted solely by larger ERN amplitudes, replicating past work[32,38]. By contrast, when responding in public, better response control was predicted by larger $P_e$ amplitudes only among participants who had previously reported being highly sensitive to social pressures to appear non-prejudiced. Importantly, the condition in which the $P_e$ strongly predicted behaviour involved monitoring the value that others put on the actions of the self. This is certainly a more complex and abstract representation of the value of actions: it is a meta-representation that enables us to reflect on the value of an action and contrast this with the value that others would place on the same action.

## Morality, reputation and the self

If we characterize the role of the arMFC as allowing the meta-cognitive process of reflecting on feelings and intentions, then we can provide a unitary account of the wide range of different tasks that activate this region. The ability to reflect on our subjective experience is of great importance for many aspects of social cognition. For example, when confronted with a moral dilemma, we base our decision on what feels like the right thing to do rather than on a logical analysis. Such decisions are associated with activity in the arMFC (0,50,17)[32]. People often reflect on their feelings for information when making decisions about what they like and dislike[102], and such reflection has been found to activate this same region (−6,55,13)[56].

An important, but often underappreciated, aspect of moral decisions is that they are not based solely on reflections about the self, but also relate to the image of the self we want to project into the minds of others: our reputation. Much social psychological research shows that there is a distinction between our actual behaviour and the image we wish to have of ourselves and to present to others[103,104]. This concept of reputation is essentially a representation of how others represent us (although note that this re-representation of subordinate knowledge structures might not be conscious or deliberative, and is therefore distinguished from metacognition). Such a representation goes beyond the first-level representations of our own attributes or the attributes of others. The representation of our own reputation requires that we close the social loop and form a second-level representation of the attributes that others apply to us. Ochsner *et al.* refer to this as reflected self-knowledge[67]. We have to think about how others think about us. This is perhaps why the same region is activated whether we are thinking about our own psychological attributes or those of others.

Self- and other-referencing, and counter-referencing are even more obviously involved when playing economic games that involve trust and reciprocity[105]. Before we invest we must decide not just whether we trust the other player, but also whether the other player trusts us. Consistent with our formulation, the arMFC is activated when playing these games, especially when participants are cooperating, as long as they believe they are playing against a person rather than a computer. In these studies, arMFC activation was observed at Talairach coordinates 5,52,10 (REF. 106) and 3,44,20 (REF. 107).

## Conclusions

The meeting of neuroscientists and social psychologists in research on the MFC has led to a remarkably rich and varied set of experimental data from which to speculate about the function of this region. Our assumption has been that the different functions instantiated in this region are not placed randomly, but form a systematic map. As part of the frontal cortex, this region is concerned with determining future behaviour. More specifically, it is concerned with determining behaviour on the basis of anticipated value. In the more caudal region of the MFC value is associated with actions, whereas in the more orbital region value is associated with outcomes. These representations become more abstract as we move forward, such that the most anterior region of the MFC is associated with metacognitive representations that enable us to reflect on the values linked to outcomes and actions (that is, thinking about thinking). These high level representations have a major role in many aspects of social cognition. Not only do they allow us to reflect on the values that other people attach to actions and outcomes, they also allow us to reflect on what other people think about us. These speculations remain to be confirmed, but we hope we have provided a framework for future research on the role of the MFC in social cognition that will permit fruitful interactions between neuroscientists and social psychologists.

## Acknowledgements

We are grateful to D. Passingham, J. Mitchell, K. Ochsner and an anonymous reviewer for their comments on early versions of this review.

## Notes

1 Cohen, S. Social relationships and health. *Am. Psychol.* **59,** 676–684 (2004).

2 Silk, J. B., Alberts, S. C. & Altmann, J. Social bonds of female baboons enhance infant survival. *Science* **302,** 1231–1234 (2003).

3 Fiske, S. T. & Taylor, S. E. *Social Cognition* (McGraw-Hill, New York, 1991).

4 Bargh, J. A. in *Handbook of Social Cognition: Basic Processes* (Eds Wyer, R. S. Jr & Srull, T. K.) 1–40 (Hillsdale, New Jersey/Lawrence Erlbaum Associates, Inc. England, 1994).

5 Devine, P. G. Stereotypes and prejudice: their automatic and controlled components. *J. Pers. Soc. Psychol.* **56,** 5–18 (1989).

6 Kihlstrom, J. F. The cognitive unconscious. *Science* **237,** 1445–1452 (1987).

7 Eslinger, P. J. & Damasio, A. R. Severe disturbance of higher cognition after bilateral frontal lobe ablation: patient EVR. *Neurology* **35,** 1731–1741 (1985).

8 Farah, M. J. Agnosia. *Curr. Opin. Neurobiol.* **2,** 162–164 (1992).

9 Ochsner, K. N. & Lieberman, M. D. The emergence of social cognitive neuroscience. *Am. Psychol.* **56,** 717–734 (2001).

**The authors propose the theoretical and methodological integration of neuroscience, cognitive science and social psychology, and introduce the new field of social cognitive neuroscience.**

10 Bush, G., Luu, P. & Posner, M. I. Cognitive and emotional influences in anterior cingulate cortex. *Trends Cogn. Sci.* **4,** 215–222 (2000).

11 Ullsperger, M. & von Cramon, D. Y. Neuroimaging of performance monitoring: error detection and beyond. *Cortex* **40,** 593–604 (2004).

**Important evidence on the connectivity of medial prefrontal cortex obtained from studies of the monkey that provides a model of anatomical connectivity of the MFC in humans.**

12 Barbas, H., Ghashghaei, H., Dombrowski, S. M. & Rempel-Clower, N. L. Medial prefrontal cortices are unified by common connections with superior temporal cortices and distinguished by input from memory-related areas in the rhesus monkey. *J. Comp. Neurol.* **410,** 343–367 (1999).

13 Carmichael, S. T. & Price, J. L. Connectional networks within the orbital and medial prefrontal cortex of macaque monkeys. *J. Comp. Neurol.* **371,** 179–207 (1996).
14 Bates, J. F. & Goldman-Rakic, P. S. Prefrontal connections of medial motor areas in the rhesus monkey. *J. Comp. Neurol.* **336,** 211–228 (1993).
15 Amaral, D. G. & Price, J. L. Amygdalo-cortical projections in the monkey (*Macaca fascicularis*). *J. Comp. Neurol.* **230,** 465–496 (1984).
16 Vogt, B. A. & Pandya, D. N. Cingulate cortex of the rhesus monkey: II. Cortical afferents. *J. Comp. Neurol.* **262,** 271–289 (1987).
17 Ray, J. P. & Price, J. L. The organization of projections from the mediodorsal nucleus of the thalamus to orbital and medial prefrontal cortex in macaque monkeys. *J. Comp. Neurol.* **337,** 1–31 (1993).
18 Petrides, M. & Pandya, D. N. Dorsolateral prefrontal cortex: comparative cytoarchitectonic analysis in the human and the macaque brain and corticocortical connection patterns. *Eur. J. Neurosci.* **11,** 1011–1036 (1999).
19 Ongur, D., Ferry, A. T. & Price, J. L. Architectonic subdivision of the human orbital and medial prefrontal cortex. *J. Comp. Neurol.* **460,** 425–449 (2003).
20 Sherwood, C. C., Holloway, R. L., Semendeferi, K. & Hof, P. R. Is prefrontal white matter enlargement a human evolutionary specialization? *Nature Neurosci.* **8,** 537–538; author reply 538 (2005).
21 Koski, L. & Paus, T. Functional connectivity of the anterior cingulate cortex within the human frontal lobe: a brain-mapping meta-analysis. *Exp. Brain Res.* **133,** 55–65 (2000).

**Provides a useful account of the connectivity of the ACC based on human functional data.**

22 Croxson, P. L. *et al.* Quantitative investigation of connections of the prefrontal cortex in the human and macaque using probabilistic diffusion tractography. *J. Neurosci.* **25,** 8854–8866 (2005).
23 Paus, T., Petrides, M., Evans, A. C. & Meyer, E. Role of the human anterior cingulate cortex in the control of oculomotor, manual, and speech responses: a positron emission tomography study. *J. Neurophysiol.* **70,** 453–469 (1993).
24 Picard, N. & Strick, P. L. Motor areas of the medial wall: a review of their location and functional activation. *Cereb. Cortex* **6,** 342–353 (1996).
25 Paus, T., Koski, L., Caramanos, Z. & Westbury, C. Regional differences in the effects of task difficulty and motor output on blood flow response in the human anterior cingulate cortex: a review of 107 PET activation studies. *Neuroreport* **9,** R37–R47 (1998).
26 Steele, J. D. & Lawrie, S. M. Segregation of cognitive and emotional function in the prefrontal cortex: a stereotactic meta-analysis. *Neuroimage* **21,** 868–875 (2004).

**A careful meta-analysis of studies activating the MFC that reveals clear functional segregation of cognitive and emotional processes.**

27 Botvinick, M. M., Cohen, J. D. & Carter, C. S. Conflict monitoring and anterior cingulate cortex: an update. *Trends Cogn. Sci.* **8,** 539–546 (2004).
28 Botvinick, M., Nystrom, L. E., Fissell, K., Carter, C. S. & Cohen, J. D. Conflict monitoring versus selection-for-action in anterior cingulate cortex. *Nature* **402,** 179–181 (1999).
29 Carter, C. S. *et al.* Anterior cingulate cortex, error detection, and the online monitoring of performance. *Science* **280,** 747–749 (1998).

30 Liddle, P. F., Kiehl, K. A. & Smith, A.M. Event-related fMRI study of response inhibition. *Hum. Brain Mapp.* **12,** 100–109 (2001).

31 Barch, D. M. *et al.* Anterior cingulate cortex and response conflict: effects of response modality and processing domain. *Cereb. Cortex* **11,** 837–848 (2001).

32 Gehring, W., Goss, B., Coles, M., Meyer, D. & Donchin, E. A neural system for error detection and compensation. *Psychol. Sci.* **4,** 385–390 (1993).

33 Brázdil, M. *et al.* Combined event-related fMRI and intracerebral ERP study of an auditory oddball task. *Neuroimage* **26,** 285–293 (2005).

34 Dehaene, S., Posner, M. & Tucker, D. Localization of a neural system for error detection and compensation. *Psychol. Sci.* **5,** 303–305 (1994).

35 Yeung, N., Cohen, J. D. & Botvinick, M. M. The neural basis of error detection: conflict monitoring and the error-related negativity. *Psychol. Rev.* **111,** 931–959 (2004).

36 Bartholow, B. D. *et al.* Strategic control and medial frontal negativity: beyond errors and response conflict. *Psychophysiology* **42,** 33–42 (2005).

37 Hajcak, G., Moser, J. S., Yeung, N. & Simons, R. F. On the ERN and the significance of errors. *Psychophysiology* **42,** 151–160 (2005).

38 Amodio, D. M. *et al.* Neural signals for the detection of unintentional race bias. *Psychol. Sci.* **15,** 88–93 (2004).

39 Walton, M. E., Devlin, J. T. & Rushworth, M. F. Interactions between decision making and performance monitoring within prefrontal cortex. *Nature Neurosci.* **7,** 1259–1265 (2004).

**Reveals an important distinction between monitoring actions and monitoring outcomes in the prefrontal cortex.**

40 Knutson, B., Taylor, J., Kaufman, M., Peterson, R. & Glover, G. Distributed neural representation of expected value. *J. Neurosci.* **25,** 4806–4812 (2005).

41 Coricelli, G. *et al.* Regret and its avoidance: a neuroimaging study of choice behavior. *Nature Neurosci.* **8,** 1255–1262 (2005).

**An important demonstration of the role of emotion (anticipated regret) in decision making.**

42 Brown, J. W. & Braver, T. S. Learned predictions of error likelihood in the anterior cingulate cortex. *Science* **307,** 1118–1121 (2005).

43 Holroyd, C. B. & Coles, M. G. The neural basis of human error processing: reinforcement learning, dopamine, and the error-related negativity. *Psychol. Rev.* **109,** 679–709 (2002).

44 Rolls, E. T. The orbitofrontal cortex. *Phil. Trans. R. Soc. Lond. B* **351,** 1433–1443; discussion 1443–1444 (1996).

45 Elliott, R., Dolan, R. J. & Frith, C. D. Dissociable functions in the medial and lateral orbitofrontal cortex: evidence from human neuroimaging studies. *Cereb. Cortex* **10,** 308–317 (2000).

46 Camille, N. *et al.* The involvement of the orbitofrontal cortex in the experience of regret. *Science* **304,** 1167–1170 (2004).

47 Fellows, L. K. & Farah, M. J. Different underlying impairments in decision-making following ventromedial and dorsolateral frontal lobe damage in humans. *Cereb. Cortex* **15,** 58–63 (2005).

48 Ridderinkhof, K. R., Ullsperger, M., Crone, E. A. & Nieuwenhuis, S. The role of the medial frontal cortex in cognitive control. *Science* **306,** 443–447 (2004).

49 Alexander, G. E., DeLong, M. R. & Strick, P. L. Parallel organization of functionally segregated circuits linking basal ganglia and cortex. *Annu. Rev. Neurosci.* **9,** 357–381 (1986).
50 Lehericy, S. *et al.* Diffusion tensor fiber tracking shows distinct corticostriatal circuits in humans. *Ann. Neurol.* **55,** 522–529 (2004).
51 Baumeister, R. F. in *The Handbook of Social Psychology* Vol. 1, 4th edn (eds Gilbert, D. T., Fiske, S. T. & Lindzey, G.) 680–740 (McGraw Hill, New York, USA, 1998).
52 Johnson, S. C. *et al.* Neural correlates of self-reflection. *Brain* **125,** 1808–1814 (2002).
53 Kelley, W. M. *et al.* Finding the self? An event-related fMRI study. *J. Cogn. Neurosci.* **14,** 785–794 (2002).
54 Lieberman, M. D., Jarcho, J. M. & Satpute, A. B. Evidence-based and intuition-based self-knowledge: an fMRI study. *J. Pers. Soc. Psychol.* **87,** 421–435 (2004).
55 Schmitz, T. W., Kawahara-Baccus, T. N. & Johnson, S. C. Metacognitive evaluation, self-relevance, and the right prefrontal cortex. *Neuroimage* **22,** 941–947 (2004).
56 Zysset, S., Huber, O., Ferstl, E. & von Cramon, D. Y. The anterior frontomedian cortex and evaluative judgment: an fMRI study. *Neuroimage* **15,** 983–991 (2002).
57 Macrae, C. N., Moran, J. M., Heatherton, T. F., Banfield, J. F. & Kelley, W. M. Medial prefrontal activity predicts memory for self. *Cereb. Cortex* **14,** 647–654 (2004).
58 Ochsner, K. N. *et al.* Reflecting upon feelings: an fMRI study of neural systems supporting the attribution of emotion to self and other. *J. Cogn. Neurosci.* **16,** 1746–1772 (2004).

**An important demonstration of the role of the MFC in emotion attributions, and a detailed review of MFC activation associated with inferring emotional responses of the self and others.**

59 Phan, K. L., Wager, T., Taylor, S. F. & Liberzon, I. Functional neuroanatomy of emotion: a meta-analysis of emotion activation studies in PET and fMRI. *Neuroimage* **16,** 331–348 (2002).
60 Lieberman, M. D. & Pfeifer, J. H. The self and social perception, in *Cognitive Neuroscience of Social Behavior* (eds Easton, A. & Emery, N.) 195–235 (Psychology Press, Philadelphia, 2005).
61 Mitchell, J. P., Heatherton, T. F. & Macrae, C. N. Distinct neural systems subserve person and object knowledge. *Proc. Natl Acad. Sci. USA* **99,** 15238–15243 (2002).
62 Mason, M. F., Banfield, J. F. & Macrae, C. N. Thinking about actions: the neural substrates of person knowledge. *Cereb. Cortex* **14,** 209–214 (2004).
63 Mitchell, J., Macrae, C. & Banaji, M. Forming impressions of people versus inanimate objects: social-cognitive processing in the medial prefrontal cortex. *Neuroimage* **26,** 251–257 (2005).
64 Iacoboni, M. *et al.* Watching social interactions produces dorsomedial prefrontal and medial parietal BOLD fMRI signal increases compared to a resting baseline. *Neuroimage* **21,** 1167–1173 (2004).
65 Gobbini, M. I., Leibenluft, E., Santiago, N. & Haxby, J. V. Social and emotional attachment in the neural representation of faces. *Neuroimage* **22,** 1628–1635 (2004).
66 Mitchell, J. P., Banaji, M. R. & Macrae, C. N. General and specific contributions of the medial prefrontal cortex to knowledge about mental states. *Neuroimage* **28,** 757–762 (2005).

**An important demonstration that activity in the MFC is associated with the inference of others' mental states, rather than specific person-related attributes.**

67 Ochsner, K. N. *et al.* The neural correlates of direct and reflected self-knowledge. *Neuroimage* **28,** 797–814 (2005).
68 Mitchell, J. P., Banaji, M. R. & Macrae, C. N. The link between social cognition and self-referential thought in the medial prefrontal cortex. *J. Cogn. Neurosci.* **17,** 1306–1315 (2005).
69 Craik, F. I. M. *et al.* In search of the self: a positron emission tomography study. *Psychol. Sci.* **10,** 26–34 (1999).
70 Frith, U. & Frith, C. D. Development and neurophysiology of mentalizing. *Phil. Trans. R. Soc. Lond. B* **358,** 459–473 (2003).
71 Premack, D. & Woodruff, G. Chimpanzee problem-solving: a test for comprehension. *Science* **202,** 532–535 (1978).
72 Fletcher, P. C. *et al.* Other minds in the brain: a functional imaging study of 'theory of mind' in story comprehension. *Cognition* **57,** 109–128 (1995).
73 Goel, V., Grafman, J., Sadato, N. & Hallett, M. Modeling other minds. *Neuroreport* **6,** 1741–1746 (1995).
74 Saxe, R., Carey, S. & Kanwisher, N. Understanding other minds: linking developmental psychology and functional neuroimaging. *Annu. Rev. Psychol.* **55,** 87–124 (2004).
75 Gilbert, D. T. in *The Handbook of Social Psychology* Vol. 2, 4th edn (eds Gilbert, D. T., Fiske, S. T. & Lindzey, G.) 89–150 (McGraw Hill, New York, USA, 1998).
76 Jones, E. E. & Davis, K. E. in *Advances in Experimental Social Psychology* (ed. Berkowitz, L.) 220–266 (Academic, New York, 1965).
77 Harris, L. T., Todorov, A. & Fiske, S. T. Attributions on the brain: neuro-imaging dispositional inferences, beyond theory of mind. *Neuroimage* **28,** 763–769 (2005).
78 Walter, H. *et al.* Understanding intentions in social interaction: the role of the anterior paracingulate cortex. *J. Cogn. Neurosci.* **16,** 1854–1863 (2004).
79 Grezes, J., Frith, C. & Passingham, R. E. Brain mechanisms for inferring deceit in the actions of others. *J. Neurosci.* **24,** 5500–5505 (2004).

**Demonstrates an interesting distinction between the role of the MFC and the pSTS in social cognition that involves mentalizing.**

80 Grezes, J., Frith, C. D. & Passingham, R. E. Inferring false beliefs from the actions of oneself and others: an fMRI study. *Neuroimage* **21,** 744–750 (2004).
81 Ochsner, K. N. & Gross, J. J. The cognitive control of emotion. *Trends Cogn. Sci.* **9,** 242–249 (2005).
82 Craig, A.D. How do you feel? Interoception: the sense of the physiological condition of the body. *Nature Rev. Neurosci.* **3,** 655–666 (2002).

**Proposes that interoceptive information is represented in an explicit form in the anterior insula.**

83 Rainville, P., Duncan, G. H., Price, D. D., Carrier, B. & Bushnell, M. C. Pain affect encoded in human anterior cingulate but not somatosensory cortex. *Science* **277,** 968–971 (1997).
84 Rainville, P. *et al.* Cerebral mechanisms of hypnotic induction and suggestion. *J. Cogn. Neurosci.* **11,** 110–125 (1999).
85 Wager, T. D. *et al.* Placebo-induced changes in fMRI in the anticipation and experience of pain. *Science* **303,** 1162–1167 (2004).
86 Salomons, T. V., Johnstone, T., Backonja, M. M. & Davidson, R. J. Perceived controllability modulates the neural response to pain. *J. Neurosci.* **24,** 7199–7203 (2004).

87 Singer, T. *et al.* Empathy for pain involves the affective but not sensory components of pain. *Science* **303,** 1157–1162 (2004).

**Reveals functional segregation of the anterior cingulate in relation to sensory and affective properties of pain.**

88 Jackson, P. L., Meltzoff, A. N. & Decety, J. How do we perceive the pain of others? A window into the neural processes involved in empathy. *Neuroimage* **24,** 771–779 (2005).

89 Morrison, I., Lloyd, D., di Pellegrino, G. & Roberts, N. Vicarious responses to pain in anterior cingulate cortex: is empathy a multisensory issue? *Cogn. Affect. Behav. Neurosci.* **4,** 270–278 (2004).

90 Donkers, F. C., Nieuwenhuis, S. & van Boxtel, G. J. Mediofrontal negativities in the absence of responding. *Brain Res. Cogn. Brain Res.* **25,** 777–787 (2005).

91 Luu, P., Tucker, D. M., Derryberry, D., Reed, M. & Poulsen, C. Electrophysiological responses to errors and feedback in the process of action regulation. *Psychol. Sci.* **14,** 47–53 (2003).

92 Gehring, W. J. & Willoughby, A. R. The medial frontal cortex and the rapid processing of monetary gains and losses. *Science* **295,** 2279–2282 (2002).

93 van Schie, H. T., Mars, R. B., Coles, M. G. & Bekkering, H. Modulation of activity in medial frontal and motor cortices during error observation. *Nature Neurosci.* **7,** 549–554 (2004).

94 Bates, A. T., Patel, T. P. & Liddle, P. F. External behavior monitoring mirrors internal behavior monitoring: error-related negativity for observed errors. *J. Psychophysiol.* **19,** 281–288 (2005).

95 Lane, R. D. *et al.* Neural correlates of levels of emotional awareness. Evidence of an interaction between emotion and attention in the anterior cingulate cortex. *J. Cogn. Neurosci.* **10,** 525–535 (1998).

96 Gusnard, D. A., Akbudak, E., Shulman, G. L. & Raichle, M. E. Medial prefrontal cortex and self-referential mental activity: relation to a default mode of brain function. *Proc. Natl Acad. Sci. USA* **98,** 4259–4264 (2001).

**A classic paper examining the functional significance of 'resting activity' in fMRI studies. The authors suggest that self-referential processes correspond to the default mode of function in the MFC.**

97 Lane, R. D., Fink, G. R., Chau, P.M. & Dolan, R. J. Neural activation during selective attention to subjective emotional responses. *Neuroreport* **8,** 3969–3972 (1997).

98 Nieuwenhuis, S., Ridderinkhof, K. R., Blom, J., Band, G. P. & Kok, A. Error-related brain potentials are differentially related to awareness of response errors: evidence from an antisaccade task. *Psychophysiology* **38,** 752–760 (2001).

99 Van Veen, V. & Carter, C. S. The timing of action-monitoring processes in the anterior cingulate cortex. *J. Cogn. Neurosci.* **14,** 593–602 (2002).

100 Eisenberger, N. I. & Lieberman, M. D. Why rejection hurts: a common neural alarm system for physical and social pain. *Trends Cogn. Sci.* **8,** 294–300 (2004).

101 Amodio, D. M., Kubota, J. T., Harmon-Jones, E. & Devine, P. G. Alternative mechanisms for regulating racial responses according to internal vs. external cues. *Soc. Cogn. Affect. Neurosci.* **1,** 26–36 (2006).

102 Schwarz, N. & Clore, G. L. Mood, misattribution, and judgments of well-being: informative and directive functions of affective states. *J. Pers. Soc. Psychol.* **45,** 513–523 (1983).

103 Devine, P. G., Monteith, M. M., Zuwerink, J. R. & Elliot, A. J. Prejudice with and without compunction. *J. Pers. Soc. Psychol.* **60,** 817–830 (1991).

104 Higgins, E. T. Self-discrepancy: a theory relating self and affect. *Psychol. Rev.* **94,** 319–340 (1987).

105 Camerer, C. F. Psychology and economics. Strategizing in the brain. *Science* **300,** 1673–1675 (2003).

106 McCabe, K., Houser, D., Ryan, L., Smith, V. & Trouard, T. A functional imaging study of cooperation in two-person reciprocal exchange. *Proc. Natl Acad. Sci. USA* **98,** 11832–11835 (2001).

**The first demonstration of a role for the MFC in trust and reciprocity games.**

107 Rilling, J. K., Sanfey, A. G., Aronson, J. A., Nystrom, L. E. & Cohen, J. D. The neural correlates of theory of mind within interpersonal interactions. *Neuroimage* **22,** 1694–1703 (2004).

108 Wimmer, H. & Perner, J. Beliefs about beliefs: representation and constraining function of wrong beliefs in young children's understanding of deception. *Cognition* **13,** 103–128 (1983).

109 Brunet, E., Sarfati, Y., Hardy-Bayle, M. C. & Decety, J. A PET investigation of the attribution of intentions with a nonverbal task. *Neuroimage* **11,** 157–166 (2000).

110 Heider, F. & Simmel, M. An experimental study of apparent behavior. *Am. J. Psychol.* **57,** 243–249 (1944).

111 Castelli, F., Happe, F., Frith, U. & Frith, C. Movement and mind: a functional imaging study of perception and interpretation of complex intentional movement patterns. *Neuroimage* **12,** 314–325 (2000).

112 Gallagher, H. L., Jack, A. I., Roepstorff, A. & Frith, C. D. Imaging the intentional stance in a competitive game. *Neuroimage* **16,** 814–821 (2002).

113 Corcoran, R., Cahill, C. & Frith, C. D. The appreciation of visual jokes in people with schizophrenia: a study of 'mentalizing' ability. *Schizophr. Res.* **24,** 319–327 (1997).

114 Gallagher, H. L. *et al.* Reading the mind in cartoons and stories: an fMRI study of 'theory of mind' in verbal and nonverbal tasks. *Neuropsychologia* **38,** 11–21 (2000).

115 Adolphs, R. Cognitive neuroscience of human social behaviour. *Nature Rev. Neurosci.* **4,** 165–178 (2003).

116 Gusnard, D. A. & Raichle, M. E. Searching for a baseline: functional imaging and the resting human brain. *Nature Rev. Neurosci.* **2,** 685–694 (2001).

117 Fransson, P. Spontaneous low-frequency BOLD signal fluctuations: an fMRI investigation of the resting-state default mode of brain function hypothesis. *Hum. Brain Mapp.* **26,** 15–29 (2005).

118 Lieberman, M. D., Gaunt, R., Gilbert, D. T. & Trope, Y. in *Advances in Experimental Social Psychology* (ed. Zanna, M.) 199–249 (Academic, New York, 2002).

119 D'Argembeau, A. *et al.* Self-referential reflective activity and its relationship with rest: a PET study. *Neuroimage* **25,** 616–624 (2005).

120 Maguire, E. A. & Mummery, C. J. Differential modulation of a common memory retrieval network revealed by positron emission tomography. *Hippocampus* **9,** 54–61 (1999).

121 Maguire, E. A., Mummery, C. J. & Buchel, C. Patterns of hippocampal-cortical interaction dissociate temporal lobe memory subsystems. *Hippocampus* **10,** 475–482 (2000).

122 Bonda, E., Petrides, M., Ostry, D. & Evans, A. Specific involvement of human parietal systems and the amygdala in the perception of biological motion. *J. Neurosci.* **16,** 3737–3744 (1996).

123 Turk, D. J. *et al.* From facial cue to dinner for two: the neural substrates of personal choice. *Neuroimage* **22,** 1281–1290 (2004).

124 Bottini, G. *et al.* The role of the right hemisphere in the interpretation of figurative aspects of language. A positron emission tomography activation study. *Brain* **117,** 1241–1253 (1994).
125 Ferstl, E. C. & von Cramon, D. Y. What does the frontomedian cortex contribute to language processing: coherence or theory of mind? *Neuroimage* **17,** 1599–1612 (2002).
126 German, T. P., Niehaus, J. L., Roarty, M. P., Giesbrecht, B. & Miller, M. B. Neural correlates of detecting pretense: automatic engagement of the intentional stance under covert conditions. *J. Cogn. Neurosci.* **16,** 1805–1817 (2004).
127 Greene, J. D., Sommerville, R. B., Nystrom, L. E., Darley, J. M. & Cohen, J. D. An fMRI investigation of emotional engagement in moral judgment. *Science* **293,** 2105–1208 (2001).
128 Heekeren, H. R. *et al.* Influence of bodily harm on neural correlates of semantic and moral decision-making. *Neuroimage* **24,** 887–897 (2005).
129 Kampe, K. K., Frith, C. D. & Frith, U. "Hey John": signals conveying communicative intention toward the self activate brain regions associated with "mentalizing," regardless of modality. *J. Neurosci.* **23,** 5258–5263 (2003).
130 Schilbach, L. *et al.* Being with virtual others: neural correlates of social interaction. *Neuropsychologia* **44,** 718–730 (2006).
131 Vogeley, K. *et al.* Mind reading: neural mechanisms of theory of mind and self-perspective. *Neuroimage* **14,** 170–181 (2001).
132 Braver, T. S., Barch, D. M., Gray, J. R., Molfese, D. L. & Snyder, A. Anterior cingulate cortex and response conflict: effects of frequency, inhibition and errors. *Cereb. Cortex* **11,** 825–836 (2001).
133 Bunge, S. A., Hazeltine, E., Scanlon, M. D., Rosen, A. C. & Gabrieli, J. D. Dissociable contributions of prefrontal and parietal cortices to response selection. *Neuroimage* **17,** 1562–1571 (2002).
134 Casey, B. J. *et al.* Dissociation of response conflict, attentional selection, and expectancy with functional magnetic resonance imaging. *Proc. Natl Acad. Sci. USA* **97,** 8728–8733 (2000).
135 Eisenberger, N. I., Lieberman, M. D. & Williams, K. D. Does rejection hurt? An fMRI study of social exclusion. *Science* **302,** 290–292 (2003).
136 Kerns, J. G. *et al.* Anterior cingulate conflict monitoring and adjustments in control. *Science* **303,** 1023–1026 (2004).

# 11 The role of gaze in dialogue

*B. J. Hedge, B. S. Everitt and C. D. Frith**

## 1 Introduction

It is widely believed that the flow of conversation in a dialogue is regulated by various nonverbal cues (Condon and Ogston 1966; Kendon 1967, 1970; Duncan 1972). Some of these cues, such as pauses and inflections, are incorporated in the speech; other cues are quite independent of speech. For example, a number of studies (Kendon 1967; Argyle et al. 1968; Kendon and Cook 1969) have suggested that eye gaze plays an important role in controlling the flow of conversation. However, a formal demonstration of this proposition has not been presented. Kendon (1967) demonstrated that significant changes in direction of eye gaze are associated with transitions from one speaker to another during a dialogue, but this does not of course imply that the pattern of eye gaze was regulating the transitions. In this paper we shall show that a simple mathematical model of gaze and speech behaviours can provide evidence of an important role for gaze in the smooth exchange of speakers in a dialogue. However, we shall also show that the role of gaze is dependent on situational factors associated with the dialogue.

Two simple but plausible assumptions can be made about the process by which a participant in a dialogue decides whether to speak or not at any given time:

1 His decision to speak or not at some given time will be made on the basis of the state of the dialogue at the immediately preceding time. This state of the dialogue would include information from the various nonverbal cues already mentioned.
2 His decision to speak or not at each point in time will be made independently of his partner's decision to speak or not in the same instant. Both partners in the dialogue can only base their decision to speak on various external cues. They have no access, except perhaps through the meaning of what is said, to each other's inner states.

Both these assumptions can readily be incorporated by modelling dialogue as a first-order Markov process. Such models for processes exhibiting sequential patterning are described in detail in Billingsley (1961), Kemeny and Snell (1960) and Chatfield (1973). If a dialogue is represented by such a process, then its state at time $t$ is completely determined by its state at time $t - 1$. That the two participants in the dialogue should act independently at each point in time is a special case of this Markov process involving additional and simplifying assumptions.

If the decision to speak at each point in time is dependent on the speech and gaze behaviours of both participants at the previous point in time then a first-order Markov process that includes information about both speech and gaze behaviours will adequately account for the sequence of events. However, a first-order Markov process that took into account only speech would not adequately account for the sequence of events. Such a result would provide evidence that gaze plays a crucial role in dialogue. If a first-order Markov process is not adequate even when both gaze and speech behaviours are considered this would imply that other additional cues are used by participants, or that a more complex time series is involved. This might be the case if the semantic content of the speech had an important role in regulating the flow of dialogue. By the same argument, if gaze and speech are sufficient to describe the dialogue it would also be required that the two participants should be acting independently. If the independence model did not fit this would imply that participants were using additional information which had not been incorporated into the model.

Thus, by attempting to fit a model of dialogue as a first-order Markov process in which the two participants act independently at each point in time it should be possible to demonstrate whether or not gaze has an important role in dialogue and whether or not additional factors other than gaze and speech are also involved. However, it is possible that the use of gaze in dialogues may also be affected by factors specific to the situation.

For example, it has been shown by Exline et al. (1965) and Schulz and Barefoot (1974) that while speaking, the time a person spends gazing towards his partner decreases as the intimacy of the conversation increases. In addition a number of studies including those of Exline and Winters (1965), Rubin (1970) and Cook and Smith (1975) have indicated that gaze behaviour varies with the degree of affiliation between conversational partners. It therefore seems likely that pairs of friends and pairs of strangers may utilize gaze cues in dialogue differently. Consequently, we have considered the fit of first-order Markov processes to dialogues between friends and between strangers involving topics differing in level of intimacy.

## 2 The experiment

### *2.1 Method*

#### *2.1.1 Subjects and procedure*

Detailed descriptions of how the conversational data considered in this paper were generated are given in Hedge (1977), but essentially audio-visual recordings were obtained from each of 64 pairs of *S*s; 32 pairs of men and 32 pairs of women. 32 men and 32 women were recruited individually and each of these was randomly paired with another of the same sex and age with whom he or she was previously unacquainted, resulting in 32 same-sex pairs of strangers. The remaining *S*s were recruited as pairs of friends of the same sex and age.

In the interview one of each pair was required to obtain information on a particular topic from the other; consequently one of each pair was allocated randomly the position of 'questioner' and the other the position of 'answerer'. The two topics of conversation considered were an intimate topic, namely 'What are your favourite ways of making love?' and an essentially non-intimate topic, namely 'Where did you last go on holiday?' Each pair was observed under one of four conditions (1) strangers talking about sex, (2) strangers talking about holidays, (3) friends talking about sex, and (4) friends talking about holidays. There were therefore, eight male and eight female pairs in each condition. *S*s were seated facing one another with the backs of their chairs fixed 2m apart. Each *S* was given a throat microphone and the 'questioner' was asked to initiate and sustain a five minute conversation on his prescribed topic (following ten minutes preparation).

### 2.1.2 *Recording and observations*

Direction of gaze was filmed using two Shibaden TV cameras arranged one behind each *S* so that when either *S* gazed at the other's eyes he appeared to be looking straight into one of the cameras. By means of a split screen video display showing a full-face view of each participant the two *S*s were viewed simultaneously on a 12″ monitor. The conversations were recorded with a Shibaden video tape recorder which, with the monitor, was in an adjoining room out of view from the *S*s.

The experimenter viewed the video tapes of the dyads some time after the actual sessions. Eye gaze and speech were scored separately for each person, so that a particular session was viewed four times, the experimenter concentrating on one aspect at a time. To ensure precise coordination of the speech and gaze behaviour of each pair, a digital clock was positioned in the experimental room so it appeared clearly in each film. This enabled all films to be synchronized to within 0.5 sec. When eye-gaze occurred the experimenter held down a button which activated a marker pen on a graphic level recorder for the duration of that event. Consequently, eye-gaze behaviour was recorded as an 'on' pattern and away gaze was recorded as an 'off' pattern by the graphic level recorder. An *S* was considered to be gazing when he was looking at the face of the other *S* (no reciprocal gaze is implied by this term). In terms of the video display this meant that the *S* was looking straight ahead and was easily and reliably observable.

A similar trace was obtained for utterances and silences. The button activating the marker pen on the graphic level recorder was held down for the duration of an *S*'s utterance, thus producing an 'on' pattern for speech and an 'off' pattern for silence. In other words, only the presence or absence of speech was recorded; no attempt was made to record the content of speech.

The data considered in this paper were obtained by sampling the states of speech and gaze for each individual in each 0.3 sec interval of the five min interview. This particular size of interval was chosen so that 97.5% of changes of state could be recorded; a longer interval would lead to situations in which changes of state could occur *within* an interval and thus fail to be recorded.

Since the conditions for adequate measurement of gaze direction are met (a real-life situation with both the distance and angle between the interactors and the observers being small; see Vine 1971), it was expected that reliable and valid observations could be made. To verify the reliability of the measurements four randomly chosen video tapes were transcribed a second time by the experimenter. The measurements were shown to be consistent both for gaze ($r = 0.89$) and for speech ($r = 0.94$).

After sampling these traces every 0.3 sec the data for each individual appears in the following form:

| | |
|---|---|
| Gaze: | 0 1 1 1 1 0 1 . . . |
| Speech: | 1 1 0 0 1 0 0 . . . |

where zero indicates the absence of the particular behaviour and unity its presence, during a 0.3 sec interval in the interview. Such data may be considered in a number of ways, those possibilities which are of interest in this paper are outlined in table 11.1.

## 3 Markovian models

A consideration of table 11.1 makes it clear that the raw data of any of the processes indicated is simply a sequence of numbers whose sequential dependency may be systematically investigated. For example, the sequence describing the speech behaviour of the dyad might appear as follows:

111122311142444111 . . .

and that describing the joint gaze and speech behaviour would be a sequence involving the numbers one to sixteen. In this paper *Markovian* models will be used to investigate these sequences. For each sequence a *transition probability matrix,* $P^{(n)}$ can be computed; the rows of this matrix represent the possible states of the process at time $t$, and the columns the possible states at time $t + n$. The elements of the matrix, $p_{ij}^{(n)}$, represent the probabilities of passing from state $i$ at time $t$ to state $j$ at time $t + n$. Particularly important in respect of this investigation, as we shall see later, is the matrix of one-step transition probabilities, $P^{(1)}$ which we shall denote by $P$, the elements, $p_{ij}$, of which give the probability of state $j$ immediately following state $i$.

The simplest model that might be considered for any of the processes is that of the *independence* of consecutive states in the sequence of observations. Such a model (which will be referred to as the zero-order Markov chain model), would imply that the rows of $P$ were identical.

The simplest departure from the zero-order Markov model would be one in which the probability of being in a particular state in any interval depended only

*Table 11.1* Behaviours to Be Investigated

| *Behaviour* | *Possible states of behaviour* | | | | |
|---|---|---|---|---|---|
| | *Speech* | | *Gaze* | | *Resulting state* |
| Individual speech | 0 | | – | | Not speaking |
| | 1 | | – | | Speaking |
| Dyadic speech | Q | A | Q | A | |
| | 0 | 0 | – | – | 1. Silence |
| | 0 | 1 | – | – | 2. A speaking |
| | 1 | 0 | – | – | 3. Q speaking |
| | 1 | 1 | – | – | 4. Simultaneous speech |
| Individual's joint speech and gaze | 0 | | 0 | | 1. Neither speaking or gazing |
| | 1 | | 0 | | 2. Speaking but not gazing |
| | 0 | | 1 | | 3. Silent gaze |
| | 1 | | 1 | | 4. Gazing and speaking |
| Joint gaze and speech of dyad | 0 | 0 | 0 | 0 | 1. Silence, neither gazing |
| | 0 | 0 | 1 | 0 | 2. Silence, Q gazing |
| | 0 | 0 | 0 | 1 | 3. Silence, A gazing |
| | 0 | 0 | 1 | 1 | 4. Silence, mutual gaze |
| | 1 | 0 | 0 | 0 | 5. Q speaking, neither gazing |
| | 1 | 0 | 1 | 0 | 6. Q speaking and gazing |
| | 1 | 0 | 0 | 1 | 7. Q speaking; A gazing |
| | 1 | 0 | 1 | 1 | 8. Q speaking, mutual gaze |
| | 0 | 1 | 0 | 0 | 9. A speaking, neither gazing |
| | 0 | 1 | 1 | 0 | 10. A speaking, Q gazing |
| | 0 | 1 | 0 | 1 | 11. A speaking and gazing |
| | 0 | 1 | 1 | 1 | 12. A speaking, mutual gaze |
| | 1 | 1 | 0 | 0 | 13. Both speaking, neither gazing |
| | 1 | 1 | 1 | 0 | 14. Both speaking, Q gazing |
| | 1 | 1 | 0 | 1 | 15. Both speaking, A gazing |
| | 1 | 1 | 1 | 1 | 16. Both speaking, mutual gaze |

*Note:* Roles played by the two individuals in the interview:

Q is questioner

A is answerer

on the state occupied in the immediately preceding interval. Such a model is termed a *first-order Markov chain;* essentially such a model is completely described by *P,* the matrix of one-step transition probabilities.

An increased departure from independence than that described by a first-order Markov chain model may be accommodated by a second-order model. Here the probability of occupying a particular state in any interval is dependent upon the states occupied in the *two* immediately preceding intervals.

Likelihood ratio tests for deciding which order model is appropriate for a particular set of data are described in Chatfield (1973); this author also outlines other informal graphical procedures that may be used for deciding on an appropriate model, when the more formal likelihood ratio tests are inapplicable; such a situation arises, essentially, when particular changes of state occur only very rarely, leading to many zero or very small entries in the observed transition matrices.

Later in this paper, in addition to determining the most appropriate Markov model for each of the processes to be investigated, we shall be interested in testing for the independence of two first-order Markov chains. If gaze behaviour is independent of speech behaviour it should be possible to predict accurately the transition matrix for the joint occurrence of gaze and speech given the transition matrices for gaze and speech considered separately. A test for this kind of independence between two first-order Markov chains is described in detail by Anderson and Goodman (1957) and Sandland (1976), but since it may be unfamiliar to many readers, it is outlined briefly in Appendix A.

## 4 Stationarity

Markovian models can only be applied to processes that are stationary. It was therefore necessary to show that the dialogues being studied had this property; that is, the probability of transition from one state to another, $p_{ij}$, should be much the same which ever section of the dialogue has been used for its estimation. Since one might well expect changes in the patterning of speech and gaze at the very beginning and end of a conversation, the five minutes of data that were analysed were extracted from the middle of a longer, seven minute conversation. To investigate the stationarity of this section of dialogue transition matrices were computed from the first 200, middle 200, and final 200, 0.3 sec intervals as well as for the total five minutes of dialogue. An informal inspection of these matrices, as shown in table 11.2, indicates that the transition probabilities were fairly constant over time,

*Table 11.2* Stationarity of Dialogue

| (a) | | | | (b) | | | | (c) | | | |
|---|---|---|---|---|---|---|---|---|---|---|---|
| 134 | 33 | 29 | 0 | 0.67 | 0.18 | 0.14 | 0.00 | 0.70 | 0.17 | 0.13 | 0.00 |
| 42 | 496 | 6 | 1 | 0.16 | 0.81 | 0.03 | 0.00 | 0.06 | 0.93 | 0.01 | 0.01 |
| 20 | 4 | 186 | 14 | 0.06 | 0.00 | 0.83 | 0.11 | 0.09 | 0.00 | 0.83 | 0.09 |
| 0 | 12 | 4 | 17 | 0.00 | 0.46 | 0.15 | 0.38 | 0.00 | 0.38 | 0.13 | 0.50 |
| (d) | | | | (e) | | | | | | | |
| 0.69 | 0.17 | 0.13 | 0.00 | 0.71 | 0.16 | 0.13 | 0.00 | | | | |
| 0.13 | 0.87 | 0.00 | 0.00 | 0.04 | 0.93 | 0.02 | 0.00 | | | | |
| 0.07 | 0.02 | 0.87 | 0.04 | 0.15 | 0.03 | 0.79 | 0.03 | | | | |
| 0.00 | 0.33 | 0.00 | 0.67 | 0.00 | 1.00 | 0.00 | 0.00 | | | | |

(a) Example of a frequency transition matrix for dialogue, calculated over the 5-minute conversation.
(b) The equivalent transition probability matrix to (a).
(c) (d) and (e) Transition probability matrices for the first, middle and final 200 sampling intervals respectively, of the 5-minute conversation.
(The large difference between the last rows of (c), (d) and (e) is essentially due to the very small number of transitions involving state 4, and should not be taken as evidence against stationarity.)

discrepancies occurring most frequently where the number of transitions between states was extremely small. The assumption of stationarity for these dialogues therefore seems justified.

## 5 Results: fitting first-order Markov processes

The minimum possible information which an individual could use to decide whether to continue speaking would be his own current speech state; this would imply that a zero-order Markov chain model was adequate to describe the process. All individuals however, departed significantly from this model. If individuals were making this decision with respect to their own previous speech state a first-order Markov chain model would be implied. Examination of table 11.3 shows that a first-order Markov process is an appropriate description of an individual's speech only for strangers discussing sex; a higher order Markov process is necessary to describe an individual's speech in all other conditions. To assess whether the groups differed in respect of the numbers of individuals for whom a first-order Markov model provided an adequate fit, a log-linear model (see Bishop et al. 1975; Everitt 1977) was fitted to these data. An adequate fit was provided by including parameters representing degree of acquaintance and interaction between degree of acquaintance and topic of conversation ($\chi^2 = 12.07$ with $df = 12$). This finding indicates that proportionally more strangers than friends are fitted by the model and that in addition, for strangers proportionally more of those discussing sex than those discussing holidays are fitted by this model, whilst for friends there is a small difference in the reverse direction. There were, however, no significant differences between males and females and none between questioners and answerers. (The actual chi-square values from which table 11.3 and subsequent tables are derived are available from the authors on request).

*Table 11.3* Fitting a First-order Markov Process to Individual Speech

| *Subjects* | *Topic of conversation* | *Sex of dyad* | *Number of individuals for whom a first-order Markov process was appropriate (N = 8)* | |
|---|---|---|---|---|
| | | | *Q* | *A* |
| Strangers | Sex | M | 7 | 5 |
| | | F | 5 | 5 |
| | Holidays | M | 2 | 3 |
| | | F | 1 | 4 |
| Friends | Sex | M | 1 | 4 |
| | | F | 0 | 0 |
| | Holidays | M | 2 | 2 |
| | | F | 1 | 2 |

*Note:* M = male; F = female; *N* = no. of dyads in each cell. Roles played by individuals in the interview: Q = questioner; A = answerer.

It was also found that for no pair of individuals in any condition could the speech process of the dyad be predicted from the separate speech behaviours of the dyad members. (The independence test described in Appendix A and used to calculate these results is strictly applicable only in cases already shown to be first-order Markov processes. However, since departures from this condition, even when significant, are likely to be small this test may still be employed to provide useful information.) Any other result would be very unexpected since conversation is essentially an interactive process. Consequently we must now consider the information afforded by the joint speech behaviour of the dyad. Examination of table 11.4 indicates that a difference arises between strangers and friends with regard to the order of Markov process necessary to describe their joint speech behaviour. Fitting a linear model to the logistic function of the proportion of people fitted, for these data it was found that an adequate fit was provided by a model involving only a parameter representing differences between strangers and friends ($\chi^2 = 7.01$ with $df = 6$). This implies simply that a first-order Markov chain model provided an adequate fit for a significantly higher proportion of strangers than friends. In other words when deciding whether to speak, strangers appear to use only information from the immediately preceding state of their dialogue whilst friends appear to use information from additional speech sources. There were however, no significant differences between type of conversation between males and females, nor was it necessary to postulate any interaction effects.

Proceding to states which include any additional information given by gaze cues we next examine whether the joint speech and gaze behaviour of an individual can be described by a first-order Markov process. Examination of table 11.5 shows that for the joint gaze-speech behaviour of both questioner and answerer a first-order Markov process is almost universally applicable. It can also be seen from table 11.5 that for the vast majority of cases an individual's joint speech and gaze behaviour cannot be predicted from his separate gaze and speech behaviours; in other words gaze and speech are not independent behaviours. Considering now the joint gaze and speech behaviour of the dyad we see from table 11.5 that

*Table 11.4* Fitting a First-order Markov Process to the Joint Speech Behaviour of the Dyad

| *Subjects* | *Topic of conversation* | *Sex of dyad* | *No. of dyads for whom a first-order Markov process was appropriate (N = 8)* |
|---|---|---|---|
| Strangers | Sex | M | 7 |
| | | F | 8 |
| | Holidays | M | 4 |
| | | F | 7 |
| Friends | Sex | M | 3 |
| | | F | 3 |
| | Holidays | M | 4 |
| | | F | 5 |

*Note:* M = male; F = female; *N* = no. of dyads in each cell.

*Table 11.5* Fitting a First-order Markov Process to the Joint Speech and Gaze Behaviours of Individuals and Dyads

| *Subjects* | *Topic of conversation* | *Sex of dyad* | *No. of individuals for whom a first-order Markov process was appropriate (N = 8)* | | | *No. of joint gaze-speech patterns which can be predicted from the independent gaze and speech process (N = 8)* | | | *No. of dyads whose joint gaze-speech patterns can be predicted from the gaze-speech processes of Q and A considered independently (N = 8)* |
|---|---|---|---|---|---|---|---|---|---|
| | | | *Q (gaze and speech)* | *A (gaze and speech)* | *Dyads (gaze and speech)* | *Q (gaze and speech)* | *A (gaze and speech)* | *Dyads (gaze and speech)* | |
| Strangers | Sex | M | 8 | 8 | 8 | 1 | 2 | 3 | 1 |
| | | F | 8 | 8 | 8 | 2 | 3 | 3 | 1 |
| | Holidays | M | 7 | 6 | 8 | 2 | 2 | 3 | 0 |
| | | F | 6 | 7 | 8 | 0 | 5 | 2 | 0 |
| Friends | Sex | M | 6 | 5 | 8 | 2 | 2 | 3 | 1 |
| | | F | 7 | 8 | 8 | 2 | 2 | 0 | 1 |
| | Holidays | M | 7 | 7 | 8 | 2 | 3 | 2 | 0 |
| | | F | 6 | 4 | 8 | 1 | 0 | 1 | 0 |

*Note:* M = male; F = female; *N* = no. of dyads in each cell. Roles played by individuals in the interview: Q = questioner; A = answerer.

a first-order Markov process is an appropriate description for this behaviour for all dyads, whether friends or strangers. It is also apparent from table 11.5 that the dyad's joint speech and gaze behaviour is not predictable from either the gaze-speech behaviours of questioner and answerer when considered independently or from independent consideration of the dyad's speech and gaze behaviours. In other words, in the interview situation considered it appears firstly that gaze and speech do not act independently, and secondly that the questioner and answerer do not act completely independently.

## 6 Discussion: fitting first-order Markov processes

The results presented in the previous section show that the gross temporal aspects of a dyad's joint gaze and speech behaviour during dialogue may be described by first-order Markov chain models. This implies that gaze-speech behaviour is generated by a process in which the state occupied at any particular instance is dependent only on the state occupied in the immediately preceding 0.3 sec time interval. In other words only a model involving the simplest departure from one assuming the complete independence of states is necessary to account for the gaze-dialogue process.

The results also appear to suggest that while strangers base their decision to speak or not at some given time solely on the speech state of the dyad in the immediately preceding time, for friends a simplification in the description of the underlying process is achieved by the use of information from the gaze state of the dyad in the immediately preceding time along with that obtained from the state of speech. That is, when only speech cues are used a second- or higher-order Markov model was necessary to describe the dialogue of friends but when their combined speech-gaze cues were used a first-order model was adequate.

From the results of the tests of independence of gaze and speech behaviours, and independence of questioner and answerer described in the previous section it would seem that the most realistic model for dialogue would be one incorporating the joint speech and gaze behaviours of the dyad rather than the component processes. This result implies that an individual's gaze behaviour is dependent on his speech behaviour.

## 7 Separate source models

The description of dyadic gaze and speech by means of first-order Markov chain models offers no explanation as to the way in which the two participants interact to generate the temporal sequences involved. An interactive model which accounted for the dyadic behaviour in terms of the individuals' separate behaviours would be more satisfying. As noted in section 1 such models would necessarily involve independent decisions from each individual at each point in time. Two possible simple 'separate source' models which present themselves are (i) complete independence of each individual, and (ii) a conditional independence model in which 'independent' decisions are made conditional on the state of the process at some earlier point in time. (Such conditional independence models have been considered previously by Jaffe et al. 1967). Each of these models was therefore considered for both dialogue and the joint gaze and speech behaviour of the dyad.

It has already been noted in section 5 that for none of the dyads observed, was dialogue predictable from the independent operation of each individual's speech. Consequently a separate source model assuming complete independence is not tenable. A simple interactive theory of the individual behaviours of each member of the dyad which *might* account for the observed first-order Markov findings for dialogue is one in which the questioner (Q) and answerer (A), make independent decisions to speak or remain silent in each interval, conditional however, on the *joint* dialogue state of the previous interval. In formal terms this 'conditional' independence model is defined as follows:

Let $q_i$ = Pr (Q speaks at time $t$ given Q was in state $i$ at time $t-1$)
$r_i$ = Pr (A speaks at time $t$ given A was in state $i$ at time $t-1$)

(where $i$ takes values from 1 to 4 and Pr denotes probability).

The parameters of the model, $q_i$ and $r_i$, $i = 1$ to 4, may be estimated from the first order transition probability matrices for dialogue, and these estimates may be used to find the transition probability matrix predicted by the model. Both of these procedures are outlined in Appendix B. The transition matrix predicted by the model was calculated for each dyad in the study and compared with the corresponding observed transition matrix. The adequacy of the model was judged for each dyad by means of the chi-square test outlined in Appendix B. The results of these tests are given in table 11.6. The conditional independence model for dialogue appears adequate for the large majority of dyads, with the notable exception of female friends discussing holidays, where a significant departure from the model was noted for all eight pairs. The implications of this finding are discussed in sections 8 and 9.

The simplest separate source model which might account for dyadic gaze and speech behaviour would be one in which participants in the interview operated

*Table 11.6* Adequacy of Separate Source Model in Describing Dialogue

| *Subjects* | *Topic of conversation* | *Number of pairs fitted by separate source model (N = 8)* | |
|---|---|---|---|
| | | *Males* | *Females* |
| Strangers | Sex | 6 | 6 |
| | Holidays | 7 | 6 |
| Friends | Sex | 5 | 7 |
| | Holidays | 4 | 0 |

completely independently of one another. However, it has already been shown (see table 11.5) that separate source models involving complete independence of individuals or of the gaze and speech processes are *not* adequate to account for the joint gaze-speech behaviour of the dyad. Consequently a more involved separate source model is required. A possible separate source model for the joint gaze and speech behaviour of the dyad which allows for the individuality of the participants may be formulated as one which postulates both the independence of an individual's speech and gaze behaviour and the independence of each individual, conditional on the joint gaze-speech state of the dyad in the previous interval. In more formal terms this conditional independence model is defined as follows:

Let $q_i^{(1)}$ = Pr (Q speaks at time $t$ given dyadic state $i$ at $t - 1$)
$r_i^{(1)}$ = Pr (A speaks at time $t$ given dyadic state $i$ at $t - 1$)
$q_i^{(2)}$ = Pr (Q gazes at time $t$ given dyadic state $i$ at $t - 1$)
$r_i^{(2)}$ = Pr (A gazes at time $t$ given dyadic state $i$ at $t - 1$)

(where $i$ takes values from 1 to 16; Pr denotes probability and dyadic state implies the joint gaze and speech behaviours of both participants).

The method for estimating these parameters from the first-order transition probability matrix of the 16 state combined dialogue and gaze process and the form the transition probability matrix would then take are described in Appendix B. The transition matrix predicted by the model was calculated for each dyad in the study and compared with the corresponding observed transition matrix. The adequacy of this model was tested for each dyad using the chi-square test described in detail in Appendix B. The results of this test are shown in table 11.7. Examination of this table indicates no significant difference between the observed and predicted transition matrices for 60 of the 64 dyads. In other words the proposed separate-source model provides an adequate account of the joint gaze and speech behaviour for the large majority of dyads in the study. This model appears to be equally applicable to both male and female pairs in all the various situations considered.

*Table 11.7* Adequacy of Separate Source Model in Describing Dyadic Gaze and Speech

| *Subjects* | *Topic of conversation* | *Number of pairs fitted by separate source model (N = 8)* | |
|---|---|---|---|
| | | *Males* | *Females* |
| Strangers | Sex | 8 | 7 |
| | Holidays | 8 | 8 |
| Friends | Sex | 8 | 8 |
| | Holidays | 7 | 6 |

(A further separate source model which might be deemed appropriate for the combined dialogue and dyadic gaze process is one in which only the individuals are assumed to operate independently; that is, it is not assumed that gaze and speech act independently. This model was considered but was found not to lead to any significant improvement in fit over the simpler model described above.)

## 8 Discussion: separate source models

A conditional independence model of the type described by Jaffe et al. (1967) was fitted to dialogue and shown to describe the data adequately for most dyads with the exception of pairs of friends discussing holidays. In other words, during dialogue strangers make their decisions to speak independently of each other but conditional on their joint state of speech in the previous instance. This however, was found not to be true for friends, particularly those discussing a neutral topic.

When a similar conditional independence model was fitted to the joint gaze-speech behaviour of dyads it was shown to be an adequate description for the great majority of dyads. The model considered implies that in each time interval an individual makes decisions to speak or to gaze independently of each other and independently of the other individual in the dyad, conditional on the joint state of the dyad in the immediately preceding time interval. This model applied to male and female pairs and in all the situations considered. Therefore the observed first-order Markov behaviour of the joint gaze-speech process of the dyad, whilst not recoverable from either the independent action of each individual's gaze-speech sequence *or* from the separate gaze and speech sequences of the dyad, is accountable for in terms of the fairly simple conditional independence model described in section 7.

Overall these results demonstrate that the gross temporal aspects of gaze and speech behaviour generated in a face-to-face interview may be explained in terms of fairly simple interactive models which enable a complex communication system to be described very concisely. In particular, the separate source model described here enables the $16 \times 16$ transition probability matrix of the process to be described in terms of only 64 parameters rather than the 240 necessary when the process is viewed simply as a first-order Markov process and no account is taken of the way in which individual participants or separate processes interact.

## 9 Final discussion

Our analysis of dialogues in terms of simple Markov chains leads to a number of conclusions about the role of gaze in dialogues. Firstly, the gaze behaviour of an individual is clearly not independent of his speech behaviour since his joint speech and gaze behaviour cannot be predicted from his gaze and speech behaviour considered separately. However this does not necessarily imply that gaze is important in controlling the flow of dialogue.

Secondly, for the dialogues of strangers, particularly when they are talking about embarrassing topics, the speech state of the two participants in the immediately preceding 0.3 seconds is sufficient to determine the next state of the dialogue. This is not true for friends. For their dialogues both speech and gaze in the immediately preceding 0.3 seconds must be taken into account. This suggests that gaze does have a role in the dialogue of friends if we assume that a decision to speak or not is based on the state of the dialogue in the preceding 0.3 seconds. From a descriptive point of view the time sequence of dialogue between friends can be described more simply if their gaze is taken into account.

Thirdly, we have shown that the requirement that the participants in a dialogue make their decisions to speak independently of one another at each time point is met, for strangers, by a conditional independence model involving only speech states. This is not true however for friends, particularly if they are discussing a neutral topic. This implies that friends must take more than speech into account when making their decisions. Evidence that gaze behaviour supplies this additional information is provided by consideration of the combined gaze-speech process of friends; in this case a conditional independence model *was* proved adequate. Consequently there is a clear indication that gaze does play a role in controlling the dialogues of friends but not those of strangers. Anyone wishing to investigate more closely the role of gaze in dialogue would therefore be well advised to study the dialogues of friends.

From a descriptive point of view all the types of dialogue investigated in this study may be adequately described by a simple conditional independence model taking into account both speech and gaze and in which the two participants make independent decisions to speak or gaze at each point in time.

Once we have decided upon an adequate and simple descriptive model of the dialogues we are interested in then we can use the parameters of that model to compare different dialogues. Dialogues that can be described by the same model may well differ in terms of the parameters of the model. In this paper we have proposed a simple and adequate model for describing a range of dialogues. Elsewhere (Hedge in preparation), an account will be presented of comparisons of dialogues in terms of the parameters of this model.

## Note

* One of us (B.J.H.) acknowledges the support of the S.S.R.C. during the course of this research.

# Appendix A

## Testing the independence of two first-order Markov chains

Let us assume that we have discrete time observations on two underlying stochastic processes $X(t)$ and $Y(t)$. The discrete time observations are assumed to be first-order Markov chains and we wish to investigate their 'independence'. Independence is here defined to mean that the vector random variables $(X(n_1), X(n_2) \ldots X(n_k))$ and $(Y(n_1), Y(n_2) \ldots Y(n_k))$ are statistically independent for every choice of observation times $n_1, n_2 \ldots n_k$. Provided the Markov chains are stationary (see Chatfield 1973), the following may be proved.

Let $P_x$ and $P_y$ be the matrices of one-step transition probabilities of the Markov chains $X$ and $Y$ respectively, and let $P$ be the corresponding matrix of the combined $X$ and $Y$ processes, the latter will be referred to as the process $Z$. Then if $X$ and $Y$ *are* independent first-order Markov chains, $Z$ is also first-order Markov with transition matrix, $P$, given by

$$P = P_y \otimes P_x \tag{1}$$

where the symbol $\otimes$ indicates the Kronecker product of matrices (see, for example, Graybill 1969). An example, involving one of the processes outlined in table 11.1 may help to clarify this equation.

Consider the questioner's speech behaviour with $(2 \times 2)$ transition probability matrix $P_q$, and similarly that of the answerer, with transition matrix $P_a$, where

$$P_q = \begin{bmatrix} p_{00}^{(q)} & p_{01}^{(q)} \\ p_{10}^{(q)} & p_{11}^{(q)} \end{bmatrix} \text{ and } P_a = \begin{bmatrix} p_{00}^{(a)} & p_{01}^{(a)} \\ p_{10}^{(a)} & p_{11}^{(a)} \end{bmatrix}$$

If the questioner and answerer act independently with respect to speech behaviour, it is fairly simple to deduce that the $(4 \times 4)$ transition probability matrix, $P_d$, for the dialogue would be given by

$$P_d = \begin{bmatrix} p_{00}^{(q)} & p_{00}^{(a)} & p_{00}^{(q)} & p_{01}^{(a)} & p_{01}^{(q)} & p_{00}^{(a)} & p_{01}^{(q)} & p_{01}^{(a)} \\ p_{00}^{(q)} & p_{10}^{(a)} & p_{00}^{(q)} & p_{11}^{(a)} & p_{01}^{(q)} & p_{10}^{(a)} & p_{01}^{(q)} & p_{11}^{(a)} \\ p_{10}^{(q)} & p_{00}^{(a)} & p_{10}^{(q)} & p_{01}^{(a)} & p_{11}^{(q)} & p_{00}^{(a)} & p_{11}^{(q)} & p_{01}^{(a)} \\ p_{10}^{(q)} & p_{10}^{(a)} & p_{10}^{(q)} & p_{11}^{(a)} & p_{11}^{(q)} & p_{10}^{(a)} & p_{11}^{(q)} & p_{11}^{(a)} \end{bmatrix}$$

$$= \begin{bmatrix} p_{00}^{(q)} & P_a & p_{01}^{(q)} & P_a \\ p_{10}^{(q)} & P_a & p_{11}^{(q)} & P_a \end{bmatrix}$$

that is

$$P_d = P_q \otimes P_a$$

Therefore under the null hypothesis of independence between the two Markov chains $X$ and $Y$, we know that the joint process, $Z$, is also Markov and that its transition probability matrix has a particular form. A test of the hypothesis, based on this result, employs the following chi-square statistic

$$x^2 = \sum_{i=1}^{c}\sum_{j=1}^{c}\left(f_{ij} - f_i p_{ij}\right)^2 / f_i p_{ij} \tag{2}$$

where $f_{ij}$ is the number of observations where the process $Z$ goes from state $i$ to state $j$ in a single step, and $f_i$ is the number of times $Z$ is observed in state $i$; $p_{ij}$ is the $ij$-th element of the matrix $P$ derived from equation (1), and $c$ is the number of possible states of the joint process, $Z$. The statistic $\chi^2$ is distributed asymptotically as a chi-square variate with $\upsilon$ degrees of freedom, where

$$u = \sum_{i=1}^{c}(s_i - 1) - k \tag{3}$$

and $s_i$ is the number of terms in the $i$-th row of $P$ which are greater than zero, and $k$ is the number of parameters in the model to be estimated.

# Appendix B

## 1 Conditional independence separate source model for dialogue

The parameters $q_i$ and $r_i$ defined in section 7 may be derived from the first-order transition probability matrix of dialogue as follows:

$$q_i = p_{i3} + p_{i4}$$
$$r_i = p_{i2} + p_{i4}$$

where the four states of dialogue are as identified in table 11.1.

Under such a model the $i$-th row of the transition probability matrix of dialogue would take the form shown in table 11.8.

### *Chi-square test*

Let us denote the predicted transition probability matrix by $\hat{P}$. Corresponding to the observed transition matrix $P$ is a matrix of transition frequencies, $f_{ij}$ and these may be used to provide a chi-square test of the adequacy of the proposed separate source model as follows:

$$x^2 = \sum_{i=1}^{4}\sum_{j=1}^{4}\left(f_{ij} - f_{i.}\,\hat{p}_{ij}\right)^2 \Big/ f_{i.}\,\hat{p}_{ij}$$

*Table 11.8* Predicted Probability of State $j$ at Time $t$ Given State $i$ at Time $t - 1$

| *State j* | *Predicted prob. of state j at time t/state i at time t − 1* |
|---|---|
| 1 | $(1 - qi)\,(1 - ri)$ |
| 2 | $(1 - qi)\,ri$ |
| 3 | $qi\,(1 - ri)$ |
| 4 | $qi\,ri$ |

where $\widehat{P}_{ij}$ are the elements of $\widehat{P}$ and $f_{i.} = \sum_{j=1}^{4} f_{ij}$ are row totals of the observed transition frequencies. The statistic $\chi^2$ is distributed asymptotically as a chi-square variate with degrees of freedom $\upsilon$, given by

$$v = \sum_{i=1}^{4} (s_i - 1) - k$$

$s_i$ is the number of terms in the $i$-th row of $P$ which are greater than zero and $k$ is the number of parameters to be estimated, which in this case is eight.

## 2 Conditional independence separate source model for the joint gaze and speech behaviour of the dyad

The parameters $q_i^{(1)}$, $r_i^{(1)}$, $q_i^{(2)}$ and $r_i^{(2)}$ defined in section 7 may be obtained from the first order transition probability matrix of the 16 state joint gaze-speech process of the dyad as follows:

$$q_i^{(1)} = p_{i5} + p_{i6} + p_{i7} + p_{i8} + p_{i13} + p_{i14} + p_{i15} + p_{i16}$$
$$r_i^{(1)} = p_{i9} + p_{i10} + p_{i11} + p_{i12} + p_{i13} + p_{i14} + p_{i15} + p_{i16}$$
$$q_i^{(2)} = p_{i2} + p_{i4} + p_{i6} + p_{i8} + p_{i10} + p_{i12} + p_{i14} + p_{i16}$$
$$r_i^{(2)} = p_{i3} + p_{i4} + p_{i7} + p_{i8} + p_{i11} + p_{i12} + p_{i15} + p_{i16}$$

where the sixteen states of the process are identified by the numbers 1 to 16 as in table 11.1.

Under such a model the $i$-th row of the transition probability matrix of the process would take the form shown in table 11.9.

### *Chi-square test*

Let us denote this matrix by $\widehat{P}$. Corresponding to the observed transition matrix $P$ is a matrix of transition frequencies, $f_{ij}$, and these may be used to provide a chi-square test of the adequacy of the proposed 'separate source' model using the following statistic:

$$x^2 = \sum_{i=1}^{16} \sum_{j=1}^{16} \left( f_{ij} - f_{i.}\, \widehat{p}_{ij} \right)^2 \Big/ f_{i.}\, \widehat{p}_{ij}$$

where $\widehat{P}_{ij}$ are the elements of $\widehat{P}$ and $f_{i.} = \sum_{j=1}^{16} f_{ij}$ are row totals of the observed transition frequencies. The statistic $\chi^2$ is distributed asymptotically as a chi-square variate with $\upsilon$ degrees of freedom where

$$v = \sum_{i=1}^{16} (s_i - 1) - k$$

*Table 11.9* Predicted Probability of State $j$ at Time $t$ Given State $i$ at Time $t-1$

| *State (j)* | *Predicted probability of state j at time t given state i at time t − 1* |
|---|---|
| 1 | $(1-q_i^{(1)})(1-r_i^{(1)})(1-q_i^{(2)})(1-r_i^{(2)})$ |
| 2 | $(1-q_i^{(1)})(1-r_i^{(1)})\,q_i^{(2)}(1-r_i^{(2)})$ |
| 3 | $(1-q_i^{(1)})(1-r_i^{(1)})(1-q_i^{(2)})\,r_i^{(2)}$ |
| 4 | $(1-q_i^{(1)})(1-r_i^{(1)})\,q_i^{(2)}\,r_i^{(2)}$ |
| 5 | $q_i^{(1)}(1-r_i^{(1)})(1-q_i^{(2)})(1-r_i^{(2)})$ |
| 6 | $q_i^{(1)}(1-r_i^{(1)})\,q_i^{(2)}(1-r_i^{(2)})$ |
| 7 | $q_i^{(1)}(1-r_i^{(1)})(1-q_i^{(2)})\,r_i^{(2)}$ |
| 8 | $q_i^{(1)}(1-r_i^{(1)})\,q_i^{(2)}\,r_i^{(2)}$ |
| 9 | $(1-q_i^{(1)})\,r_i^{(1)}(1-q_i^{(2)})(1-r_i^{(2)})$ |
| 10 | $(1-q_i^{(1)})\,r_i^{(1)}\,q_i^{(2)}(1-r_i^{(2)})$ |
| 11 | $(1-q_i^{(1)})\,r_i^{(1)}(1-q_i^{(2)})\,r_i^{(2)}$ |
| 12 | $(1-q_i^{(1)})\,r_i^{(1)}\,q_i^{(2)}\,r_i^{(2)}$ |
| 13 | $q_i^{(1)}\,r_i^{(1)}(1-q_i^{(2)})(1-r_i^{(2)})$ |
| 14 | $q_i^{(1)}\,r_i^{(1)}\,q_i^{(2)}(1-r_i^{(2)})$ |
| 15 | $q_i^{(1)}\,r_i^{(1)}(1-q_i^{(2)})\,r_i^{(2)}$ |
| 16 | $q_i^{(1)}\,r_i^{(1)}\,q_i^{(2)}\,r_i^{(2)}$ |

and $s_i$ is the number of terms in the $i$-th row of $\widehat{P}$ which are greater than zero, and $k$ is the number of parameters in the model to be estimated, which in this case is 64.

## References

Anderson, T. W. and L. A. Goodman, 1957. Statistical inference about Markov chains. Annals of Mathematical Statistics 28, 89–110.

Argyle, M., M. Lalljee and M. Cook, 1968. The effects of visibility on interaction in a dyad. Human Relations 21, 3–17.

Billingsley, P., 1961. Statistical methods in Markov chains. Annals of Mathematical Statistics 32, 12–40.

Bishop, Y. M. M., S. E. Fienberg and F. W. Holland, 1975. Discrete multivariate analysis. M.I.T. Press.

Chatfield, C., 1973. Statistical inference regarding Markov chain models. Applied Statistics 22, 7–20.

Condon, W. S. and W. D. Ogston, 1966. Sound film analysis of normal and pathological behaviour patterns. Journal of Nervous and Mental Disorders 143, 338–347.

Cook, M. and J. M. C. Smith, 1975. The role of gaze in impression formation. British Journal of Social and Clinical Psychology 14, 19–25.

Duncan, S., 1972. Some signals and rules for taking speaking turns in conversations. Journal of Personality and Social Psychology 23, 283–292.

Everitt, B. S., 1977. The analysis of contingency tables. London: Chapman and Hall.

Exline, R. V. and L. C. Winters, 1965. Affective relations and mutual glances in dyads. In: S. S. Tomkins and C. Izard (eds.), Affect, cognition and personality. New York: Springer.

Exline, R. V., D. Gray and D. Schuette, 1965. Visual behaviour in a dyad as affected by interview content and sex of respondent. Journal of Personality and Social Psychology 1, 201–209.

Graybill, F. A., 1969. Introduction to matrices with applications in statistics. Belmont, Calif.: Wandsworth Publishing Company.

Hedge, B. J., 1977. The effects of situational constraints and individual differences on gaze and mutual gaze during dialogue. Ph.D. thesis. University of London.

Jaffe, J., S. Feldstein and L. Cassotta, 1967. Markovian models of dialogic time patterns. Nature 216, 93–94.

Kemeny, J. C. and J. L. Snell, 1960. Finite Markov chains. Princeton, N.J.: D. Van Nostrand.

Kendon, A., 1967. Some functions of gaze direction in social interaction. Acta Psychologica 26, 22–63.

Kendon, A., 1970. Movement coordination in social interaction. Acta Psychologica 32, 100–125.

Kendon, A. and M. Cook, 1969. The consistency of gaze patterns in social interaction. British Journal of Psychology 60, 481–494.

Rubin, A., 1970. Measurement of romantic love. Journal of Personality and Social Psychology 16, 265–273.

Sandland, R. L., 1976. Application of methods of testing for independence between two Markov chains. Biometrics 32, 629–636.

Schulz, R. and J. Barefoot, 1974. Non-verbal responses and affiliative conflict theory. British Journal of Social and Clinical Psychology 13, 237–243.

Vine, I., 1971. Judgement of direction of gaze – an interpretation of discrepant results. British Journal of Social and Clinical Psychology 10, 320–331.

# 12 Predictive coding

## An account of the mirror neuron system

*James M. Kilner, Karl J. Friston and Chris D. Frith*

### Introduction

The notion that actions are intrinsically linked to perception was proposed by William James, who claimed, "every mental representation of a movement awakens to some degree the actual movement which is its object" (James 1890). The implication is that observing, imagining, or in anyway representing an action excites the motor program used to execute that same action (Jeannerod 1994; Prinz 1997). Interest in this idea has grown recently, in part due to the neurophysiological discovery of "mirror" neurons. Mirror neurons discharge not only during action execution but also during action observation, which has led many to suggest that these neurons are the substrate for action understanding.

Mirror-neurons were first discovered in the premotor area, F5, of the macaque monkey (Di Pellegrino et al. 1992; Gallese et al. 1996; Rizzolatti et al. 2001; Umilta et al. 2001) and have been identified subsequently in an area of inferior parietal lobule, area PF (Gallese et al. 2002; Fogassi et al. 2005). Neurons in the superior temporal sulcus (STS), also respond selectively to biological movements, both in monkeys (Oram and Perrett 1994) and in humans (Frith and Frith 1999; Allison et al. 2000; Grossman et al. 2000) but they are not mirror-neurons, as they do not discharge during action execution. Nevertheless, they are often considered part of the mirror neuron system (MNS; Keysers and Perrett 2004) and we will consider them as such here. These three cortical areas, which constitute the MNS, the STS, area PF and area F5, are reciprocally connected. In the macaque monkey, area F5 in the premotor cortex is reciprocally connected to area PF (Luppino et al. 1999) creating a premotor-parietal MNS, and STS is reciprocally connected to area PF of the inferior parietal cortex (Harries and Perrett 1991; Seltzer and Pandya 1994) providing a sensory input to the MNS (see Keysers and Perrett 2004 for a review). Furthermore, these reciprocal connections show regional specificity. Although STS has extensive connections with the inferior parietal lobule, area PF is connected to an area of the STS that is specifically activated by observation of complex body movements. An analogous pattern of connectivity between premotor areas and inferior parietal lobule has also been demonstrated in humans, both directly (Rushworth et al. 2006) and indirectly (Iacoboni et al. 2001, 2005). In addition, a sequential pattern of activation in the human MNS has been demonstrated during action-observation that is consistent with the proposed pattern of anatomical connectivity (Nishtani and Hari 2000, 2002).

Mirror-neurons and the MNS have been the focus of much interest since their discovery because they have been proposed as a neural substrate that could enable us to understand the intentions of others through the observation of their actions (Gallese and Goldman 1998). Actions can be understood at many different levels. After Hamilton and Grafton (2007) here we will consider actions that can be described at four levels. (1) The intention level that defines the long-term goal of an action. (2) The goal level that describes short-term goals that are necessary to achieve the long-term intention. (3) The kinematic level that describes the shape of the hand and the movement of the arm in space and time. (4) The muscle level that describes the pattern of muscle activity required to execute the action. Therefore to understand the intentions or goals of an observed action, the observer must be able to describe the observed movement at either the goal level or the intention level having only access to a visual representation of the kinematic level. Although mirror neurons have been proposed as the neural substrate that could enable us to understand the intentions or goals of an observed action (Gallese and Goldman 1998) little is known about the neural mechanisms underlying this ability to 'mind read'. Gallese (2006) recently noted that " . . . we do not have a clear neuroscientific model of how humans can understand the intentions promoting the actions of others they observe". Therefore, the question remains, if mirror-neurons do mediate understanding of actions done by others how do they do it?

Rizzolatti and Craighero (2004) suggested, "The proposed mechanism is rather simple. Each time an individual sees an action done by another individual, neurons that represent that action are activated in the observer's premotor cortex. This automatically induced, motor representation of the observed action corresponds to that which is spontaneously generated during active action and whose outcome is known to the acting individual. Thus, the mirror-neuron system transforms visual information into knowledge".

## Generative and recognition models

Although this proposed mechanism is 'simple' in conception it is non-trivial in terms of implementation. It is unclear how the visual information from an observed action maps onto the observer's own motor system and how the goal of that action is inferred (Gallese et al. 2004; Iacoboni 2005; Jacob and Jeannerod 2005; Saxe 2005). Implicit in this and many descriptions of the MNS is the idea that visual information is transformed as it is passed by forward connections along the MNS network from low-level representations of the movement kinematics to high-level representations of intentions subtending the action. In this scheme, the observation of an action drives the firing of neurons in the STS, which drives activity in area PF, which in turn drives activity in area F5 (Fig. 12.1a). Formally, this is a recognition model that operates by the

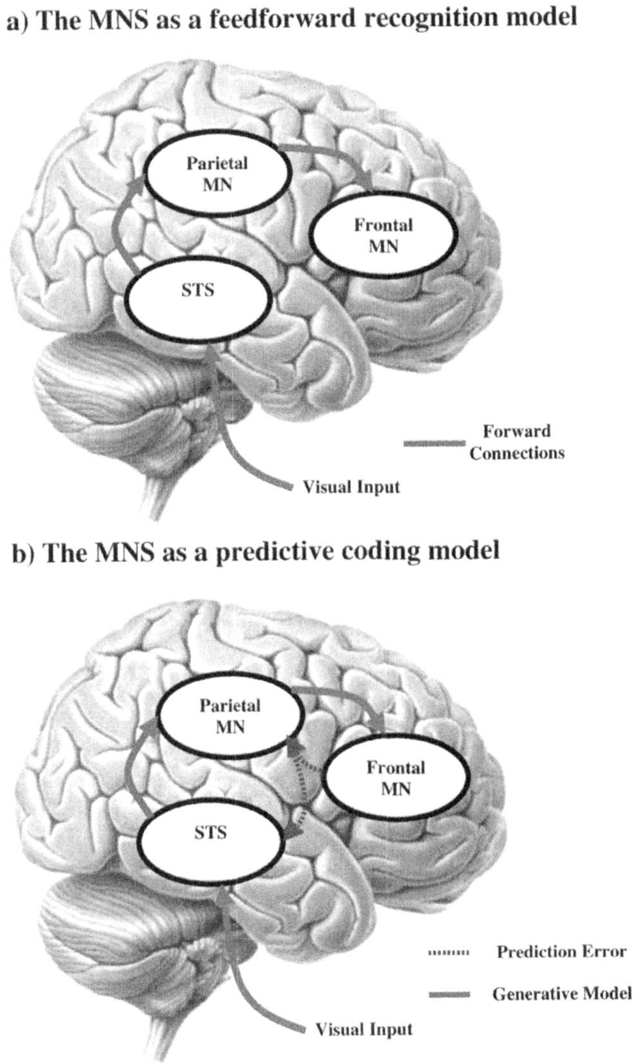


*Figure 12.1* Schemas of the mirror-neuron system. (See figure in colour plate section.)

inversion of a generative model, where the generative model produces a sensory representation of the kinematic level of an action given the information at the goals or intentions level. Generative models can be framed in terms of a deterministic non-linear generative function

$$u = G(v, \theta).$$

Here $v$ is a vector (i.e., a list) of underlying causes and $u$ represents some sensory inputs. $G(v, \theta)$ is a function that generates inputs from the causes given some parameters of the model, θ. In the case of action execution/observation the causes, $v$ are the long-term intentions or goals of the action. The parameters, $\theta$, correspond to the connection strengths in the brain's model of how the inputs are caused. These are fixed quantities that have to be learned, presumably through development. The inputs, $u$ is the visual signal corresponding to the sight of the executed action. This generative model will produce an estimate of the visual consequence of an executed action given the cause or goals of that action. By inverting this generative model it is possible to infer the cause or goals of an action given the visual input. However, is there any evidence that such generative models exist?

All executed actions have a sensory consequence. For example when we reach and grasp a bottle of wine there will be a change in our proprioceptive signal as we move, there will be a change in our tactile signal as we touch the bottle of wine, there will be change in the visual signal as we observe the action we are executing and there may be a change in the auditory signal as we pick up the bottle of wine. It is now generally accepted that when we execute a movement we predict the sensory consequences of that movement through generative or forward models (Wolpert et al. 1995, 2003; Wolpert and Miall 1996). These predictions can then be used to finesse motor control problems induced by delayed feedback and sensory noise. In short, forward models that generate predicted kinematics from motor commands are considered an integral part of motor execution. The suggestion here is that these generative models can be inverted to infer the causes given the data.

One of the obvious problems with such a model is that this scheme will only work when the processes generating the sensory inputs from the causes are invertible, i.e., when one sensory input is associated uniquely with one cause. In general, this is not the case since the same sensory input can have many causes. In the specific case of action-observation the same kinematics can be caused by different goals and intentions. For example, if, while walking along the street, someone suddenly waves his arm, is he hailing a taxi or swatting a wasp? A trivial example of this is given by the generative model $u = v^2$. In this example knowing $u$ does not uniquely determine $v$, which could be negative or positive. The nature of this ill-posed problem has been demonstrated empirically in the MNS. Mirror-neurons in area F5 that discharge when a monkey is observing a reach and grasp action also discharge when the sight of end point of this movement is occluded (Umilta et al. 2001). Critically, this result shows that mirror-neurons in area F5 are not simply driven by the visual representation of an observed movement. Therefore, if the inversion of a generative model is not sufficient to explain how we can understand others' actions through observation, then how can this be achieved? The question remains, if mirror-neurons do mediate understanding of actions done by others how do they do it?

## Predictive coding and the MNS

The perspective we propose here is that the role of the mirror-neuron system in reading or recognising the goals of observed actions can be understood within a predictive coding framework. Predictive coding is based on minimizing prediction error through recurrent or reciprocal interactions among levels of a cortical hierarchy (Box 12.1). In the predictive coding framework, each level of a hierarchy employs a generative model to predict representations in

### Box 12.1

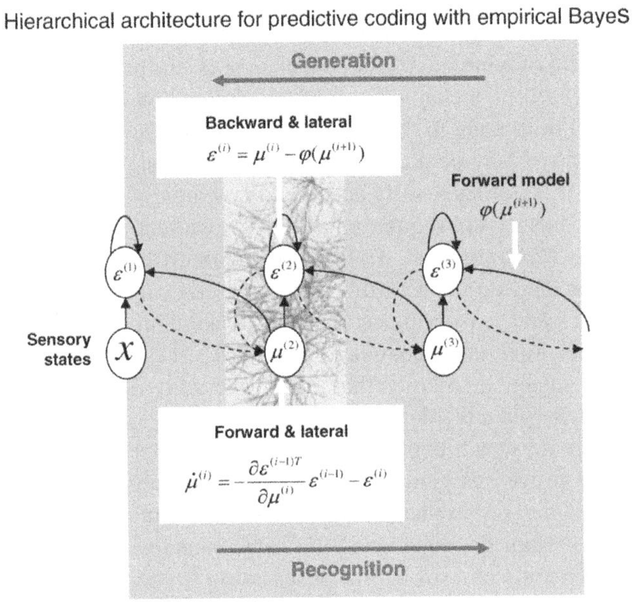


*Figure 12.2* Hierarchical architecture for predictive coding with empirical BayeS. (See figure in colour plate section.)

The empirical Bayesian perspective on perceptual inference suggests that the role of backward connections is to provide contextual guidance to lower levels through a prediction, $\varphi$ of the lower level's inputs. Given this conceptual model, a stimulus-related response can be decomposed into two components corresponding to the transients evoked in two functional subpopulations of units. The first encodes the conditional expectation of perceptual causes, $\mu$. The second encodes prediction error, $\varepsilon$. Responses are evoked in both, with the error units of one level driving appropriate changes in conditional expectations through forward connections. These expectations then suppress error units using predictions that are mediated by backward connections. These predictions are based on the brain's generative model of how sensory states are caused.

the level below. This generative model uses backward connections to convey the prediction to the lower level where it is compared to the representation in this subordinate level to produce a prediction error. This prediction error is then sent back to the higher level, via forward connections, to adjust the neuronal representation of sensory causes, which in turn change the prediction. This self-organising, reciprocal exchange of signals continues until prediction error is minimised and the most likely cause of the input has been generated. It can be shown that this scheme is formally equivalent to empirical Bayesian inference, in which prior expectations emerge naturally from the hierarchal models employed (see Box 12.2; Friston 2002, 2003, 2005). It should be noted that the prediction addressed in predictive coding is predicting the sensory effects from their cause. This is about the mapping between the cause (motor commands to grasp) and the sensory (i.e., visual or proprioceptive) expression or effect of that cause. It is not about forecasting (i.e., predicting the sensory states in the future, given the sensory state now), aka prospective coding (see Schütz-Bosbach and Wolfgang Prinz 2007 for a review of this topic).

For the MNS this means that anatomically the areas engaged by movement observation are arranged hierarchically and the anatomical connections between

**Box 12.2 Predictive coding and empirical Bayes**

Predictive coding is a framework that, in a hierarchical setting, is equivalent to empirical Bayesian inference. Schemes for identifying the causes of sensory input that are based entirely on bottom-up, forward connections, such as the feedforward recognition model in Figure 12.1a, are ill-posed when the generative model linking sensations and causes cannot be inverted. This can occur when there are inherent ambiguities in the way sensations are generated (*e.g.*, visual occlusion). However, identification is possible for noninvertible generative models by incorporating constraints and prior information. This is equivalent to full Bayesian inference. Although full Bayes enables recognition with noninvertible generative models it creates a new problem for the brain. Namely, the brain cannot construct prior expectations *de novo*; these have to be learned and adapted to the current experiential context. Statistical solutions are available for this problem using empirical Bayesian inference, in which priors are estimated from data. Empirical Bayesian inference harnesses the hierarchical structure of a generative model, treating the estimates at one level as priors on the subordinate level. This provides a natural framework within which to treat cortical hierarchies in the brain, each level providing constraints on the level below. This approach models the world as a hierarchy of systems where supraordinate causes induce and moderate changes in subordinate causes. These priors offer contextual guidance towards the most likely cause of the sensory input. This scheme can be implemented with simple architectures that have a degree of biological plausibility (see Box 12.3).

these areas are reciprocal. In terms of functional anatomy it means that the prediction error encoding higher-level attributes will be expressed as evoked responses in higher cortical levels of the MNS. For action observation the essence of this approach is that, given a prior expectation about the goal of the person we are observing, we can predict their motor commands. Given their motor commands we can predict the kinematics on the basis of our own action system. The comparison of this predicted kinematics with the observed kinematics generates a prediction error. This prediction error is used to update our representation of the person's motor commands (Fig. 12.1b). Similarly, the inferred goals are updated by minimising the prediction error between the predicted and inferred motor commands (see Box 12.1). By minimizing the prediction error at all the levels of the MNS, the most likely cause of the action will be inferred at all levels (intention, goal, motor and kinematic). This approach provides a mechanistic account of how responses in the visual and motor systems are organised and explains how the cause of an action, can be inferred from its observation.

## Generative models in motor control

Predictive coding is particularly appropriate for understanding the function of the MNS; predictive coding provides an established computational framework for inferring the causes (intentions, goals and motor commands) of sensory inputs (observed kinematics). It is now generally accepted that forward or generative models play a critical role in motor control (Wolpert et al. 1995, 2003; Wolpert and Miall 1996). The suggestion here is that these same models are used to infer motor commands from observed kinematics produced by others during perceptual inference (see Chater and Manning 2006 for a similar heuristic in the domain of language perception). Box 12.3 illustrates the formal similarities and differences between action-optimisation and action-perception. In execution, motor commands are optimised to minimise the difference between predicted and desired kinematics, under the assumption that the desired kinematics (i.e., goals) are known. Conversely, in action-perception, these goals have to be inferred. However, in both optimisations a forward model of motor control is required. In the predictive coding account of the MNS, the same generative model used to predict the sensorial effects of our own actions can also be used (with appropriate transformations) to predict the actions of others (see Friston 2005 for a description of the relationship between forward and inverse models and predictive coding).

There have been several previous accounts that have proposed the use of forward and inverse models in action-observation (Keysers and Perrett 2004; Wolpert et al. 2003; Miall 2003). "Skilled motor behaviour relies on the brain learning both to control the body and predict the consequences of this control. Prediction turns motor commands into expected sensory consequences, whereas control turns desired consequences into motor commands. To capture this symmetry, the neural processes underlying prediction and control are termed the forward and inverse internal models, respectively" (Flanagan et al. 2003). First, forward and

**Box 12.3**

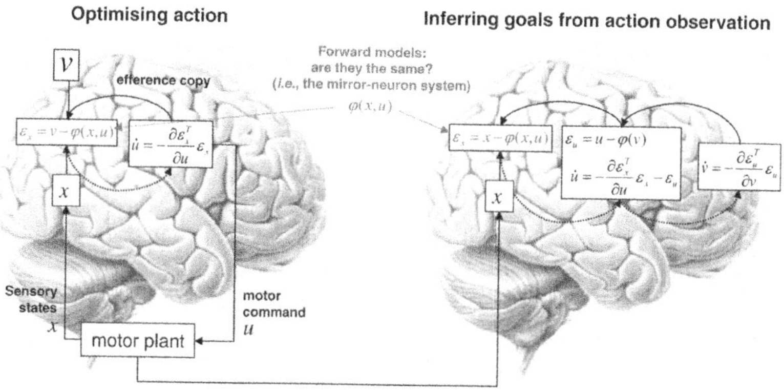


*Figure 12.3* (See figure in colour plate section.)

Simplified scheme for **motor control:** The motor plant receives commands ($u$) and changes the sensory input ($x$). These commands are constructed by a controller (inverse model) to minimise the difference between the desired trajectory of the states ($v$) and those predicted by the forward model. The forward (predictor) model is a function of the [efference] copy of the motor command. In this case, the goal is known and only $u$ is optimised. The inverse model or controller is represented as a recognition function that minimises prediction error by gradient descent (the dot above a variable means rate of change).

Simplified scheme for **action-perception:** A hierarchical generative or forward model of sensory states is inverted to infer their [unknown] causes. These causes include the motor commands ($u$) of the observed agent that are inferred by minimising the difference between the observed and predicted states (using a forward model of the motor plant). The agent's goals are inferred by minimising the error between the inferred commands ($u$) and those predicted by their forward model, which is a function of goals.

inverse models have been proposed as an account of imitation; the inverse model (mapping kinematics to motor signals) is identical to feedforward recognition model of the MNS (shown in Fig. 12.1a). The logic is that the inverse model can be used as recognition model and therefore infer the cause of an observed action. Once the cause of the observed kinematics is inferred the action can then be imitated. Second, the HMOSIAC model for motor control has recently been proposed as a model for understanding social interactions (Wolpert et al. 2003). The links between this model and the predictive coding account exist at a number of levels. In the HMOSIAC model several predictor-controller pairs are organised hierarchically. The predictor (forward) model is employed to predict the input in a subordinate module and the controller is used to adjust the predictor to maximise the prediction.

Although these generalisations of forward-inverse models in motor control to imitation and social interactions are exciting, they are formally distinct from, and more complicated than, the predictive coding account of the MNS. In predictive coding there is no separate inverse model or controller; a forward model is simply inverted by suppressing the prediction error generated by the forward model. This inversion depends on the self-organising, reciprocal exchange of signals between hierarchical levels (see Box 12.1). This simplicity translates into an algorithmic architecture that could be implemented plausibly by the brain (and for which there is a considerable amount of anatomical and physiological evidence). Indeed Miall (2003) when describing the HMOSIAC model wrote, "Quite how this multi-level controller could be generated neurally is not yet clear, but the link with mirror-neurons seems appealing." In contrast, the predictive coding account has been described in some detail at the neural level (see Friston 2002, 2003, 2005).

## An example of the predictive coding account of the MNS

Within predictive coding, recognition of causes is simply the process of jointly minimizing prediction error at all levels of a cortical hierarchy. The most likely cause of an observed action (i.e., motor commands, goal or intention) can be estimated from the visual representation of the observed movement. An intuitive example is given in Fig. 12.4. Here we use the predictive coding account of the MNS to address the Dr. Jekyll and Mr Hyde thought-experiment described in Jacob and Jeannerod (2005). In this thought-experiment, one is invited to watch identical movements, made by Dr. Jekyll and Mr Hyde. In both cases one observes the same person, taking hold of a scalpel and applying it to a human body. However, in one case Dr. Jekyll is using the scalpel to cure a patient but in the other Mr Hyde's aim is to inflict pain. Jacob and Jeannerod argue that the MNS is incapable of distinguishing between these two intentions, as the observed movement is identical in both cases. This is certainly true for the bottom-up inverse or recognition model described in Fig. 12.1a but it is not true for the predictive coding scheme. The observed kinematics can be explained at a number of levels that are hierarchically organised, the visual representation of the kinematics, the underlying motor signals, the short-term goal (e.g., to grasp the scalpel), and the long-term intention ('to cure' or 'to hurt'). These three levels are shown schematically in Fig. 12.4a. In predictive coding, the intentional level predicts a goal that in turn predicts the kinematic representation of the motor acts. At each level the predicted activity is compared to the actual activity and any difference is projected back-up the hierarchy as a prediction error (see Box 12.1). In the case where both intentions produce identical movements there are identical prediction errors and therefore

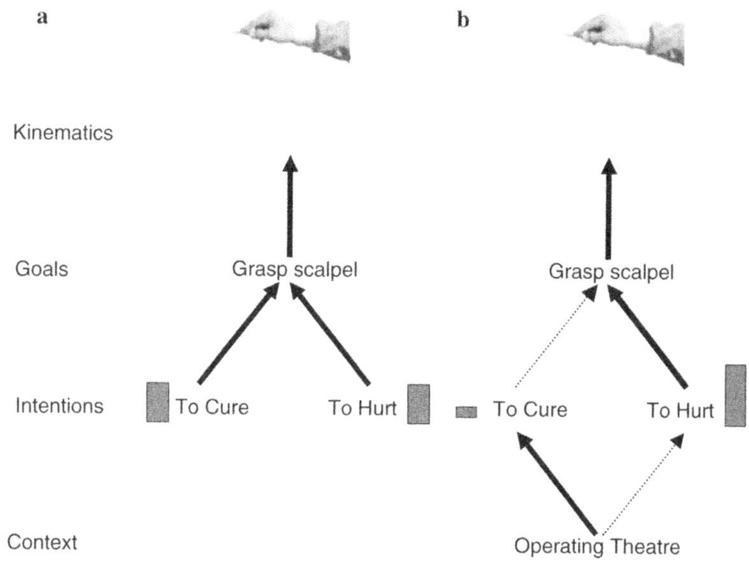


*Figure 12.4* Examples of the predictive coding account of the MNS. Here we consider four levels of attribution in an example hierarchy of the MNS; kinematics, goal, intention and context. In **a** action-observation is considered in the absence of a context, in **b** the identical action is observed but now in the context of an operating theatre. The *bars* depict the level degree of prediction error. In **a** both intentions predict identical goals and kinematics and therefore the prediction error is identical in both schemes. In this case the model can not differentiate between the intentions causing the action. In **b** the context causes a large prediction error for the goal 'to hurt' and a small prediction error for the goal 'to cure'. In this case the model can differentiate between the two intentions.

the predictive coding account cannot infer a unique intention from the observed movement. However, in contradistinction to the bottom-up model, the predictive coding model also has to explain sensory information pertaining to the context in which the movement has been observed. This induces high-level sensory causes that provide empirical priors on action-perception; for example, a therapeutic intention explains the action and the visual scenery, if seen in an operating theatre (Fig. 12.4b). This does not mean that context is coded by mirror-neurons but rather the MNS is part of a larger hierarchy, where intentions are encoded. In this scheme, the intention that is inferred from the observation of the action now depends upon the prior information received from a context level. In other words, if the action was observed taking place in an operating theatre there would be a large prediction error for the intention 'to hurt' and a smaller prediction error for the intention 'to cure'. The prediction error would be the same at all other levels of the hierarchy for the two intentions. By minimising the overall prediction error the MNS would infer that the intention of the observed movement was to cure. Therefore, the MNS is capable of inferring a unique intention even if two intentions result in identical movements. This observation is supported empirically. Mirror-neurons in area PF have been shown to have differential patterns of firing when viewing movements that are virtually identical at the kinematic level, but differ at the level of intention. In this task there is a contextual cue, the object that is grasped, that informs the monkey of the intention of the action to be observed. Within the predictive coding account the MNS will always be able to infer the most likely intention of an observed action, given the observer's priors.

## Summary

Social interaction depends upon our ability to infer beliefs and intentions in others. Impairments of this ability can lead to major developmental and psychiatric disorders such as autism (Dapretto et al. 2006; Oberman et al. 2005) and schizophrenia (Arbib and Munhenk 2005). It has been suggested that the MNS could underlie this ability to 'read' someone else's intentions. Here we have proposed that the MNS is best considered within a predictive coding framework. One of the attractions of predictive coding is that it can explain how the MNS could infer someone else's intentions through observation of their movements. Within this scheme the most likely cause of an observed action is inferred by minimising the prediction error at all levels of the cortical hierarchy that is engaged during action-observation. Central to testing the predictive coding account of the MNS is that the nodes of the cortical hierarchy are well characterised both anatomically and functionally. From the existing literature we can assume that any MNS network will include areas of ventral premotor cortex, inferior parietal lobule and STS. However, the function of each node in the MNS and the hierarchical organisation of the MNS are not known. Implicit in many accounts of the MNS is the notion that the area F5 is the highest level of the hierarchy. This is the hierarchical arrangement shown in Fig. 12.1. However, there is no direct evidence to support this view and the results of recent studies suggest that the inferior parietal lobule area may be superordinate to premotor areas in the MNS hierarchy (Hamilton and Grafton 2006; Fogassi et al. 2005). Specifically, the theory underlying the predictive coding account of the MNS is independent of the hierarchical organisation. The predictive coding account of the MNS specifies a precise role for the MNS in our ability to infer intentions and formalises the underlying computations. It also connects generative models that are inverted during perceptual inference with forward models that finesse motor control.

## Acknowledgments

The Wellcome Trust funded this work.

## References

Allison T, Puce A, McCarthy G. Social perception from visual cues: role of the STS region. Trends Cogn Sci. 2000; 4:267–278. [PubMed: 10859571]

Arbib MA, Mundhenk TN. Schizophrenia and the mirror-neuron system: an essay. Neuropsychologia. 2005; 43:268–280. [PubMed: 15707911]

Chater N, Manning CD. Probabilistic models of language processing and acquisition. Trends Cogn Sci. 2006; 10(7):335–344. [PubMed: 16784883]

Dapretto M, Davies MS, Pfeifer JH, Scott AA, Sigman M, Bookheimer SY, Iacoboni M. Understanding emotions in others: mirror-neuron dysfunction in children with autism spectrum disorders. Nat Neurosci. 2006; 9:28–30. [PubMed: 16327784]

Di Pellegrino G, Fadiga L, Fogassi L, Gallese V, Rizzolatti G. Understanding motor events: a neurophysiological study. Exp Brain Res. 1992; 91:176–180. [PubMed: 1301372]

Flanagan JR, Vetter P, Johansson RS, Wolpert DM. Prediction precedes control in motor learning. Curr Biol. 2003; 13(2):146–150. [PubMed: 12546789]

Fogassi L, Ferrari PF, Gesierich B, Rozzi S, Chersi F, Rizzolatti G. Parietal lobe: from action organization to intention understanding. Science. 2005; 308:662–667. [PubMed: 15860620]

Friston KJ. Funtional integration and inference in the brain. Prog Neurobiol. 2002; 68:113–143. [PubMed: 12450490]

Friston KJ. Learning and inference in the brain. Neural Netw. 2003; 16:1325–1352. [PubMed: 14622888]

Friston K. A theory of cortical responses. Philos Trans R Soc Lond B Biol Sci. 2005; 360:815–836. [PubMed: 15937014]

Frith CD, Frith U. Interacting minds – a biological basis. Science. 1999; 286:1692–1695. [PubMed: 10576727]

Gallese, V. Embodied simulation: from mirror neuron systems to interpersonal relations. In: Bock, G.; Goode, J., editors. Empathy and fairness. Novartis Foundation; San Diego: 2006.

Gallese V, Goldman A. Mirror-neurons and the simulation theory of mind reading. Trends Cogn Sci. 1998; 2:493–501. [PubMed: 21227300]

Gallese V, Fadiga L, Fogassi L, Rizzolatti G. Action recognition in the premotor cortex. Brain. 1996; 119:593–609. [PubMed: 8800951]

Gallese, V.; Fogassi, L.; Fadiga, L.; Rizzolatti, G. Action representation and the inferior parietal lobule. In: Prinz, W.; Hommel, B., editors. Attention and performance XIX. Common mechanisms in perception and action. Oxford University Press; Oxford: 2002. p. 247–266.

Gallese V, Keysers C, Rizzolatti G. A unifying view of the basis of social cognition. Trends Cogn Sci. 2004; 8:396–403. [PubMed: 15350240]

Grossman E, Donnelly M, Price R, Pickens D, Morgan V, Neighbor G, Blake R. Brain areas involved in perception of biological motion. J Cogn Neurosci. 2000; 12:711–720. [PubMed: 11054914]

Hamilton AF, Grafton ST. Goal representation in human anterior intraparietal sulcus. J Neurosci. 2006; 26:1133–1137. [PubMed: 16436599]

Hamilton, AF.; Grafton, ST. The motor hierarchy: from kinematics to goals and intentions. Sensorimotor Founds. of Higher Cog. 2007; 22:381–408.

Harries MH, Perrett DI. Visual processing of faces in temporal cortex: physiological evidence for a modular organization and possible anatomical correlates. J Cogn Neurosci. 1991; 3:9–24.

Iacoboni M. Neural mechanisms of imitation. Curr Opin Neurobiol. 2005; 15:632–637. [PubMed: 16271461]

Iacoboni M, Koski LM, Brass M, Bekkering H, Woods RP, Dubeau MC, Mazziotta JC, Rizzolatti G. Reafferent copies of imitated actions in the right superior temporal cortex. Proc Natl Acad Sci USA. 2001; 98(24):13995–13999. [PubMed: 11717457]

Iacoboni M, Molnar-Szakacs I, Gallese V, Buccino G, Mazziotta JC, Rizzolatti G. Grasping the intentions of others with one's own mirror neuron system. PLoS Biol. 2005; 3(3):e79. [PubMed: 15736981]

Jacob P, Jeannerod M. The motor theory of social cognition: a critique. Trends Cogn Sci. 2005; 9:21–25. [PubMed: 15639437]

James, W. Principles of psychology. Holt; New York: 1890.

Jeannerod M. The representing brain-neural correlates of motor intention and imagery. Behav Br Sci. 1994; 17:187–202.

Keysers C, Perrett DI. Demystifying social cognition: a Hebbian perspective. Trends Cogn Sci. 2004; 8:501–507. [PubMed: 15491904]

Luppino G, Murata A, Govoni P, Matelli M. Largely segregated parietofrontal connections linking rostral intraparietal cortex (areas AIP and VIP) and the ventral premotor cortex (areas F5 and F4). Exp Brain Res. 1999; 128:181–187. [PubMed: 10473756]

Miall RC. Connecting mirror neurons and forward models. Neuroreport. 2003; 14(17):2135–2137. [PubMed: 14625435]

Nishitani N, Hari R. Temporal dynamics of cortical representation for action. Proc Natl Acad Sci USA. 2000; 97(2):913–918. [PubMed: 10639179]

Nishitani N, Hari R. Viewing lip forms: cortical dynamics. Neuron. 2002; 36(6):1211–1220. [PubMed: 12495633]

Oberman LM, Hubbard EM, McCleery JP, Altschuler EL, Ramachandran VS, Pineda JA. EEG evidence for mirror-neuron dysfunction in autism spectrum disorders. Brain Res Cogn Brain Res. 2005; 24:190–198. [PubMed: 15993757]

Oram MW, Perrett DI. Responses of anterior superior temporal polysensory (STPa) neurons to biological motion stimuli. J Cogn Neurosci. 1994; 6:99–116.

Prinz W. Perception and action planning. Eur J Cogn Psych. 1997; 9:129–154.

Rizzolatti G, Craighero L. The mirror-neuron system. Annu Rev Neurosci. 2004; 27:169–192. [PubMed: 15217330]

Rizzolatti G, Fogassi L, Gallese V. Neurophysiological mechanisms underlying the understanding and imitation of action. Nat Rev Neurosci. 2001; 2:661–670. [PubMed: 11533734]

Rushworth MFS, Behrens TEJ, Johansen-Berg H. Connection patterns distinguish three regions of human parietal cortex. Cereb Cortex. 2006; 16:1418–1430. [PubMed: 16306320]

Saxe R. Against simulation: the argument from error. Trends Cogn Sci. 2005; 9:174–179. [PubMed: 15808499]

Schütz-Bosbach; Wolfgang Prinz. Prospective coding in event representation. Cogn Proc. 2007; 8.2:93–102.

Seltzer B, Pandya DN. Parietal, temporal, and occipital projections to cortex of the superior temporal sulcus in the rhesus-monkey: a retrograde tracer study. J Comp Neurol. 1994; 343:445–463. [PubMed: 8027452]

Umilta MA, Kohler E, Gallesse V, Fogassi L, Fadiga L, Keysers C, Rizzolatti G. I know what you are doing. A neurophsyiological study. Neuron. 2001; 31:155–165. [PubMed: 11498058]

Wolpert DM, Doya K, Kawato M. A unifying computational framework for motor control and social interaction. Philos Trans R Soc Lond B Biol Sci. 2003; 29(358):593–602. [PubMed: 12689384]

Wolpert DM, Ghahramani Z, Jordan MI. An internal model for sensorimotor integration. Science. 1995; 269:1880–1882. [PubMed: 7569931]

Wolpert DM, Miall RC. Forward models for physiological motor control. Neural Netw. 1996; 9:1265–1279. [PubMed: 12662535]

# 13 Optimally interacting minds

*Bahador Bahrami, Karsten Olsen, Peter E. Latham, Andreas Roepstorff, Geraint Rees and Chris D. Frith*

To come to an optimal joint decision, individuals must share information with each other and, importantly, weigh that information by its reliability[1,2]. It has been well established that isolated individuals can accurately weigh information when combining different sources of sensory information[3,4,5]. Little is known, however, about how, or even whether, two individuals can accurately combine information that they communicate with each other. To investigate this issue, we examined the behavior of pairs of individuals in a simple perceptual decision task, and we asked how signals from the same sensory modality (vision) in the brains of two different individuals could be combined through social interaction.

Work on perceptual decision-making has shown that when combining information from different senses, individuals have access not just to magnitudes of sensory signals, but also to their probability distributions, or at least to their means and variances[3,4,5,6,7,8]. However, this may not be true for interpersonal communication. Whereas probability distributions arising from different sensory modalities are available within an individual's brain, it is not clear whether such distributions can be passed directly to another person or what types of information can be communicated. To answer this, we considered four models[9], each of which proposes that different types of information could be communicated, and quantitatively compared the predictions of those models to empirical data in a low-level visual decision-making task.

The first model proposes that nothing except the decision about the visual stimulus is communicated, and when there is disagreement, the joint decision is no better than a coin flip (CF model). This strategy is expected from previous work on collective decision-making without feedback[10]. The second model proposes that nothing except the decision is communicated, but that pairs of individuals learn, from trial-to-trial feedback, which of them is more accurate, so they eventually use that individual's decisions [the behavior and feedback (BF) model]. This model was motivated by previous work showing that collective decisions are dominated by the most competent group member in situations where clear feedback about "the truth" (in our case, the correct answer) is available[11,12]. The third model, put forward here for the first time, proposes that confidence, which we define as an internal estimate of the probability of being correct[13], is communicated [the weighted confidence sharing (WCS) model][9]. Finally, the fourth model proposes that the mean and standard deviation of the sensory response to the stimulus about which the decision is made are communicated [direct signal sharing (DSS) model]. This model is used to account for multisensory integration within an individual[3,4] and also for collective decisions in groups[14]. To anticipate our findings, we determined that the WCS model was quantitatively consistent with our empirical data, whereas the other three models were not.

Our empirical data were obtained from pairs of participants (dyads) who viewed brief visual displays containing a faint target (contrast oddball; Fig. 13.1A) in either the first or second viewing interval[9]. We performed a series of four experiments, each of which followed very similar procedures. Initially, each participant chose the interval that they thought contained the target, without consulting the other. Individual decisions were then shared, and if participants disagreed, they discussed the matter until they reached a joint decision. Subsequently, both participants were informed of the correct choice (with the exception of experiment 4 in which no feedback was given). Individual and dyad psychometric functions (Fig. 13.1B, left and middle panels) were fit with a cumulative Gaussian function, from which we extracted the slope $s$. The slope provided an estimate of sensitivity (the steeper the slope, the higher the sensitivity). More sensitive observers were, by definition, more reliable in their estimates of contrast.

The four models made different predictions for the relation between the slope of the psychometric function for each individual and the collective dyad; thus, by comparing predicted and observed dyad slopes, we could distinguish the models. For each of the four models[9], we computed the predicted dyad slopes, $S_{\text{dyad}}^{\text{model}}$, in terms of the individual slopes, $s_1$ and $s_2$, of observers 1 and 2. For the CF model, the predicted dyad slope is related to the individual slopes by

$$S_{\text{dyad}}^{\text{CF}} \approx \frac{s_1 + s_2}{2} \tag{1}$$

for the BF model by

$$S_{\text{dyad}}^{\text{BF}} = \max\left(s_1, s_2\right) \tag{2}$$

for the WCS model by

$$S_{\text{dyad}}^{\text{WCS}} \approx \frac{s_1 + s_2}{2^{1/2}} \tag{3}$$

and for the DSS model by

$$S_{\text{dyad}}^{\text{DSS}} = \left(s_1^2, s_2^2\right)^{1/2} \tag{4}$$

These equations provide upper bounds on performance for each model: For example, Eq. 3 provides the largest possible dyad slope, given that participants share only confidence. If the dyads reach that slope, then they are Bayes optimal, given the model assumptions, where by "Bayes optimal" we mean that participants

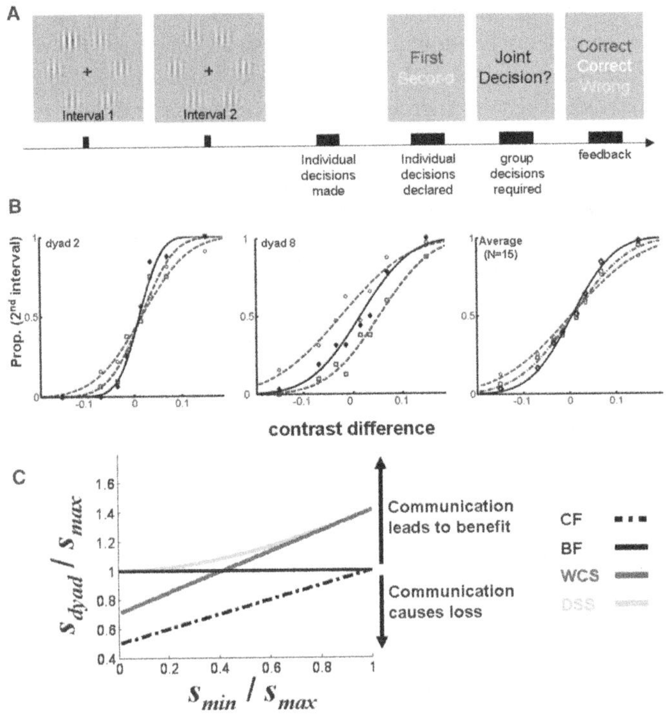


*Figure 13.1* (**A**) Experimental paradigm. Each trial consisted of two observation intervals. In each interval, six vertically oriented Gabor patches were displayed equidistantly around an imaginary circle (duration: 85 ms). In either the first or second interval, there was one oddball target that had slightly higher contrast than all of the others (in this example, upper-left target in interval 1). (**B**) Two example psychometric functions and the group average in experiment 1. The proportion of trials in which the oddball was reported to be in the second interval is plotted against the contrast difference at the oddball location (i.e., contrast in the second interval minus contrast in the first). A highly sensitive observer would produce a steeply rising psychometric function with a large slope. Open circles, performance of the less sensitive observer ($s_{min}$) of the dyad; open squares, performance of the more sensitive observer ($s_{max}$); and black diamonds, performance of the dyad ($s_{dyad}$). The dashed curves are the best fit to a cumulative Gaussian function[9]; the solid black curve is the prediction of the WCS. $N = 15$ dyads. (**C**) Predictions of the four models (see Eqs. 1 to 4). The *x* axis shows the ratio of individual sensitivities ($s_{min}/s_{max}$), with values near one corresponding to dyad members with similar sensitivities and values near zero to dyad members with very different sensitivities. The *y* axis shows the ratio of dyad sensitivity to the more sensitive member ($s_{dyad}/s_{max}$). Values above the horizontal line indicate communication benefit; in this range the dyad is better than the more sensitive observer. The black, rising line, which corresponds to the WCS model, is above the horizontal line only if $s_{min}/s_{max}$ is larger than ~0.4, reflecting the prediction that communication by WCS is beneficial only if dyad members have approximately the same competence. The grey curve, which corresponds to the DSS model, never crosses the black horizontal line, so for this model, communication will invariably be beneficial. The dot-dashed and solid black, horizontal lines indicate the CF and BF models, respectively. (See figure in colour plate section.)

made decisions that maximized their probability of being correct, given their model assumptions.

Fig. 13.1C shows the predictions (from Eqs. 1 to 4) for the collective benefit (the ratio $s_{dyad}/s_{max}$) versus relative sensitivity ($s_{min}/s_{max}$), where $s_{min}$ and $s_{max}$ are the minimum (less sensitive) and maximum (more sensitive) of the individual slopes, respectively. The models clearly make different predictions, but to distinguish them requires experiments with a broad range of $s_{min}/s_{max}$; we would need to investigate dyad members with nearly identical performance ($s_{min}/s_{max} \sim 1$), as well as those with very different performance ($s_{min}/s_{max} << 1$). Experiments 1 and 2 were performed to test the model predictions in different ranges of $s_{min}/s_{max}$.

In experiment 1, participants viewed identical stimuli, and individual sensitivities of the dyad members were similar ($s_{min}/s_{max} > 0.5$) (Fig. 13.2B). The CF model (Eq. 1 and Fig. 13.1C, black dot-dashed line) predicted that dyad sensitivity would never be higher than that of the better participant. The BF model (Eq. 2 and Fig. 13.1C, black, horizontal line) predicted that dyad sensitivity would be as good as that of the better participant. In contrast, the WCS model (Eq. 3 and Fig. 13.1C, rising, black line) and DSS model (Eq. 4 and Fig. 13.1C, grey curve) both predicted that, within the relative sensitivity range tested here ($s_{min}/s_{max} > 0.5$), dyad sensitivity would be higher than that of the better participant.

We found that the dyad slope was significantly larger than that of the better participant [$t(14) = 5.24, p < 10^{-3}$, paired $t$ test]. Thus, these data ruled out both the CF (Fig. 13.2A; $p < 10^{-5}$) and BF (Fig. 13.2A; $p < 10^{-3}$) models, for which the dyad slope can be no larger than that of the better participant, and instead favored the sharing models ($p > 0.1$), for which the dyad can outperform the individuals. The sharing models were also able to accurately predict, via Eqs. 3 and 4, the dyad slopes on a case-by-case basis. Thus, communication conferred a significant benefit, and, at least on this task, two heads did perform better than one.

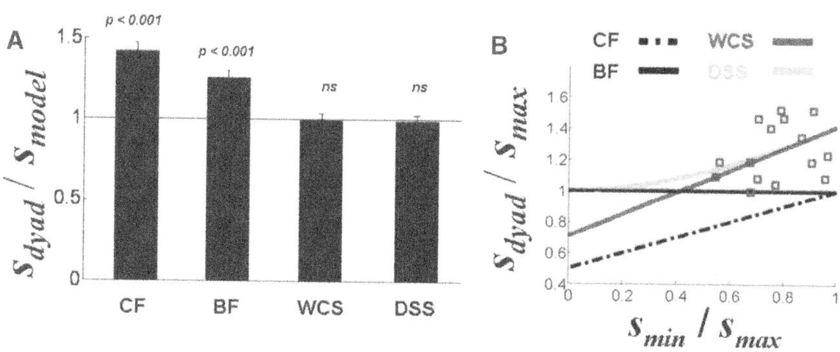


*Figure 13.2* Results of experiments 1. (**A**) Plot of the ratio of the dyad slope to the slope predicted by each model. The BF model comparison also depicts collective benefit over the more sensitive observer. Error bars indicate SEM ($N = 15$). (**B**) Distribution of data points and model predictions. Collective benefit ($s_{dyad}/s_{max}$) is plotted against relative sensitivity ($s_{min}/s_{max}$). Each open square represents one dyad. (See figure in colour plate section.)

Experiment 1 favored the WCS and DSS models, but was not able to distinguish between them. For the range of relative sensitivities tested in experiment 1, the two models made very similar predictions (Fig. 13.2B). To distinguish the models, we sought to study dyads with very different individual sensitivities ($s_{min}/s_{max} << 1$) for which the WCS model (Fig. 13.1C, red line) made a counterintuitive prediction: If one participant's sensitivity was no better than ~40% of the other's (e.g., $s_{min}/s_{max} < 2^{1/2} - 1 \approx 0.4$), then two heads should do worse than the better one ($s_{dyad}/s_{max} < 1$), even when individuals accurately communicated their confidence. In contrast, the DSS model (Fig. 13.1C, green curve) invariably predicted a benefit for dyads, consistent with the fact that when signals are directly available (as in multisensory integration within a single brain), putting them together is never worse than either one alone[4].

We tested these predictions in experiment 2. In randomly chosen trials, we surreptitiously reduced one or the other (or both) participants' sensitivity by adding a substantial amount of noise to their stimuli[9] without having told the participants about this manipulation. The four noise regimes were randomized, so on each trial, noise was given to both participants ("equal" condition), to one but not the other (both possibilities combined together as the "unequal" condition), or to neither participant ("none" condition). For each participant and dyad, four psychometric functions (corresponding to the four noise regimes) were constructed, and the slopes were estimated. Figure 13.3 shows that, in equal and none conditions – in which participants received identical amounts of noise – robust group benefits were obtained [Fig. 13.3A; for equal condition: $t(10) = 2.50$, $p = 0.03$, paired $t$ test; for none condition: $t(10) = 3.38$, $p = 0.007$, paired $t$ test]. This replicated the results of experiment 1. However, in the unequal condition, dyads did not perform better than the better participant, and reliable group benefit was not observed [Fig. 13.3A; $t(21) = 0.68$, $p = 0.54$, paired $t$ test].

In all three conditions, the results were consistent with the predictions of the WCS model (Fig. 13.3B). Importantly, the majority of the data points for which $s_{min}/s_{max} < 0.4$ fell below the black line in Fig. 13.3D, indicating that, in these instances, two heads did worse than the better one. The DSS model, on the other hand, was rejected in the unequal condition [Fig. 13.3C; $t(21) = 4.52$, $p < 10^{-3}$, paired $t$ test]. Moreover, randomized addition of noise resulted in a wide range of relative sensitivity, and a highly significant linear correlation was observed between collective benefit and relative sensitivity [Fig. 13.3D; dotted line $R^2 = 0.51$, $F_{42,1} = 43.22$, $p < 10^{-7}$] with a slope ($0.6 \pm 0.09$) and intercept ($0.74 \pm 0.05$) that were very close to the slope ($1/2^{1/2} \approx 0.71$) and intercept ($1/2^{1/2} \approx 0.71$) predicted by the WCS model.

In these experiments, two aspects of social information contributed to collective decision-making: communication and feedback. However, the experiments could not tell us whether either or both types of information were necessary for collective benefit in sensitivity. To address this issue, we conducted two more experiments: Experiment 3 tested whether communication was necessary, whereas experiment 4 tested whether feedback was necessary. We found that communication was necessary, but, surprisingly, feedback was not.

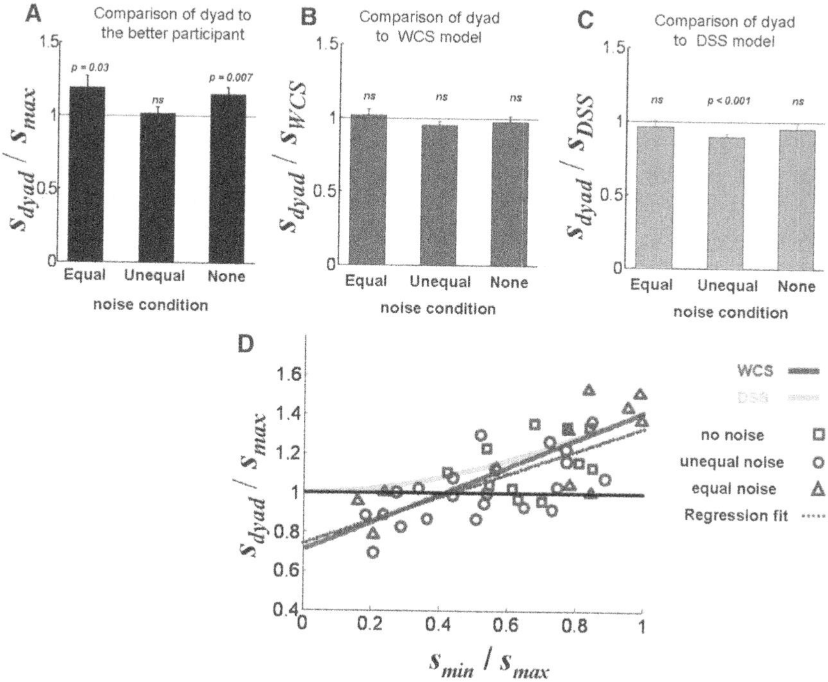


*Figure 13.3* Results of experiment 2. (**A**) Ratio of the dyad slope to the maximum individual slope for the three noise conditions (equal, unequal, and none; see main text). The line at $s_{dyad}/s_{max} = 1$ corresponds to the case in which the dyad is performing exactly as well as the more sensitive member. Values above and below the line correspond to benefit and loss due to communication, respectively. ns, not significant. (**B**) Ratio of the dyad slope to the slope predicted by the WCS model, the latter denoted $s_{WCS}$. This ratio was not significantly different from zero for any of the noise conditions. (**C**) Ratio of the dyad slope to the slope of the DSS model. For the unequal noise condition, this ratio was significantly smaller than 1 ($p < 10^{-4}$). (**D**) Distribution of data points and model predictions (the latter taken from Fig. 13.1C). Collective benefit ($s_{dyad}/s_{max}$) is plotted against relative sensitivity ($s_{min}/s_{max}$). Each dyad contributed four sets of data points (triangles for equal, squares for none, and circles for unequal conditions). The solid black, horizontal line indicates the boundary of collective benefit (see Fig. 13.1C). In (A) to (C), error bars denote SEM ($N = 11$ data points for equal and none conditions; $N = 22$ for unequal condition). (See figure in colour plate section.)

It is conceivable that, even if the participants were not able to communicate their confidence on each trial, they would still be able to estimate each other's average reliability (defined explicitly as the slope of the psychometric curves; see Fig. 13.1B), not through direct trial-by-trial interaction and confidence sharing, but by accumulating information about one another's accuracy through feedback. Armed with such an estimate, dyads might conceivably be able to match the performance of those that did communicate, and so match the performance of the WCS model. On theoretical grounds, we did not expect this; instead, we expected performance without communication to match the BF model. We hypothesized that trial-by-trial communication was necessary and that feedback alone would not be sufficient for achieving collective benefit.

Experiment 3 tested this prediction using the same paradigm as experiment 1, modified so that participants were now not allowed to communicate anything but their choice. Whenever the participants disagreed in their decision, one of the two (chosen randomly by the computer) made a decision individually by arbitrating between their own choice and that of the other participant. Feedback about the correct choice was then given to both participants[9]. The results were unequivocal. In contrast to experiment 1, dyad sensitivity did not exceed that of the more sensitive observer [Fig. 13.4A, left bar; $t(13) = 0.18$, $p = 0.85$, paired $t$ test], as predicted by the BF model. More important, dyad sensitivity was significantly lower than the upper bound predicted by the WCS model [Fig. 13.4B, left bar; $t(13) = 5.91$, $p < 10^{-4}$, paired $t$ test], demonstrating that knowledge of current choice and previous outcomes was not adequate for the dyads to reach the level of performance observed in experiment 1, expected from the WCS model.

Experiment 3 showed that communication was necessary and that feedback alone was not sufficient for dyads to achieve a collaboration benefit. However, the results do not address the question of whether communication alone, without feedback, is sufficient for achieving collaboration benefit. Could dyads achieve any group benefit at all without ever receiving any objective feedback about the accuracy of their decisions? This is an important question, because feedback is not

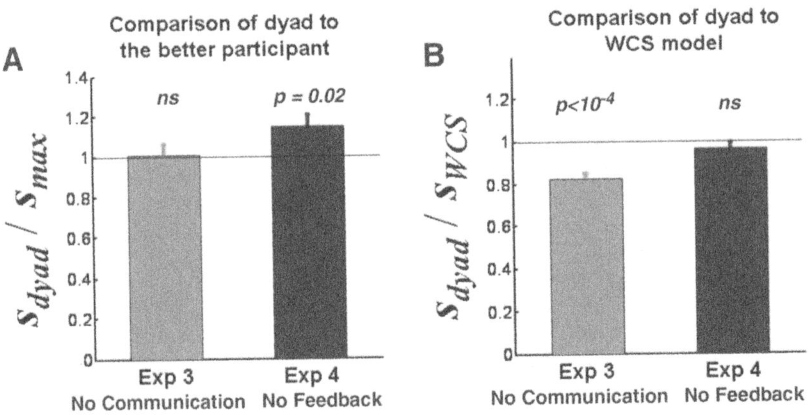


*Figure 13.4* Results of experiments 3 and 4. *y*-axis conventions are the same as in Fig. 13.3, A and B. (**A**) Collective benefit ($s_{dyad}/s_{max}$) is plotted for experiment 3 (left, without communication) and for experiment 4 (right, without feedback). (**B**) Ratio of the dyad slope to the slope predicted by the WCS model for experiment 3 (left, without communication), and experiment 4 (right, without feedback). In all panels, error bars denote SEM ($N = 14$ for experiment 3; $N = 11$ for experiment 4). (See figure in colour plate section.)

formally incorporated in the confidence-sharing model[9]. Taking this model seriously at face value, one may make the extremely counterintuitive assumption that, as long as accurate communication of confidence is ensured, dyad benefit can still be achieved without any feedback (that is, without any definitive knowledge of decision outcomes).

In experiment 4, we removed the feedback stage of the task to test this prediction[9]: After the joint decision was made (either automatically in the agreement trials or after interaction in the disagreement trials), the participants were not told the correct answer. All other aspects of the experiment were identical to experiment 1. Consistent with our prediction, even without feedback, the dyads nevertheless achieved a significant collaboration benefit [Fig. 13.4A, right bar; $t(10) = 2.68$, $p = 0.022$, paired $t$ test], and dyad sensitivity was statistically indistinguishable from the prediction of the confidence sharing model [Fig. 13.4B, right bar; $t(10) = 1.16$, $p = 0.27$, paired $t$ test]. These findings indicate that objective feedback was not necessary, and communication alone was sufficient for achieving collective benefit.

Our results show that interactive decision-making between two individuals can significantly improve perceptual sensitivity, but, importantly, only for similarly sensitive observers. Moreover, such joint behavior is Bayes optimal under the assumption that participants accurately communicate their internal estimate that they are correct. Our findings show that human-to-human interpersonal communication is adequately rich to permit sharing of subjective estimates of confidence, and humans are adequately perceptive to make optimal use of this information. Moreover, communication of trial-by-trial confidence is necessary for collective benefit, but, somewhat surprisingly, feedback about decision outcomes is not.

Quantitatively, we tested four models, and only one – the WCS model, in which participants communicated only an internal estimate of their reliability on each trial – was consistent with the data. Of the three models that were not consistent with the data, one, the DSS model, posited that participants communicated both the perceived contrast and their estimate of its reliability on each trial. That model was rejected because it outperformed the dyads in experiment 2. This leaves open the possibility that the participants did communicate contrast and reliability, but used that information suboptimally, which seems unlikely, as we never observed any dyads explicitly communicating contrast and reliability separately. However, our data cannot definitively rule out this idea, and further research is needed to distinguish between optimal use of WCS versus suboptimal DSS.

The general consensus from extensive earlier work on collective decision-making is that groups rarely outperform their best members[11,15]. Even in one of the rare cases in which consistent collaborative benefit was established, group performance failed to reach the bound predicted by the proposed ideal combination of individual decisions[14]. That study employed the DSS model (see Eq. 4) to estimate the ideal, expected group sensitivity. As shown in experiments 1 and 2, however, the predictions of that model deviate significantly from empirical data if individuals' sensitivities differ markedly. In particular, experiment 2 demonstrated the detrimental side effect of collective decision-making based on Bayesian combination of confidence: Individuals with very different sensitivities are best advised to avoid collaboration and instead should rely entirely on the more sensitive individual. In fact, the WCS model and the results of experiment 2 (Fig. 13.3D) set a quantitative limit on the usefulness of cooperation that, to our knowledge, is not predicted by current economic and social theories of collective decision-making[15]. An important next step for future research is to test the generality of this limit in other types of dyadic interactions.

Our findings have direct bearing on studies in social psychology that have discovered numerous situations in which groups fail to do better than their individuals. Many explanations for such "process loss" have been proposed, such as reduced effort in the presence of others [e.g., "social loafing"[16]], interpersonal competition[11], and groupthink[17]. Our results raise the rather different possibility that, when the communicated evidence (perceived contrast) cannot be separated from its reliability (slope), such failures of collective decision-making may be the natural consequence of a perfectly reasonable strategy (for instance, WCS). Indeed, we know all too well about the catastrophic consequences of consulting "evidence" of unknown reliability on problems as diverse as the existence of weapons of mass destruction and the possibility of risk-free investments[18].

## References and notes


1 L. Bovens, S. Hartmann, *Bayesian Epistemology* (Oxford Univ. Press, Oxford, 2003).
2 S. Nitzan, J. Paroush, *Collective Decision Making: An Economic Outlook* (Cambridge Univ. Press, Cambridge, 1985).
3 D. Alais, D. Burr, *Curr. Biol.* **14,** 257 (2004).
4 M.O. Ernst, M.S. Banks, *Nature* **415,** 429 (2002).
5 K.P. Körding, D.M. Wolpert, *Nature* **427,** 244 (2004).
6 S. Deneve, P.E. Latham, A. Pouget, *Nat. Neurosci.* **4,** 826 (2001).
7 D.M. Green, J.A. Swets, *Signal Detection Theory and Psychophysics* (Wiley, New York, 1966).
8 W.J. Ma, J.M. Beck, P.E. Latham, A. Pouget, *Nat. Neurosci.* **9,** 1432 (2006).
9 For details of methods, models, and additional results, see the supporting material on *Science* Online.
10 G.W. Hill, *Psychol. Bull.* **91,** 517 (1982).
11 R. Hastie, T. Kameda, *Psychol. Rev.* **112,** 494 (2005).
12 P.R. Laughlin, A.L. Ellis, *J. Exp. Soc. Psychol.* **22,** 177 (1986).
13 In our model, this internal estimate of the probability of being correct is a function of the ratio of stimulus contrast in a given trial to its standard deviation. The standard deviation is found by fitting a cumulative Gaussian to the participant's psychometric function.
14 R.D. Sorkin, C.J. Hays, R. West, *Psychol. Rev.* **108,** 183 (2001).
15 N.L. Kerr, R.S. Tindale, *Annu. Rev. Psychol.* **55,** 623 (2004).
16 B. Latané, K. Williams, S. Harkins, *J. Pers. Soc. Psychol.* **37,** 822 (1979).
17 M.E. Turner, A.R. Pratkanis, *Organ. Behav. Hum. Decis. Process.* **73,** 105 (1998).

18 We thank D. Bang for generous help with data collection in experiments 2 and 4 and F. Scharnowski for his insightful comments in the early stages of the project. This work was supported by the European Union MindBridge project (B.B.), the Danish National Research Foundation and the Danish Research Council for Culture and Communication (A.R. and C.D.F.), the Gatsby Charitable Foundation (P.E.L.), and the Wellcome Trust (G.R.). Support from the MIND Lab UNIK initiative at Aarhus University was funded by the Danish Ministry of Science, Technology and Innovation.

# 14 Supra-personal cognitive control and metacognition

*Nicholas Shea, Annika Boldt, Dan Bang, Nick Yeung, Cecilia Heyes and Chris D. Frith*

## A novel framework for metacognition research

Converging theoretical and empirical research suggests that most animals implicitly represent properties of their cognitive processes and use these for cognitive control (see Glossary[1,2,3])[4,5,6]. This challenges the view that only humans have metacognition[7], which is broadly defined as 'cognition about cognition', and raises the question why humans, unlike other animals, not only implicitly but also explicitly represent properties of their cognitive processes.

In this opinion article, we propose a 'dual systems' framework for thinking about metacognition. In our framework, metacognition is composed of a cognitively 'lean' system, system 1 metacognition, which operates implicitly and is for the control of processes within one agent (intra-personal cognitive control), and a cognitively 'rich' system, system 2 metacognition, which is likely to be unique to humans and is for the control of processes within multiple agents (supra-personal cognitive control). Whereas the former system is found in many animals, the latter system is likely to be unique to humans. Our 'lean' account of metacognition clarifies the minimal requirements for metacognition and thereby offers a conceptual anchor in a literature where there are many conflicting assumptions about what counts as metacognition. Further, our 'rich' account of metacognition addresses why humans evolved the ability to explicitly represent properties of their cognitive processes: by sharing and discussing these representations, agents can engage in novel forms of adaptive group behaviour and build cumulative culture.

## Glossary

**Cognitive control:** cognitive mechanisms responsible for guiding thought and behaviour in accordance with current goals and intentions.

**Conscious:** here we use the term in the sense of access consciousness[1]. A representation is access conscious just in case it can be used, without further processing, for verbal report, inferential reasoning, storage in episodic and semantic memory, and by other 'consuming' systems.

**Metacognition:** use of metacognitive representations (often, but not exclusively, for purposes of cognitive control).

**Metacognitive information:** information about a property of a cognitive process, for example, the variance in the firing rate of a population of neurons in visual cortex. Information is just a matter of correlation, strong or weak, and need not be used or represented.

**Metacognitive representation:** a representation of a property of a cognitive process, for example, the reliability of a perceptual representation. Metacognitive information that is represented and used for cognitive control is thereby a metacognitive representation, for example, the variance in the firing rate of a population of neurons in visual cortex can form the basis of a representation of the probability that the perceptual representation is correct (cf. object level representation).

**Object level representation:** a representation that is not at the meta-level, that is, that does not concern cognitive processes as such. Examples include representations of the nature, location, or value of a stimulus. (Similarly, correlates of such properties, whether represented or not, carry 'object level information'.)

**System 1 (type 1 cognitive processes):** a label for a number of cognitive systems that operate autonomously and do not require working memory. A system 1 process is typically fast, automatic, associative, effortless, and non-conscious. System 1 processes tend not to cause or suffer much interference when combined with one another or the performance of other tasks[2,3].

**System 2:** a label for a cognitive system that relies on working memory and is typically slower, serial, rule-based, more effortful, and conscious. Because of its limited capacity, processes relying on system 2 tend to disrupt each other[2,3].

### *Metacognition and its relation to cognitive control*

The broad definition of metacognition as 'cognition about cognition' is often interpreted widely[8], to include any cognitive process that receives information from and has a controlling influence on another cognitive process[9,10]. So-construed, metacognition would encompass every type of cognitive control. We define metacognition more narrowly, as control processes that make use of one or more metacognitive representations, that is, representations of a property of a cognitive process (Boxes 14.1 and 14.2).

**Box 14.1 Metacognition in humans**

Metacognition can be assessed with a range of different paradigms. Perceived (in)correctness of a first-order decision is often measured retrospectively through explicit second-order confidence or error detection judgements[58,59]. Moreover, post-decision wagering requires participants to place a wager on a just made decision, assuming higher bets will follow from higher confidence[60]. Another measure often used in reward paradigms is opt-out or uncertainty response, which allow the participant to skip a response, obtaining a smaller but guaranteed reward[61]. All these judgements are diagnostic of task performance, meaning higher confidence on correct compared with error trials. This leads to the question as to what metacognitive information is being represented by system 1 and system 2 metacognition. Studies have identified a range of candidates, which can be divided into two classes: directly accessed and inferred[39,62].

Direct access models assume that metacognition is based on the same information as the decision itself or some property of the decision. There are cases of direct access system 1 metacognitive representations that are based on exactly the same information as the decision. For example, Gigerenzer and colleagues suggested that both decision making and confidence are based on the validity of an activated cue[63]. A similar assumption is made by type 2 signal detection theory[64]; in this class of direct access models, confidence corresponds to the quantity of decision evidence accumulated for one response option. Other properties of the decision evidence have been suggested to play a role, such as its quality. Both Peirce's model of confidence[65] and Kiani and Shadlen[4] suggest a combination of both[58,59]. The idea that external variability affects confidence has also been suggested[59], meaning that more variable stimuli lead to lower levels of confidence. Others have suggested cognitive conflict as a basis for metacognition[13,17], which is based on the idea of competing response tendencies. The evidence in favour of the unchosen choice option also plays a role in mismatch models, which assume that metacognition is based on an internal matching process of the intended action with the actually performed one[66,67], as well as prediction errors[46]. Similarly, the balance-of-evidence hypothesis is another example of direct access models, according to which, confidence is a function of the evidence for the chosen and the unchosen option[68].

In contrast to direct access models, inferential models assume that metacognition is based on information external to the first-order decision-making process. For example, an individual may learn that information from conflicting or variable sources of evidence leads to slower responses[69], and thus infer her confidence from response times, either approximated internally[70,71] or through the observation of one's own or another individual's response movement. Several other inferential models, rooted in the metamemory literature, assume that metacognition is based on ease of processing, that is how accessible a representation is[72], how fluently it can be processed[73], or how familiar it is[74]. Another inferential hypothesis is the self-consistency model (SCM[39,75]), based on the consensuality principle, which assumes participants have implicit knowledge of what response others would give and approximate their confidence accordingly.

**Box 14.2 Metacognition in non-human animals**

There is compelling evidence that non-human animals are more likely to seek additional information[76,77], to opt out of making decisions[4,5,78,79,80] and to make lower post-decision wagers[67,81] under conditions in which a human observer would describe them as uncertain; for example, when the animal is required to make a difficult rather than an easy visual discrimination, or to remember an event over a long rather than a short interval. Some recent studies of monkeys[67], rats[5,78], and pigeons[79] have also indicated, using transfer tests and single neuron recording, that this type of metacognitive behaviour can be regulated by internal rather than external cues; for example, that it covaries more precisely with neural signals from the orbitofrontal cortex or the supplementary eye fields than with external stimulus values.

These data suggest that animals from a wide range of species are capable of system 1 metacognition. As we have characterised it, system 1 metacognition is undemanding (see subsection 'Only some forms of cognitive control involve metacognition' below). It could be mediated by simple reinforcement learning[cf. 7,82]. However, the current data do not show that animals are capable of system 2 metacognition: that they are able to infer or to learn, using system 2, the metacognitive significance of system 1 cues. Even in the most compelling experiments[e.g. 60,78], it is possible that a 'high confidence' internal system 1 signal, X, automatically triggered reward-seeking behaviour – and thereby reduced the probability of information-seeking, opt-out, and low post-decision wagers – without the animal having to use a system 2 process to learn that, in the presence of X, reward-seeking behaviour tends to be successful.

For example, a perceptual process may use the mean firing rate of a population of neurons in visual cortex to represent a perceived property such as the length of a line. Crucially, the variance of the firing rate across the population indicates the extent to which the neurons 'agree' about the line length and thus carries information about the reliability of the perceptual representation (metacognitive information)[11]. We propose that, if the latter type of information is used to control the relative influence of the perceptual representation on cognition[12], then it counts as a metacognitive representation, and the use of this representation for cognitive control should be considered to be an instance of metacognition. As well as choosing which sensorimotor dispositions are allowed to drive behaviour, metacognition thus conceived can be involved in distributing resources between rival processes[13], in emotion regulation[14], in guiding memory retrieval[9], allocating study time[9], and so on.

### *Only some forms of cognitive control involve metacognition*

Although all metacognition is a form of cognitive control, only some forms of cognitive control are metacognitive. Cognitive control need not make use of metacognitive representations and can be guided instead by object level representations, for example, of value or of abstract goals[15,16]. By contrast, other control processes do make use of metacognitive representations, for example, they represent that mutually inconsistent actions have been activated, which prompts the use of cognitive control processes in response selection[10,17].

Thus, our first conclusion is that, if metacognition is defined carefully, metacognition does not encompass every type of cognitive control. What, then, is distinctive about metacognition, beyond its defining feature – the use of metacognitive representations? One possibility is that metacognition is only found in the cognitive control processes carried out by higher executive systems. In considering this possibility and suggesting an alternative, we make use of the well-known distinction between system 1 and system 2[3]. However, our proposal does not depend on the details of dual systems theory, and it is consistent with other theories of higher-level executive function [18,19,20]. The dual-systems model draws on evidence that there is a distinctive form of cognitive processing, type 2 processing or system 2, with respect to which various functional features tend to cluster together, underpinned by their reliance on a capacity-limited generalised working memory system[2,3,21]. System 2 handles problems serially, takes time to operate and is affected by general working memory load. Its effectiveness correlates with individual differences in measures of general intelligence. By contrast, system 1 processes can act quickly, with many operating autonomously in parallel, and are little affected by general working memory load. System 2 representations are characteristically explicit, that is, conscious, whereas system 1 representations need not be.

Are metacognitive processes simply those control processes that are carried out by system 2? Unfortunately, things do not fall out so neatly. Much cognitive control takes place outside system 2[22,23]. For example, experimental subjects can inhibit responses to stimuli of which they remain unaware due to visual masking[22] and slow down after errors they do not know they have made[24]. These system 1 types of control can make use of metacognitive representations such as decision uncertainty[25,26], for example, as evident in a neuropsychological patient whose behaviour shows adaptation to the prevailing difficulty of the task even though she has no conscious experience of mental effort[25]. Non-human animals are similarly capable of using metacognitive information[27] (Box 14.2). That, however, leaves us with a pressing puzzle. If system 1 metacognition is so pervasive, in humans and other animals, what role is there for system 2 metacognition?

## A hypothesis about the distinctive function of system 2 metacognition

Our answer to the puzzle – what is the role of system 2 metacognition? – will be that it comes into its own when the action-driving systems to be controlled are found in two different agents: that is, in cases of 'supra-personal cognitive control'.

Within a single agent, domain-general processes of learning, which are part of system 1, can quickly establish – through experience – the best way to prioritise the inputs to and outputs from competing sensorimotor systems (Figure 14.1). Such processes can use system 1 metacognitive information – for example, variance of a distribution, time to completion of a process, activation of incompatible response tendencies (Box 14.1) – to improve those trade-offs, just as they can learn to use any other type of relevant cue. The result will be a form of control that is

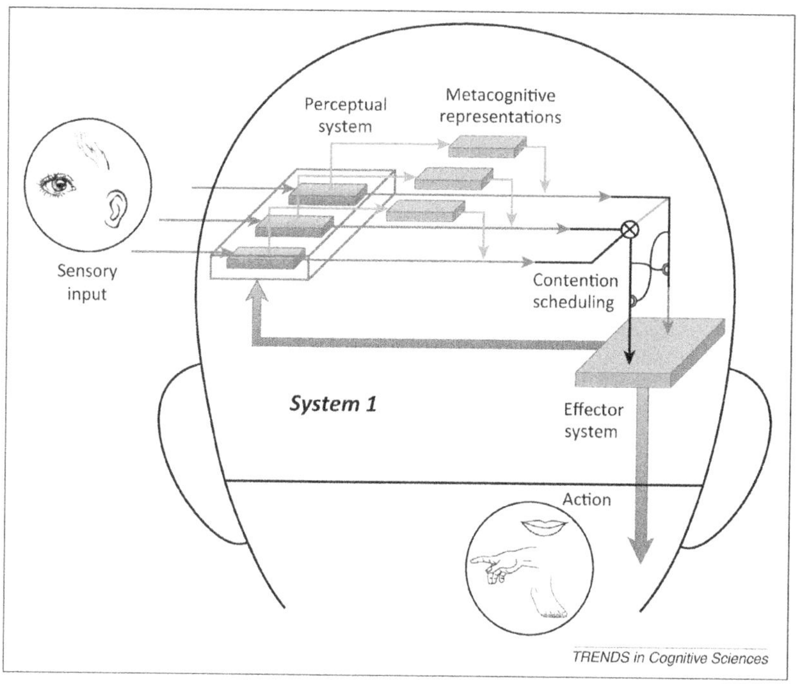


*Figure 14.1* System 1 metacognition with a single agent. The control of cognitive processes in an individual's system 1 occurs automatically and at a sub-personal level[3]. Contention scheduling, a term introduced by Norman and Shallice[18], refers to a mechanism for resolving competition between processes that overlap in their effector system requirements. Metacognitive representations reflect the properties of the functioning of these cognitive processes. System 1 uses metacognitive representations to improve control. An example of such representations would be the reliability of sensory signals. Cognitive processes estimated to be more reliable can be given greater weight[12]. (See figure in colour plate section.)

implemented within system 1 processing and relies on metacognitive representations – that is, a system 1 form of metacognition.

When sensorimotor systems have to be coordinated between two or more interacting agents it is no longer possible for learning automatically to make use of all and any metacognitive information located anywhere within the different agents: my system 1 learning processes have direct access to the metacognitive information in my head, but not to the metacognitive information in your head, and vice versa. Some forms of coordinated action do not depend on metacognitive representations, for example, bodily movements can be synchronised relying only on object level information (e.g., about the location and trajectory of limbs)[28,29]. But inter-agent control will typically be more effective when it can use metacognitive representations, if relevant metacognitive representations within system 1 processes in each agent are selected for broadcast to the other agent, so that decisions about which sensorimotor processes to deploy can be taken in a space of shared metacognitive information. This, we suggest, is the distinctive role of system 2 metacognition: to select metacognitive information for broadcast, in the service of controlling the sensorimotor systems of two or more agents involved in a shared task – that is, for supra-personal cognitive control (Figure 14.2).

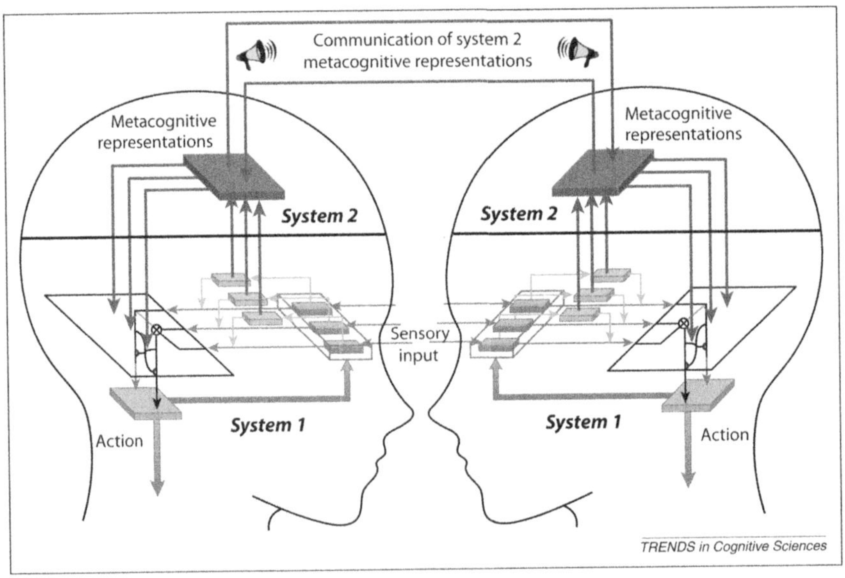


*Figure 14.2* System 2 metacognition for cognitive control across two agents. System 2 metacognitive representations are derived from information in system 1, but they are in a form available for verbal report. For example, the reliability of a sensory signal can be reported in terms of confidence. When agents are cooperating, these reports can be used to optimise control by, for example, giving more weight to the more confident observer[32]. Via system 2, verbal reports can also have long-term effects on the functioning of system 1[57]. (See figure in colour plate section.)

Ours is different from the hypothesis that metacognition is for mentalising – that is, perceiving or inferring other people's mental states[30,31]. The first difference is that the representations concern one's own cognitive processes in the first instance, rather than those of another. The second difference is that communicating metacognitive representations plays a central role. To caricature: the mentalising story says that metacognition is there to allow agent A to infer that agent B has seen a rabbit; according to us, system 2 metacognition is there to allow agent A to communicate that his visuomotor fix on the rabbit is pretty reliable at present.

## How system 2 metacognition works

### *System 2 metacognition plays a central role in group decision making*

According to our hypothesis, system 2 metacognition should play a central role in group decision making. Indeed we find that joint perceptual decision making is significantly more effective when participants communicate metacognitive representations about the stimuli[32,33]. When deciding whether to trust witness testimony, (mock) jurors make considerable use of a witness's confidence and other metacognitive representations (e.g., calibration of confidence and accuracy)[34]. People also communicate metacognitive representations when they are synchronically coordinating complex actions (e.g., communications about confidence used in team sports)[35,36]. System 2 metacognition can also be used diachronically, for example, making it possible for people to discuss how metacognitive representations should be deployed, affecting their own cognitive control[37]. Control strategies based on metacognitive representations, for example, what to do when memory fails, can be the subject of explicit instruction. For example, a person can learn socially that, following failure to produce items in a verbal fluency task to name animals, a good strategy is to consider subcategories of animals (farm animals, pets, etc.)[38].

### *Three types of work done by system 2 metacognition*

We can distinguish three different types of work done by system 2 metacognition. First (W1), it makes metacognitive representations available for verbal report and hence for communication. Second (W2), system 2 metacognition works out the significance of metacognitive representations that have been broadcast or selected for communication, that is, what the individual or group should do (e.g., try harder, start again, give low weighting to that person's opinion) when a metacognitive representation has a certain range of values (e.g., indicates disfluency or lack of confidence). Although system 1 processes already contain some metacognitive representations which system 2 metacognition can select to make available ('direct access'[39]), a third type of work done by system 2 metacognition (W3) is to construct or infer metacognitive representations from multiple sources of (sometimes weak) metacognitive information (Box 14.1, Figure 14.2).

In addition, we can, as mentioned above, distinguish between synchronic and diachronic supra-personal cognitive control. In cases of synchronic coordinated agency, metacognitive representations are used to improve the performance of two or more people when working on the same task at the same time. Metacognitive representations can also be used diachronically in teaching other agents how to think and act in the future, to improve subsequent performance in coordinated action[40], and possibly also in solitary tasks[41]. The interpretation of metacognitive representations, and what to do about them, can be altered through discussion with others, enabling the generation of cultural consensus and regulation concerning what the cues mean and why some instructions are more appropriate than others. For example, using system 2 metacognition, groups develop and pass on theories about system 1 processes (about how to think)[37]. Learnt reliance on shared metacognitive representations can be effective even though people can be very unreliable in reporting some of the object level information used by system 1 processes. For example, people are wildly incorrect about the object level information used by the system 1 processes involved in catching a ball, but can still share metacognitive information to facilitate joint performance[35,42].

When is system 2 metacognition direct and when is it inferred (W3)? We suppose that direct access will be used where the information is available, for example, confidence in perceptual decision making; and inferred otherwise, for example, in predictive ease of learning judgements[9,43] (Box 14.1). If direct, there should be a reasonably tight correlation between the subject's reports (e.g., of accuracy) and objective measures[44,45]. If system 2 has to infer the metacognitive significance of system 1 cues there is more room for error.

### *Examples and limitations of system 2 metacognition*

One central source of metacognitive representations is the prediction errors generated and used by many system 1 processes to guide learning[46]. When relied on to guide learning and behaviour prediction errors can represent the reliability of another of the system's representations (e.g., of the value of an option) and lead that representation to be revised for the future[47]. Large prediction errors may produce feelings of perceptual disfluency[48] or action selection disfluency[49]. System 2 can learn the significance of these feelings and use them for cognitive control.

System 2 has limited processing capacity, thus it can only make use of a limited number of metacognitive representations. That number should decrease as other demands on general working memory increase. And indeed there is some evidence that under cognitive load subjects switch from relying on several raw cues to depending on a single summary[50]. An example of such a summary is the z-score (derived from the mean and the standard deviation of the internal perceptual representation) communicated by subjects in social psychophysics experiments[32], although it is not known whether subjects could have communicated the raw cues independently. In some cases, the raw cues on which summaries are based may no longer be available. However, this mandatory fusion occurs relatively late in development (~12 years[51]), suggesting that adults could learn to unpack the summary if necessary.

## The function of system 2 metacognition

### *The functional claim about system 2 metacognition comes in various strengths*

We have suggested that system 2 metacognition is for supra-personal cognitive control. The functional claim – what system 2 metacognition is 'for' – comes in several strengths. A modest claim is that system 2 metacognition is functionally involved in cases of inter-agent cognitive control; in situations where two or more people successfully coordinate their actions to achieve an outcome that depends on sensorimotor processes found in both. A bolder hypothesis is that this is the evolutionary purpose of system 2 metacognition: that the ability to represent metacognitive information in system 2 evolved to allow people to engage in more sophisticated cooperative projects and coordination tasks.

### *The hypothesis that system 2 metacognition evolved for supra-personal cognitive control*

There is not scope here to properly assess the evolutionary claim, but we will note an empirical consequence. Humans are a distinctively cooperative mammal, engaging in coordinated behaviour to an extent that is markedly different from even our closest primate cousins[52,53]. If the ability to use system 2 to select, construct, and broadcast metacognitive representations arose in humans in response to selection pressure for increasingly complex forms of coordinated action, then in non-human animals we would not expect to find a system 2 that processes metacognitive representations (Box 14.2). One possibility is that non-human animals do not have a system 2 at all. Alternatively, non-human animals may have system 2 functions, such as maintenance in working memory and selective attention[54,55], that do not involve the use of metacognitive information. In this case, what evolved in the hominin line was the capacity to take metacognitive representations in system 1 and turn them into metacognitive representations for system 2.

According to this evolutionary hypothesis, supra-personal coordination was the origin of system 2 metacognition. Using conscious metacognitive representations to control one's own individual behaviour is probably the most obvious manifestation of system 2 metacognition in everyday life. But on our account, using metacognitive representations about one's own cognitive processes for intrapersonal cognitive control came second, and arose as a side effect of the selection of system 2 metacognition for interpersonally coordinated action. The picture is of cooperation becoming a central feature of the human way of life, in the form of fluidly coordinated joint action and diachronically organised cooperative projects, both controlled by a supra-personal system of cognitive control. This system directs resources and activity between a variety of different sensorimotor processes that are distributed across agents. It relies on selected metacognitive representations which, because they are shared among the agents involved, enable more efficient and complex forms of coordinated action. The selection and sharing occurs not only synchronically, while a particular episode of coordinated action is in progress, but also diachronically, as system 2 metacognition allows experts to teach novices how to use metacognitive representations in future episodes of coordinated and solitary tasks.

The selection processes favouring the emergence of system 2 metacognition could have been genetic and/or cultural. To the extent that the evolutionary processes were genetic, rather than cultural, one would expect: (i) little cross-cultural variation in the extent and content of system 2 metacognition, especially when people are tested in coordinated action tasks and when adults are teaching children; and (ii) that metacognitive competence would emerge early and independently of instruction. If these predictions are false[56], it would suggest a role for cultural selection in the evolution of system 2 metacognition (see section on 'Empirical predictions' below).

### *An (even) more radical evolutionary hypothesis about system 2 metacognition*

The evolutionary claim about the function of system 2 metacognition in turn comes in various strengths. So far, we have suggested that it was the ability to represent metacognitive information in system 2 that was selected. This allows that early hominins may already have had system 2 in place, and perhaps also natural language (which may or may not be separable from the presence of system 2). However, it is worth noting that a much more radical evolutionary claim could also be entertained: that system 2 itself evolved to perform the function of selecting, constructing, and broadcasting metacognitive representations in the service of suprapersonal cognitive control. A yet further evolutionary question on which we do not venture to speculate is the relation of these various evolutionary steps to the emergence of consciousness.

## Empirical predictions

We suggest several empirical predictions against which our hypothesis can be tested. The first concerns linguistic communication. It follows from our functional hypothesis that some forms of joint action are significantly aided by communication of metacognitive representations selected by system 2 metacognition. Thus, in a novel task requiring two or more agents to act jointly in pursuit of some goal (i.e., not one where an action plan has been automatised in system 1 processes in both agents), blocking the linguistic communication of metacognitive information should have a selective detrimental effect on performance, in a way that blocking the linguistic communication of object level information about the task does not.

Similarly, in such a novel coordination task, cognitive load should selectively impair performance, and should do so via an effect on the (accuracy or range) of communicated metacognitive information. By contrast, where automatic/autonomous/implicit processes rely on metacognitive information in directing behaviour or resources between sensorimotor processes, increased cognitive load should cause relatively little impairment.

A third prediction concerns individual differences. Performance in the types of novel coordination tasks just described should correlate with individual differences in measures of general intelligence.

Our final prediction concerns non-human animals. If, contrary to our hypothesis, non-human animals have system 2 metacognition, they should be able to learn that reward-seeking behaviour is successful after making decisions that are unlikely to be correct (low confidence) and unsuccessful after making decisions that are likely to be correct (high confidence). This could be tested by, for example, using a reverse transfer test after training in a wagering task.

## Concluding remarks

As yet the evidence for our hypothesis is limited and there are many outstanding questions (Box 14.3). The two key components, for which there is some preliminary evidence, are: (i) that system 2 metacognition is very malleable and readily influenced by instructions and beliefs[56,57]; and (ii) that exchange of system 2 metacognitive representations can create advantages for the group[32]. If tests of our empirical predictions provide further support, it would suggest that metacognition is a specific form of cognitive control and is not unique to system 2. Metacognitive information such as decision uncertainty is used to modulate ongoing thought and behaviour in the absence of awareness. These implicit metacognitive representations enable the many different processes that make up system 1 to work together in an optimal manner. However, when metacognitive representations are explicit in system 2 they can be readily used to enable several people to work together in an optimal manner, for example, by sharing information about decision confidence. We suggest that explicit metacognitive representations exist for this reason. This role is possible, first because the representations are in verbal form suitable for sharing, and second because they can modify the functioning of system 1. On the basis of metacognitive signals emerging from system 1, accounts are developed in system 2 designed to explain and control the functioning of system 1. These accounts can be sketchy and inaccurate, like any narrative, but are constantly updated and sometimes improved through discussion with others. This process provides a mechanism for modification of behaviour through instructions and cultural expectations. These are powerful forces that alter behaviour of whole groups of people and provide a mechanism for the emergence of cumulative culture.

**Box 14.3 Outstanding questions**

- Is there a specific format for system 2 metacognitive representations designed to enable a common supra-personal metric (e.g., confidence as signal mean*precision)?
- Can cognitive control be improved through inter-personal exchange of system 2 metacognitive representations?
- Can the interpretation of system 2 metacognitive representations be changed/corrected through discussion (e.g., learning that perceptual fluency indicates familiarity)?
- What are the distinctive features of group decision making in humans in comparison to eusocial animals such as ants and bees?
- Are there cultural differences in the use of system 2 metacognitive representations?

## Acknowledgements

We are grateful to All Souls College for hosting and funding the series of seminars on metacognition from which our ideas have emerged. We are also grateful to all the speakers and participants of the seminars, but should make clear the ideas we present are not intended to represent any consensus of these participants. This work was supported by All Souls College, University of Oxford; the Economic and Social Research Council (A.B.); the Calleva Research Centre for Evolution and Human Sciences (D.B.); and the Wellcome Trust (CDF).

## References

1 Block, N. (2005) Two neural correlates of consciousness. *Trends Cogn. Sci.* 9, 46–52
2 Kahneman, D. (2003) A perspective on judgment and choice: mapping bounded rationality. *Am. Psychol.* 58, 697–720
3 Evans, J.S.B.T. and Stanovich, K.E. (2013) Dual-process theories of higher cognition advancing the debate. *Perspect. Psychol. Sci.* 8, 223–241
4 Kiani, R. and Shadlen, M.N. (2009) Representation of confidence associated with a decision by neurons in the parietal cortex. *Science* 324, 759–764
5 Kepecs, A. *et al.* (2008) Neural correlates, computation and behavioural impact of decision confidence. *Nature* 455, 227–231
6 Komura, Y. *et al.* (2013) Responses of pulvinar neurons reflect a subject's confidence in visual categorization. *Nat. Neurosci.* 16, 749–755
7 Terrace, H.S. and Son, L.K. (2009) Comparative metacognition. *Curr. Opin. Neurobiol.* 19, 67–74
8 Carruthers, P. (2009) How we know our own minds: the relationship between mindreading and metacognition. *Behav. Brain Sci.* 32, 121–182 (p. 170)
9 Metcalfe, J. (2009) Metacognitive judgments and control of study. *Curr. Dir. Psychol. Sci.* 18, 159–163

10 Fernandez-Duque, D. *et al.* (2000) Executive attention and metacognitive regulation. *Conscious. Cogn.* 9, 288–307
11 Drugowitsch, J. and Pouget, A. (2012) Probabilistic vs. non-probabilistic approaches to the neurobiology of perceptual decision-making. *Curr. Opin. Neurobiol.* 22, 963–969
12 Ernst, M.O. and Banks, M.S. (2002) Humans integrate visual and haptic information in a statistically optimal fashion. *Nature* 415, 429–433
13 Davelaar, E.J. (2009) Conflict-monitoring and (meta)cognitive control. In *Connectionist Models of Behaviour and Cognition II. Proceedings of the 11th Neural Computation and Psychology Worksho* (Mayor, J. *et al.*, eds), pp. 91–102, WorldScientific
14 Davis, E.L. *et al.* (2010) Metacognitive emotion regulation: children's awareness that changing thoughts and goals can alleviate negative emotions. *Emotion* 10, 498–510
15 Shenhav, A. *et al.* (2013) The expected value of control: an integrative theory of anterior cingulate cortex function. *Neuron* 79, 217–240
16 Sakai, K. (2008) Task set and prefrontal cortex. *Annu. Rev. Neurosci.* 31, 219–245
17 Yeung, N. (2013) Conflict monitoring and cognitive control. In *Oxford Handbook of Cognitive Neuroscience* (Vol. 2) (Ochsner, K. and Kosslyn, S.M., eds), pp. 275–299, Oxford University Press
18 Norman, D.A. and Shallice, T. (1986) Attention to action: willed and automatic control of behaviour. In *Consciousness and Self-regulation (Advances in Research and Theory, Vol. 4)* (Davidson, R.J. *et al.*, eds), pp. 1–18, Plenum
19 Desimone, R. and Duncan, J. (1995) Neural mechanisms of selective visual attention. *Annu. Rev. Neurosci.* 18, 193–222
20 Dehaene, S. and Naccache, L. (2001) Towards a cognitive neuroscience of consciousness: basic evidence and a workspace framework. *Cognition* 79, 1–37
21 Kahneman, D. (2011) *Thinking Fast and Slow,* Macmillan
22 Sumner, P. *et al.* (2007) Human medial frontal cortex mediates unconscious inhibition of voluntary action. *Neuron* 54, 697–711
23 Custers, R. and Aarts, H. (2010) The unconscious will: how the pursuit of goals operates outside of conscious awareness. *Science* 329, 47–50
24 Logan, G.D. and Crump, M.J.C. (2010) Cognitive illusions of authorship reveal hierarchical error detection in skilled typists. *Science* 330, 683–686
25 Naccache, L. *et al.* (2005) Effortless control: executive attention and conscious feeling of mental effort are dissociable. *Neuropsychologia* 43, 1318–1328
26 Bach, D.R. and Dolan, R.J. (2012) Knowing how much you don't know: a neural organization of uncertainty estimates. *Nat. Rev. Neurosci.* 13, 572–586
27 Summerfield, C. and Yeung, N. (2013) Oh, rats! Post-error behavioral adjustment in creatures great and small. *Nat. Neurosci.* 16, 1715–1716
28 Richardson, M.J. *et al.* (2007) Rocking together: dynamics of intentional and unintentional interpersonal coordination. *Hum. Mov. Sci.* 26, 867–891
29 Hasson, U. *et al.* (2012) Brain-to-brain coupling: a mechanism for creating and sharing a social world. *Trends Cogn. Sci.* 16, 114–121
30 Byrne, R. and Whiten, A. (1989) *Machiavellian Intelligence: Social Expertise and the Evolution of Intellect in Monkeys, Apes and Humans,* Oxford Science Publications
31 Herrmann, E. *et al.* (2007) Humans have evolved specialized skills of social cognition: the cultural intelligence hypothesis. *Science* 317, 1360–1366
32 Bahrami, B. *et al.* (2010) Optimally interacting minds. *Science* 329, 1081–1085
33 Fusaroli, R. *et al.* (2012) Coming to terms quantifying the benefits of linguistic coordination. *Psychol. Sci.* 23, 931–939

34 Tenney, E.R. *et al.* (2007) Calibration trumps confidence as a basis for witness credibility. *Psychol. Sci.* 18, 46–50

35 Poizat, G. *et al.* (2009) Analysis of contextual information sharing during table tennis matches: an empirical study of coordination in sports. *Int. J. Sport Exerc. Psychol.* 7, 465–487

36 Lausic, D. *et al.* (2009) Intrateam communication and performance in doubles tennis. *Res. Q. Exerc. Sport* 80, 281–290

37 Job, V. *et al.* (2010) Ego depletion – Is it all in your head? Implicit theories about willpower affect self-regulation. *Psychol. Sci.* 21, 1686–1693

38 Hurks, P.P.M. (2012) Does instruction in semantic clustering and switching enhance verbal fluency in children? *Clin. Neuropsychol.* 26, 1019–1037

39 Koriat, A. (2012) The self-consistency model of subjective confidence. *Psychol. Rev.* 119, 80–113

40 Bahrami, B. *et al.* (2012) Together, slowly but surely: the role of social interaction and feedback on the build-up of benefit in collective decision-making. *J. Exp. Psychol. Hum. Percept. Perform.* 38, 3–8

41 Payne, B.D. and Manning, B.H. (1992) Basal reader instruction: effects of comprehension monitoring training on reading comprehension, strategy use and attitude. *Read. Res. Instr.* 32, 29–38

42 Reed, N. *et al.* (2010) Implicit knowledge and motor skill: what people who know how to catch don't know. *Conscious. Cogn.* 19, 63–76

43 Meiser, T. *et al.* (2007) Metacognitive inferences in source memory judgements: the role of perceived differences in item recognition. *Q. J. Exp. Psychol.* 60, 1015–1040

44 Brewer, W.F. and Sampaio, C. (2012) The metamemory approach to confidence: a test using semantic memory. *J. Mem. Lang.* 67, 59–77

45 Overgaard, M. and Sandberg, K. (2012) Kinds of access: different methods for report reveal different kinds of metacognitive access. *Philos. Trans. R. Soc. Lond. B: Biol. Sci.* 367, 1287–1296

46 Friston, K. (2010) The free-energy principle: a unified brain theory? *Nat. Rev. Neurosci.* 11, 127–138

47 Shea, N. (2012) Reward prediction error signals are meta-representational. *Nous* http://dx.doi.org/10.1111/j.1468–0068.2012.00863.x

48 Yue, C.L. *et al.* (2013) When disfluency is – and is not – a desirable difficulty: the influence of typeface clarity on metacognitive judgments and memory. *Mem. Cogn.* 41, 229–241

49 Chambon, V. and Haggard, P. (2012) Sense of control depends on fluency of action selection, not motor performance. *Cognition* 125, 441–451

50 Hoffman, Y. *et al.* (2011) Explicit memory for unattended words the importance of being in the 'no'. *Psychol. Sci.* 22, 1490–1493

51 Nardini, M. *et al.* (2010) Fusion of visual cues is not mandatory in children. *Proc. Natl. Acad. Sci. U.S.A.* 107, 17041–17046

52 Tomasello, M. (2009) *Why We Cooperate*, MIT Press

53 Sterelny, K. (2012) *The Evolved Apprentice*, MIT Press

54 Matzel, L.D. and Kolata, S. (2010) Selective attention, working memory, and animal intelligence. *Neurosci. Biobehav. Rev.* 34, 23–30

55 Dickinson, A. (2012) Associative learning and animal cognition. *Philos. Trans. R. Soc. Lond. B: Biol. Sci.* 367, 2733–2742

56 Mayer, A. and Träuble, B.E. (2013) Synchrony in the onset of mental state understanding across cultures? A study among children in Samoa. *Int. J. Behav. Dev.* 37, 21–28

57 Rigoni, D. *et al.* (2011) Inducing disbelief in free will alters brain correlates of preconscious motor preparation: the brain minds whether we believe in free will or not. *Psychol. Sci.* 22, 613–618
58 Pleskac, T.J. and Busemeyer, J.R. (2010) Two-stage dynamic signal detection: a theory of choice, decision time, and confidence. *Psychol. Rev.* 117, 864–901
59 Yeung, N. and Summerfield, C. (2012) Metacognition in human decision-making: confidence and error monitoring. *Philos. Trans. R. Soc. Lond. B: Biol. Sci.* 367, 1310–1321
60 Pasquali, A. *et al.* (2010) Know thyself: metacognitive networks and measures of consciousness. *Cognition* 117, 182–190
61 Smith, J.D. *et al.* (2012) The highs and lows of theoretical interpretation in animal-metacognition research. *Philos. Trans. R. Soc. Lond. B: Biol. Sci.* 367, 1297–1309
62 Schwartz, B. (1994) Sources of information in metamemory: judgments of learning and feelings of knowing. *Psychon. Bull. Rev.* 1, 357–375
63 Gigerenzer, G. *et al.* (1991) Probabilistic mental models: a Brunswikian theory of confidence. *Psychol. Rev.* 98, 506–528
64 Higham, P.A. *et al.* (2009) Investigating strength and frequency effects in recognition memory using type-2 signal detection theory. *J. Exp. Psychol. Learn. Mem. Cogn.* 35, 57–80
65 Peirce, C.S. (1877) Illustrations of the logic of science: the probability of induction. *Popular Sci. Monthly* 12, 705–718
66 Charles, L. *et al.* (2013) Distinct brain mechanisms for conscious versus subliminal error detection. *Neuroimage* 73, 80–94
67 Middlebrooks, P.G. and Sommer, M.A. (2012) Neuronal correlates of metacognition in primate frontal cortex. *Neuron* 75, 517–530
68 Kepecs, A. and Mainen, Z.F. (2012) A computational framework for the study of confidence in humans and animals. *Philos. Trans. R. Soc. Lond. B: Biol. Sci.* 367, 1322–1337
69 Hanks, T.D. *et al.* (2011) Elapsed decision time affects the weighting of prior probability in a perceptual decision task. *J. Neurosci.* 31, 6339–6352
70 Moreno-Bote, R. (2010) Decision confidence and uncertainty in diffusion models with partially correlated neuronal integrators. *Neural Comput.* 22, 1786–1811
71 Zylberberg, A. *et al.* (2012) The construction of confidence in a perceptual decision. *Front. Integr. Neurosci.* 6, 79
72 Koriat, A. (1993) How do we know that we know? The accessibility model of the feeling of knowing. *Psychol. Rev.* 100, 609–639
73 Castel, A.D. *et al.* (2007) Illusions of competence and overestimation of associative memory for identical items: evidence from judgments of learning. *Psychon. Bull. Rev.* 14, 107–111
74 Hertzog, C. *et al.* (2010) Episodic feeling-of-knowing resolution derives from the quality of original encoding. *Mem. Cogn.* 38, 771–784
75 Koriat, A. (2011) Subjective confidence in perceptual judgments: a test of the self-consistency model. *J. Exp. Psychol. Gen.* 140, 117–139
76 Call, J. (2010) Do apes know that they could be wrong? *Anim. Cogn.* 13, 689–700
77 Beran, M.J. and Smith, J.D. (2010) Information seeking by rhesus monkeys (*Macaca mulatta*) and capuchin monkeys (*Cebus apella*). *Cognition* 120, 90–105
78 Foote, A.L. and Crystal, J.D. (2007) Metacognition in the rat. *Curr. Biol.* 17, 551–555
79 Adams, A. and Santi, A. (2011) Pigeons exhibit higher accuracy for chosen memory tests than for forced memory tests in duration matching-to-sample. *Learn. Behav.* 39, 1–11

80 Templer, V.L. and Hampton, R.R. (2012) Rhesus monkeys (*Macaca mulatta*) show robust evidence for memory awareness across multiple generalization tests. *Anim. Cogn.* 15, 409–419

81 Kornell, N. *et al.* (2007) Transfer of metacognitive skills and hint seeking in monkeys. *Psychol. Sci.* 18, 64–71

82 Le Pelley, M.E. (2012) Metacognitive monkeys or associative animals? Simple reinforcement learning explains uncertainty in nonhuman animals. *J. Exp. Psychol. Learn. Mem. Cogn.* 38, 686

# Index

Made in the USA
Coppell, TX
13 June 2023

18062450R00157